A Third Way

HARVARD EAST ASIAN MONOGRAPHS 438

A Third Way

*The Origins of China's Current
Economic Development Strategy*

Lawrence C. Reardon

Published by the Harvard University Asia Center
Distributed by Harvard University Press
Cambridge (Massachusetts) and London 2020

Printed in the United States of America

The Harvard University Asia Center publishes a monograph series and, in coordination with the Fairbank Center for Chinese Studies, the Korea Institute, the Reischauer Institute of Japanese Studies, and other faculties and institutes, administers research projects designed to further scholarly understanding of China, Japan, Vietnam, Korea, and other Asian countries. The Center also sponsors projects addressing multidisciplinary and regional issues in Asia.

A Study of the Weatherhead East Asian Institute, Columbia University

The Studies of the Weatherhead East Asian Institute of Columbia University were inaugurated in 1962 to bring to a wider public the results of significant new research on modern and contemporary East Asia.

Library of Congress Cataloging-in-Publication Data

Names: Reardon, Lawrence C., author.
Title: A third way : the origins of China's current economic development strategy / Lawrence C. Reardon.
Description: Cambridge, Massachusetts : Harvard University Asia Center,
2020. | Series: Harvard East Asian monographs ; 438 | Includes bibliographical references and index.
Identifiers: LCCN 2020034595 | ISBN 9780674247888 (hardcover)
Subjects: LCSH: China—Economic policy—1949-1976. | Mixed economy—China—History—20th century. | Communism—China—History—20th century.
Classification: LCC HC427.9 .R385 2020 | DDC 338.951—dc23
LC record available at https://lccn.loc.gov/2020034595

Index by Randa Dubnick

Printed on acid-free paper

Last figure below indicates year of this printing
26 25 24 23 22 21 20

For Professor Thomas Bernstein, my family, and close friends, who have been so supportive over the past thirty-five years.

Contents

Tables

Preface

In 1984 I received a two-year fellowship from the National Academy of Sciences' Committee for Scholarly Communications with the People's Republic of China (CSCPRC) to conduct fieldwork on China's foreign economic policy at Peking University. Getting off the bus in Tiananmen Square, I was amazed by its enormity and the iconic picture of Mao Zedong hanging at the Tiananmen Gate. Nearly twenty years before, Mao Zedong had been standing on the gate's balcony reviewing a million Red Guards waving their Little Red Books and chanting, "Mao zhuxi wansui!" (Long live Chairman Mao!).

But this was a new China, Deng Xiaoping's China. Remnants of the Cultural Revolution were fading. People still wore the blues and greens of revolutionary China, but the *fuwuyuan* (salesperson) was scooping face cream from a big barrel in the Haidian state store while customers were strapping new television sets on the backs of their Feige (Flying pigeon) bicycles. A statue of Mao watched over those entering the Peking University library, but the Maoist slogans painted on the buildings surrounding the library were gradually fading. Liberation trucks, light blue Shanghai cars, and bicyclists were everywhere, but every so often a brand-new black Audi with military plates or a new Volkswagen Santana would emerge from the mayhem. Taxis were found only in certain key locations, like the Jianguo and Friendship Hotels that only foreigners could enter. But the private markets were bustling with sellers of fresh local apples and pears. People would earn money by mending clothes or fixing your bike. Street venders sold *tanghulu*, candied hawberries on a very long stick, while the local Uighur merchants were roasting *yangrouchuar* (lamb kebab) or exchanging foreign exchange certificates for renminbi.

I returned to the square with the rest of the Peking University foreign students to witness the thirty-fifth anniversary celebration on 1 October 1984, which was really a celebration of Deng's new China. I could barely see Deng Xiaoping, standing in the same spot that Mao had occupied. But there was a palpable sense of excitement and joy in the crowd as people felt that the political maelstrom had subsided and a new era of reforms was dawning. Within the year, the urban reforms were transforming living standards in the capital, as people could buy vegetables from the south during the winter, and not just *dabaicai* (cabbage). Beijing residents attended the first fashion show since the 1949 revolution, with real Chinese models, while Hou Dejian packed the Capital Indoor Stadium in the city with a crowd of young fans who went wild when he sang "Descendants of the Dragon." As a foreign student in Beijing, I found it was still difficult to conduct research about Chinese reforms. However, I learned to use my American Southerner's manners to get along with Beijing's people. I also took advantage of work I got with Chinese film companies that hired me to act and to do translation, and even enjoyed a month of filming on Hainan Island. Having escaped the cold and dusty winter in Beijing, I was enthralled by my trip to China's south and the wild beauty of the underdeveloped island, which included children in ragged clothes but also newly paved roads and a large number of imported cars waiting to be shipped to the mainland.

When I first arrived at the Shenzhen special economic zone (SEZ) in the spring of 1985 with a Peking University delegation that included economists from the Soviet Union, Deng Xiaoping had recently completed his first *nanxun* (southern tour) and declared the zones to be a success that other coastal cities should emulate. Factories and high-rises surrounded the old town, while farmers wearing conical bamboo hats tended their rice fields and lychee trees along the four-lane road that wound its way from Luohu to Guangzhou. Having been appointed as a foreign expert to teach political economy and English at Shenzhen University from 1986 to 1988, I experienced firsthand the dramatic changes in the Shenzhen SEZ. The symbol of Shenzhen was an image of oxen pulling a stump out of the ground, which could be interpreted as the new Shenzhen pulling China into the twenty-first century. The zones were a true experimental hothouse for China's coastal development strategy, where policy makers tested various economic reforms, including apartment ownership, employment bonuses, and other market-style policies. The best and brightest flocked to Shenzhen, in part because of its reputation for "Shenzhen efficiency" but also because professionals could arrange to reunite with their spouse and live as a family in one of the city's large, newly built apartments with such modern amenities as air conditioning. People wanted change, and Shenzhen was at the epicenter of this transformation—at least until the late 1980s.

This study analyzes the special period in China's development when Chinese elites decided to harness the financial and technological strengths of the international market to accelerate the nation's transformation into a major global economic power. My time in southern China coincided with Premier Zhao Ziyang's directive to break down barriers between bureaucracies by publishing internal government policies and regulations. Some of these collections became available in bookstores in Guangzhou and Shenzhen, and I felt like a kid in a candy store. I also had in-depth conversations with scholars at the Guangzhou Academy of Social Sciences and Jinan and Shenzhen Universities, as well as with colleagues at the Universities Service Centre in Hong Kong. I initially explored ideas about Chinese economic development strategies in *The Reluctant Dragon: Crisis Cycles in Chinese Foreign Economic Policy* (2002), which traced the circuitous path of China's development as it cycled between large-scale import substitution industrialization and closed-door, semi-autarkic strategies, from 1949 to 1978. Expanding on that work, this study makes use of new research on Stalin's development ideas and Zhao Ziyang's comprehensive collection of policy documents and speeches (published by Chinese University Press in 2016) to analyze China's adoption of a "third way" in developing its opening strategy, from 1979 to 1988.

I sincerely thank CSCPRC for funding and support during my first two years of fieldwork in Beijing. I remain deeply indebted to the faculty and staff of Columbia University's Weatherhead East Asian Institute; they have been my primary source of inspiration since 1979. Carol Gluck and the Weatherhead East Asian Institute again supported me during the publication process for this book. While attending a recent event at the institute honoring Dr. Dorothy Borg, I sat next to my adviser and friend Andrew Nathan, who told me to always look at the bigger picture and who continues to inspire the next generation of China scholars. I also thank James Reardon-Anderson, who was not only my teacher at the Johns Hopkins School of Advanced International Studies but also my supervisor when I was managing Columbia's China/Japan Documentation Center. I am deeply grateful to the faculty and staff of Peking University's Economics Department and Foreign Students Office; Jinan University's Research Institute on the SEZs, Hong Kong, and Macao; the Guangdong Academy of Social Sciences; the Economics and English Departments of Shenzhen University; and the Universities Service Centre for China Studies, which is now at the Chinese University of Hong Kong. I also must thank Harvard's Fairbank Center for Chinese Studies, where I delivered early versions of some chapters, and the Woodrow Wilson Center and George Washington University, where I carried out my initial research as a Luce Foundation Faculty Fellow. Since 1991, I have been teaching at the University of New Hampshire, where the administration, faculty, staff, and graduate students have been so supportive of my scholarship over the years. I am deeply grateful for their encouragement and patience, especially David Larson, who treated me like a son, constantly pressured me to get my work done, and introduced me to the restorative effects of a Maine camp and the energy, intelligence, and love of border collies.

So many people and institutions have aided me along this journey. However, I want to thank in particular Tom Bernstein and Dorie Solinger, who have always taken time to read my chapters, helped me focus my argument, and inspired me to work harder. Tom's recent work on Stalinist influences on Chinese economic development has been especially insightful and has transformed my thinking. Ezra Vogel's *Canton under Communism* was the very first academic study I read on China, and his work on Guangdong and Deng Xiaoping continues to guide my thinking. He was particularly supportive of this current study, reading chapters and suggesting publication venues. Bob Graham and Kristen Wanner of Harvard University Asia Center have done a phenomenal job overseeing the publication process, and Julie Hagen has been a meticulous copyeditor. I am deeply grateful to Randa Dubnick for her meticulous work in compiling the index, and to her husband Mel who continues to inspire me to work harder. Finally, I want to thank my family, especially my parents Rosemary and Larry

Reardon, who remain with me in spirit. I still use the *Pinyin Chinese-English Dictionary* that my dad bought for me in June 1980. I miss having my mom read my manuscripts but realize that she commented on a very early version of this work when it was my dissertation.

LCR
Portsmouth, NH

Abbreviations

BOC	Bank of China
CAC	Central Advisory Committee
CCP	Chinese Communist Party
CDIC	Central Discipline Inspection Commission
CITIC	China International Trust and Investment Corporation
CMSN	China Merchants' Steam and Navigation Company
CPPCC	Chinese People's Political Consultative Conference
CYL	Communist Youth League
ECPB	export commodity processing base
EPZ	export processing zone
ETDZ	economic and technological development zone
FDI	foreign direct investment
FEC	foreign exchange certificate
FFYP	First Five-Year Plan
FTZ	free trade zone
GLF	Great Leap Forward
GVIAO	gross value of industrial and agricultural output
GVIO	gross value of industrial output
HAR	Hainan Administrative Region
ISI	import substitution industrialization
MFT	Ministry of Foreign Trade

MOFERT	Ministry of Foreign Economic Relations and Trade
NEP	New Economic Policy
NIDZNATs	National Industrial Development Zones for New and Advanced Technology
NPC	National People's Congress
OCIE	overseas Chinese investment enterprise
PBOC	People's Bank of China
PLA	People's Liberation Army
RMB	renminbi
SEZ	special economic zone
SFIC	State Foreign Investment Control Commission
SIEAC	State Import-Export Administrative Commission
SIEC	State Import-Export Commission
SOE	state-owned enterprise
SPC	State Planning Commission

Note to the Reader

Internal Chinese policy collections are comprehensive, lightly edited, and provide unprecedented details about the internal policy process. To cite these documents, I have adapted the Chinese system of policy identification. For example, the CCP Central Committee and State Council initiated China's opening process on 15 July 1979 by issuing the official document (*gongwen*) entitled "The Approval and Transmittal of the 'Two Reports of the Guangdong and Fujian Provincial Committees Concerning the Implementation of Special Policies and Flexible Measures in Foreign Trade Activities.'" While the Central Committee and the State Council approved the document, the primary issuing unit (*bianzi*) for this document was the Central Committee (Zhongfa) and not the State Council (Guofa). The issuing unit assigns each document a sequence number (*xuhao*) with the year of issuance (*niandu*). For example, the document just mentioned is labeled "Zhongfa (1979) 50 *hao*," which I translate as Central Committee document 1979.50; I use a similar numbering system for documents released by other issuing units at the central government and provincial levels and have left the bureaucratic acronym of the issuing unit in the original Chinese.

Important Actors Encountered
along China's Third Way

Chen Yun (1905–95)

Among the "eight elders" of the Chinese policy elites, Chen Yun was the most powerful promoter of the balanced, planned-growth approach of bureaucratic Stalinism, which inspired his policy choices as vice premier (1954–64), first secretary of the Central Commission for Discipline Inspection (1978–87), and second chairman of the CCP Central Advisory Commission (1987–92).

After working in Shanghai as a union organizer, Chen Yun spent time in Moscow in the early 1950s learning the intricacies of state planning and became the major proponent of bureaucratic Stalinism as outlined in Stalin's *Economic Problems of Socialism in the USSR* (1951) and the Soviet *Political Economy Textbook* (1954). Having witnessed Mao's harsh treatment of former party leaders Gao Gang and Rao Shushi after 1953, Chen Yun acted strategically to avoid Mao's wrath.[1] While he and Zhou Enlai blocked many of Mao's normative ideas in 1956, he was unable to counter Mao's push for the Great Leap Forward (GLF) in 1958.

Following Mao's destruction of the Yan'an Roundtable and the GLF economic crisis, Chen Yun joined with Zhou Enlai, Liu Shaoqi, and others to form a bureaucratic Stalinist opinion group to advocate the use of the market to overcome the GLF's economic chaos. In the early 1970s, Chen and the bureaucratic Stalinists renewed their cooperative efforts to resuscitate the economy after the Cultural Revolution and to reinstate the Four Modernizations import substitution industrialization (ISI) approach. He had a close relationship with Deng Xiaoping and facilitated his rehabilitation in 1973 and 1977. Later, suffering from poor health, including cancer surgery in October 1979, Chen Yun depended on his allies, including Li Xiannian, Yao Yilin, and Zhao Ziyang, to formulate and implement his vision of bureaucratic Stalinism and the economic readjustment policies of the early 1980s.[2]

Throughout the 1980s, Chen Yun directly confronted Deng's "rash advance" approach to development. Some viewed Chen Yun as slavishly devoted to preserving the command economy. Zhao Ziyang believed that Chen Yun had the most sophisticated knowledge of economics among those in the first generation of bureaucratic Stalinists, and that he "believed in allowing for as lively a market as possible within the structure of a planned economy."[3] Chen Yun never adopted the radical approaches to marketization that Deng Xiaoping proposed. From the 1950s to the 1990s he consistently followed a moderate, bureaucratic Stalinist path in promoting a balanced, planned economy that was supplemented by markets. This became known as "the bird in the cage approach," in which the market is restrained by the plan.[4]

Deng Xiaoping (1904–97)

Before he became the paramount leader of the second generation of party elites as well as one of the elite eight elders in the late 1970s, Deng Xiaoping studied and worked in France, where he took menial jobs at various French factories, making ordnance, artificial flowers, rubber galoshes, and Renault automobiles.[5] Besides learning firsthand about Western technology, management techniques, and the problems of capitalism, Deng also learned to become a revolutionary by participating in the Communist Youth League in Europe. In 1926 Deng arrived in Russia for a year-long stay at Moscow's Sun Yat-sen University of the Toilers of China. The Soviet Union had experienced five years of economic recovery and growth under Lenin's New Economic Policy (NEP), which established a limited number of regional commodity markets and imported foreign capital and technology to modernize the agricultural, industrial, and petrochemical industries.[6] According to Ezra Vogel, "The fundamentals of the NEP, a market economy under Communist leadership, were similar to those of the economic policies that Deng would carry out when he was in charge of China's Southwest Bureau in 1949–52 and those that he would reintroduce in the 1980s."[7]

An ambitious soldier in the Chinese Communist Revolution, Deng moved, after the war, from directing the party in southwestern China to Beijing, where he rose to become Mao's right-hand man during the Anti-Rightist Campaign and the Great Leap Forward. Like Mao, Deng was not an economist. But he joined with Liu Shaoqi, Zhou Enlai, and Chen Yun to oppose radical Stalinism in 1961 and became a strong proponent of bureaucratic Stalinism's remunerative approach and the Four Modernizations ISI approach. Chen Yun eventually tempered Deng's enthusiastic promotion of Hua Guofeng's New Great Leap strategy of large-scale ISI. In promoting a policy readjustment, Deng appointed a third generation of Chinese leaders, such as Zhao Ziyang, to experiment with outwardly oriented coastal development and special economic zones. While Deng's two *nanxun* trips to southern China in 1984 and 1992 reinforced the international Leninist economic paradigm change promoted by Zhao, Deng did not advocate changing the Stalinist political or social paradigm and its support of party hegemony.

Mao Zedong and Deng Xiaoping were neither technocrats nor economists but visionaries, with unrivaled abilities to lead the party-state. They strongly believed in the importance of maintaining the power of the paramount leader and the party's hegemony. They were loyal to fellow elites if they were useful for gaining or maintaining power. They had a penchant for spittoons and grandiose policy initiatives designed to accelerate China's economic growth; Mao is remembered as the "Great Helmsman" at the vanguard of the revolution. Deng is often described as the pragmatic architect of China's opening strategy who invoked cat analogies. Like Mao, Deng did not get bogged down by economic realities but focused on economic possibilities.[8] Mao and Deng were responsible for creating great improvements in China's standard of living, but also for the deaths of tens of millions of people during the GLF and the subjection of Chinese citizens to decades of political persecution.

Just as Mao Zedong promoted "rash advance" in the 1950s to accelerate domestic development, Deng Xiaoping enthusiastically promoted

Mao's rash advance throughout the Great Leap Forward period. While implementing the GLF Deng stated, "We should have a grand prospect of Socialism, and a fondness for the grandiose. . . . Now our direction is clear and definite. As long as we have enthusiasm, we can develop socialism quickly, and not make the mistakes of opportunists."[9] Although tempered by Chen Yun from the late 1970s to the 1990s, Deng often employed a similar grandiose rash-advance approach when expanding the domestic marketplace and opening China to the international economy.[10]

In the 1980s, during the transition to the Third Way, Deng adopted a more international Leninist viewpoint in which he mixed Lenin's NEP market policies with Mao's rash-advance enthusiasm. Deng's rash-advance attitude and unbridled enthusiasm to open China to the outside world eventually co-opted the moderate view of Chen Yun and led to China's shift to a consultative economic paradigm. But, like Mao, Deng steadfastly upheld the hegemony of the party over the state.

Hu Yaobang (1915–89)

Like his mentor Deng Xiaoping, Hu Yaobang was a Kejia (Hakka), but he was from a poor family and was a survivor of the Long March and Yan'an, where he was assigned to the Second Field Army. Hu followed Deng to Sichuan, where Hu oversaw the land reform process in northern Sichuan. Deng later brought him to Beijing, where he was appointed first secretary of the Communist Youth League in 1953. After following Deng's example of supporting Hua Guofeng's New Great Leap in the late 1970s, Hu focused on political reforms and played only a limited role in economic policy making in the 1980s.

Zhao Ziyang described Hu as having an older concept of economic growth that emphasized production statistics, growth rates, and mass campaigns, rather than economic efficiency. Nevertheless, Hu Yaobang strongly supported Deng Xiaoping's international Leninist approach to opening China and adopting a more consultative economic paradigm. However, he disagreed with Deng and the first generation regarding the Stalinist political and social hegemony of the party and argued for a new consultative approach. For this reason, when Central

Committee document 1987.3 was issued 19 January 1987, Deng criticized Hu Yaobang for six major mistakes, including encouraging bourgeois liberalization, questioning the legitimacy of the Chinese Communist Party, opposing "leftist" ideas, promoting high economic growth rates, and opposing the use of normative slogans.

Hua Guofeng (1921–2008)

Hailing from Mao's home province and as his appointed successor from 1976 to 1981, Hua was a transitional paramount leader. While his "Two Whatevers" approach was derided by some as adhering too closely to Mao Zedong's radical Stalinism, he was a bureaucratic Stalinist who promoted Zhou Enlai's Four Modernizations and its large-scale ISI development strategy. Although Deng Xiaoping was especially supportive of the expensive ISI schemes, Chen Yun and Li Xiannian convinced Deng to readjust the New Great Leap approach. Yet they expanded many of Hua's key opening policies, including the initial focus on processing and assembly manufacturing, foreign investment, and export processing zones.

Li Xiannian (1909–88)

Li Xiannian was truly one of the eight elders, as his continuous role in formulating and implementing China's economic policy was extraordinary. Unlike Deng, Li did not favor Mao's more normative approach to economic development. As vice chairman of the State Council's Finance and Economics Committee, Li reestablished his working relationship with Chen Yun that was first forged during the Long March. Li sided with Zhou Enlai, Chen Yun, and others to oppose Mao's rash-advance approach in 1956 and again in the early 1960s. In 1958, Li adopted a survivor strategy by following Zhou Enlai's example of voicing self-criticisms. Such a defensive approach allowed Li to avoid Mao's wrath and gained him his appointment to the Central Secretariat in May 1958.[11] However, as the GLF was entering one of its acute starvation phases in 1959, Li—along with Deng Zihui and Liao

Luyan—convinced Mao to reestablish private agricultural plots and livestock to augment production on the people's communes.[12] Li also proposed that sideline agricultural production bases be established to guarantee food supplies for the urban areas.[13]

Li argued that foreign trade was very beneficial to China's development and criticized those who promoted a more autarkic, revolutionary Stalinist approach. Li joined a three-person Foreign Trade Command Post in August 1959 to divert scarce commodities to the export sector and recentralize the foreign trade system.[14] To encourage production, Li argued against a normative development approach and promoted a more remunerative approach, including enticing producers to supply the state with necessary export goods by providing them with scarce grain reserves and sugar.[15] By the early 1960s Li had joined Zhou Enlai, Chen Yun, and the other bureaucratic Stalinists to reestablish their approach to development, and to feed the starving people by importing grain from overseas.[16] To finance grain imports, China's remaining debts to the Soviet Union, and the small-scale ISI program envisioned in the Four Modernizations plan of 1963, Li vigorously advocated various export promotion programs, especially the Import Production Inputs to Produce Exports Program (*Yijin yangchu*).[17] Li argued that China had to target capitalist countries to import needed industrial equipment, although he cautioned that doing business with Western countries was complicated, as China would have to respect contracts and Western demands for high-quality exports.[18]

Like Zhou Enlai, Li remained in power during the Cultural Revolution to implement Mao's semi-autarkic Third Front strategy. Li Xiannian, along with the head of the State Planning Commission, Yu Qiuli, managed the chaotic economy during the Cultural Revolution and throughout the 1970s. After 1971, Zhou Enlai, Li Xiannian, Yu Qiuli, and Chen Yun readjusted the economy to overcome the economic chaos of the Third Front development strategy. Li argued in 1973, for instance, that the state had to invest equally in military and civilian industries.[19] Li Xiannian worked closely with Chen Yun to formulate the Four-Three ISI Plan in 1973 and promoted Hua Guofeng's New Great Leap as a continuation of Zhou Enlai's bureaucratic Stalinism and its large-scale ISI.[20]

Li's ideas concerning Hua's large-scale ISI program changed when Chen Yun persuaded the bureaucratic Stalinist elites of the dangers of Hua's ISI strategy, and submitted a self-criticism for his own participation in the New Great Leap in 1977–78.[21] In 1979 Li joined Yao Yilin to work under Chen Yun as vice chairmen of the State Council Finance and Economics Committee (Caizheng Jingji Weiyuanhui) and was especially influential during the three-year readjustment period. While often in his shadow, Li continued to side with Chen Yun in the 1980s to promote the moderate bureaucratic Stalinist development model II, which he had promoted under Zhou Enlai from the 1950s to the 1970s, and to temper Deng's desire to establish state capitalism.

However, Zhao Ziyang argues that Li increasingly felt estranged from the other elites, "feeling that his work had been rejected, [and] often expressed his displeasure at the direction of China's economy. Li rhetorically asked, '[I]f whatever is being done now is all correct, then was the past work all wrong?' He always opposed reform and often complained about it."[22] This feeling of rejection coincided with Li's reduced role in economic policy formulation, which occurred after March 1980 when the Party Standing Committee established the Central Finance and Economic Leading Group (Zhongyang Caizheng Jingji Lingdao Xiaozu].[23] Li Xiannian was relegated to following a former subordinate, Zhao Ziyang, as he assumed responsibility, as premier, for the implementation of Chen Yun's bureaucratic Stalinist vision of economic readjustment.[24] Eventually Li was appointed China's president in 1983, which, in comparison with his previous key roles in economic decision making, was a sinecure. However, as one of the surviving first generation of bureaucratic Stalinists, he strongly disliked Zhao Ziyang and was increasingly critical of Zhao's economic and political reforms.[25]

Mao Zedong (1893–1976)

China's first paramount Communist leader, Mao was not an economist but was an early proponent of Stalin's *Short Course of the History of the All-Russian Communist Party (Bolshevik)*, known simply as the *Short Course*. Mao admired the use of normative incentives and its emphasis on class struggle. While initially accepting Soviet advice on balanced growth and large-scale ISI development, he promoted Stalin's earlier approach as embodied by the Great Leap Forward. China needed to become self-reliant and to implement a semi-autarkic development strategy so that it could stand on its own "two legs."

Zhao Ziyang (1919–2005)

Zhao Ziyang was the primary proponent of the international Leninist approach. As Guangdong Party Secretary Tao Zhu's talented protégé, Zhao learned about the reality of the revolutionary Stalinist approach as he oversaw the implementation of the Guangdong land reform campaigns and the Great Leap Forward in the 1950s. Like Deng, he sought the truth by adopting a more radical vision of bureaucratic Stalinism. He resurrected the Guangdong private markets in the early 1960s and implemented the Sichuan agricultural decentralization experiments in the mid-1970s.

During this period Zhao learned about the economic importance of the overseas Chinese community, especially after the party admitted its flawed implementation of the Guangdong land reform campaigns of the early 1950s and its poor treatment of overseas Chinese communities. Zhao gained a greater understanding of export promotion schemes as he helped to inaugurate the first China Export Commodity Trade Fair in spring 1957, which became China's primary venue for promoting exports.[26] While speaking to a meeting of the State Council in September 1981, Zhao gave the other Political Bureau and State Council members a firsthand account of the Chinese economic migrants who had continued to brave the treacherous border areas to escape to Hong Kong.[27] And when Guangdong and Fujian opened their doors to foreign direct investment in the early 1980s, Zhao Ziyang could personally explain to the leadership the vast potential of overseas Chinese investment.

Zhao states that his trip to Western Europe in 1979 had a great impact on his views of the marketplace. He was amazed that European farmers living in arid regions were prosperous. Zhao realized that Western European economies had not pursued self-reliant development but "instead relied on trade with the outside world and utilized their strengths to export their goods in exchange for what they needed."[28] Zhao became the primary architect of the coastal development strategy, including the SEZs, the fourteen open coastal cities and their economic and technological development zones, the Hainan SEZ, and accession to the international General Agreement on Tariffs and Trade. While Zhao understood the importance of opposing a rash advance to gain favor from Chen Yun, and put forward fundamental policies that transformed the revolutionary economic paradigm, he failed to appreciate Deng's emphasis on maintaining the party's political hegemony. Following the June Fourth Incident at Tiananmen Square and his house arrest, Zhao's memoirs were spirited out of Beijing and his collected works were published in Hong Kong.

Zhou Enlai (1898–1976)

Zhou became the first premier of the People's Republic of China in 1949; until 1958 he was also the first foreign minister. Having studied and worked in Japan and France, Zhou was one of the primary proponents of Stalin's moderate bureaucratic approach of balanced growth, remunerative incentives, and import substitution industrialization. He had learned never to confront Mao directly or to challenge his rash-advance approach of radical Stalinism. Instead, he worked closely with Chen Yun to offset Mao's more radical policies. In 1960, to recover from the GLF, he backed the establishment of China's first export processing zones; he also promoted large-scale ISI with the Four Modernizations development strategy in 1963, and the Four-Three large-scale ISI strategy of 1973.

INTRODUCTION

Elite Learning and China's Third Way

He who learns but does not think is lost. He who thinks
but does not learn is in great danger.

子曰, 学而不思则罔, 思而不学则殆.
—Confucius, *Lunyu* 2.15

During the first three decades of communist rule in the People's Republic of China, Chinese elites steadfastly supported the long-term goals of the comprehensive Stalinist political, economic, and social paradigm. Those goals included building a strong national defense, developing a self-sufficient economy, and guaranteeing the Communist Party's hegemony over the state, the economy, and the people.[1] This comprehensive approach guided Mao and the PRC leadership for thirty years and imbued the thinking of the party membership, the bureaucracy, and the people with a revolutionary purpose and an agenda for action.

However, the elites held differing opinions concerning the strategies for achieving the goals of the Stalinist economic paradigm. Their differences resulted in a cycling between two Chinese variations of Stalinism from the 1950s to 1970s. Mao promoted the "first way" of normative semi-autarkic development (development model I), which used ideology and mobilization techniques characteristic of revolutionary Stalinism (practiced in the Soviet Union from 1929 to 1934) to implement the Great Leap Forward (GLF), the Third Front, and the Cultural Revolution. Zhou Enlai, Chen Yun, and eventually Deng Xiaoping promoted the "second way" (development model II): a strategy of remunerative, import substitution industrialization (ISI) adapted from the bureaucratic Stalinist model (1934–53). These ideas inspired Chinese leaders to formulate the Four Modernizations strategy and its variations, the Four-Three ISI Plan (Sisan fang'an) and the new Ten-Year ISI Plan.[2]

By the late 1970s and early 1980s, Chinese elites realized the limitations of adapting model II and its bureaucratic Stalinist approach. Partly inspired by the Soviet Union's New Economic Policy (NEP; 1921–29), they initiated experiments with a new "Third Way" for China's development (development model III). Chen Yun adapted a more moderate version of bureaucratic Stalinism, which promoted balanced growth that relied primarily on the state plan and command economy, supplemented by the market. Deng Xiaoping adopted a more radical version of bureaucratic Stalinism that experimented with outward-oriented development, special economic zones (SEZs), and a greater role for the market. And in the 1990s, Chinese elites had shifted to a new consultative economic paradigm while adapting policies of the older Stalinist political and social paradigms.

Ideational Learning: The Origin of Chinese Development Ideas

Following its defeat in the first Opium War (1839–42), the Chinese empire was forced to open to the global economy. To adapt to the changed environment, Chinese elites borrowed ideas from abroad, following the Qing dynasty's Self-Strengthening Movement that promoted *ti yong*: protecting Confucian values as China's essence (*ti*) while using foreign technology to modernize the country (*yong*). After 1949, elites in the PRC preserved China's essence by adapting Confucian concepts with Marxism-Leninism–Mao Zedong Thought and used foreign learning from the Soviet Union to modernize the state.[3] Understanding the Soviet development ideas explains the process of Chinese ideational learning from the 1950s to the 1980s and the origins of China's Third Way.

The basic ideational learning process focuses on individuals, their Weltanschauung, and how they promote their policy preferences by joining with like-minded individuals to influence policy formation over time. Mark Blyth hypothesizes that economic ideas create institutional change by reducing leadership uncertainty during periods of crisis; they also act as an organizing principle for interest groups and provide a tool with which to dismantle and rebuild state, business, and labor institutions while reducing uncertainty by providing a blueprint for change.[4] Expanding upon Blyth's approach, this study links individual views as expressed in currently available primary resources (speeches, policy opinions, chronologies, and autobiographies) with the formation of elite opinion groups coalescing around specific preference choices.

Chinese elites studied Soviet writings and economic policies and adapted the basic ideas to formulate policies for China's countryside and urban areas. Traveling, working, and studying abroad also influenced the elites' worldview and the policy choices they adopted. They formed opinion groups around a collective preference for a specific economic model for developing China. Notably, their preferences and strategies were not static but evolved over time, reflecting the fluctuation of internal political dynamics and incremental learning based on perceived successes and mistakes in policy implementation.

Development Model I: Mao, Revolutionary Stalinism, and the Consensus Strategy

Revolutionary Stalinism, especially its focus on industrial-sector development and normative means to inspire "communist man," strongly influenced Mao's economic development ideas and his policy preferences.[5] To understand Mao's concept of economic development, one first must understand the evolution of Stalin's ideas.

Considering "the necessity of flexible tactics for the greater cause," Stalin supported Lenin's New Economic Policy in 1921. While the NEP

entailed a partial restoration of the private economy and private ownership, Stalin argued that the party must maintain its hegemony over
the state.[6] Following Lenin's death in 1924, Stalin exiled Trotsky, ousted
the NEP's greatest supporter, Bukharin, from the Political Bureau, and
implemented the "Great Turn" away from the NEP.[7] With the precipi-
tous drop in grain procurement in 1927–28, Stalin feared that the kulaks,
or "petty-peasant" farmers, would threaten the party's power. He was
also concerned that the NEP had not promoted the "industrial prole-
tarians."[8] In an "earth-shattering speech" delivered in Siberia in 1928,
Stalin replaced the NEP's mixed market economy with coercive administrative controls in order to collectivize the Soviet countryside. Stalin
also used persuasion to mobilize the peasantry, promote the socialist
transformation, and increase education levels among the people.[9]

While Stalin's collectivization measures resulted in mass starvation in the early 1930s, the newly established Soviet command economy
eventually recovered and grew tremendously by the mid-1930s. Stalin
described this revolutionary Stalinist model in his *Short Course of the
History of the All-Russian Communist Party (Bolshevik)*, or simply *Short
Course*, which became the core text in China for CCP elites, cadres,
and members, as well as university students, about the "true" path of
Marxism-Leninism. Even after Nikita Khrushchev repudiated Stalin
at the Twentieth Soviet Party Congress in 1956, Mao continued to promote the ideas of the *Short Course*, including Stalin's emphasis on class
struggle, and the work remained required reading for high-level cadres
during the Socialist Education Movement of 1963.[10]

Mao admired Stalin's blueprint for radical socialist transformation
in agriculture and industry and had gained two decades of experience
implementing such radical change in Jinggangshan, the Chinese Soviet
Republic, and to a lesser extent in the Shaan-Gan-Ning region during
the 1930s and 1940s.[11] However, Mao initially argued that Stalin's guide
to establishing a strong communist state was not appropriate for
China's agrarian-based revolution.[12] Chinese party elites had adopted
a democratic centralism and a united-front approach in Yan'an in the
1930s and 1940s to gain support from all of China's social classes, in
order ultimately to achieve a communist victory. Most important, Mao
was unwilling to promote a revolutionary strategy put forward by one
of his primary political challengers, Wang Ming, who believed in a

closer relationship with the Comintern, promoted a more orthodox Marxism-Leninism, and enjoyed Stalin's strong support as the rightful CCP leader.[13]

While Mao absorbed and adapted Stalin's revolutionary approach during the next three decades to formulate his views on normative development, political realities hindered the comprehensive implementation of Stalin's revolutionary ideas until the late 1950s.[14] Realizing that the party would assume control of a country ravaged by civil war, hyperinflation, and foreign intrigue, Mao and China's leaders adapted the revolutionary concepts outlined in Stalin's *Short Course* to the Chinese situation.[15] Mao described his adaptation of Soviet methods as "accepting all that is good, and firmly rejecting all that is bad."[16] Mao continued to ponder the policy problems he first had encountered when implementing his radical approach to socialist transformation at Jinggangshan and his later, more moderate policies in Yan'an.[17] He incorporated Stalin's totalitarian tactics and normative approach to mobilize the masses' sense of nationalism and communism and thus accelerate development. The inspired Chinese people "were the determining factor," he believed, that could overcome all problems and easily achieve economic self-reliance.[18] Mao especially appreciated Stalin's emphasis on the hegemonic party structure, class conflict, and accelerated socialist transformation.[19] He thus considered Stalin's *Short Course* a blueprint for the way to achieve remarkable economic growth.[20] Mao thus adapted Stalin's *Short Course* and its emphasis on normative incentives to China's realities to produce a unique Chinese approach that would achieve high growth rates in agricultural and industrial output.[21]

After Ivan Arkhipov and his team of Soviet experts arrived in China in late 1949, Mao must have been disappointed that Arkhipov did not promote revolutionary Stalinism as outlined in the *Short Course*. Instead of emphasizing class struggle and a radical, socialist transformation of agricultural and industry, Arkhipov argued for a more balanced bureaucratic Stalinist development model, which the Soviet Union adopted following the economic debacle of the early 1930s and had imposed on its new satellite states in Eastern Europe.[22] The Russian advisers argued for a moderate approach to socialist transformation in which private property and markets initially coexisted with the Chinese state sector. They subsequently directed the Chinese to study Stalin's 1951 treatment of Marxist-Leninist development, *Economic Problems of Socialism in the USSR*, which recognized that markets could exist under socialism and would gradually be phased out as higher stages of communism were achieved.[23]

Rejecting his earlier radical approach to socialist transformation, in *Economic Problems of Socialism in the USSR*, Stalin promoted a moderate, bureaucratic Stalinism model in which the pace of socialist transformation was dependent on a country's level of development. Stalin had learned that the violence resulting from Soviet collectivization in the early 1930s could threaten Communist Party hegemony in the Eastern European and Chinese economies. As an incentive to adopt the new path, he also offered political and security guarantees, technical advice, and low-interest loans to procure Soviet technology and turnkey projects.

As China was underdeveloped, it needed to achieve socialist transformation in a gradual fashion.[24] Stalin sent a cable to Mao in 1948 stating that the CCP should not abolish private land ownership and nationalize lands, nor should the party confiscate the wealth of the bourgeoisie.[25] Mao did not reject Stalin's newer bureaucratic model, which was strongly supported by the Chinese elites who had studied in the Soviet Union during the NEP, including the Vice Chairman of the Central People's Government Liu Shaoqi and the future ambassador to the Soviet Union, Zhang Wentian. Liu and Zhang, in particular, agreed with Stalin that China initially should focus on its agricultural sector, which should undergo a slower-paced collectivization to allow the development of the private agricultural sector.[26] Perhaps reflecting on his experience living in the Soviet Union, Liu argued in May 1949 that China had established "state capitalism, in which there is long-term cooperation between the private sector and the state. We want many long-term cooperative endeavors, in which both private and public sectors benefit. This cooperation is freely undertaken." The result, according to Liu, would be one in which "everyone eats when there is rice, and everybody profits when there is money."[27] In June 1949 Liu Shaoqi traveled to Moscow to open negotiations for a one-year trade agreement that was signed the following month. Liu highly praised the Soviet model for its technical expertise and financing capabilities, which would accelerate China's development.[28]

Mao thus made a tactical compromise. He accepted Arkhipov's slower bureaucratic methods to achieve the Stalinist economic paradigm, which did not call for the complete and immediate collectivization of the countryside as Stalin had done in Russia in January 1930.[29] In negotiating the Treaty of Friendship, Alliance, and Mutual Assistance with the Soviet Union, Mao withstood Stalin's attempts at humiliation and dominance during the negotiation process in Moscow between December 1949 and February 1950.[30] He accepted the establishment of joint Sino-Russian stock companies, such as those established in Xinjiang for mining and petroleum production, and preferential access for the Soviets to the Chinese Changchun Railroad and the naval ports at Dalian and Lüshun.[31] Mao also accepted Stalin's order to reduce the projected growth rates of the First Five-Year Plan (FFYP) and the amount of Chinese imports from the Soviet Union.[32] Realizing that Stalin questioned the authenticity of the Chinese revolution, Mao's negotiation strategy was "first I argued against any proffered proposal with which I disagreed. Second, if they persisted in supporting the proposal, I accepted but with reservations. This was because I took into consideration the entire interest of socialism."[33]

Mao and the Yan'an Roundtable thus reached a compromise concerning policies implemented after 1951; they reflected a mixture of bureaucratic and revolutionary Stalinism. Chinese elites thus adapted bureaucratic Stalinism, which included the Soviet model of central planning and formulation of the FFYP. They also adapted revolutionary Stalinism by promoting a limited socialist transformation, including the establishment of small rural collectives, based on the Soviet experience.[34] And they agreed to accelerate Chinese industrialization by importing Soviet turnkey projects and technology, just as Stalin had done in the late 1920s.[35]

However, Mao had not given up on revolutionary Stalinism and its normative strategies. He remained unsatisfied with the slow pace of socialist transformation in the economy and with China's dependency on the Soviet Union, while his Yan'an Roundtable colleagues continued to promote the more bureaucratic, balanced path. This difference of opinion eventually corroded both the consensus strategy and the Yan'an Roundtable. By the mid-1950s, Mao was promoting his normative, "rash advance" development approach, based on revolutionary

Stalinism and the *Short Course*. Embracing the concept of self-reliance, with secondary support from abroad, Mao's vision resulted in the Great Leap Forward, the Third Front, and the Cultural Revolution.[36]

Development Model II:
Adapting Bureaucratic Stalinism

In contrast to Mao, who fervently believed in revolutionary Stalinism, Zhou Enlai, Liu Shaoqi, Chen Yun, and the other Yan'an Roundtable members embraced Stalin's new bureaucratic approach to economic development, with its gradual approach to socialist transformation and its use of remunerative means to motivate "economic man" to accelerate modernization.[37] By the mid-1930s, Stalin declared that class struggle had achieved the socialist transformation of the Soviet Union's industrial and agricultural sectors. In reality, Stalin had allowed a limited return of the markets by the mid-1930s, approving household agricultural plots, reestablishing free markets, and permitting the sale of agricultural goods once state quotas were met.[38] Stalin subsequently promoted a more balanced economic development model that emphasized an extensive centralized planning bureaucracy, which Trotsky criticized in *The Revolution Betrayed* as "the Soviet Thermidor [which was] a triumph of the bureaucracy over the masses."[39]

Thus, instead of teaching how to collectivize the countryside, Soviet experts in the early 1950s were promoting Stalin's new approach, described in his *Economic Problems of Socialism in the USSR*, to teach Chinese bureaucrats how to organize key state economic sectors and allow a limited role for the market. Zhou Enlai called "for all to come under the economic plan, which we can revise and supplement frequently because of incomplete statistics and other issues."[40] The February 1951 expanded meeting of the Political Bureau approved Zhou Enlai's suggestion and established a six-person "Leading Small Group," composed of Zhou Enlai, Chen Yun, Bo Yibo, Li Fuchun, Nie Rongzhen, and Gong Shaowen, to focus all efforts to oversee the drafting of the FFYP.[41] In August 1952 Chen Yun and others traveled to Moscow, where the Chinese delegation held talks with Stalin, participated in economic training sessions, and visited several large industrial enterprises.[42] The party subsequently centralized control over all aspects of domestic and international economic exchange, placing high restrictions on foreign trade and foreign investment while establishing a limited socialist market economy that utilized remunerative policies; the bureaucratic Stalinists even promoted competition among China's private entrepreneurs in 1952.[43] The newly established State Planning Commission (SPC) eventually produced the FFYP in 1954. Following Stalin's advice concerning socialist transformation, the plan moderated Mao's radical view by advocating a more gradual transition.

In light of the consensus strategy on development in the early 1950s, proponents of both revolutionary and bureaucratic Stalinism embraced the selective importation of Soviet and Eastern European technology and equipment, which allowed China to reduce manufactured imports and achieve the long-term goals of the Stalinist economic paradigm.[44] Because of Mao's cooperative attitude toward "elder brother" Stalin, the Chinese and Soviets eventually signed agreements between 1953 and 1954 to construct 156 large-scale ISI projects, which developed China's indigenous industries by importing Russian manufacturing technology, and to decrease China's dependence on imports. As a result of the so-called 156 Projects, Mao argued, "The Chinese people will, with their efforts to learn from the advanced experience and latest technical achievements of the Soviet Union, be able to gradually build up their own powerful heavy industry."[45] In addition to the importation of technology and turnkey projects, the Chinese elites sent 8,000 Chinese scientists, engineers, and students to study in the Soviet Union and welcomed 7,000 Soviet experts to guide the construction of their new industrial infrastructure.[46]

The Contradiction between Revolutionary and Bureaucratic Stalinists

Following the death of Stalin, Mao sent a telegram of condolence to the Soviet people in September 1953. While Mao publicly acknowledged Stalin's wish that China would have a "gradual transition to socialism," he was privately critical of the relatively slow pace of China's economic development.[47] Freed by Stalin's passing to promote his older radical strategy, Mao tried to convince the other members of the Yan'an Roundtable to alter their consensus strategy and fully adopt development model I, based on revolutionary Stalinism, to promote faster change. He attacked those he considered to be too close to Stalin, specifically Gao Gang.[48]

Mao was committed to employing his normative interpretation of revolutionary Stalinism to achieve the comprehensive Stalinist paradigm. He simply believed that by following the general guidelines of the *Short Course*, he could discard all remnants of the previous capitalist, semifeudal, semicolonial society and pull China out of its morass. After Khrushchev criticized Stalin at the Twentieth Party Congress of the Soviet Union in February 1956, Mao rejected the consensus development strategy reached with the other elites of the Yan'an Roundtable, instead arguing that China "must be very specific when studying the Soviet Union. We do not want to study the Soviet example when we carry out land reforms or transformation of industry or commerce."[49] In Mao's first version of his "On the Ten Great Relationships" speech to the April 1956 Political Bureau meeting, he openly criticized the "blind copying of Soviet agricultural policies" and the consensus strategy's emphasis on investment in heavy industry and the military during times of peace, and the Soviet administrative methods designed to encourage economic growth.[50]

Mao and like-minded elites coalesced in the mid- to late 1950s to form the revolutionary Stalinist opinion group. In December 1955 he criticized those cadres who maintained a model II, bureaucratic Stalinist approach as being too conservative and acting like "women with bound feet" (*xiaojiao nüren*) by advocating only balanced development.[51] Mao argued for a "rash advance" (*maojin*) because, he said, China "must hurry and achieve faster, greater and better results in all work projects" and surpass the economic goals of the fifteen-year economic plan.[52] While Mao gradually became less sanguine about achieving the communist stage, he remained firm in his criticism of the bureaucratic Stalinist approach of the FFYP.[53] Mao echoed Stalin's *Short Course* by stating, "The objective reality of development is not balance. Constant breaching of equilibrium is a good thing. Do not promote balance in your work. Those units that do, have a problem."[54]

Reacting to the FFYP's dependence on the Soviet Union and its slavish adherence to bureaucratic Stalinism, the revolutionary Stalinist opinion group promoted a semi-autarkic development strategy that relied on China's own innate abilities—China's "communist man"—to transform the state into a strong, self-sufficient economy.[55] The international marketplace was no longer necessary, because under the FFYP China had already imported the basic technological tools of development, just as Stalin had implemented a large-scale ISI program in the Soviet Union of the early 1930s.[56] Mobilized by the Communist Party and its ideology, the Chinese people could now stand on their own two feet. While Mao believed that foreign technology could supplement Chinese development efforts, China would rely primarily on the Chinese people and the use of indigenous technologies suitable to Chinese development.[57] Only in this fashion would China create a strong, prosperous, and self-reliant nation.

Without directly confronting Mao, Premier Zhou Enlai, Chen Yun, and others adapted their bureaucratic Stalinism to address some of Mao's concerns and to emphasize remunerative policies, a limited socialist market economy, and an ISI development strategy for achieving the Stalinist economic paradigm.[58] Many of the first generation of Communist Party elites had studied and worked overseas and in China's cosmopolitan areas, such as Shanghai. While wary of the exploitative power of foreign market economies, they believed that the financial and technical knowledge found in the international marketplace could supplement the economic base provided by the FFYP to ensure long-term domestic development. They thus championed the continuation of bureaucratic Stalinism and its ISI strategy for self-reliance. Holding a more conservative view of balanced development, they argued that China should pursue "more, faster, better," but added the words "more economically." In June 1956 Zhou told Chen Yun, "We can no longer just try to prevent rash advance but must oppose it! If rash advance continues, we will lose contact with reality, the masses, and our current needs and possibilities. We don't want to throw cold water on the masses, but we also cannot let the demands of a minority of activists become the needs of the masses."[59]

True to the slower paced, remunerative version of bureaucratic socialism, Zhou Enlai and Chen Yun argued that China would require fifteen years to establish a comprehensive industrial system. They thus implemented a slower development approach, which lasted from the 1956 Eighth Party Congress to the Third Plenum of September/ October 1957. Recognizing the adamant opposition to his normative approach, Mao destroyed the Yan'an Roundtable and its norm of consensus by the late 1950s, disciplined Zhou and Chen Yun, and implemented his normative vision of rash advance, the Great Leap Forward.[60]

Prodded by a deep concern over the economic chaos and rampant starvation that resulted from Mao's rash-advance strategy of the late 1950s and by the demise of the Yan'an Roundtable, Zhou Enlai, Chen Yun, and other elites came together after the late 1950s to form a bureaucratic Stalinist opinion group. While never directly challenging Mao, they adapted the remunerative concepts of bureaucratic Stalinism and Soviet economic practices whenever they were in power, to accelerate China's recovery from Mao's disastrous economic policies and the reimplementation of the ISI strategy.

For the next two decades, both elite opinion groups—the revolutionary and the bureaucratic Stalinists—supported the long-term goals of the Stalinist economic paradigm. Yet the actual strategies used to achieve the paradigm's long-term goals cycled between semi-autarky and ISI, reflecting the shifting political power of the two groups and their preferred variation of Stalinism.[61] Thus, the elites were engaged not in collective learning but in divergent learning, or "the adoption of different new policy understandings by members of a group," as each group, when in power, followed its preferred development strategy.[62]

Adapting Development Model II

The bureaucratic Stalinism opinion group promoted four distinct adaptations of development model II's ISI strategy, based on lessons learned incrementally between 1956 and 1978. By evaluating policy implementation whenever they held power, the bureaucratic Stalinists learned the strengths and weaknesses of various policy adaptations. The knowledge they accumulated contributed to the elites' recognition of paradigm anomalies and their eventual adoption of the Third Way, the consultative economic development paradigm.

Sharing a deep concern about Mao's development model I and his adaptation of revolutionary Stalinism, the bureaucratic Stalinists argued for model II's moderate growth strategy and a continuation of its remunerative interpretation of bureaucratic Stalinism, including its technocratic ISI development strategy.[63] At the Eighth Party Congress, Zhou and Chen Yun gained tacit support from the other key economic leaders, such as Liu Shaoqi, Li Fuchun, Li Xiannian, and Bo Yibo, to implement a slower path toward development that entailed three five-year plans to establishing a "comprehensive industrial system."[64]

Diversifying ISI Sourcing, 1956–57

As China still had to import 40 percent of its industrial needs from abroad after the FFYP, Zhou took advantage of the Eisenhower administration's "peaceful evolution" strategy toward China and its lack of embargo enforcement.[65] Zhou increased China's imports from Japan, Great Britain, and West Germany, and decreased spending on imports from the Soviet Union from US$705 million to US$640 million.[66] While diversifying China's ISI partners, Zhou Enlai continued to rely on the Soviet Union, whose technology and expertise had been a core building block in developing China's economy. He signed a US$1.25 billion agreement with the Soviet Union to build seventy-eight new ISI projects, including chemical factories, petrochemical complexes, power generation plants, and machinery manufacturing plants.[67]

To finance the ISI projects, China exported goods through Hong Kong and tapped overseas Chinese investment capital to develop areas around the Pearl River Delta. According to Zhou, Hong Kong was to become "our base for making economic connections with foreign countries, for attracting foreign capital and earning foreign exchange."[68] In a meeting of the State Council on 6 April 1957, Zhou argued that China could use either Hong Kong or foreign capital to modernize mainland factories.[69] Beijing allowed overseas Chinese investment, and overseas Chinese investment enterprises (OCIEs) were established so that Chinese businesspeople living overseas could invest in schools and factories in their hometowns and elsewhere.[70] Finally, in spring 1957, the government held the first Guangzhou Trade Fair to promote Chinese exports, to help pay for Chinese ISI projects.[71]

This first major adaptation of the ISI strategy is intriguing. While successfully thwarting Mao's initial rash-advance initiative, which had strong autarkic overtones, Zhou Enlai, Chen Yun, Zhu De, and the other bureaucratic Stalinists accommodated Mao's concerns about overreliance on the Soviet Union. In signing a second agreement to import Soviet technology, Zhou diversified China's ISI technology sourcing within the confines of the flexible international economic sanctions, to prevent China's overreliance on a single technology source. Zhou's promotion of Hong Kong as both a base from which to sell its exports to the Western marketplace and a source of capital investment also had far-ranging consequences. While these initiatives were temporarily superseded by Mao's GLF strategy, they demonstrated that the bureaucratic Stalinists acknowledged the positive role of the international marketplace in accelerating domestic development.

If overseas Chinese investment in the mainland had continued, it is possible that the GLF crisis could have triggered a complex learning process resulting in a fundamental change in the development paradigm. Such paradigm changes were taking place in South Korea and Taiwan in the early 1960s as elites there began to experiment with outwardly oriented export-driven development. Yet such change was not forthcoming in China, as Mao and the revolutionary Stalinist coalition successfully destroyed the Yan'an Roundtable consensus in the late 1950s and ended experimentation with overseas Chinese investment in order to implement Mao's development model I, the Great Leap Forward.

Export Product Procurement, 1959–64

Chinese elites undertook a second major adaptation of development model II's ISI strategy in the wake of the GLF disaster. Unable to effect a comprehensive readjustment program until after fall 1960, Zhou Enlai and the bureaucratic Stalinists implemented a series of readjustment measures in the foreign economic sector, starting in December 1958.[72] They prevented a drastic expansion of exports, recentralized control over all foreign trade activities, separated the foreign trade system from the domestic economy, and placed the highest priority on the acquisition, processing, and exporting of all export goods (Wu Youxian, or the Five-Priority policy).[73] Eventually policy elites diverted from the domestic economy any commodity needed to fulfill the export plan, following a method known as *yi qi, er xiang, san chao* (first, squeeze; second, replace; third, exceed), which exacerbated domestic food shortages.[74] Finally, in 1960 Chinese elites temporarily froze debt repayments to the Soviet Union and other creditors, which had been complicated by the growing Sino-Soviet schism.[75]

Yet these plan-oriented administrative measures were not enough to guarantee sufficient export supplies to enable repayment of foreign creditors for the ISI projects, to finance the wheat imports that Zhou Enlai had approved on December 30, 1960, or to restart the ISI strategy.[76] To guarantee raw-material supplies needed for exports, the bureaucratic Stalinists approved a series of measures to "motivate" individual producers. These included increasing procurement prices for various agricultural crops for both the domestic and export markets, allocating scarce consumer goods to encourage specific export production, and providing capital to industries to expand export production (the Chukou gongyepin shengchan zhuanxiang daikuan, or Specialized Loan Program for Industrial Export Production). In addition to these remunerative measures, Zhou Enlai in early 1960 approved the establishment of export commodity processing bases (*jingji chukou jiagong jidi*, or ECPBs), which, according to Chen Yun, could guarantee the supply of high-quality agricultural and industrial items required for exports.[77] The combination of administrative and remunerative measures adopted in the early 1960s allowed China to repay ISI debts to the Soviet Union and finance grain imports to feed China's starving millions.

At a September 1963 conference, Premier Zhou Enlai and the bureaucratic Stalinists subsequently introduced the second major adaptation of development model II—the Four Modernizations plan, which was their attempt to replace Mao's vision of a semi-autarkic, rash-advance strategy. The Four Modernizations was a long-term ISI strategy that "by the end of the twentieth century would complete the building of a strong socialist state that enjoyed a modernized agricultural sector, a modernized industrial sector, a modernized national defense sector, and a modernized science and technology sector."[78] This adaptation augmented the command economy's ability to finance ISI by introducing remunerative export promotion measures and export processing zones (EPZs).

By the mid-1960s, Mao replaced the Four Modernizations strategy with his semi-autarkic Third Front strategy of economic development, which he implemented in tandem with the political mobilization of the Cultural Revolution.

Expanding the Export Product Mix, 1971–75

Following the death of Lin Biao in September 1971, Zhou Enlai reasserted control over the State Council and, with Mao's approval, rehabilitated the surviving bureaucratic Stalinists. Zhou and the bureaucratic Stalinists then set about dismantling Mao's development model I and the semi-autarkic Third Front strategy, which had led to the investment of large amounts of capital to develop production facilities in more protected areas of China's inland provinces.[79] Zhou revived development model II's Four Modernizations and formally introduced the Four-Three ISI Plan in February 1972. This US$4.3 billion ISI program included the importation of large-scale manufacturing—steel complexes such as the Wuhan Steel Works, electrical generation plants, chemical fiber and fertilizer plants, and jet engine assembly plants—from Western European and Japanese suppliers. In 1973, Chen Yun announced that China desired to import US$300 million worth of technology from the United States to produce steel. According to Zhou Enlai, the development strategy's long-term goal was for China to realize a comprehensive modernized economy by 2000.[80]

To finance development model II's new ISI strategy, the bureaucratic Stalinists revived and adapted the administrative and remunerative measures designed to guarantee export procurement in the early 1960s. Having determined that the Specialized Loan Program for Industrial Export Production had been effective in the early 1960s, the bureaucratic Stalinists revived and expanded the program. They implemented a short-term foreign-exchange loan program for the foreign trade corporations, established an investment fund for export commodity production, and revived and expanded the bonus scheme for agricultural exports.[81]

The bureaucratic Stalinists also argued for developing China's export market by producing high-demand export items that met international standards. Chen Yun argued that foreign loans could finance the ISI projects that would achieve the long-term goal of self-reliance.[82] Zhou Enlai thus approved the use of foreign loans to finance the importation of a steel rolling plant from West Germany and other new ISI projects. With the phenomenal rise in the international price of petroleum, in 1974 Li Xiannian approved the sale of Chinese petroleum and gold reserves as well as the use of foreign trade loans, to finance ISI projects.[83] The bureaucratic Stalinists revived and expanded the ECPBs and approved experimentation with a variety of different forms, including export production bases for individual agricultural or sideline export commodities, specialized factories, and comprehensive bases for export commodity production. Many of the new EPZs produced products specifically for the Hong Kong/Macao and Japanese markets. The new comprehensive export bases, such as the one established in Foshan, Guangdong, produced a variety of agricultural and light industrial goods for export. These bases were the direct forerunners of the SEZs.

In 1973 Deng Xiaoping returned from forced exile to assume the vice premiership, resuming his positions on the Central Military Commission and in the Political Bureau.[84] With Zhou Enlai suffering from terminal bladder cancer, Deng had assumed responsibility for day-to-day State Council affairs by January or February 1975.[85] Deng continued to implement Zhou's development model II and its Four-Three ISI program.[86] However, Deng Xiaoping, Chen Yun, and Li Xiannian were unable to carry out innovative new financing measures when Mao Zedong's wife Jiang Qing and her allies attacked their economic strategy as following a "traitorous, capitulationism line," "giving foreign concessions to outside countries," and selling China's national resources (petroleum, coal, and cotton textiles) to foreign enemies.[87]

Deng was once again forced to resign.

Active Use of Foreign Investment, 1976–78

Following Mao Zedong's death in September 1976 and the subsequent arrest of Jiang Qing and the "Gang of Four," Premier Hua Guofeng, Li Xiannian, and Chen Yun faced severe economic disruptions caused by the Third Front and Cultural Revolution as well as the devastating Tangshan earthquake, including production input shortages and infrastructure and transportation problems; more than one-third of China's state-owned enterprises (SOEs) incurred economic losses.[88] However, Mao's death also hastened the demise of development model I and the revolutionary Stalinist opinion group. Two decades of dramatic policy swings that characterized the divergent, incremental-learning model also ended, allowing the bureaucratic Stalinists to focus solely on expanding Zhou's development model II without fear of criticism.

At the March 1977 Central Party Work Conference, Hua attempted to delay Deng's return to power, arguing, "Criticizing Deng and attacking the rightist reversal of verdicts were decided by our Great Leader Chairman Mao Zedong. It is necessary to carry out these criticisms."[89] In response, Chen Yun strongly advocated Deng's return to power. Chen was joined by many of Deng's military and political colleagues and subordinates, such as General Chen Zaidao and Liu Bocheng, in requesting Deng's reinstatement.[90] By summer 1977, Deng had regained positions in the party, the state, and the military, while Chen Yun continued to promote his bureaucratic Stalinist approach to economic renewal, which was first adopted during the post-GLF period of the early 1960s.[91]

The Central Committee subsequently approved the SPC's new adaptation of development model II in February 1978, the Ten-Year Plan, which was first outlined in Zhou Enlai and Deng Xiaoping's January 1975 Government Work Report. Zhou and Deng's original Ten-Year Plan covered 1975 to 1985 and authorized the importation of foreign technology to achieve "the comprehensive modernization of agriculture, industry, national defense, and science and technology" by 2000.[92] Hua's ISI program was much larger in scope than Zhou's Four-Three ISI Plan of the early 1970s, as it authorized the importation of 120 large-scale turnkey plants, valued at more than US$6.5 billion.[93] As outlined in Yu Qiuli's State Planning Commission report of July 1977, the program called for the construction of a nuclear power plant, hydroelectric power stations, various types of petrochemical plants for industry and agriculture, synthetic textile plants, and large-scale steel complexes, including Shanghai's Baoshan Steel complex that was to cost US$4.8 billion in foreign exchange plus RMB 21.4 billion to finance the infrastructure.[94] By 1978 China had signed contracts worth US$7.8 billion to import ISI turnkey projects; building the infrastructure necessary for the proposed projects would cost another US$5 billion.[95]

Hua Guofeng initiated the first steps to China's opening to the outside world by inviting the leader of Yugoslavia, Marshal Tito, to visit China in August 1977. Much to the dismay of General Secretary Brezhnev of the Soviet Union, Tito had reestablished ambassadorial relations with China in 1970; Tito visited China after stops in Moscow and Pyongyang in August 1977 and reestablished party relations with China by March 1978.[96] Hua and the Central Committee allowed Chinese policy makers and academics to study Eastern European economies, especially their utilization of Western technology, innovative factory-management reforms, promotion of science and technology, capital construction plans, and agricultural-sector improvements.[97] Tito's visit also opened the door to greater interaction between China and Yugoslavia; the two countries exchanged more than a hundred military, trade, and academic delegations between August 1977 and August 1978, increasing the value of their bilateral trade from US$30 million in 1976 to US$200 million in 1978.[98]

Between July 1977 and June 1980, Hua approved travel abroad for 360 delegations from the State Council and 472 delegations from various science and education institutions in hopes of using foreign knowledge to further China's long-term growth.[99] In 1978 Hua sent abroad thirteen officials with the rank of deputy premier and several hundred other important cadres. As one of the officials recounted, "We thought capitalist countries were backward and decadent. . . . When we left our country and took a look, we realized things were completely different."[100] According to Teiwes and Sun, three of these delegations fundamentally transformed China's economic policies: SPC vice chairman Lin Hujia's visit to Japan, SPC vice chairman Duan

Yun's visit to Hong Kong and Macao, and Vice Premier Gu Mu's month-long inspection tour of fifteen European cities in France, Switzerland, West Germany, Denmark, and Belgium in the summer of 1978.[101] Gu Mu described in vivid detail the various modern factories he visited, the container loading facilities in Bremen, the modern airport facilities, and the Europeans' high standards of living. Gu Mu suggested that China could take advantage of the Europeans' willingness to loan billions of dollars of capital and copy the Western countries' practice of "establishing industrial processing zones closed off from surrounding areas, where foreign businesses could invest and establish factories under a tax-free regime, with production directly exported."[102] Duan Yun "suggested converting Bao'an and Zhuhai counties into a prefecture governed directly by Guangdong and with the authority to engage in foreign trade directly with Hong Kong and Macao; people from the two colonies would be free to come and go and to participate in the industrial processing bases being established."[103] Just as Zhou Enlai and Chen Yun had promoted textile production and exports in 1972 and 1973, Gu Mu suggested that China could modernize its textile industries to spur domestic growth and foreign exports, to pay off foreign loans used to finance new ISI projects.[104]

Hua Guofeng followed up on Gu Mu's trip and Tito's 1977 visit by taking an inspection tour of Romania, Yugoslavia, and Iran in August 1978. On returning to Beijing, Hua enthusiastically recounted that "those countries accepted foreign currency, had joint ventures with foreign companies, carried on compensation trade (countertrade in which investments are repaid from their profits), and brought in foreign technology—all without any loss of sovereignty. Hua commented that the factories he had seen in Eastern Europe, while not as large as those in China, were far more efficient. The conclusion was obvious: China should follow the examples of Eastern Europe and bring in more foreign technology."[105]

Both Hua and the vice delegation head and future premier Zhao Ziyang were fascinated by Yugoslavian enterprise-management reforms. During his eight-day visit to Yugoslavia, Hua Guofeng broke with previous Maoist critiques and praised the Yugoslavian self-management system as a Marxist system of management.[106] Such Eastern European management reforms inspired Hua and Zhao to carry out similar modifications in China.[107] In September 1978 *Renmin ribao* reported on Hua's Romanian trip and especially the Romanians' methods for strengthening enterprise management, including bonuses and greater enterprise autonomy.[108]

Unlike under the nativist xenophobia of just four years before, China's policy makers were allowed to consider formulating more profound domestic and foreign economic reforms based on the Eastern European experience. Inspired by others and by his own trip abroad, Hua adapted his "Two Whatevers" approach to incorporate small-scale experiments with the household contract system, compensation trade, cooperative production, the use of commercial loans for smaller projects, and equity joint ventures.[109] In 1978 Hua was the first Chinese leader to approve the use of multilateral aid, by requesting technical assistance from the United Nations Development Programme, which eventually allocated US$15 million in 1979 to finance twenty-seven projects.[110] Gu Mu's suggestions for using foreign capital and other initiatives were discussed during the State Council's Ideological Discussion Conference on how to speed up the Four Modernizations, convened from 6 July to 9 September 1978. The conference's recommendations for using large amounts of foreign capital to finance ISI projects were incorporated into the 1979 and 1980 economic plans by the National Planning Conference convened on 5 September 1978.[111] By November 1978, China had established its first joint venture, with a Hong Kong catering company. Hua was thus the first to approve joint ventures with Western capitalists.[112]

Speaking to the National Planning Conference on 9 September 1978, Li Xiannian repeated the bureaucratic Stalinist strategy to achieve the long-term goal of self-reliance: China needed to promote a large expansion of its exports to finance the importation of the foreign technology. Recognizing China's lack of foreign exchange, Li Xiannian added that China should not expand the scale of domestic infrastructure investment nor import any technology or mechanical equipment that China itself could produce. Duplicating its experience with Russia in the 1950s, China once again needed to rely on foreign experts and advisers to help with the purchasing and installation of new technology and send its technicians abroad to study the technology. To finance these imports, China had to expand its traditional exports; expand the export of petroleum, coal, and minerals; and develop new machinery and power-generating equipment, chemical products, light textiles, and complete equipment sets. In contrast to previous approaches, the bureaucratic Stalinists would use compensation trade and renovate existing older industries to reduce domestic investment costs and meet economic-plan goals.[113] Li Xiannian also added, "We should have the guts and the ability to boost development by utilizing their technology, equipment, funds and management expertise. We cannot afford to lose this rare opportunity. Self-reliance does not mean shutting ourselves behind closed doors and turning a blind eye to advancements in foreign countries."[114]

While he did not attend the meetings, Deng was especially intrigued by the Europeans' willingness to finance China's ISI dreams.[115] According to Vogel, Deng responded to the conference's recommendation to import US$18 billion in ISI projects by asking, "Why not US$80 billion?"[116] Deng thus fully shared Hua Guofeng's and Li Xiannian's enthusiasm for using foreign capital to accelerate the ISI program and to break away from Mao's nativist view. During his talk at the Jilin Work Conference one week after the close of the Ideological Discussion Conference on the Four Modernizations, Deng stated,

> There are many circumstances that didn't exist in Comrade Mao Zedong's lifetime. If the Central Committee doesn't consider the problem and make up its mind in light of the current circumstances, many problems will not be able to be confronted nor resolved. For instance, during Comrade Mao Zedong's lifetime, we also wanted to expand economic and technical exchange abroad. This included developing economic and trade relations with some capitalist countries, even attracting foreign capital, carrying out equity joint ventures, etc. However, at that time conditions weren't right and people blocked us. . . . After a few years of hard work, the current international situation is much better than that of the past. Foreigners may also cheat us and take advantage of our backwardness. For instance, they may inflate the price of a set of equipment or sell us seconds at prime quality prices. This is all possible. But, we have a good situation which hadn't been enjoyed in the past. What is the point of holding high the banner of Mao Zedong Thought if we cannot make up our mind and do things just because Comrade Mao Zedong had not said them in the past? This is to say that we must act on the basis of current realities and fully exploit these advantageous conditions and

realize the goals of the Four Modernizations put forth by Comrade Mao Zedong and announced by Comrade Zhou Enlai. . . . There are changes occurring every day in the world today; new situations and problems are constantly appearing. It will not work for us to close our door to such things, not use our minds and forever be bogged down in backwardness. We are a poor country in comparison with countries of the world today and are part of the Third World. We also belong to the less developed portion of the Third World. . . . We must speed up development of productive forces in light of the new beneficial conditions and make the material livelihood of the people.[117]

Just as Deng had strongly supported Mao's revolutionary Stalinist approach in the Great Leap Forward in the 1950s, he strongly supported Hua Guofeng's attempt to take advantage of "the new beneficial conditions" to establish a New Great Leap Forward in the fall of 1978. However, while declining to invoke the older GLF's slogan, "Daring to think, daring to act" (*Gan xiang, gan gan*), Deng argued for the radical use of foreign capital to finance large-scale ISI projects. No doubt Deng felt a sense of vindication, having suffered from endless criticism by Jiang Qing and the revolutionary Stalinists for his promotion of greater interactions with the outside world in the mid-1970s.[118]

Deng became convinced of the utility of Hua's New Great Leap Forward during his official visit to Japan in October 1978.[119] Having established solid relations with visiting Japanese delegations in the mid-1970s, Deng was feted with the highest honors in Japan and met with both Emperor Hirohito and Prime Minister Tanaka.[120] Participating in the ratification of the Sino-Japanese Peace and Friendship Treaty, Deng made it clear that China had set aside its wartime anger, as well as territorial disputes such as the sovereignty issue concerning the Diaoyutai/Senkaku Islands. According to Vogel, Deng visited Japan "like Xu Fu, to find a 'secret magic drug,'" which in this case was Japan's successful pathway to modernization. Thus, Deng was especially attentive when visiting Nissan's Zama automobile plant, the Kimitsu Steel Works near Tokyo, the Matsushita factory in Osaka, and when riding Japanese hovercraft and the bullet train. Deng was deeply impressed by Japan's economic development, its scientific advancements, and its management techniques. He argued, "We must firmly grasp management. Just making things is not enough. We need to raise the quality." During his trip to Singapore in November 1978, Deng was also impressed by the way the Singaporeans had permitted foreign direct investment (FDI) and how this benefited the workers and the state.[121] Throughout the 1980s Deng consistently repeated the themes of modernizing China's scientific capabilities and management techniques and making use of foreign investment, which he had learned from observing Japan and Singapore's modernization in 1978.[122] Deng combined these ideas of outward-oriented development with the Leninist NEP approach to arrive at the international Leninist approach, which became an integral part of the Chinese Third Way.

In working to achieve China's version of modernization, Deng viewed Hua's New Great Leap as one way to establish a large-scale modern industrial foundation and promote foreign management techniques that would ignite an internal economic revolution. However, Deng's radical tendencies were tempered by moderates among the first generation of bureaucratic Stalinist elites, such as Chen Yun, who was adamantly opposed to Hua Guofeng's New Great Leap strategy. Chen Yun was alarmed that Hua's closest economic advisers, Li Xiannian and Yu Qiuli, were enthusiastically supporting the program.[123] Chen strongly opposed the decisions reached at the July–September 1978 State Council Ideological Discussion Conference on using foreign capital to speed up the Four Modernizations and its ISI program;[124] he revealed his thinking publicly in his speech criticizing Hua's development strategy at the 21 March 1979 Political Bureau meeting. He chastised Hua for "only considering to borrow money and only look[ing] at the fast development of other countries."[125] Chen was concerned that China would be paying exorbitant interest rates and thus should rely only on commercial loans for small projects.[126] Chen Yun thus advocated a severe reduction of Hua's mega-ISI program and the use of low-interest World Bank loans and concessional financing for any crucial ISI projects.[127]

Chen Yun was seeing red. Hua's Ten-Year Plan required China to achieve a gross value of industrial output of more than 10 percent per annum, and would make up 21 percent of the total national capital construction investment for ten years.[128] To finance the ISI plan,

Beijing planned to withdraw RMB 2 billion from provincial budgets, expand the older export promotion schemes, implement limited experiments with foreign capital investment, increase petroleum production for export, reduce central financial support of the provinces, and assume foreign exchange debt, which in 1979 was estimated to be around US$10 billion. Such reallocations of resources would still fail to overcome severe shortages in construction materials and petroleum.[129] Chen Yun realized that the Cultural Revolution and the revolutionary Stalinists had severely disrupted the Chinese economy. According to a July 1977 State Council circular, the debt owed by SOEs soared to 37.2 percent in 1976 from 10 percent in 1970.[130] The State Council had frozen bank accounts and reduced overall government domestic spending and foreign aid.[131] Within the domestic economy, China confronted continuous agricultural shortfalls, transportation bottlenecks, and increasing shortages in raw materials and energy supplies.[132] These domestic economic difficulties had a deleterious impact on the nation's ability to produce agricultural and industrial products for export, resulting in China's failure to fulfill contracted exports to Hong Kong.[133]

Chen Yun discreetly lobbied Deng, Li Xiannian, and the other members of the first generation of bureaucratic Stalinist elites. In his speech to the Central Work Conference on 10 December 1978, Chen put forward several themes that he would repeat throughout the 1980s.[134] First, Chen argued that the party's primary concern was an adequate food supply, echoing his 1960 warning that "the most dangerous situation is not to have food." China must first import food to feed its people, he said, as "only then will general stability be achieved."[135] Later, in a December 1981 speech to provincial and municipal party secretaries, Chen Yun stressed that food supplies should always be given paramount importance over construction projects:

> Another important guideline for our economic work is: (1) we must enable one billion people to eat, and (2) we must carry out socialist construction. The state has no future if it solely focuses on eating, as once supplies are depleted there is nothing left. After guaranteeing that there will be enough food, we must use our remaining energies to carry out

construction. Thus, we don't want to fall short of food supplies, but we also don't want to eat too well. If we eat too well, we will not have enough strength to carry out construction. There is a limitation when raising living standards: there is only so much money. You cannot raise living standards too high. We must aim first to eat and second to build.[136]

Chen also warned that the various agricultural responsibility plans first pioneered by Wan Li in Anhui "might [make it] appear that the plan is not needed. In reality, it is not this way."[137] Full marketization of the countryside would not guarantee food supplies to all Chinese people, as the capitalist instincts of the market would sacrifice the needs of the people.

Second, Chen Yun argued that new ISI projects should be "carried out in an orderly fashion, and not ineptly implemented because of poor planning." Implying that Hua Guofeng's New Great Leap Forward was seriously flawed, Chen argued that one could not compare China's steel production with that of Japan, Germany, Great Britain, and France, as they enjoyed far more sophisticated infrastructure and far more advanced technology. He also argued that China could not compare itself with Taiwan and South Korea, as they had received U.S. aid over the years. In his December 1981 speech to provincial and municipal party secretaries, Chen Yun argued, "State construction must regard the entire country as a chessboard and must carry out our work according to the plan. Supplies that must be allocated must be allocated by the state plan. The pace of national construction must be staggered, there must be emphasis on heavy and light industry, all in accordance with the national plan."[138]

Having learned to formulate a state plan in the Soviet Union in the early 1950s, Chen Yun continued to believe that only the principles of moderate, balanced growth embodied in the state plan could bring about steady growth. Chen Yun's balanced approach to development restrained Deng's radicalism, brought an end to Hua Guofeng and his New Great Leap, and instituted a three-year period of readjustment. Deng and Chen's collaborative efforts realized a safer pathway to economic development by promoting limited experimentation with new forms of investment, such as the SEZs and wholly foreign-owned joint ventures of the 1980s.

While the New Great Leap was rejected, Hua Guofeng's foreign economic innovations became the foundation for China's opening to the outside world. Hua had approved a limited number of processing and assembly projects, initiated compensation trade agreements, and permitted FDI in new construction for foreign companies. These initiatives were expanded to include cooperative production, equity joint ventures, 100 percent foreign-owned ventures, and the acceptance of capital from foreign governments and international organizations; in this key respect, Hua completely broke with Mao's semi-autarky and Zhou's limited overseas Chinese investment of the 1950s and early 1960s to herald a new era in foreign economic policy.[139]

Hua also accepted the April 1978 report of the State Planning Commission and the Ministry of Foreign Trade (MFT) that proposed the establishment of export processing zones in the areas on the mainland opposite Hong Kong and Macao.[140] Zhou Enlai first advocated these types of zones in early 1960, resulting in the establishment of export-commodity processing bases in the early 1960s that were revived and expanded in the early 1970s.[141] Eventually approved in July 1979, the SEZs became China's primary laboratory for transforming the Stalinist economic paradigm. Many of China's best and brightest professionals moved to the zones, where they could take advantage of the economic, social, and even political reforms, ranging from apartment ownership, greater media freedom, and the reduced role of the party in noneconomic organizations.

Development Model III: The Chinese Third Way

Lenin's concept of state capitalism was implemented through the New Economic Policy, which established a mixed Soviet economy in the 1920s that made use of market-oriented remunerative and administrative tools as well as FDI and international trade to bring about economic recovery and growth. In the 1980s, Lenin's concept of state capitalism became the theoretical basis for China's Third Way development model. Some scholars, including Lüthi, treat the concept as a unique model; Friedman argues that Zhou Enlai and others promoted some elements of the NEP approach in promoting Titoism.[142]

Lenin and the Bolsheviks responded to the advent of the Russian Civil War in 1917 by establishing "war communism" in 1918 to guarantee supplies to their troops and to feed the Russian population under their control. The Bolsheviks initiated centralized economic control by nationalizing and militarizing industrial and agricultural labor. Yet war communism also created serious food and fuel shortages, transport bottlenecks, and a drastic decline in industrial production.

Threatened by the ongoing civil war, peasant rebellions, and millions of Russians dying from famine and typhus between 1919 and 1921, Soviet elites confronted a severe economic crisis.[143] Lenin rejected war communism as having "been forced upon the country by extreme want, ruin and war, to regularize the socialist exchange of products."[144] He pulled back from accelerating the socialist transformation that would have forced all agricultural production to collective exchanges.

Lenin initiated the NEP in 1921 to introduce the Russian people to the future collective economy, establishing a mixed market economy that replaced administrative fiat with remunerative market mechanisms to increase production.[145] As Davies writes, "The central feature of NEP was the right of individual peasants to sell their products freely, locally or nationally, to private traders, direct to individuals, or to state agencies. Trade was resumed on a national scale, with most retail trade in private ownership."[146] Lenin argued that the promotion of industrial and agricultural growth even by means of private capitalism, even without cooperatives or without transforming this capitalism directly into state capitalism, would still do more for the cause of socialist construction in Russia than those who would "ponder over" the purity of communism, draw up regulations and instructions from state capitalism and the cooperatives, but do nothing practical to stimulate trade.[147] The party and state control over the industrial and agricultural economy established during war communism remained in place; the party retained control of the large industrial firms and financial institutions and controlled foreign investment and international trade.

Chinese communist leaders witnessed the NEP's implementation during the 1920s and its role in igniting Soviet economic recovery.[148] Liu Shaoqi arrived in Moscow in 1921 to study at the Communist University of the Toilers of the East, where he observed the initial implementation of Lenin's NEP solution to relieve the famine afflicting the new Soviet state. Following the Shanghai Massacre of 1927 and the end of the First United Front, Liu and Zhou Enlai traveled to Moscow in 1928 to attend the CCP's Sixth Congress. They witnessed an economy transformed into a mixed economy enjoying relative abundance and vibrancy.[149] Zhou, who previously had studied in Japan and Western Europe and had a relatively sophisticated knowledge of market economies, praised the NEP in the journal *Shaonian* (Youth), stating that nationalization of industry had allowed the Russians time to recover from the civil war and the First World War and to rebuild their agricultural and industrial sectors.[150] Deng Xiaoping also studied in Moscow, attending the Moscow Sun Yat-sen University in 1926 after working and studying in Western Europe for several years.[151] Deng walked through Moscow markets filled with fresh produce from the countryside, saw the shelves of local stores filled with products from SOEs and private firms, and relived his time in France by enjoying the cafés scattered around the streets of Moscow.[152] These Chinese elites had experienced the power of the market while in Europe, and this had a lasting impact on their view of development.[153] Beginning with their attempt to establish sideline agricultural plots and the Anhui household contracts system in 1961, Liu Shaoqi and Deng Xiaoping gradually turned away from supporting Mao's radical normative economic strategy, eventually joining Zhou Enlai and Chen Yun to adopt NEP-style ideas about using market-oriented, remunerative measures to promote economic recovery following the economic failures of Mao's GLF and Cultural Revolution.[154]

As for FDI and international trade, Liu Shaoqi argued in a March 1950 directive drafted for the Central Committee that Lenin had approved several concessionary agreements with foreign corporations during the NEP period. The Chinese elites, he said, should consider signing "concessionary contracts involving certain enterprises, joint venture agreements, and even joint stock companies" with the Soviet Union, Eastern European countries, and capitalist countries.[155] China established joint ventures with the Soviet Union in Xinjiang in 1950, approved the establishment of OCIEs in Guangdong and Fujian beginning in the early 1950s, and allowed Chinese investors living overseas to invest in their hometowns.[156] However, Mao and the revolutionary Stalinists eliminated the OCIEs because they regarded such foreign investment policies as endangering the goal of development model I to establish a semi-autarkic economy. Later, to finance development model II's large-scale ISI program in the 1970s, the bureaucratic Stalinist elites focused on improving the quantity and quality of Chinese exports. In addition, Li Xiannian called for the use of foreign trade loans to finance ISI projects in September 1974, and in 1975 Deng Xiaoping called for more creative use of foreign capital, including deferred payments and other loan schemes.[157] Again the revolutionary Stalinists vilified such measures as the result of a "comprador bourgeois ideology."[158]

After Mao's death, China's bureaucratic Stalinist elites realized the chaotic nature of Mao's development model I and the limits to adapting development model II, especially in light of the "economic miracle" taking place in the East Asian economies and the diminishing returns of ISI development.[159] While publicly promoting Zhou Enlai's Four Modernizations mantra to demonstrate policy legitimacy and continuity, the bureaucratic Stalinists were motivated to experiment with innovative tools to finance development model II, with its smaller ISI component in the late 1970s, and reach a new consensus on first- and second-order policy adaptations. Chen Yun famously described the process in his 16 December 1980 speech to a work conference as "crossing the river by feeling the stones."[160] Deng Xiaoping reaffirmed this approach in his 6 October 1984 speech on China's cooperation with the international economy. While policy elites in Beijing initiated many small- or large-scale experiments, local and provincial elites undertook various initiatives as well. Elite support at all levels was critical for all policy experiments, especially those that challenged the logic of the Stalinist economic paradigm.

Malle argues that Lenin initiated the NEP in 1921 in response to an economic crisis, "without a precise program regarding the scope of the new policy measures and their connotations."[161] In the same way, the bureaucratic Stalinists responded to China's economic dilemma of the late 1970s; they were not testing a new economic paradigm. Wan Li and Zhao Ziyang's experimentation with the agricultural contract responsibility system was their response to local agricultural problems; the elite's adoption of the contract system nationwide was their response to the immediate problems posed by the state's agricultural problems, and a purposeful experiment with a new plan.[162] Just as the export promotion experiments of the late 1950s were a response to China's inability to repay the Soviet Union for the 156 Projects, the bureaucratic Stalinists adapted and experimented with foreign economic policies, beginning in the late 1970s, in order to finance the remaining small-scale ISI program and develop new sources of income for future ISI projects. They were not rejecting the inward-oriented ISI strategy but were altering it to reflect the domestic economic problems of the moment and the availability of foreign capital.

Initial Steps along China's Third Way

The concept of a third or middle way has been part of Western political discourse for decades and describes the adaptation of market-economy policies to achieve progressive demands for social justice and equality.[163] In the 1980s the popularity of the neoliberal policies of Margaret Thatcher in the United Kingdom, Helmut Kohl in West Germany, and Ronald Reagan in the United States deeply disturbed social democrats, who thus reevaluated their classical approaches to social democratic policies. According to Anthony Giddens, neoliberals also confronted an inherent contradiction between their emphasis on the free market and the importance of the family and the state.[164] As a result, during the 1990s Britain's Tony Blair and the New Labour movement, Germany's Gerhard Schröder and the Seeheimer Kreis, and William Clinton and the New Democrats in the United States all promoted a new centrist approach to governing that was "in favour of growth, entrepreneurship, enterprise and wealth creation but it [was] also in favour of greater social justice and it [saw] the state playing a major role in bringing this about."[165] Yet this was a "Western" third way, embedded in the capitalist market system and reflecting Western democratic traditions.

In contrast, the evolution of China's Third Way is unique to China's command-economy experience. After 1976 Hua Guofeng, Li Xiannian, Deng Xiaoping, and Chen Yun initially strengthened the development model II approach to achieve the comprehensive Stalinist paradigm. Influenced by thirty years of experimentation and policy debate, elites had learned the limitations of the previous bureaucratic Stalinist, top-down command-economy approach and feared that the party might lose control. As Naughton argues, the decentralization experiments of the 1980s that relaxed the state monopoly over industry transformed China from a command to a market economy; those reforms, in contrast, were implemented in a gradual fashion, which was "a resilient, 'natural' way to transform an economic system."[166] With the 1980s experiments, elites delegated greater decision-making authority to ministries, localities, and individuals, who fully took advantage of their new economic freedoms. While Beijing elites retained ultimate authority, they had learned to establish a more consultative relationship with China's major economic actors and as a result ignited tremendous economic growth in the coastal areas beginning in the 1980s.

More recently, the concept of consultative authoritarianism "is used to describe a regime that creates formal channels for citizens to voice their policy concerns. Consultative authoritarianism implies greater citizen influence and participation than command authoritarianism."[167] It has been used to explain why civil society has evolved in China since the 2000s as a tool of the party, strengthening authoritarianism, and not as a catalyst for democracy. This study expands Teets' brief argument that the origins of consultative authoritarianism started with the decentralization experiments of the 1980s, which gave local government limited political power but more significant administrative and economic control, and which were intended to increase the ability of local government to regulate local markets and provide public services. Decentralization theoretically increases the provision of public goods because local governments know better the needs of their citizens and can provide services more cost effectively, and creates more responsive institutions by bringing government decision makers into closer proximity to the affected constituency.[168]

Before the development of modern Chinese civil society in the 2000s, the party and state first loosened control over China's provinces, municipalities, firms, and individuals. Beginning in the early 1980s, elites began to experiment with NEP-style policies of state capitalism, including decentralization and a greater role for the market. This decentralization brought about an end to the totalitarian, top-down Stalinist paradigm, which had maintained the hegemony of the party and government planning. It established a new consultative system that taught the Beijing elites that they could safely allocate greater decision-making powers to lower levels of government, which in turn were increasingly responsible for financing their own operations. Those at the lower levels of government were thus highly motivated to provide feedback to the Beijing elites about policy effectiveness. Provinces, municipalities, and firms strengthened the central government by reporting their positive and negative experiences with policy implementation.[169] Initiated during a time of economic readjustment in the early 1980s, Beijing elites learned that the decentralization experiments lifted the financial burden of the command economy from Beijing by reallocating economic responsibilities to the lower levels. And by the 2000s, Teets argues, the lower-level elites learned that they could cooperate with various groups emerging in the new civil society to share the responsibility of carrying out Beijing's unfunded mandates.

From their initial establishment in the late 1970s, the zones challenged the basic tenets of the Stalinist political, economic, and social paradigm, in which the party maintained control over all aspects of life, including the domestic and international marketplaces. Elites could safely carry out the decentralization experiment in Guangdong and Fujian, as they could isolate any disruptive influences on China's major economic centers in Shanghai and the northeast. The elites used the success of the provincial decentralization and zonal experiments of the 1980s to shift from the inwardly oriented Stalinist economic paradigm to a new Third Way promoting an outwardly oriented, consultative economic paradigm. They empowered coastal provincial and municipal governments, industries, and entrepreneurs to engage in the domestic and international markets, and even permitted wholly foreign-owned ventures to operate inside China. They also agreed to explore China's accession to the General Agreement on Tariffs and Trade (GATT), which is now called the World Trade Organization (WTO). This change in the economic paradigm and its greater economic pluralism initiated the country's shift to a post-totalitarian state that has become one of the most important political, economic, and military players in the world in the twenty-first century.[170]

Although the revolutionary Stalinists criticized Deng's attempt to employ foreign capital in the mid-1970s, the political atmosphere changed after Mao's passing in 1976, and Chen Yun thus argued, "Because capital is not enough, we can borrow from abroad."[171] The financing crisis of the late 1970s forced elites to question the wisdom of one of China's long-term goals: self-reliance. They experimented with Lenin's state capitalism concept, which eventually replaced the older Chinese Stalinist economic paradigm with a new remunerative, consultative economic paradigm. Yet this Chinese Third Way also retained and adapted China's older Stalinist social and political paradigm.[172]

Initial steps taken in the late 1970s led China's bureaucratic Stalinist elites to transform the comprehensive Stalinist paradigm in which the party maintained full control over the state, the economy, and society. With the passage of the "Resolution on Certain Questions in Our Party's History since the Founding of the PRC" in 1981, the bureaucratic Stalinists formally rejected the revolutionary Stalinist approach of development model I.[173] After accepting the idea that China was in an "initial stage of socialism," Chinese elites followed the Leninist NEP model and loosened hegemonic control over the economy. They thus initiated a sectorial paradigm shift that resulted in China's transition from an inward-looking totalitarian state to a post-totalitarian state adopting an outward-looking consultative economic model while retaining the party's control over the political and social sectors.

The Chinese Third Way did not emerge out of the sea fully formed, as Botticelli depicted the birth of Venus. The Chinese Third Way evolved during the transition period of the 1980s, after decades of success and failure with the Soviet-model development. Deng Xiaoping, Zhao Ziyang, and the bureaucratic Stalinists perceived the shortcomings of those development approaches and were daring enough to gamble with a new NEP-style approach. Their initial steps down the Third Way path were circuitous and characterized by disagreements and compromises. Chen Yun was concerned about economic stability and retaining the state plan. Hu Qiaomu was alarmed by the emergence of a new class of Chinese businesspeople who resembled the Russian private entrepreneurs who emerged between 1921 and 1929. Yet their concerns did not prevent the emergence of the Chinese Third Way and China's opening to the outside world.

Methodology and Approach

To study China's experience of learning and experimentation in its post-1979 economic development, and to explain it in *A Third Way*, I used the "process tracing" method, which "attempts to identify the intervening causal process—the causal chain and causal mechanism—between an independent variable and the outcome of the dependent variable."[174] With this method I analyzed the evolution of elites' opinions on economic policy and their promotion of a particular vision of development during the policy adoption, implementation, and adjustment process.

To examine and understand the relationship between elite opinions and the policy process, I relied on a variety of primary and secondary sources collected in China and Hong Kong since the 1980s. Analyzing elite views is always a challenge in authoritarian states such as China's, where the party is constantly rewriting history to suit the current party leader. After he became paramount leader in the early 1980s, Deng Xiaoping, not Hua Guofeng, was given credit for initiating and expanding the economic opening strategy. In 2018, celebrated as the fortieth anniversary of the opening decision, the party rewrote history again to demote Deng and expand the role of General Secretary Xi Jinping's father, Xi Zhongxun, who along with Yang Shangkun had proposed Guangdong as an experimental laboratory for economic and foreign trade reforms.[175] The most blatant rewriting of history is the complete omission of the true architect of the opening strategy of the 1980s, Premier Zhao Ziyang, who has been airbrushed out of history, including in Political Bureau member Li Lanqing's 2009 autobiography, *Breaking Through: The Birth of China's Opening-Up Strategy*.

Thus, I was careful when using openly available collections of the writings and speeches, reminiscences, and biographies of Deng Xiaoping, Chen Yun, Li Xiannian, and others. Whenever possible I relied on internally circulated collections of speeches, such as those edited by the Chinese Academy of Social Sciences, the Central Archival Library, and the Central Committee's Office of Documentary Research, including *Zhonghua Renmin Gongheguo jingji fagui xuanbian, 1979.10–1981.12* (Collection of economic laws and regulations of the People's Republic of China, October 1979–December 1981) and *Sanzhong quanhui yilai zhongyao wenxian xuanbian* (Selected important documents issued since the Third Plenum), which provide authoritative compilations of speeches given during the early period. I augmented these collections with the chronicles issued by the Central Committee's Office of Documentary Research, although they lack the detail and insight of the valuable two-volume *Zhou Enlai nianpu (1949–1976)* (A chronicle of Zhou Enlai's life [1949–1979]), published in 1997. I also depended on the two major works on Deng Xiaoping, the biography written by Alexander Pantsov with Steven Levine (2015), which is especially strong on Deng's life during the pre-1979 period, and the biography by Ezra Vogel (2011), who emphasizes Deng's political life during the 1980s and 1990s.

However, the most comprehensive and authoritative collection of speeches and policy documents is *The Collected Works of Zhao Ziyang*, published by Chinese University Press in 2016. The 498 writings in this four-volume collection include policies, speeches, reports, letters, and written policy comments issued between 1980 and 1989, when Zhao was the Chinese state premier and the party general secretary. I found that the primary documents were enhanced by reading Zhao's autobiography, *Prisoner of the State: The Secret Journal of Premier Zhao Ziyang*, which was transcribed from thirty cassette tapes that Zhao recorded around the year 2000 during his house arrest and published in the West in 2009, four years after his death. Although I also examined competing viewpoints from Chen Yun, Li Peng, Deng Liqun, and other conservatives, I fully acknowledge that this study focuses to a greater extent on Zhao Ziyang and his coastal development strategy to explain the elites' learning process.

To demonstrate and analyze the linkage between elite learning and policy formulation, I used a variety of internal policy collections that document formal and informal meetings, formal written communications, and inspection and investigation reports from the Central Committee, the State Council, and various government and provincial ministries. With the aim of breaking down the barriers to communication and cooperation between the central bureaucracies, in the mid-1980s Premier Zhao Ziyang promoted greater openness in bureaucratic procedures, including the publication of various restricted policy collections. In addition to collections issued by individual State Council ministries, I relied on State Council Office records for information on the SEZs and on the State Council General Office Secretariat internal policy collection entitled *Yanhai chengshi kaifang he tequ gongzuo wenjian xuanbian* (A selection of public documents relating to the opening of the coastal cities and the SEZs). First published in May 1986, with subsequent issues covering policies of the late 1980s and 1990s, these volumes contain the core Central Committee and State Council documents related to China's opening to the outside world, especially of coastal cities, the use of foreign capital, the importation of foreign technology and equipment, import and export management, the use of foreign exchange and banking, customs regulations, and import and export tariffs. I translated many of the key Central Committee documents in two special issues of *China Law and Government* entitled "China's Coastal Development Strategy, 1979–1984." Other important collections include *Duiwai jingji falü zhengce huibian* (A selection of foreign economic laws and policies), issued by the Zhejiang Provincial Government Department and its Foreign Trade Office in 1985.

The most important official documents in this study often include an initial commentary from the issuing unit that may have been issued as a circular (*tongzhi*), a report comment (*pishi*), or an approval and transmittal notice (*pizhuan*).[176] Central Committee document 1979.50, for example, was originally a report submitted by the Guangdong and Fujian provincial party committees on 6 June 1979 that was subsequently approved and transmitted by the Central Committee and State Council on 15 July 1979. The *pizhuan* is quite lengthy and provides insight into the elites' thinking as they established the policy's key goals, including the acceleration of the Four Modernizations and the establishment of a ten-year target for foreign exchange earnings. The document also specifies the exact amount of money that Guangdong would turn over to the central government and the amount that the central government would pay out to the poorer Fujian province. They agreed to a phased opening of the export zones, starting with the two areas of Shenzhen and Zhuhai; after a trial period, Xiamen and Shantou would be opened. Subsequent to this document, this study analyzes the official documents that authorized the expansion of the coastal development strategy, including the establishment of the fourteen coastal cities and the Hainan SEZ.

Beginning in the early 1980s, Chinese elites embarked on the Chinese Third Way by experimenting with various policy innovations that directly and indirectly influenced the evolution of the coastal development strategy. To gain a greater understanding of these initiatives, I primarily relied on another internal document published in 1986 by the Chinese Economic Publishing House titled *Zhonghua Renmin Gongheguo jingji guanli dashiji* (A chronicle of the PRC's economy and administration). While it lacks certain details such as the document sequence number, this chronicle covers elite speeches and comments, conferences, and meetings, as well as names and descriptions of economic and administrative policies issued by the Central Committee, the State Council, and its ministries, from October 1949 to December 1985. Internal studies were especially invaluable, especially Tan Qingfeng, Yao Xuecong, and Li Shusen's *Waimao fuchi shengchan shijian* (The practice of supporting foreign trade production), which provides invaluable analysis of China's export promotion measures.

Viewing the adaptation of policies from the elites' own perspective allows us to partially open the "black box" of decision making to see a more complete picture of the opening experiment throughout the 1980s. With that goal in mind, I have divided *A Third Way* into the following chapters, each tracing a distinct phase in the complex learning process undertaken by Chinese elites as they worked toward China's development.

Chapter 1: Empowering the Coastal Provinces, 1978–81

In the first phase—crisis—Chen Yun and Deng Xiaoping criticized Premier Hua Guofeng's large-scale ISI strategy for exacerbating the country's economic crisis and endangering the party's control over the state. In the second phase—readjustment—Deng resurrected the consensus norm initiated during the Yan'an Roundtable period before 1957. Elites promoted a second generation of leaders, including Zhao Ziyang and Hu Yaobang, who readjusted the entire Ten-Year Plan and discovered new ways to finance the new, smaller ISI development strategy, including the "active" use of foreign capital.

The third phase was characterized by adaptation and experimentation. During this time the bureaucratic Stalinists adapted various plan-oriented export promotion policies, including expansion of the ECPBs first established in 1960. With the adoption of Central Committee document 1979.50 on 15 July 1979, bureaucratic Stalinists gave provincial authorities greater decision-making rights in economic planning and foreign trade, foreign investment projects, foreign trade revenue, commodity pricing and supplies, and the banking and labor sectors.

Chapter 2: Initiating the Special Economic Zones, 1980–81

Document 1979.50 also approved the trial operation of the first SEZs, which represented a completely new experiment with decentralization, foreign financing, and outward-oriented development. Beijing approved various types of SEZ investment incentives, including preferential tax treatment, greater retention of foreign exchange profits, and the ability to import items unavailable on the domestic economy. The newly empowered regional leaders were often inexperienced and sought innovative and sometimes illegal means to raise development capital and foreign investment, including entrepôt trade and smuggling, to meet the nearly insatiable domestic demand for foreign goods such as watches, calculators, electronics, and automobiles.

Chapter 3: Review and Adjustment of the SEZ Experiment, 1981–83

The fourth phase of reviewing and adjusting policy grew out of two major conferences sponsored by the Central Committee and State Council in Beijing in March 1980 (resulting in Central Committee document 1980.41) and in May–June 1981 (Central Committee document 1981.27). Local provincial and SEZ officials reported on the experiment's progress, leading to the promulgation of corrective policies and the expansion of the SEZ experiment. However, by January 1982 Guangdong's large-scale smuggling operations had alarmed Beijing elites, who feared that party members were involved in serious economic crimes. Chen Yun successfully convinced Deng to review the decentralization policy, resulting in a moratorium on new SEZs and the construction of a border fence to separate the Shenzhen SEZ from the interior economy.

The first generation of bureaucratic Stalinists subsequently formed two elite opinion groups: the international Leninists and the moderate bureaucratic Stalinists, with Deng Xiaoping as the paramount leader. Deng maintained the Third Plenum consensus and compromised with Chen Yun and the moderate bureaucratic Stalinists by adopting a "balanced" approach in policy experiments. Although elites continued to learn, differences of opinion persisted and influenced economic policy review and adjustment measures.

Chapter 4: Coastal Expansion, 1983–88

In the fifth phase, policy expansion, Deng Xiaoping traveled to Guangdong, Fujian, and Shanghai in 1984 to signal his approval of Zhao Ziyang's international Leninist vision of coastal development. Central Committee document 84.13 acknowledges that the opening of fourteen coastal cities to the international marketplace would attract foreign investment and increase production of "foreign goods" that could be sold in China's domestic marketplace. While elites reprimanded Hainan authorities for their large-scale importation of foreign automobiles and luxury items, they learned how to transform Hainan from a simple natural-resource base into an important building block for China's coastal development strategy. China's elites were now pursuing an outward-oriented development strategy, which engaged the global economy and accepted global norms of international economic behavior.

Chapter 5: Initiating China's Third Way

After 1978, Chinese elites no longer considered the outside world as an enemy but saw it as a potential partner in development. This chapter analyzes the sixth and final policy adoption phase of the developmental learning process, based on the perceived success of the coastal development and other domestic economic decentralization experiments in urban and rural China. Chinese elites agreed by the late 1980s to reject inwardly-oriented strategies and adopt Zhao Ziyang's outward-oriented, coastal development strategy and initiate internal discussions on GATT admittance.

Conclusion: Spillover and the Stalinist Paradigm

The Chinese Third Way of development entailed a shift from the comprehensive Stalinist paradigm characteristic of the Chinese totalitarian state to a consultative economic paradigm characteristic of a post-totalitarian regime. This was a sectoral paradigm shift, as the first generation of Chinese elites decided to retain and adapt the political and social Stalinist paradigm of the 1950s. When the second generation of elites, including Hu Yaobang and Zhao Ziyang, attempted to harmonize economic experiments with China's Stalinist political and social paradigms by reducing the role of the party in political and social policy, Deng Xiaoping and the first generation replaced them with a new third generation of leaders made up of technocrats less interested in political and social reforms.

CHAPTER ONE

Empowering the Coastal
Provinces, 1978–80

Mao's death in 1976 initiated China's transition to an early post-totalitarian state, a form of rule characterized by limited political, economic, and social pluralism; a less pervasive ideology; reduced emphasis on mobilization; and party leaders who are often technobureaucrats rather than charismatic figures.[1]

Guided by a spirit of cooperation and compromise, throughout the 1980s China's leaders formulated and implemented decentralization experiments in the rural, urban, and industrial sectors.[2] Based on their accumulated learning from the previous three decades of ISI development, the elites saw that the Stalinist economic paradigm, with its command economy and its inward-oriented ISI strategy, had severe limitations.[3] To build a strong and prosperous China, the state needed to alter one of its fundamental long-term goals and relinquish the party's control of the state economy—while maintaining control in the other sectors. Although they differed on how to transform the Stalinist economic paradigm, the elites engaged in continuous discussion, learning, and compromise in the spirit of the new Third Plenum consensus, which created a cautious, but stable, environment for policy experimentation. Thus they began the complex learning process and initiated the shift from a Stalinist economic paradigm to a consultative economic paradigm.

Complex Learning Phase One: Political and
Economic Crisis, 1976–80

With the death of China's first paramount leader, Mao Zedong, on 9 September 1976, Chinese leaders faced their most important crisis since the country's founding in 1949. Hua Guofeng joined with the first generation of bureaucratic Stalinists to bring down the remaining revolutionary Stalinists—Jiang Qing, Zhang Chunqiao, Wang Hongwen, and Yao Wenyuan, the so-called Gang of Four. To reestablish the party's legitimacy and Hua's leadership of the party and state, all problems resulting from the disastrous Third Front and the Cultural Revolution were blamed on the Gang of Four, despite the party's culpability in the deaths of millions of people since the Great Leap Forward.

Although scholars argue that a crisis motivates policy makers to institute reforms, it is often the *perception* of crisis and the surrounding political and economic conditions that determine whether reform and learning can take place.[4] Despite their initial enthusiastic support for Hua's version of development model II and the Four Modernizations, Deng Xiaoping, Chen Yun, and Li Xiannian used the high economic costs of the New Great Leap plan in the late 1970s to persuade party members that Hua's replacement was necessary.

Having convinced Deng of the economic dangers of Hua's grandiose ISI vision, Chen Yun criticized Hua's desire to "catch up with the other countries in eight to ten years." Dependence on foreign capital to finance the ISI projects was dangerous, Chen believed, as China lacked the ability to finance the Ten-Year Plan, which could cost nearly US$300 billion.[5] Most important, Chen Yun informed his revolutionary cohort that the ISI program had become problematic, as China lacked the industrial capacity and advanced technology to absorb the ISI projects.[6] Planners had seriou sly underestimated the cost to build the ISI projects. And once in operation, the ISI projects often lacked the ability to obtain spare parts, raw materials, and the qualified technical and managerial personnel they needed to operate efficiently.[7]

Political unrest, beginning in 1978 with the Democracy Wall Movement in Beijing—where people posted signs such as Wei Jingsheng's *dazibao* (large-character poster) declaring the need for a "Fifth Modernization" of democracy—led to Deng's suppression of the movement in 1979 and his enunciation of the Four Cardinal Principles. The bureaucratic Stalinists realized that an economic crisis could create more political turmoil and threaten the party's control of the state.[8] And it was in the midst of these circumstances that the high costs of the Ten-Year Plan threatened to create just such a crisis. Fearing political chaos, the leadership replaced Hua Guofeng and assumed control, and then completely readjusted Hua's development model II. Nevertheless, even with the readjusted ISI program implemented in the early 1980s, the bureaucratic Stalinists questioned the effectiveness of development model II, whose high costs and low return no longer offered an appropriate pathway for China's development.

Complex Learning Phase Two: Third Plenum Consensus and Readjustment

During the readjustment phase, phase two in the complex learning process, the bureaucratic Stalinists readjusted the previous second-order adaptations of their political, economic, and social policies to mitigate the deleterious effects of crisis. After the death of Mao and the demise of the revolutionary Stalinist coalition, the bureaucratic Stalinists formed the Third Plenum consensus, which revived the consensus norm of the Yan'an Roundtable. Deng replaced the divergent, incremental learning of the previous two decades with a system for collective, continuous learning. For the next decade, the first and second generations of elites sought to compromise, despite their different attitudes, on policy initiatives and experiments for China's economic reforms, with Deng as the moderating paramount leader.

In reasserting the party's hegemony over the state by promoting the Four Cardinal Principles in 1979, Deng formally broke with his former mentor and declared Mao's partial culpability for the revolutionary-Stalinist excesses carried out while implementing development model I.[9] During this initial period of leadership consolidation, Deng's primary goal was to strengthen a strong cooperative relationship with the remaining bureaucratic Stalinist elites and to invigorate the party by appointing a second generation of party leaders to implement their strategy. Compared with Mao, Deng had a greater ability to tolerate and accommodate different economic policy viewpoints among the first generation of elites.[10] Deng replaced the Yan'an Roundtable of the 1950s with a new Third Plenum consensus, composed of the eight elders of the first generation of bureaucratic Stalinists, to formulate the overall policy strategy (*fangzhen*). They in turn chose a second generation of Chinese leaders, including Hu Yaobang as party general secretary and Zhao Ziyang as premier, to formulate and implement their strategy's policy initiatives (*zhengce*).

Despite outwardly appearing to be a new generation of party leadership, the bureaucratic Stalinists maintained strict control over the direction of the party-state in the 1980s through their positions on the Central Advisory Committee (CAC) and the Central Discipline Inspection Commission, which were established by the Twelfth Party Congress in September 1982 and enshrined in the 1982 CCP constitution. According to Article 22, CAC members were required to "have a party standing of forty years or more, have rendered considerable service to the party, have fairly rich experience in leadership, and to enjoy fairly high prestige inside and outside the party." As a member of the Political Bureau Standing Committee the CAC chairman "puts forward recommendations on the formulation and implementation of the party's principles and policies and gives advice upon request, assists the Central Committee in investigating and handling certain important questions, propagates the party's major principles and policies inside and outside the party, and undertakes such other tasks as may be entrusted to it by the Central Committee." The Central Committee regarded the CAC as a "political assistant and consultant"; CAC members could participate in the Central Committee plenary meetings and participate in Political Bureau sessions.[11] As Deng stated in his speech to the CAC's first plenary session in September 1982, the CAC was a temporary bridging organization that would not "hinder" the work of the Central Committee or the lower-level provincial organizations. "If we take a correct attitude, we shall help them in their work. If we act inappropriately, we may have a bad effect."[12] Deng said the CAC would exist for a decade or so, until the party instituted a more formal retirement system.

Many of the bureaucratic Stalinists became the key members of the CAC, including those who had survived the Cultural Revolution and returned in the 1980s to oversee and guide China's economic transformation.[13] While Deng Xiaoping had stepped down as first vice premier in 1980, he controlled policy strategy as the paramount leader, through his chairmanship of the CAC from 1981 to 1987 and his chairmanship of the Central Military Commission from 1983 to 1990. The first generation of Chinese bureaucratic Stalinists included a significant number of cadres who had studied and worked overseas in Asia and in Europe in the 1920s, including Deng Xiaoping. The experience of living and working in Europe, Japan, and Shanghai had given these elites a great appreciation for technology and the role it played in the modernization of Western Europe and Japan.

Despite the bureaucratic Stalinists' past involvement in the formulation of Hua's large-scale ISI program, Chen Yun convinced Deng and the other leaders that the ISI economic plan had to be radically readjusted. Without a clear long-term path to guide them, Chinese leaders readjusted the entire Ten-Year Plan and implemented a three-year period of "readjustment, reform, reorganization, and improving standards" (*tiaozheng, gunggu, chongshi, tigao*) that included the reduction or elimination of many of the large-scale ISI projects.[14] Because of his continued support for the large-scale ISI strategy, in August 1980 Yu Qiuli lost his positions as head of the State Planning Commission and the State Council's Small Leadership Group on Imports and Exports. Gu Mu was subsequently appointed leader of the State Foreign Investment Control Commission (SFIC) and the State Import-Export Commission (SIEC).[15]

Based on academic discussions at the April 1979 Wuxi Conference and policy-oriented discussions at the Central Work Conference that same month, Chen Yun and Li Xiannian's Finance and Economy Commission guided the readjustment program, which first focused on readjusting the 1979 economic plan, correcting "proportional imbalances" within various economic sectors, and reducing capital construction.[16] Not all large-scale ISI projects were eliminated. Despite Chen Yun's objections to a project based on the GLF concept of "taking steel as the key link," the massive Baoshan Iron and Steel Corporation survived the readjustment cuts of the early 1980s, and by 2012–14 it was ranked fourth among the world's largest steel-producing companies.[17] Echoing the cautious bureaucratic Stalinist approach of Chen Yun, Li Xiannian argued to delay reimplementation of the large-scale ISI strategy until 1985. During the interim period, China would import key technology or projects that required "less coal, less electrical demand, less investment, [and] have a quicker return on investment and a greater ability to earn foreign exchange."[18]

Li's proposed 1985 reimplementation of the large-scale ISI strategy was never adopted. By the early 1980s a growing number of elites realized that the ISI strategy in place since the early 1950s was no longer effective. The cost of the ISI projects had grown exponentially from what was projected in the original 156 Soviet-assisted Projects, the Four Modernizations strategy of the early 1960s, and the Four-Three Plan and Ten-Year ISI Plan of the 1970s. Hua Guofeng had planned to finance the ISI plan with large amounts of foreign capital, which Li Xiannian and the elites had initially supported but eventually rejected.[19] However, the core problem was the ineffectiveness of the ISI strategy. The 156 Soviet-assisted Projects had provided China with a modern industrial infrastructure. By the 1970s, the Chinese encountered various problems in bringing the Four-Three Plan projects online, including construction problems, importation of inappropriate technology, the high cost of building the necessary infrastructure, duplication of facilities, poor-quality imports, the need for spare parts, lack of qualified technical personnel, and return-on-investment.[20]

During this period, elites reviewed reports on Zhou Enlai's early-1970s ISI projects, which were now in operation. More than two-thirds of the turnkey plants were losing money. There were massive overruns as the State Planning Committee failed to import the correct technology or spare parts. The technology in place was often inappropriate, and there were not enough qualified technicians or managers to run the turnkey operations. In the case of Wuhan Steel, China imported a 1.7-meter steel rolling mill project between 1975 and 1978 from West Germany and Japan at a cost of RMB 3.89 billion. The State Council criticized its cost overruns and the insufficient preparatory work that resulted in a lack of electricity, raw materials, and sufficient transportation. Coupled with low productivity, the plant was projected in

1979 as meeting just 18 to 40 percent of its planned steel production targets.[21] Thus at the April 1979 Central Work Conference Li Xiannian agreed with the goals of development model II, setting "self-reliance as the primary goal and external assistance as a supplementary." Li argued that China had to prioritize its ISI program to "increase the country's power and strengthen national defense." China lacked technicians but enjoyed a surplus of labor; thus, it was unnecessary to import labor-saving technology.[22]

Chen Yun aptly described the changing attitude of the first generation of bureaucratic Stalinists when he stated in the late 1970s: "Because capital is not enough, we can borrow from abroad."[23] Even plan-oriented Stalinists desperate to find new sources of investment capital were beginning to doubt the inward-oriented development strategy, including the ISI strategy and China's long-term goal to achieve self-reliance. Having traveled abroad in the mid- to late 1970s to Eastern and Western Europe and the United States, Deng Xiaoping and other key elites admired the economic progress achieved by those economies, which relied on a more outward-oriented strategy, using the international marketplace and foreign capital to achieve a greater integration with the global economy. The Chinese political and economic crisis of the late 1970s forced some of the first generation of bureaucratic Stalinists to question the inward-oriented ISI development strategy. Influenced by his training in the Soviet Union, Chen Yun had adapted the plan-oriented development strategy implemented since the 1950s by allowing in foreign investment, foreign technology, and foreign capital. Influenced by his study in Lenin's Russia and his travels overseas in the 1970s, Deng Xiaoping allowed Premier Zhao Ziyang to decentralize China's economy and to search for a third development mode, China's Third Way.

Complex Learning Phase Three: Adaptation of Plan-Oriented Policies

The bureaucratic Stalinists revived and adapted the remunerative policies they had initiated during the post-GLF period to empower local producers to increase domestic production. Within the foreign policy sector, they also adapted foreign trade policies they had first implemented in the early 1960s to finance China's ISI program and other import needs.

Beginning with State Council document 1979.202, issued in August 1979, Chinese leaders reaffirmed the "Five Priority" policy, which placed the highest priority on export production, especially the Importation of Materials to Develop Export Industries program (*Yijin yangchu*), which authorized exporters to retain some foreign trade earnings and avoid payment of certain taxes. Leaders strengthened policies to reduce costs for export production and expanded financing opportunities for export manufacturers. They also established new loan schemes for developing export goods, including improvements in product manufacturing, quality, variety, and packaging. They approved loans to renovate existing production facilities, allowed localities to retain some foreign exchange, provided tax incentives to increase exports, reduced or eliminated customs duties on imports and exports, devalued the RMB, and changed the internal settlement rate. They also updated the "trial procedures" first promulgated in 1973 that gave priority to a variety of export promotion schemes including the specialized export commodity processing bases.[24] These were adaptations of plan-oriented export promotion strategies enacted over the past two decades that used remunerative measures to motivate export producers.

Yet their grandest decentralization experiment was enshrined in Central Committee document 1979.50, promulgated on 15 July 1979, which authorized decentralization policies for Guangdong and Fujian provinces, including the granting of greater decision-making authority over FDI.[25] As part of the revolutionary Stalinist Third Front strategy, state investment had been minimized in coastal and border regions. In August 1966 Lin Biao proposed a "political frontier defense" (*zhengzhi bianfang*) strategy as part of the revolutionary Stalinists' Third Front development plan. Political Frontier Defense work teams assumed power from local party officials and conducted campaigns to "seize spies." Economic development of the frontier areas was of secondary importance, and production was so disrupted that "commune members and others were not able to engage in their regular work, which meant that some lands remain uncultivated, crops failed and the standard of living dropped." The relevant slogan was,

"'Don't build before the war, build after the war.'"[26] After a decade of neglect, the growth rates of the coastal regions were low, infrastructure was falling apart, and unemployment had led to massive migrations to Hong Kong.[27]

However, Guangdong and Fujian leaders argued that their provinces were in a special position to "expand foreign economic trade, reform the economic management structure, and accelerate its economic development" because they enjoyed easy access to capital, management, and technical expertise from their relatives living in Hong Kong.[28] Elites realized that their experiment could be contained in what was considered an unimportant corner of China's command economy. Yet the region's geographical proximity to Hong Kong, Taiwan, and the overseas Chinese community living in Southeast Asia and around the world meant it could become a dependable source of investment and growth. While agricultural reforms implemented in Sichuan and Anhui were being expanded nationwide, the first major provincial decentralization experiment took place in Guangdong and Fujian provinces.

As the chairman and vice chairman, respectively, of the Guangdong Provincial Party Committee, Xi Zhongxun and Yang Shangkun used their strong connections with Deng Xiaoping to promote the Guangdong experiment. Reporting to the Central Work Conference held in November 1978 before the Third Plenum, Xi Zhongxun described Guangdong's greatest problem as its agricultural sector, which had been crippled by the political upheavals of the previous decade, leaving the people "without full stomachs" and causing widespread shortages on the domestic market.[29] His solution was to "liberate" thinking and implement a more comprehensive agricultural policy that was focused on more than grain production numbers. Guangdong needed to develop more cash crops, implement the agricultural contract system, increase provincial investment in agriculture, and develop the rich agricultural resources of Hainan Island.

Most important, Xi argued, Guangdong had to develop closer economic relations with Hong Kong and Macao by encouraging greater overseas Chinese investment.[30] He pointed out that by October 1978 Guangdong had already signed one hundred different agreements with

Hong Kong and Macao, worth more than US$33.5 million, dealing with technology imports, assembly and processing, equipment, and so on.

> However, our thinking isn't liberated enough. There are too many rules and regulations. Organizational turnaround time and work efficiency are very low. We must quickly change this situation, otherwise we won't be able to carry out business and [may] even start to lose money. The provincial committee has already decided to set up a specialized office that will purely be responsible for this work. We suggest that the central government consider the following: in view of the good relations between Guangdong and Hong Kong/Macao, we hope that we can establish an office in Hong Kong that will enable us to study and investigate various issues and establish direct relations with Hong Kong and Macao businesspeople. Any economic activities related to export processing, compensation trade, etc., would be handled directly by Guangdong, thus reducing unnecessary bureaucracy.[31]

Xi also wanted his colleagues to take advantage of overseas Chinese, who since the 1950s had demonstrated their willingness to invest in their ancestral homeland. They were interested not just in profits in processing and assembly; they also invested in luxury hotel facilities for overseas Chinese visiting Guangzhou, Shantou, Zhaoqing, and elsewhere; built or repaired schools in their ancestral towns; established social welfare organizations; and constructed new residences in Guangzhou, which some overseas Chinese investors hoped to link with Hong Kong by building a superhighway, reducing transit time from the Shenzhen border from four hours to one.

The success of this provincial-level decentralization experiment was crucial to realizing a new approach to China's development strategy, which leaders hoped would no longer be financed solely by Beijing but also by the provinces and foreign investors. The Central Committee approved various measures in 1978 and 1979 to allow foreign investors greater access to the Chinese market, including the establishment of SEZs, first in Shenzhen and Zhuhai in July 1979 and subsequently in Shantou and Xiamen in 1980. The Central Committee and State Council also approved various decentralizing measures in both the domestic and foreign trade sectors. Beijing's leaders assumed a greater advisory role by decreasing the central government's intervention in local economic affairs, hoping this "laissez-faire" attitude would stimulate greater capital formation, which in turn would finance the ISI development strategy and regional development.

Decentralizing the economic system meant that some localities, enterprises, and individuals would "become better off before others." In the foreign trade sector, the new leadership hoped that this strategy would "bring into full play" the strengths of China's major export regions, just "like the eight immortals crossing the sea, each showing their special prowess" (*baxian guohai, gexian shentong*).[32] The leaders thus adopted State Council document 1979.202, which outlined various foreign trade decentralization initiatives, and State Council document 1979.233, which granted special foreign trade rights to Beijing, Tianjin, and Shanghai. Their most daring experiment was Central Committee document 1979.50, which delegated greater authority to Guangdong and Fujian provinces in the domestic economic and foreign trade sectors.

Despite the never-ending rhetoric describing the momentous decisions of the Third Plenum of 1978, the bureaucratic Stalinists did not embark on a new path toward export development as adopted by the other East Asian "miracle" economies. Instead, in the early 1980s China's bureaucratic Stalinists remained committed to the inward-oriented development regime and the ISI Four Modernization development strategy originally promoted by Premier Zhou Enlai and Chen Yun. According Gu Mu, Central Committee document 1979.50

> primarily was intended to implement policies of contracted responsibility for fiscal affairs, of proportional retention of any increases in foreign trade export earnings, and to give the two provinces a bit more decision-making authority in the foreign trade activities, so that they could bring into full play their advantages in being close to Hong Kong/Macao, in having many overseas Chinese [investors], and in having relatively ample supplies of some natural resources. This would thus enliven the economy as quickly as possible. Furthermore, it was one of the initial steps forward in reforming the economic structure and was able to probe into some aspects of reforms.[33]

Thus, as originally conceived, the SEZs were more akin to the OCIEs and the export commodity processing bases of the previous two decades. As Shenzhen party secretary and mayor Liang Xiang stated, "In the initial period of the establishment of the SEZ, our attention was more taken up by solving the labor employment problem, bringing prosperity to the local economy, and stabilizing social order along the border areas. Moreover, due to the influence of the patterns of 'export processing zones' and 'free trade zones' of foreign countries, we thought that the SEZ should be closed to the interior and thus neglected economic combination with the interior. The structure of the SEZ also followed the pattern of the interior."[34]

Not until the crisis of late 1981 did the elites seriously reconsider China's inward-oriented development regime and the experimental role of the SEZs. In an article written on early SEZ policy formulation, Thomas Chan, E. K. Y. Chen, and Steve Chin argued,

> The SEZs were generally considered by the central authorities as part of a policy package for foreign trade and were seen as a local experiment that would have few or no direct and immediate consequences for national economic policies. Thus, the SEZs were not consciously linked with the reform of the national economic system undertaken since early 1979.... The elevation of the SEZs from a strictly local experiment to an issue of national concern came in the second half of 1981 and the beginning of 1982 in the form of a crisis in which the very existence of the SEZs was under threat.[35]

While the most daring experimentation in the domestic and foreign trade sectors was safely confined to SEZs, the lessons learned from China's SEZ experimentation had a profound impact on China's overall economic development strategy during the 1980s. The leadership learned that they could transform China's inward-oriented ISI command economy into a more outward-oriented, state-directed market economy like the development regimes adopted in most of East Asia, which were defined by a more consultative economic relationship with the provinces and local producers.

Decentralization of the Domestic Sector

After assuming power in 1949, the new Stalinist leadership attempted to centralize decision-making power, such as in fiscal affairs.[36] However, Chinese leaders gradually realized that "ours is a country with a large area, many people, and a relatively underdeveloped communications [system]. . . . We already have the ability to distribute to the local government some powers in fiscal economic work that are appropriate for local government management."[37] Thereafter, the country underwent a series of decentralization and recentralization campaigns, including the disastrous Great Leap Forward.

During his speech to the April 1979 Work Conference, Li Xiannian described the economic management structure of the late 1970s as "too centralized and the Plan [as] too rigid. There is a state monopoly of control over the country's revenues and expenditures, its purchasing and acquisition, and its importing and exporting. The 'eating from the same big pot' way of thinking is rampant and no one speaks of economic efficiency. This greatly restricts and inhibits the enthusiasm, the willingness to take the initiative, and the creativity of the central government departments, localities, enterprises, individual staff members, and workers."[38] The bureaucratic Stalinists had learned that the bureaucracy's commanding role in the economy had to be reduced to bring "into full play the enthusiasm of the central government and the localities . . . [as well as] guarantee and promote the smooth implementation of general economic readjustment."[39]

The decentralization campaign initiated in the late 1970s was to prove unique. For the first time, guiding Maoist tenets, such as those expressed in the "Ten Great Relationships" or in such phrases as "Continue the revolution under the leadership of the proletariat," were rejected.[40] The leadership adopted a new definition of egalitarianism, arguing that the old inequalities among the people had for the most part been resolved. Thus, decentralization could be carried out with the purpose of achieving an economic goal and not a political one.

This position was most clearly enunciated in Deng Xiaoping's closing remarks to the November-December 1978 Central Work Conference. On 13 December 1978 Deng stated, "In economic policy, it is my opinion that we should permit some areas, enterprises, workers, and peasants to gain higher incomes first, through hard and diligent work, and to have a better life. If some people's lives become better before others [*xian haoqilai*], they are bound to create a massive model force, influencing their neighbors and causing other areas and units to learn from them. In this way, we can cause a constant, wavelike development of the national economy and bring about speedier prosperity for all the peoples of China."[41] Based on this principle, the new leadership rejected previous normative policies directed against indigenous "capitalists."[42] In fact, the leaders encouraged their resurgence by reducing the state's interventionist role in the marketplace. Such decentralization allowed the coastal areas to develop at a faster pace, allowed industrial and agricultural producers to retain a larger percentage of their profits, and encouraged the development of the collective sector and individual entrepreneurs.[43]

Li Xiannian's April 1979 Work Conference speech again articulated the new leadership's altered views by proposing various methods that would allow "some to become better off."[44] He proposed several principles to guide economic reform: the use of the market mechanism, the expansion of enterprise autonomy, the delegation of greater authority to the localities, the simplification of the administrative structure, and the employment of more economic levers of management.[45] Li Xiannian was particularly critical of the relationship between the central government and the localities. He stated that "powers that ought to be disbursed are not, some that should be centralized are not, some that should be lenient are not and some that should be stricter are not. The duties and jurisdiction between central government departments and localities, as well as between departments, are unclear. The administrative organization is overstaffed, different levels overlap, and efficiency is low." Li thus proposed that, in the future, the "authority to formulate and promulgate national policies, laws, and decrees must be centralized under the central government. Central government departments will carry out primary management responsibility for major construction projects and for procurement, production, and sales of key industries of national importance. [Localities will be allotted] even more authority over planning, fiscal matters, basic construction, materials, labor, etc. Central government departments will help localities successfully accomplish tasks that the localities must manage."[46]

The implementation of a system of "unified leadership, with management undertaken at various levels," was "a major issue related to the national economy," as Li saw it.[47] Initially guided by the Small Research Group on Economic Structural Reform, the new leadership adopted far-ranging policies to decentralize the economy, especially in the agricultural and industrial sectors. Li informed the Work Conference that "the State Council . . . is preparing to organize immediately the various relevant powers to establish several small groups to include comrades working in the central government and the localities and those involved in theoretical and practical work." On 17 June 1979 the Finance and Economy Commission established four research groups, each assigned to one of the following areas: (1) economic structural reform, headed by Zhang Jinfu; (2) economic structure, led by Ma Hong; (3) technical imports; and (4) economic theory. These four groups were transformed into the Office of Economic Structural Reform (Jingji Tizhi Gaige Bangongshi) in May 1980; it was renamed the State Economic Structural Reform Committee (Guojia Jingji Tizhi Gaige Weiyuanhui) in May 1982 by the NPC.[48]

Decentralization of the Foreign Trade Sector

The new leadership also decentralized the government's fiscal relationship with individual provinces and its control over the foreign trade sector.[49] The central government had dominated foreign trade since the 1950s. In 1953, fifteen different specialized foreign trade import-export corporations were established (*waimao zhuanye jinchukou gongsi*) under the newly formed Ministry of Foreign Trade.[50] Eventually the corporations took over the privately owned export concerns after the 1956 socialist transformation period, to prevent the "tendency toward free capitalist competition"; the MFT "system" assumed responsibility for all foreign trade after August 1958.[51]

From 1974 to 1978, Beijing adopted different measures to decentralize foreign trade management. For instance, China's provinces, cities, and autonomous regions (except Tibet) directly shipped and delivered goods and handled foreign exchange transactions. In certain cases, localities, using their retained foreign exchange funds, directly ordered foreign goods through the various foreign trade corporations or

China's Ministry of Finance representative in Hong Kong. State Council ministries established export supply corporations (*chukou gongying gongsi*), responsible for the delivery of foreign trade goods or supplies to the MFT.[52] By the late 1970s the state foreign trade corporations still controlled more than 60 percent of foreign trade activities.[53] This division of production and marketing undermined China's international market competitiveness, encouraged inefficiency, and exacerbated irrational pricing of exports, which increased the domestic production losses assumed by the state.[54]

While accompanying Hua Guofeng on his inspection tour of Eastern Europe in August 1978, Zhao Ziyang realized the importance of breaking the control of foreign trade organizations. To that end, Zhao advocated empowering individual enterprises to conduct foreign trade.[55] However, no significant changes in the foreign trade structure were made until 1988, after Zhao Ziyang successfully pushed for the adoption of an outward-oriented economy.

To increase exports that would finance the ISI development strategy, the bureaucratic Stalinists decided by the 1979 April Work Conference to decentralize the foreign trade management structure and eventually empower individual firms to conduct foreign trade. Between July and September 1979, the CCP Central Committee and State Council issued three very important documents concerning decentralization: State Council document 1979.202, on 13 August 1979, regarding the planned economy and foreign trade; document 1979.233, on 14 September 1979, concerning the foreign trade activities of three major coastal cities; and Central Committee document 1979.50, on 15 July 1979, that decentralized foreign trade power to Guangdong and Fujian and established the SEZs.

STATE COUNCIL DOCUMENT 1979.202

State Council document 1979.202 is an extremely important document outlining China's nationwide efforts to expand and adapt plan-oriented measures to promote exports and experiment with decentralizing foreign trade.[56] To break the monopolistic control of the foreign trade corporations, document 1979.202 called for "a division of management of export commodities" in which the individual government departments and localities would be responsible for conducting a greater range of export trade activities.[57] The number of ports authorized to carry out foreign trade was expanded under regulation 5, which resulted in the opening of eight ports along the Yangtze River in 1980.[58] To facilitate their trade activities, regulation 3 granted localities greater flexibility in using locally generated foreign exchange revenue to import technology and equipment; regulation 9 outlined in detail the foreign exchange retention scheme for localities.[59]

Coinciding with initiatives adopted in the domestic economy to establish enterprise-type companies, regulation 4 authorized "the establishment of specialized trading companies [*zhuanye maoyi gongsi*]" in the various localities.[60] In 1979, thirteen import-export companies were established; nineteen more were established in 1980. These companies were responsible for the export of locally produced goods as well as imports for the region; certain companies were permitted to produce and export their products.[61]

In addition, certain government departments established export companies outside the MFT system. Beijing, Tianjin, and Shanghai municipalities—as well as the provinces of Guangdong, Fujian, Hebei, and Liaoning—established foreign trade corporations (*duiwai maoyi zonggongsi*). The localities were even permitted to establish corporations in foreign countries and Hong Kong (regulation 13); corporations were established in Hong Kong to represent Guangdong (Yuehai Gongsi), Fujian (Huamin Gongsi) and Tianjin (Jinlian Gongsi). Regulation 7 allowed individual production units to engage in a greater range of foreign trade activities. This included sending trade delegations abroad and inviting foreign businessmen to China.

STATE COUNCIL DOCUMENT 1979.233

While document 1979.202 was implemented on a nationwide scale, State Council document 1979.233 and Central Committee document 1979.50 were designed for specific geographical areas where more radical experimental measures would have the greatest potential for expanding export trade. Document 1979.233 was the product of an August 1979 Export Work Conference that sought different ways to expand the export production of Beijing, Tianjin, and Shanghai.[62] Those three cities traditionally had supplied the largest percentage of the nation's exports. In 1979 alone, the conference estimated, 22 percent of the nation's total export revenues—or US$2.88 billion—would be earned by the three cities.

"To achieve in a short amount of time the transformation of the three cities into important export bases with strong international competitive ability," and to raise the proportion of export commodity procurement to total commodity procurement to 50 percent by 1985 (for Shanghai and Tianjin), the new leadership decided to give greater decision-making authority to the local municipal leadership. In May 1979 the new leadership also decided to experiment with industrial management reforms, including granting expanded foreign trade privileges to eight different enterprises in the three cities.[63] By the August Tri-City Export Work Conference that year, those rights were expanded to include a greater role for the localities themselves. According to document 1979.233, the three cities could approve "compensation trade and imports of technology and equipment of US$3 million and below." Bank of China branches located elsewhere could approve only up to US$1 million.[64]

To streamline export work and eliminate bureaucratic redundancies, the three cities were given authority to establish foreign trade corporations and import-export corporations, which were to be the primary regulatory bodies for the cities' foreign trade activities. For instance, the Shanghai Foreign Trade Corporation, established in December 1979, managed fifteen import-export branch corporations and four specialized branch corporations, and provided various other foreign trade services.[65] The trading of important and large-volume items would still be managed by the MFT; the local foreign trade corporations would be responsible for the export and import of all other products.

To respond more promptly to international market demands, the three cities were to formulate their own foreign trade procurement and export revenue plans and carry out other export activities, including the *Yijin yangchu* program, after meeting planned quotas.[66] Chinese leaders authorized the three cities to experiment with a new type of export enterprise that integrated production and trade (*gongmao jiehe*).[67] They also could approve the sending of personnel abroad to engage in foreign trade activities, using local foreign exchange.

CENTRAL COMMITTEE DOCUMENT 1979.50

The most radical experiments were conducted in the coastal areas furthest from Beijing but closest to China's traditional window to the outside world: the southeast Chinese coast. By July 1979 the bureaucratic Stalinists had decided that Guangdong and Fujian would be the first provinces granted the right to formulate "all the plans for production, basic construction, technology planning [*jicuo*], finance, materials, foreign trade, commodity circulation, labor wages, science and technology, culture, education, health, etc." Responsibility for managing units involved in "agriculture, industry, communications, commerce, culture and education, science and technology, and health in general" would be transferred to the two provinces.[68] Fiscal management was decentralized. Guangdong would use a hybrid method of "dividing revenue and expenditure between the central and local governments, rendering a definite revenue quota to the central government." Fujian would receive a set subsidy from the central government [*ding'e buzhu*], "which would remain unchanged for five years."[69] Furthermore, the two provinces would be responsible for the distribution of "State Plan–controlled" materials, the management of provincial commercial affairs, the determination of labor allocation and wage readjustments, and setting the prices for many goods.

The new leadership in Beijing allowed the local Guangdong and Fujian officials five years to prove the decentralization scheme successful. Not only would the local officials use their newly derived powers within this interim period to enliven the two domestic economies, but they also would take full advantage of their newly acquired foreign trade privileges to expand foreign exchange revenue sources. However, the MFT would maintain control of export products that had export quota restrictions, were imported or exported on a large scale, or were subject to "an international market monopoly or fierce competition." The two provinces would "plan and manage (their) own foreign trade under the unified general and specific foreign trade policies and the plans of the central government."[70]

The provinces thus enjoyed full control over export and import needs, circumventing the then "current division of labor in port management of commodities," and they shared joint control over the various branch offices of the central government's foreign trade corporations. They could not only "conduct direct transactions in foreign trade" but also "decide the pricing of imported materials that use the local foreign exchange"; establish companies "combining production and sales, industry and trade and domestic and foreign sales"; "examine and approve all processing and assembly projects, compensation trade, and equity joint ventures undertaken within the province that do not relate to the comprehensive balance of the national [economy]"; and approve to varying degrees exit and entry visas, as well.[71]

Each province would contract to remit a set amount of foreign exchange that was based on "the actual 1978 foreign exchange revenue derived from foreign trade." During the first two years of implementation, the provinces could retain any foreign exchange income that exceeded the 1978 base figure. After the initial two-year period, the provinces would retain 70 percent of excess earnings from foreign trade and 100 percent of excess foreign exchange earnings from non-trade activities.

Chinese leaders authorized the provinces to formulate their own foreign exchange revenue and expenditure plans. To ensure a more constant supply of capital "that [would] be beneficial in developing export commodity production, processing [and] assembly, [and] compensation trade," the two provinces asked Beijing to issue "a set amount of RMB and foreign exchange loans" for provincial use. Document 1979.50 also authorized the two provinces to establish China International Trust and Investment Corporation–type investment companies to "carry out foreign business activities such as attracting overseas Chinese and foreign capital, importing advanced technology and equipment, [and] running companies." The companies could deal directly with the Bank of China, overseas Chinese investors, and commercial and foreign government banks, as well as establish representative offices to carry out business in Hong Kong and Macao.

Many of the foreign trade rights and privileges granted to Guangdong and Fujian by document 1979.50 were later granted to Beijing, Tianjin, and Shanghai by State Council document 1979.233. Yet there was one major exception. Central Committee document 1979.50 authorized the establishment of SEZs only in Guangdong province.

Decentralization and the Special Economic Zones: Tools of State Supervision

Of the decentralization measures approved by the new leadership in 1979, Central Committee document 1979.50 is the most far-ranging, especially regarding SEZ management. State intervention was limited to a supervisory and coordinating role; the localities were responsible for SEZ development and financing. The state used three major tools to guide and supervise SEZ development: directives of the Central Committee leadership, regulations issued by the SIEC and the Ministry of Communications for the Shekou Industrial Zone inside the Shenzhen SEZ, and reports issued by provincial work conferences. The Central Committee's SEZ directives dealt with the most important issues, such as establishing and defining the general purpose of the zones. Party vice chairman and State Council vice premier Li Xiannian approved a request by the Guangdong Revolutionary Committee—the provincial government—and the Ministry of Communications to initiate the Shekou Industrial Zone project on 31 January 1979.[72] Deng Xiaoping approved the SEZ project during the 1979 April Work Conference.[73] To comply with the readjustment plans, in his talk at the 16 December 1980 Central Committee Work Conference Deng also called for a slowdown in SEZ construction.[74] Chen Yun was even more severe in December 1981. He stated that there was an overriding need to "summarize the experiences of the SEZs" and argued against the establishment of additional zones.[75]

The SIEC and the Ministry of Communications were responsible for primary oversight of the zones, even though document 1979.50 gave overwhelming control to the provincial and local governments. The SIEC formally was established on 30 July 1979 by the NPC.[76] Together with the SFIC, the SIEC was the major State Council organ responsible for general foreign trade and investment activities. As head of both the SIEC and the SFIC, Vice Premier Gu Mu assumed primary responsibility for SEZ development. Born in Shandong Province in 1914, Gu Mu rose from his position as a local party secretary in the Jinan Municipal Committee to chairman of the State Capital Construction Commission in 1964. Appointed vice premier in 1975, he was one of the senior economic leaders responsible for formulating the national development strategy in the late 1970s. His month-long inspection tour of fifteen European cities had inspired Hua Guofeng and the leadership to promote the acceleration of ISI development and the New Great Leap Forward. Unlike the head of the State Planning Commission, Yu Qiuli, Gu Mu quickly fell in line with Chen Yun's readjustment initiatives. He continued to play a major role in formulating economic policy up to 1982, when Zhao Ziyang assumed greater power.[77]

Gu Mu was personally involved in all the SEZ decisions. Together with party vice chairman Li Xiannian, he listened to the 31 January 1979 report on the Shekou Industrial Zone submitted by the Ministry of Communications and the Guangdong Revolutionary Committee. Gu Mu subsequently was assigned by Li Xiannian to "gather the relevant comrades together and handle the problem."[78] After the April 1979 Work Conference, Gu Mu led a work team to Guangdong and Fujian in May to discuss provincial draft reports that would form the basis of Central Committee document 1979.50.[79] He also was the primary Central Committee representative at several work conferences about Guangdong and Fujian provinces held between 1979 and 1982.[80] Considering Gu Mu's many obligations, SIEC vice chairman and chief secretary Jiang Zemin assumed responsibility for routine SEZ matters. In presenting the "Regulations of Guangdong Province on Special Economic Zones" to the fifteenth plenary meeting of the NPC Standing Committee on 21 August 1980, which formally approved the establishment of the SEZs, Jiang Zemin laid out the early goals of the zones.

The SEZs are structured quite differently from the interior areas and have been allowed to speed up their opening by fully utilizing foreign capital and technology to develop their industries, agriculture, livestock, cultivation, tourist industries, housing construction, high-tech research industries, and other endeavors. Because an SEZ is a bit larger than the typical export processing zone, it will be more comprehensive in its economic undertakings, which is why it is called an economic zone and is distinguished by its use of capital. There are now more than seventy different EPZs around the world, the majority of which are doing quite well. Things have gone quite well in our preparations to build the Shenzhen SEZ, especially the Shekou Industrial Zone, which has developed rather quickly and [has] already demonstrated excellent prospects.[81]

Between 1980 and 1982 Jiang led several work teams to inspect the zones. By 1982 he was appointed mayor of Shanghai, and he became the general secretary of the CCP in 1989.[82]

The second major organization supervising SEZ affairs was the Ministry of Communications and its Hong Kong affiliate, China Merchants' Steam and Navigation Company (CMSN). Established in 1872 during the Qing dynasty, CMSN originally was to compete with foreign interests, specifically the British shipping monopoly, along the China coast. After 1949 the PRC Ministry of Communications transformed CMSN into a socialist state enterprise representing China's shipping interests in Hong Kong. On 12 October 1978, the CCP Central Committee approved the Ministry of Communications' plan to diversify CMSN's traditional shipping activities in Hong Kong and Macao.[83] CMSN expanded into various industrial and commercial ventures and was granted greater decision-making powers. Five years later, CMSN handled one-tenth of the materials imported by Hong Kong and one-third of China's overseas shipments. CMSN also managed more than 100 companies, including Hong Kong's largest ship repair facility, with capital assets estimated at HK$8 billion.[84]

The CMSN was directly in charge of the Shekou Industrial Zone, which was the progenitor of the Shenzhen SEZ. On 9 October 1978, Minister of Transport and Communications Ye Fei submitted the "Request for Instructions on Full Utilization of the China Merchants' Steam and Navigation Company" for the revitalization of the ministry's CMSN based in Hong Kong, including the ability to apply for US$5 million from Chinese banks; Li Xiannian recommended the request, as it was consistent "with Chairman Hua's directive to 'unshackle the mind a little more, be a little bolder, find more ways to get things done, and step it up a bit faster.'"[85] The new CMSN leader, Yuan Geng, proposed the establishment of the Shekou Industrial Zone in 1978, to be located in the adjacent county of Bao'an. This solution would mitigate CMSN's high production costs and develop China's coastal region near Hong Kong. At the time, it was reported,

> when one turned on the television, there almost always was a news report on young people from the interior fleeing across the border and escaping. Every time [Yuan Geng] saw scenes on TV of large groups of young men

and women from the interior who had been caught by the British police in Hong Kong, being escorted one by one in handcuffs, he felt an indescribable feeling in his heart. Afterward, when he went to Shekou looking for a place to locate the industrial zone, he felt even more disturbed by what he saw and heard. At that time, Shekou was seen as providing an opening for those who wanted to escape, and many youths from the interior had swarmed into the area. From Shekou Bay, they would risk their life to swim to Hong Kong; many would be engulfed by the uncaring ocean waves and their corpses washed up on the beaches, where they decomposed and emitted stinking odors. The first task of the Preparatory Construction Command Post after it was set up in the Shekou Industrial Zone was to collect the corpses, which were lying exposed in this desolate place. In the next few months, they collected more than 100 corpses.[86]

CMSN desired to take advantage of the mainland's cheaper land and labor rates and expand its operations in Bao'an, an area adjacent to the Hong Kong colony. On 6 January 1979 the Ministry of Communications and the Guangdong Revolutionary Committee submitted a request to Vice Premier Li Xiannian.[87] In his discussions with Gu Mu, Yuan Geng, and Peng Deqing, Li stated, "What we should do now is to put the strengths of Hong Kong and the mainland together, and make the most of foreign capital in our construction work. This should be done not just in Guangdong, but in Fujian, Shanghai, and some other places as well. . . . Don't count on me for money to buy ships and build docks. You've got to get it done by yourselves. Live or die, that's your business."[88]

Following Li's approval, Vice Premier Gu Mu initiated discussions in Beijing concerning the establishment of the industrial zone, which eventually was situated on 2.14 square kilometers of land in western Shenzhen on the Nanshan Peninsula.[89] According to CMSN's Yuan Geng, the proposed size of the industrial zone was intentionally small, "since at that time people's ideas weren't liberated enough."[90] Six months after Li authorized the Shekou Industrial Zone, the Central Committee approved document 1979.50, which established the SEZ incorporating the Shekou Industrial Zone. Guangdong and Shenzhen authorities subsequently agreed to grant CMSN sole authority over Shekou.[91] While this relationship was troublesome at times, it insulated Shekou from many problems encountered by the rest of Shenzhen.[92]

With the intervention at various times of Premier Hu Yaobang and SIEC vice minister Jiang Zemin, the Shekou Industrial Zone was established in the early 1980s, complete with a working port and a shopping center.[93] Yuan Geng approved a series of new reforms, starting with the issuance of bonus payments to local zone workers in 1979. He was "the first in China to introduce a new personnel system whereby staff members had to compete for job vacancies," and he oversaw the first direct election of members of the Shekou Industrial Zone's Management Committee in 1983, approved by General Party Secretary Hu Yaobang.[94] Yuan Geng also approved the promulgation of a new slogan for the industrial zone, "Time is money, and efficiency is life."[95] While embodying the spirit of zonal reform, the slogan challenged the basic tenets of thirty years of the Stalinist economic paradigm; critics thus accused Shekou, along with the SEZs, of promoting capitalist exploitation and draining the "lifeblood" of the country. Only after Deng Xiaoping personally visited the zones in early 1984, extolled their accomplishments, and publicly approved Shekou's motto did criticism abate.[96] The approved motto was prominently displayed on the Shekou float as it went past the Tiananmen Square reviewing stand during celebrations of the thirty-fifth anniversary of the founding of the PRC in October 1984.

A similar area, albeit not as important, was the Shahe Industrial Zone. Shahe also was established in 1979 in the Shenzhen SEZ and was not directly under the Shenzhen government. The Overseas Chinese Enterprise Company established Shahe, which was operated by the Guangdong Provincial Overseas Chinese Affairs Committee, a division of the State Council's Office for Overseas Chinese Affairs. The 12.6-square-kilometer site was established in an area between downtown Shenzhen and Shekou, on the road from Shenzhen to Guangzhou. Its purpose was to attract overseas Chinese investment.[97]

The third important tool the central government could use to guide and supervise SEZ policy was the convening of annual conferences. These were forums for central government officials, to help them understand SEZ progress and formulate SEZ development strategy. At them, Guangdong and Fujian officials conferred on specific policy problems and petitioned for changes in specific central government policy guidelines.

Three major conferences were held between 1980 and September 1982, before the Twelfth Plenum of the CCP. The first was a provincial conference held in Guangzhou in 1980, from March 24 to 30. At the meeting, Vice Premier Gu Mu, central ministry representatives, party leaders of Guangdong and Fujian provinces, and representatives of the Hong Kong/Macao Work Committee reviewed the implementation of document 1979.50. A summary of the conference was issued on 16 May 1980 as Central Committee document 1980.41.[98] The second was a work conference convened by the State Council between 27 May and 14 June 1981. This conference sought to define the purpose of the SEZs and resulted in Central Committee document 1981.27.[99] Among the various policies discussed, the conferees agreed that "management structure and policies in the SEZ can differ from those of the interior." The Central Committee Secretariat convened the third and last conference before the Twelfth Plenum from 11 to 13 February 1982, in Beijing. Top party, government, and military leaders attended this important meeting, which was called to discuss the struggle against criminal activities in the zones and "to sum up" the SEZ experience. This conference resulted in Central Committee document 1982.17, issued on 1 March 1982, written in language reminiscent of the Cultural Revolution.[100]

Following the issuance of State Council document 1985.46 approving the decentralization experiment and extending the SEZs for another five years, SEZ work conferences were to be held annually to monitor SEZ development.[101] Besides defining the purpose of the zones, the resulting work conference reports outlined general policies to be implemented by other State Council departments in support of the SEZs. Implementation of the policies, many of which were first mentioned in document 1979.50, required the cooperation of various State Council departments, including the General Customs Administration, the Ministry of Foreign Trade, and the Ministry of Commerce. Cooperation was not always forthcoming.

Among their general guidelines, the early conference reports emphasized protecting foreign business investments, extending preferential custom rates for SEZ imports, simplifying entry and exit procedures, and reforming salary and employment systems. To attract foreign investors, document 1979.50 guaranteed that foreign businesses "operating a factory [would] receive the guarantee of our country's law." The state also permitted the repatriation of profits. Document 1980.41 sweetened the deal by stating, "To attract investment from overseas Chinese and foreign businessmen, income taxes, land use fees, and salaries can be a bit lower than those in Hong Kong and Macao. Initially, the income tax rate is set at 15 percent. The number of years for land use should be set flexibly according to different situations."[102]

Document 1979.50 declared that "a preferential tax system will be implemented for imported materials needed by the special zone and for exported commodities." Document 1980.41 specifically stated:

> The machines, equipment, spare parts, raw materials, and other production materials should be allowed to be imported duty free; in principle the domestic economy would supply goods used in daily life. Those necessary items used in daily life, which the domestic economy truly has difficulty supplying, can be imported upon approval and customs duties levied. Some items can be imported on a reduced or duty-free basis. . . . The imported raw materials and components of commodities, which use imported raw materials and are then processed and re-exported, should be imported duty free. From now on, we must gradually implement a method of paying duty imports and returning the paid duties upon export. Duty exemptions also will be granted to the coal and petroleum imported to relieve the energy problems of the two provinces and to approved technology and equipment imported by Sino-foreign joint ventures.[103]

Documents 1979.50 and 1980.41 also proposed a general simplification of entry and exit procedures for foreigners and Chinese personnel dealing in SEZ business affairs. With the issuance of document 1981.27, the local SEZ governments and management committees could approve exit and entry permits for Chinese individuals and foreigners.

Document 1979.50 had stated that salaries in the SEZs "can be higher than the average national or Guangdong levels." With the adoption of Document 1981.27, the salary reform was expanded so that "management structure and policies in the SEZ can differ from those of the interior." According to document 1981.27, "The staff and workers of SEZ enterprises are under a contract system. Enterprises have the right to fire, to hire on a trial basis and to fire. We want to transform slowly the methods of having a low salary with lots of supplements. The Shenzhen and Zhuhai wage zones will be raised to the tenth level. Enterprise salaries can be split into a basic wage and fluctuating wage." Deng Xiaoping agreed in April 1979 that the state would only provide policy guarantees for running the SEZs. Central Committee and State Council directives, policies approved by the SIEC and the Ministry of Commerce, and reports issued by the various conferences were the major tools for outlining such SEZ policies and supervising their implementation.

Provincial Management of the SEZ Experiment

While Beijing had oversight responsibilities, provincial government organizations directly managed Guangdong and the SEZs from 1979 to 1982. The only exception occurred within Shenzhen. Of the total 327.5-square-kilometer area of Shenzhen, Shekou (2.14 square kilometers) was managed by CMSN under the Ministry of Communications, and Shahe (12.6 square kilometers) was directly managed by the Overseas Chinese Enterprise Company.

Although Xi Zhongxun and Yang Shangkun continued to promote the decentralization experiment, both leaders left Guangdong in September 1980 to assume high level positions in Beijing.[104] Ren Zhongyi, described by Vogel as "*the* great provincial entrepreneur of the reform period," was appointed first party secretary of Guangdong and was in charge overall, and principle regional defender of, the Guangdong provincial decentralization experiment and the SEZs.[105] After August 1980 the Guangdong Provincial Administration of the SEZs (Guangdong-sheng Jingji Tequ Guanli Weiyuanhui) was established, with offices in each zone. The primary officials in charge of SEZ work between 1979 and 1982 were two local Cantonese officials, Liu Tianfu and Wu Nansheng. Fujian's provincial-level officials managed SEZ development by establishing the Xiamen SEZ Management Committee on 26 November 1980.[106] Liu Tianfu had been first appointed a secretary of the Guangdong Provincial Committee and vice governor in the early 1960s; he regained both posts in the 1970s and replaced Xi Zhongxun as governor in 1981.[107]

As the senior local provincial official, Liu personally was involved with the initial establishment of the SEZs. For instance, he collaborated with CMSN in establishing the Shekou Industrial Zone.[108] Liu also accompanied Vice Premier Gu Mu on his May 1979 inspection trips to Shenzhen and Zhuhai in preparation for document 1979.50 and the establishment of the two zones.[109] Wu Nansheng was the cadre most intimately involved in SEZ development during the 1979–82 period.[110] He was appointed a full secretary of the Guangdong Provincial Party in 1978.[111] Then, in August 1980, Wu was appointed head of the Guangdong Provincial Administration of the SEZ and concurrently held the post of first party secretary and chairman of the Revolutionary Committee of Shenzhen Municipality.[112] He is credited with formulating the Guangdong SEZ regulations approved by the NPC in August 1980, popularizing the term "special economic zone," and expanding their number to include Shantou.[113]

Wu Nansheng's primary administrative tool for managing the SEZs was the Guangdong Provincial Administration of the SEZs, which was authorized by the "Regulations of Guangdong Province on Special Economic Zones." The State Council approved the regulations on 16 December, and they were adopted by the Guangdong People's Congress on 27 December 1979 and formalized by the NPC on 26 August 1980.[114] According to Article 24, the Shenzhen SEZ was under the direct jurisdiction of the Guangdong provincial administration; branch offices of the administration were opened in Shantou on 29 August 1980 and in Zhuhai on 28 October 1980.[115] The Shenzhen SEZ management committee was empowered to:

1. Draw up development plans for the special zones and organize their implementation.
2. Examine and approve investors' projects in the special zones.
3. Deal with the registration of industrial and commercial enterprises in the special zones, and with land allotment.
4. Coordinate the working relations among the banking, insurance, taxation, customs, frontier inspection, postal, telecommunications, and other organizations in the special zones.
5. Provide staff and workers needed by the enterprises in the special zones and protect the legitimate rights and interests of these staff members and workers.

6. Run education, cultural, health, and other public welfare facilities
    in the special zones.
7. Maintain law and order and protect, according to law, the persons
    and properties in the special zones from encroachment.[116]

To facilitate provincial administrative control, on 26 November 1981
the NPC Standing Committee "authorized the People's congresses
and the standing committees of Guangdong and Fujian Provinces to
formulate various specific economic regulations for their respective
SEZs . . . and to report such regulations to the Standing Committee of
the National People's Congress and the State Council for the record."[117]

Thus, management of the SEZs was decentralized. The state supervised and guided SEZ development, but the province was responsible
for managing actual zonal affairs, including planning as well as industrial and commercial development. Eventually the province formulated
and approved specific economic legislation. Wu Nansheng was the primary Guangdong provincial leader responsible for SEZ affairs. He and
his deputy at the Guangdong Provincial Administration of the SEZs,
Qin Wenjun, reported directly to Gu Mu and Jiang Zemin at the SIEC.[118]

The Center-Province Relationship

We can gain an understanding of the dynamics of this decentralized
relationship by analyzing the establishment of the four different SEZs.
As a result of the Third Front and its "political frontier defense" strategy, the front-line coastal areas of Guangdong and Fujian were economically devastated. Between 1978 and 1979, Bao'an's population had
dropped from 334,000 to 313,000. The average Bao'an resident earned
RMB 537 in 1978, while the average national income was RMB 585.[119]
In 1975 Beijing had established an ECPB in Guangdong's Huiyang Prefecture, just north of Hong Kong, that produced export goods for Hong
Kong that ranged from live chickens and lychees to fireworks and
bricks.[120] Yet the Huiyang ECPB was unable to staunch the wave of
economic migrants.

Starting in 1977, various State Council ministries, including the
State Planning Commission and the MFT, planned to establish a new

type of ECPB in Bao'an opposite Hong Kong and in Zhuhai opposite Macao that would encourage development of the border economy and reduce the exodus of economic migrants. On 3 June 1978, Hua Guofeng approved the "Report on an Economic Inspection Tour of Hong Kong and Macao"; as the second secretary of the Guangdong Provincial Party Committee, Xi Zhongxun inspected the areas and submitted on 23 October 1978 the "Report on a Tentative Plan for Building Foreign Trade Bases and Urban Development in Bao'an and Zhuhai counties."[121] The State Council approved these tentative plans on 14 February 1979 with the adoption of State Council document 1979.38, which coincided with the invasion of Vietnam.[122] The State Council allocated RMB 150 million to set up this new type of ECPB, which "would be developed into a very substantial Export Commodity Production Base that combines both the industrial and agricultural sectors, into a tourist area which will attract Hong Kong and Macao tourists and into a new type of border city. This [program] would simply be called the "three developments" (*sange jiancheng*).[123] The State Council approved the transformation of Bao'an (22 February 1979) and Zhuhai (3 March 1979) into municipalities; Shenzhen submitted its plan to develop the "border economy" while Zhuhai held a work conference between 25 and 27 March 1979 on the same topic.[124] As mentioned previously, the Ministry of Communications and the Guangdong Revolutionary Committee simultaneously approached Vice Premier Li Xiannian to approve the establishment of the Shekou Industrial Zone in Bao'an.

After March 1979, Guangdong party leaders Xi Zhongxun and Yang Shangkun elaborated on these ideas. They proposed that Guangdong be allowed "to expand foreign economic trade, reform the economic management structure, and accelerate its economic development." Xi Zhongxun also agreed with Party Secretary Wu Nansheng that Shantou should also be considered a new type of ECPB.[125] Deng approved the special policies and the establishment of special zones, stating that using overseas Chinese financing in Guangdong and Fujian "won't turn us into capitalists, because the money won't go into the pockets of Comrade Hua Guofeng or others among us. Ours is ownership by all the people. I just can't see that things would go wrong if we allow the eighty million people of Guangdong and Fujian to get rich first. . . . Why don't we call them 'special zones'? That was the

Shaanxi-Gansu-Ningxia Border Region in the beginning."[126] In "Some Initial Ideas on the Trial Operations of Export Special Zones in Shenzhen, Zhuhai and Shantou," drafted in May 1979, Guangdong leaders originally included Shantou among the three Guangdong sites.[127] Fujian leaders considered various sites besides Xiamen, including Xinglin near Zhangzhou and Langqi Island near Fuzhou.[128]

Although the two provincial reports submitted in June 1979 to the Central Committee suggested the building of four zones, Central Committee document 1979.50 approved only two zones on 15 July 1979. "Shenzhen and Zhuhai cities will first put the export special zones [sic] into trial operation. After gaining experience, we will then consider establishing them in Shantou and Xiamen." At the second session of the Fifth National People's Congress, held on 23 June 1979, Hua Guofeng, not Deng Xiaoping, told the Guangdong delegation that he and the other central authorities had agreed "to grant Guangdong with some incentive policies and more decision-making power" because of its ability to attract investment from Hong Kong and Macao.[129]

The period of "gaining experience" was very short. During the interim four-month period, provincial officials continued to lobby for the establishment of four zones. On 16 December 1979 the State Council approved the establishment of a third special zone in Shantou. Wu Nansheng convened an Export Special Zone Work Conference in Guangzhou on 31 October 1979, inviting the party secretaries of Shenzhen, Zhuhai, and Shantou together with various provincial government leaders. After the conclusion of the conference, Wu Nansheng submitted a report to the Central Committee and State Council entitled, "Outline of the Report on Several Problems in Establishing the SEZs." Reportedly, this document argued for the establishment of a special zone in Shantou.[130]

In response, SIEC chairman Gu Mu visited Shantou a few weeks later, on 23 November 1979. Accompanied by Wu Nansheng, the two leaders discussed the establishment of a special zone in Shantou. Gu Mu was apparently persuaded by Wu's argument; perhaps he was swayed by the promises of Singapore industrialist Luo Xinquan, Hong Kong industrialist Tang Bingda, and other overseas Chinese to invest in a Shantou special zone.[131] Subsequently Wu Nansheng traveled to Beijing to report on 16 December 1979 on the progress of the SEZs and his ideas on establishing a zone in Shantou. The "leading comrades" of the State Council agreed in principle to the proposed special zone management regulations and the construction of the Shantou zone.[132] The establishment of Shantou was formally announced on 16 May 1980 with the publication of Central Committee document 1980.41, which also formally changed the term from export special zone (*chukou tequ*) to special economic zone (*jingji tequ*).[133]

Although Fujian officials lobbied for the establishment of the fourth SEZ in Xiamen, Beijing approved only a feasibility study for a Langqi Island zone near Fuzhou, in Central Committee document 1980.41. In addition to Chen Yun's opposition to the Xiamen SEZ, Beijing officials realized that Fujian provincial officials would encounter major bureaucratic and financial obstacles in establishing the special zone. Situated opposite Taiwan, the province had been a frontline post for the protection of the mainland from foreign and the Republic of China on Taiwan's aggression, and the People's Liberation Army retained a strong influence within this poor province. Only after 1982 did the Xiamen SEZ become operational.

Guangdong provincial officials also succeeded in expanding the actual size of the SEZs. Shenzhen originally was planned to be "similar to those EPZs abroad. It would have an area a little over three square kilometers and would be separated from the nonprocessing zone by a steel fence with clearly demarcated boundaries. During the day, workers from the nonprocessing zone would enter the zone to work and would leave at night."[134] When the NPC promulgated the "Regulations of Guangdong Province on Special Economic Zones" in August 1980, the size of the Shenzhen SEZ had expanded to 327.5 square kilometers. The other two Guangdong SEZs experienced expansion on a smaller scale in the 1980s.[135] The most dramatic expansion was approved in 1985, when the Fujian provincial government requested that the Xiamen SEZ be expanded from the 2.5-square-kilometer Huli industrial zone to cover 131 square kilometers that encompassed both Xiamen and Gulangyu.[136]

During the initial period from 1979 to 1982, under the rubric of decentralized rule, Beijing acceded to many of the provincial requests for developing the SEZs. The provinces assumed responsibility for the implementation of SEZ policy. Beijing supervised general policy implementation and coordinated the efforts of the two provinces.

Beijing's coordinating role is evident in the 1980 and 1981 conference reports. For instance, Beijing determined the priority of SEZ development for the two provinces. Beijing emphasized in document 1980.41 that provincial officials "should first concentrate [their] energies on the successful construction of the Shenzhen Special Economic Zone and second, on Zhuhai's construction. . . . Planning must first be carried out for the Shantou and Fujian SEZs. After the proper preparations are in order, there will be a gradual implementation of the plans." Thus, Beijing suggested that Guangdong first focus on Shenzhen.[137] After gaining experience in SEZ construction, Guangdong and Fujian could develop the other three zones.

Beijing also "guided" the development strategy of each zone. According to document 1979.50, the two approved zones of Shenzhen and Zhuhai would "first gradually accumulate capital by carrying out processing and assembly projects, light industrial processing, and tourism. After which, we can initiate projects that entail a higher degree of processing." As the number of zones increased, Beijing determined the exact role each would play. Shenzhen and Zhuhai would be developed into comprehensive zones. This idea was first proposed in document 1980.41, which stated, "Initially, construction should begin on those projects requiring little investment, [that] have quick and high returns. While developing the processing export industry, we must concurrently develop under the right conditions the housing, tourist, and other facilities."[138]

More than one year later, with the adoption of document 1981.27, Beijing's idea was more clearly stated: "Shenzhen and Zhuhai SEZs should be developed into a comprehensive type of special zone engaged in industry, commerce, agriculture, animal husbandry, housing, tourism, etc. The international market will influence its market and prices. We thus must pay attention to resolving the various new accompanying problems in economic management."

Initially the purpose of the Shantou and Xiamen SEZs was ambiguous. Unlike Shenzhen, they were located in established cities with an industrial base. Document 1980.41 proposed that "we must fully bring into play the older industrial bases of Guangzhou, Shantou, Foshan, Fuzhou, and Xiamen. We must fully tap their current potential and energetically develop exports of light industrial and machinery products."

This idea of developing the older industrial infrastructure was expanded by document 1981.27, and the exact role of the two SEZs was defined:

> Xiamen and Shantou SEZs currently should be constructed as SEZs emphasizing export processing and simultaneously developing their tourist industries. Within these two SEZs, only factory buildings will be constructed. Living accommodations for staff and workers will rely on the older city areas. The supply of commodities and price management in general can be maintained at the same levels as the non-SEZ areas. To bring fully into play the beneficial conditions of the existing cities, preferential treatment enjoyed by the SEZs will be extended to imported production materials and the payment of income taxes for the older enterprises within Xiamen, Shantou, and Zhuhai, using foreign capital to transform the older urban areas as long as their purpose is to export.[139]

The development strategy for Xiamen and Shantou thus was less ambitious than that for Shenzhen and Zhuhai. Not only were they to be smaller in size, but they were to be developed as EPZs, like others elsewhere in the world economy.

By 1982, the decentralized management of the SEZs was changed. Although the provinces were allowed to maintain their decision-making powers, Chen Yun persuaded Deng Xiaoping to rein in the SEZs and strengthen Beijing's supervisory role.

CHAPTER TWO

Initiating the Special
Economic Zones, 1980–81

The so-called opening of China to international trade and finance in 1978 was initially intended to finance the readjusted ISI development strategy and not as a full-scale adoption of the outward-oriented development practiced by many East Asian economies. As in previous decades, the bureaucratic Stalinists continued their inward-oriented development regime, which isolated the Chinese domestic market from international trade and financial forces, except under very strict controls.

Yet those strict controls were contradicted by Beijing's decentralization policies, which allowed southeastern China to open a small window to the international marketplace. Lacking central government funding, yet free from Beijing's oversight, local SEZ leaders in the region developed the real estate and tourist industries to finance basic construction within the zones. More importantly, local elites took advantage of the huge, pent-up domestic demand for foreign goods and created a flourishing entrepôt trade, both legal and illegal. By breaching internal barriers and engaging the foreign economy, the large-scale importation carried out in the zones exacerbated domestic inflation, adversely affected native industries, and increased the outward flow of foreign exchange. These factors reduced the central state's ability to finance its development strategy and threatened the ideological "purity" of the party and the masses.

The entrepôt trade was a manifestation of a much larger problem facing the new central government leadership: the desire of the newly empowered localities to place their parochial self-interest above the needs of the state.

The Effect of Decentralization on Foreign Economic Policy, 1980–81

The decentralization measures and other reforms adopted in 1979 had a positive effect on Chinese exports in the early 1980s (Table A). Total exports rose 40.2 percent that year, to US$13.7 billion. This annual growth rate in exports was second only to the 69 percent jump in exports between 1972 and 1973. This growth in exports was accomplished despite the world economic recession of the early 1980s.[1] By 1982 China was the eighteenth-largest exporter in the world, having risen ten places over its 1980 position and sixteen places over its 1976 position.[2]

The foreign trade decentralization measures had a similar yet more intense effect on SEZ policy implementation. To paraphrase a Cantonese saying, Beijing was far away; thus, the SEZs prospered. Although reliable statistics are lacking for SEZ imports and exports during the 1979–1982 period, available indicators show definite growth.[3] This is especially true of the Shenzhen SEZ, which was the first SEZ to be developed. The population in the Shenzhen SEZ grew from 70,900 people in 1979 to 128,600 in 1982. Shenzhen's average income rose from RMB 152.2 in 1979 to RMB 393 in 1982. The gross value of industrial and agricultural output for Shenzhen rose from RMB 50.32 million in 1979 to RMB 320.32 million in 1982, with the most dramatic change occurring in the gross value of industrial output, which rose from RMB 29.66 million in 1979 to RMB 299.12 in 1982.[4] Speaking at the NPC Standing Committee in November 1981, Jiang Zemin reported:

Toward the end of June 1981, Shenzhen Municipality had signed 720 economic contracts, [and] 76 percent of those projects had come under construction or commenced production. Of these 720 contracts, 17 were for wholly foreign-owned projects, 7 were equitable joint ventures with Chinese and foreign investment; and 623 were processing, assembling

Table A
Selected Export/Import Figures (US$100 million)

Year	Total exports		Total imports	
	Value	% change	Value	% change
1978	97.45	28.4	108.93	51.0
1979	136.58	40.2	156.75	43.9
1980	182.72	33.8	195.50	24.7
1981	208.93	14.3	194.82	-0.3
1982	218.19	4.4	174.78	-10.3

SOURCE: Zhongguo Duiwai Jingji Maoyi Nianjian Bianji Weiyuanhui, *Zhongguo duiwai maoyi nianjian, 1984* [China's foreign economic trade yearbook, 1984], IV-3, IV-4.

and compensation trade projects, totaling HK$2.458 billion in investment, and bringing in 6,000 sets of machinery and equipment. By the end of that month, HK$500 million had been put to use, the completed buildings had topped 500,000 square meters in floor space, 17,500 people had landed new jobs, the fees paid for the finished projects and the profits shared between the parties concerned had totaled HK$161 million, and foreign investors had been reimbursed with a total of HK$13.65 million [in] equipment imports.[5]

Jiang Zemin's statistics for foreign trade and SEZ growth are impressive. Unfortunately, decentralization also had many unintended side effects. The statistics masked the pandemonium in Chinese foreign trade between 1980 and 1982.[6] In a series of questions and answers first published in 1982 by the major military paper *Jiefang junbao*, the authors succinctly stated, "The reasons for the 'chaotic' situation are very complicated. Sometimes experience was lacking. Many [administrators] were like green recruits brought up to the front [*xinbing shangzhen*]; a large number of problems occurred because the appropriate management measures had failed to keep up with structural changes; in addition, there were some people who only cared about their area or department in procuring foreign exchange. They ignored the general situation, didn't calculate the costs involved, and exacerbated the chaos in procurement, exports and imports, and so on."[7] This apt analysis in *Jiefang junbao* is also applicable to the problems facing the Shenzhen SEZ: namely, bureaucratic intransigence and an inexperienced local bureaucracy. The solutions to these problems would have long-term ramifications for SEZ development.

Central Bureaucratic Intransigence

Decentralization is a gradual process. The top leadership may approve reform initiatives, but actual implementation depends on various levels of bureaucracy, which the bureaucratic Stalinist leadership had strengthened over the decades.

Implementation of the SEZ policy depended on the cooperation of the central bureaucracy in Beijing. According to Central Committee document 1980.41, the SIEC, the State Council Office on Hong Kong/ Macao, the General Customs Administration, and the Ministries of Foreign Affairs and Public Security were called on to formulate and approve specific measures for the SEZs. Document 1981.27 asked central government departments to "deeply understand the situation," declaring: "They must actively help the two provinces to conduct timely research and resolve relevant problems. When the various departments of the State Council issue directives, they should consider the special circumstances of the two provinces. The two should be separately treated according to the spirit of the two Central Committee documents."[8]

Yet central bureaucracies were slow to formulate measures. This was a problem endemic not just to foreign trade reform but to reform policy implementation in general. In a 10 June 1980 article in *Renmin ribao*, the noted economist Xue Muqiao stated that the 1979 reforms had encountered three major problems: (1) The ideas and habits of the cadre were difficult to change; (2) areas implementing experimental policies were forced to deal with outside units carrying out the older policies; and (3) a general reform plan did not exist. SEZ policy was no exception.

Central Committee document 1979.50 stipulated that "detailed rules and regulations for the specific management methods will be set forth at the earliest possible date." Yet promulgation of policies often was blocked. Guo Yunzhang of the Zhuhai SEZ Management Committee complained in 1982, "Currently a unified understanding of constructing the SEZ has yet to be achieved. Some comrades fear the SEZs will become 'colonies,' and that Zhuhai will become a 'neighborhood' of Macao. They fear the 'restoration' of capitalism, etc. Some comrades are not very enthusiastic about SEZ construction. Some departments not only do not actively support SEZ development but even erect barriers. This has caused great problems in developing the work of SEZ construction." Clearly the SIEC was aware of bureaucratic obstacles. Central Committee document 1981.27 states, "The primary problem currently existing is that some regulations of the Central Committee documents have yet to be fully carried out. Management work and specific measures have yet to meet current need. . . . Comrades from the central government departments and from the two provinces have all stated that we must continue to free ourselves of old ideas, be brave in our efforts, sum up our experiences and achieve new results."[9] To facilitate policy implementation, it calls on "the two provinces [to] organize specialized groups and quickly formulate, based on complete research and investigation, various types of local laws and regulations based on the authority invested by the state."[10]

In addition, document 1981.27 suggests the authorization of the Guangdong and Fujian People's Congresses to approve special legislation for the SEZs. The NPC Standing Committee granted such authorization on 26 November 1981.[11] In the post-1982 period, this solution only partially resolved central bureaucratic inefficiency and opposition.

Inexperience

A key to the success of any project is to have capable personnel. Most Shenzhen SEZ cadres were local county officials who lacked the inventiveness to implement the SEZ experiment. Their faults, including their strong desire to make a profit, partially caused the initial chaos in Shenzhen's development. The situation gradually changed as talented cadres and technicians from the interior transferred to the SEZs after 1982.

The Shenzhen SEZ originally was designated a "first category area directly under provincial management" (*diqu yiji de shengxiashi*) in November 1979.[12] Wu Nansheng was appointed first party secretary and chair of the Shenzhen Revolutionary Committee. Because he also retained his position as the provincial party secretary in charge of SEZ affairs, he was often preoccupied managing provincial SEZ matters in Guangzhou. Wu thus delegated authority for Shenzhen's daily affairs to the secretary of the Shenzhen Party Standing Committee, Zhang Xunfu.[13]

Zhang Xunfu originally was appointed as Bao'an county's first party secretary. After the State Council transformed Bao'an into a Shenzhen municipality in February 1979, Zhang and the other "Old Bao'an" bureaucrats retained their positions and managed SEZ affairs. Even after the area's designation as a "first category area directly under provincial management," local bureaucrats maintained control of SEZ affairs.[14]

The Old Bao'an bureaucrats lacked the economic or management expertise needed to carry out the SEZ experiment. According to one senior provincial party official, many of them "were incapable of furthering contemporary economic construction and possessed traditional bureaucratic work methods"; they established an economic structure in Shenzhen "following the pattern of the interior."[15] According to a 1984 speech by Liu Bo, a member of the Standing Committee of the Shenzhen Communist Party, the early Shenzhen SEZ

> basically continued to use the original administrative structure and methods, and there were many abuses. The most prominent problem was that the various administration levels involved themselves in matters that were none of their business or carried out poor or ineffective management. Decision-making power was too centralized, there were too many bureaucratic organizations; industry and government weren't separated; administrative lines of authority were divided; there were too many levels of bureaucracy; these problems led to low efficiency and bureaucratism. . . . It didn't matter how well one did one's job, since there was an "iron rice bowl." Leadership post appointments were for life and based on seniority.[16]

Even Shekou, the most "advanced" section of the Shenzhen SEZ with the strongest connections with Hong Kong, encountered major problems with cadre inexperience and provincialism. In a speech given on 8 June 1984, Yuan Geng of Shekou's Management Committee stated, "Some of our cadre asked some visiting Englishmen from Cambridge University, 'How many bridges have you built?' . . . While reporting to Comrade Gu Mu, one of our cadre stated that after he had been to Hong Kong, his thinking was liberated. Not only did he have 180-degree turnaround in his thinking, but a 360-degree one. Comrade Gu Mu asked him: 'Comrade, where exactly are you turning?' Some of our cadre also asked American businesspeople, 'English people speak English. What language do you Americans speak?'"[17] Despite Shenzhen's location next to Hong Kong and the area's ability to receive Radio Television Hong Kong broadcasts, for example, the cadres and the people remained relatively isolated from the outside world.[18]

The core problem was that sophisticated party cadres in Guangzhou did not want to be transferred to Shenzhen. They considered the area not only a "backwater" but also a potentially dangerous assignment. Though Deng Xiaoping directly supported the SEZ policy, it still was a daring idea. Such an assignment could be costly to one's career if Beijing decided to cancel the SEZs for ideological reasons.[19]

The situation in Shenzhen began to change in 1981 when a major provincial reshuffling and realignment of the administrative structure occurred. In July, Central Committee document 1981.27 announced the separation of Shenzhen from Bao'an county. The Shenzhen municipality was elevated to the same administrative status as Guangzhou (*banshengji shi*) and placed directly under the Guangdong provincial government.[20] Thereafter, Shenzhen municipality was responsible for the administration of Bao'an county.[21]

Liang Xiang was transferred from his post in Guangzhou to replace Wu Nansheng as first party secretary of Shenzhen in February 1981.[22] Liang, who was born in Kaiping county, Guangdong, in 1919, was an experienced party operative. Having taught in the Central Party School and served as a county and municipal party secretary in northeast China, Liang was transferred to Guangdong after 1949. By the late 1970s he had served as a member of the Standing Committee of the Guangdong Communist Party (until August 1978), a vice chair of the Guangdong Revolutionary Committee (December 1978 to January 1980), and second party secretary and vice mayor of Guangzhou.[23]

Strongly supported by Guangdong party secretary Ren Zhongyi, Liang Xiang had the proper party and government connections to pursue corruption in Shenzhen.[24] He had served as a senior bureaucrat since the 1950s and established excellent connections throughout the Cantonese bureaucracy. In 1981 he was simultaneously appointed vice governor of Guangdong and first party secretary of Shenzhen; on 15 October 1981 he consolidated his control by also being appointed mayor of Shenzhen. Liang Xiang considered himself like a bull struggling to uproot a tree, which is the symbol of the Shenzhen SEZ.[25] In this role he was very effective. Under his leadership the Shenzhen SEZ embarked on various innovative reforms that were publicized throughout the country, including professionalizing the municipal government and empowering the mayor's office.[26] Deng Xiaoping later would remark to leaders of the Sichuan Provincial Party Committee: "The ideas of Shenzhen mayor Liang Xiang are very innovative [*jiefang*]. You all should go to the Shenzhen SEZ to take a look around."[27] His innovative style would later serve him well in his capacity as governor and vice party secretary of Hainan Island, a new province established in 1988 that would become China's largest SEZ.

Financing: The Irrelevance of the "Shekou Model"

As a product of the readjusted ISI strategy, the SEZs originally were designed to rely on foreign investment to develop their infrastructure and industries. Funding from domestic sources, especially the central government, would play only a limited role. As Deng Xiaoping directed in 1979, "Since the central authorities lack funds, we call on you to find a way out."[28] The only area that would achieve this objective to the satisfaction of the Beijing leadership was the Shekou Industrial Zone in the Shenzhen SEZ.

The Shekou Industrial Zone, established in January 1979 and located on the Nanshan Peninsula in the Shenzhen SEZ, was under the direct control of the China Merchants' Steam and Navigation Company of Hong Kong. Shekou's top leadership was made up of experienced businesspeople from CMSN affiliates in Hong Kong. Although initially problems were encountered in recruiting competent cadres from the interior, Shekou management was permitted to test and hire applicants nationwide after August 1980. According to Yuan Geng,

> In August 1980, we sent an emergency telegram to the Ministry of Communications. We asked for an immediate halt of transfers [to Shekou] of nonspecialized personnel, recent graduates, and average bureaucrats. The Central Government Organization Ministry gave support to our carrying out direct testing nationwide. During the same year, over 800 people in Guangzhou, Wuhan, and Beijing signed up for the examinations. We chose more than 50 people. More than ten employers [danwei] refused to allow our candidates to leave.[29]

Shekou and CMSN relied on the zone's parent organization, the Ministry of Communications, to resolve any problems they encountered with the central government bureaucracy. According to several agreements concluded in 1979, Shekou was insulated from both Guangdong's provincial bureaucracy and the Shenzhen municipal bureaucracy. As for financing, Shekou and CMSN had access to RMB 50 million in profits retained by CMSN in Hong Kong; two-thirds of its development capital came from the company in Hong Kong.[30] CMSN subsidiaries in Hong Kong also invested in Shekou, thus guaranteeing its steady access to Hong Kong capital and management expertise. In addition, CMSN's involvement in the Shekou project assured potential foreign businesspeople of Shekou's healthy investment environment.

Construction of Shekou's basic infrastructure began in February 1979 and was completed by May 1981.[31] Shekou signed several agreements with Hong Kong and foreign interests that included projects to construct shipping containers, to forge specialty steel products, produce machinery products, and so on. By 1981 Shekou had "twenty-four projects involving foreign capital with planned investment reaching over HK$400 million."[32]

Shekou was so successful that Premier Zhao Ziyang approved the idea of the "Shekou model" during his August 1981 visit to the industrial zone. Each SEZ was to use Shekou as a template for development.[33] Sun Ru, the most important Guangdong economist working

on SEZ development during this period, summarized the Shekou
model as follows:

> CMSN's first step was to dismantle the overlapping bureaucracy among
> numerous offices, sections, and so on. They only opened a central office,
> the General Engineering Office, General Accounting Office, and 13 spe-
> cialized companies. The specialized companies were all independent
> accounting units responsible for profits and losses; all business matters
> are decided on by the board of directors and the managers they ap-
> pointed. They dismantled overstaffed bureaucracies; in administrative
> management, they also dismantled the bureaucratic practice of report-
> ing on every matter, regardless of its significance, and eliminated
> mutual squabbling. This greatly increased work efficiency. Third, in
> construction work, they drew up a general plan for the whole area.
> According to this general plan, they first carried out infrastructure proj-
> ects (specifically, what we often call "five connections and one leveling"
> [wutong yiping]). This created optimal conditions for the operations of
> foreign business investment [projects]. The fourth is the formulation
> and announcement of various laws, regulations, and preferential meth-
> ods that protected the legitimate interests of foreign and Hong Kong
> capital. They attached great importance to contracts and protecting
> their credit; they energetically absorbed foreign and Hong Kong capital
> and imported advanced capital that was suitable to our [country's]
> needs.[34]

Unfortunately, neither the Shenzhen SEZ nor any of the other three SEZs
could copy the Shekou model. Shenzhen lacked experienced leadership
and was plagued with bureaucratic problems. As we will see, Shenzhen
also lacked Shekou's easy access to Hong Kong investment capital.

Financing problems were compounded by the large-scale nature
of Shenzhen SEZ construction. Shenzhen leaders planned to develop
the Luohu district first, located in downtown Shenzhen at the Hong
Kong–China border. Roughly the size of Shekou (two square kilometers), the Luohu development district was designed on a much grander
scale, to accommodate 120,000 people housed in more than one hundred buildings, each over eighteen stories tall. Yet Luohu was only a
small part of the Shenzhen SEZ, which altogether was 327.5 square kilometers in size. Development was planned for other areas of Shenzhen,

Table B
Shenzhen SEZ Capital Construction Investment (RMB in millions)

Year	State inv.	State loans	Ministry/ prov.[a]	Domestic ent.[b]	City/ county	SEZ ent.	Foreign inv.
1979	23.9	n/a	12.2	n/a	6.3	2.1	5.5
1980	33.0	7.0	13.2	n/a	9.6	8.1	53.9
1981	22.7	31.6	24.4	2.9	33.4	20.0	135.3
1982	47.4	202.9	57.9	19.1	64.0	50.0	191.1
1983	43.7	334.1	70.2	n/a	78.0	97.1	222.1

SOURCE: SJTN, 1986: 247.

NOTE: Amounts rounded to nearest hundred thousand.

[a] Funds raised by individual central government ministries and provinces (including Guangdong and Fujian).

[b] Enterprises located in China's interior [Neilian Qiye].

as well. According to the second draft of the Shenzhen development plan, approved in 1981, the SEZ's population was to expand to 400,000 by 1990.[35] The local leadership needed to find local financing for the development of Luohu and the rest of the Shenzhen SEZ.

Financing Shenzhen Development

Beijing lacked capital to develop the zones. Zou Erkang, the vice mayor of Shenzhen, explained the early financial situation for the Shenzhen SEZ in 1985, stating that "shortly after the establishment of the SEZ, our country was in a period of economic readjustment. The central authorities clearly stated that they only provided policies guiding the construction in Shenzhen, but would not give money."[36] Although Chen Yun and the bureaucratic Stalinists had readjusted the economic plan and reduced national government expenditures after 1979, they also realized that the SEZs needed a certain amount of financial help. Document 1979.50 stated, "Needed investment [for SEZ construction] will be resolved by fiscal allocations, bank loans, and absorption of foreign businessmen's capital." The state directly allocated RMB 23.9 million in 1979 for capital construction projects (Table B).

The state decided to increase financial support for the SEZs in 1980. Certain national economic reform policies (increasing the primary agricultural products procurement price, the agricultural side-products sales price, and salaries and bonuses) had an inflationary effect on the domestic economy. As Central Committee document 1980.41 states, "Owing to the readjustment of salaries and prices of agricultural and sideline products, there has been a large reduction in the fiscal revenues of the two provinces and a few problems with construction capital. . . . The state shall provide the appropriate allowances and support in fiscal matters and credit."

Beijing thus set a basic revenue figure of RMB 1 billion for the amount Guangdong would send to the state; in reverse, Beijing increased the Fujian subsidy to RMB 150 million. Shenzhen and Zhuhai retained their fiscal revenues until 1985, which was an extension of the original three-year grace period. All foreign-exchange earnings from the SEZs above the 1978 base figure were to be channeled into SEZ construction until 1985; all revenue from SEZ land development was also to be used for SEZ development. In addition, Beijing promised in document 1980.41 to continue its financial support for construction projects that the state "directly or indirectly" managed and for the operational costs of central ministry facilities "entrusted to the localities to manage." The People's Bank of China (PBOC) and the Chinese People's Construction Bank would provide loans (in RMB) for provincial construction. The state promised to subsidize convertible-currency loans with floating interest rates over 10 percent and to provide US$200 million in foreign currency loans to provincial enterprises engaged in compensation trade.

However, by 1981 the central government reduced the SEZ funding allocation, as the national economic readjustment begun in 1979 had not been successful. By 1980, "finances continually incur[red] a deficit, banks greatly increased issuance of notes, there [was] too much currency on the market, and there [was] commodity price inflation."[37] As for capital construction, Beijing declared "the current scale . . . is far too large, projects [are] far too many with too many overduplications, and [it faced] a comparatively serious situation with unchecked construction. There is also a great waste in construction capital utilization, with poor results."[38]

Beijing thus implemented several macroeconomic measures to re-adjust the national economy and balance the 1981 fiscal budget.[39] In compliance with the leadership's call for greater readjustment during the 1980 National Planning Conference (16 November to 21 December) and the Central Committee Work Conference (16 to 25 December), the State Council "adopt[ed] definitive measures to control currency issu-ance, stabilize market prices for commodities, guarantee the smooth implementation of economic readjustment and consolidate and de-velop a stable and unified political situation."[40] These measures in-cluded tightening credit, reducing the amount of circulating funds, and strengthening cash management. To limit capital construction to RMB 30 billion in 1981, the central leadership also severely restricted the scale of national and local capital construction.[41]

The call for reduced capital expenditures had a direct effect on SEZ construction. During the December 1980 Work Conference Deng Xiao-ping stated, "We want to continue to carry out the decision to establish economic zones in Guangdong and Fujian provinces. Yet steps and measures must be in compliance with the readjustment. Our steps can be taken a bit more slowly."[42] Consequently, state funding for SEZ con-struction was reduced from RMB 33 million in 1980 to RMB 22.7 mil-lion in 1981. Document 1981.27 did approve "an appropriate increase in credit to meet the RMB needs of SEZ construction." State loans for construction increased from RMB 7 million in 1980 to RMB 31.6 mil-lion in 1981.[43]

The central government in Beijing thus was responsible for provid-ing policy and limited financial assistance to the SEZs. Indirect aid from central government ministries and investment from outside provincial industries was also kept to a minimum (see Table B). Shenzhen mayor Liang Xiang explained in 1985 that the leadership intentionally isolated the SEZs from the interior economy.[44] Document 1980.41 thus stated, "Primarily, the special economic zone is relying on overseas-Chinese and foreign capital to carry out construction. In general, the central government departments and various areas are not allowed to manage enterprises within the SEZ, except those that have been permitted to participate in a few equity joint ventures with foreign concerns. Guang-dong Province must strictly keep this in check. If some units locating to Shenzhen and Zhuhai bring chaos to the construction plan, then they must immediately be stopped."[45] Beijing did not officially allow large-scale investments from China's interior until after 1982.

Guangdong and Fujian provincial leaders primarily relied on locally generated funds and foreign investment to finance SEZ development. Initially, local officials depended on fees earned from simple reprocessing agreements with Hong Kong businesspeople. As document 1979.50 stated, "We must first gradually accumulate capital by carrying out processing and assembly projects, light industrial processing, and tourism. After that, we can initiate projects that entail a higher degree of processing."

According to Hu Youqing, an economist at Jinan University's Research Institute on the Economies of Hong Kong, Macao, and the SEZs, this period of development lasted until summer 1980. Hu stated that from mid-1979 to mid-1980, the Shenzhen SEZ

> primarily was engaged in processing foreign supplied materials and agricultural cultivation. This included processing clothing, plastic items or hardware, vegetables, fish and shrimp cultivation, etc. This situation is related to the initial start of the SEZ. The investment environment was lacking, and foreign businessmen still had a wait-and-see attitude toward China's "opening" policy. The SEZ thus engaged only in processing projects involving little investment, few risks, and quick returns. During this period many projects were initiated, but most were simple processing ventures with little investment: for instance, the Shenzhen Clothing Factory, the Shekou Wanxia Clothing Factory, the Shatoujiao Ornamental Flower Factory, the Shenzhen Handicraft Factory, and other processing factories. There was a total investment of approximately HK$100,000.[46]

By May 1980, local and central planners had realized that the development of simple processing and assembly ventures would not generate the foreign capital necessary to build the basic SEZ infrastructure. According to document 1980.41, the solution was to develop sectors of the SEZ economy that required little domestic investment but would attract the greatest foreign investment. "We must fully use the current infrastructure during the construction of the SEZs. Initially, construction should begin on those projects requiring little investment, [and that] have quick and high returns. While developing the processing export industry, we must concurrently develop under the right conditions the housing, tourist, and other facilities." To attract such foreign investment, document 1980.41 proposed that "the management structure and policies in the SEZ can be different from those of the interior. Principally, the SEZ is carrying out regulation by the marketplace. . . . [I]ncome taxes, land use fees, and salaries can be a bit lower than those in Hong Kong and Macao. Initially, the income tax rate is set at 15 percent. The number of years for land use should be set flexibly according to different situations." Bonds and stocks would be issued to attract foreign capital; Shenzhen enterprises could accept foreign loans, especially buyers' credit, with the approval of the SIEC. While continuing restrictions against domestic concerns investing in the SEZs, Central Committee document 1981.27 allowed "Chinese organizations based in Hong Kong and Macao to invest in the SEZs or to jointly invest with foreign businessmen." FDI also could be used to develop "SEZ airports, harbors, railroads, communications and other enterprises and undertakings."[47]

So that foreign investment would be used efficiently, document 1981.27 announced the development of two different types of SEZs: a comprehensive zone and an export processing zone. The Shenzhen and Zhuhai SEZs, which were the first SEZs to be developed, would each become "a comprehensive type of special zone engaged in industry, commerce, agriculture, animal husbandry, housing, tourism, etc. Its market and prices will be influenced by the international market." Document 1980.41 authorized Shantou and Xiamen to build smaller SEZs that specialized in export processing factories and tourism and relied on the older city areas to provide housing for workers. Thus, foreign investment would finance the general infrastructure of Shenzhen and Zhuhai, which were large, underdeveloped areas. In the Shantou and Xiamen SEZs, foreign investment would be more focused and limited.

Measures authorized in documents 1980.41 and 1981.27 effectively encouraged foreign investment in SEZ construction, which rose in the Shenzhen SEZ from RMB 5.5 million in 1979 to RMB 53.9 million in 1980 and RMB 135.3 million in 1981. The proportion of foreign investment to total capital construction investment in the Shenzhen SEZ saw a corresponding rise from 11 percent in 1979 to 43.2 percent in 1980 and 50 percent in 1981.[48] Judging from these statistics, the leaders of the

Shenzhen SEZ complied with Deng Xiaoping's directive to "find a way" of financing SEZ development. Since the central authorities lacked funds, as Deng had said, Guangdong officials had to attract the foreign capital needed to develop Shenzhen's infrastructure in the 1979–80 period.

To resolve the initial problems in SEZ development caused by decentralization, Beijing leaders applied various solutions. Guangdong and Fujian provinces were authorized to approve SEZ legislation, to overcome central bureaucratic intransigence. To rectify the inexperience of the local cadres, Liang Xiang was appointed as a full-time administrator for SEZ–communist party affairs. In addition, Shenzhen was upgraded to the same administrative status as Guangzhou. Finally, the lack of adequate central financing motivated provincial and local leaders to exploit indigenous capital investment sources. It was the methods of financing SEZ development that attracted the attention of—and criticism from—the leadership in Beijing.

The Unintended Results of SEZ Financing

Of all the problems facing SEZ development in the early 1980s, financing was the most crucial. Beijing's strategy of providing policy but not funding for the SEZs was appropriate for constructing the Shekou Industrial Zone. However, it was unsuitable for Shenzhen. Shenzhen lacked the qualified personnel, the simplified bureaucratic structure, and the easy access to Hong Kong capital that Shekou enjoyed. In addition, the scale of construction and the need for capital in Shenzhen were much greater.

The Shenzhen leadership realized that the simple export processing ventures carried out in the zone between 1979 and 1980 would not provide all the necessary capital. To address the shortfall, a second stage of SEZ development, initiated between 1980 and 1982, emphasized low investment and quick returns. Local leaders turned to foreign capital earned from the real estate market, tourist industries, and entrepôt trade to develop the rest of Shenzhen. Reliance on these three sources created both political and economic problems, however. The solutions would have a major influence on SEZ policy implementation in the 1980s.

Problems with the Real Estate and Tourism Sectors

Between 1979 and 1982, during Shenzhen's initial period of construction, 1,168 projects used foreign and Hong Kong capital. Planned foreign investment totaled HK$8.59 billion; twelve projects were worth more than HK$100 million each. During the second stage of SEZ development, most projects were "large housing and tourist ventures initiated in the zone. These were carried out to meet the feeding and housing needs of tourists and investors and [were] an important component in the SEZs' urban modern transformation. In addition, these [were] ventures with quick returns, high profits, and little risk. They met the demands of investors during the early period. During this period, the projects were large-scale cooperative ventures and 100 percent foreign-owned ventures. This is the reason the amount of [foreign] investment in the zone was high."[49] Of total foreign investment in the Shenzhen SEZ, 83 percent was in real estate (cooperative land development, residential housing) and tourism; that figure was 75 percent in the Zhuhai SEZ (Table C).[50]

In the spirit of the Shekou model, Shenzhen developers signed major agreements with Hong Kong investment groups to develop specific tracts of land. The Shenzhen SEZ Development Corporation and the Hopewell Group of Hong Kong concluded the largest land development deal on 23 November 1981. Hopewell proposed to develop Futian into a residential, commercial, and industrial center housing 700,000 people. It also agreed to invest HK$2 billion in providing the basic infrastructure for the thirty-two-square-kilometer area west of Luohu. Agreements with other Hong Kong investment groups were also reached, including an agreement with the Hong Kong Corporation to develop the older section of Shenzhen municipality.[51]

In addition, SEZ developers sought Hong Kong capital to develop the tourist industry. Tourism was regarded as an effective way to attract potential foreign investors to the SEZ; it led to the development of various SEZ industries and services vital to tourism (food, transport, hotels, construction); and most important, it earned foreign exchange. SEZ planners thus decided to exploit the zone's open beaches, lands, and reservoirs to attract weekend visitors from Hong Kong. The tourist

Table C
Shenzhen and Zhuhai SEZ Investment, January 1979–February 1982

Area	No. projects with foreign investment	Amount invested (HK$ million)	Percent of total foreign investment in SEZ
Shenzhen SEZ investment			
Industry	763	861.42	10.3
Agriculture/ husbandry	313	117	1.4
Cooperative land development	3	4400	53
Commerce	30	331.92	4
Communications/ transport	13	11.52	0.14
Residential housing	13	1580	19
Tourism	11	890	10.7
Other	2	100.6	1.8
Zhuhai SEZ investment			
Industry	191	46.82	19.4
Agriculture	13	4.36	1.8
Commerce	29	8	3.3
Tourism	8	15.79	6.5
Land development/ residential housing	15	164.57	68.1
Other	22	2.23	0.9

SOURCE: "Shenzhen, Zhuhai yinjin waizi, gangzi de hangye goucheng jiqi jingying fangshi" [Business composition and management methods of foreign and Hong Kong capital invested in Shenzhen and Zhuhai], in Sun Ru, *Qianjinzhong de Zhongguo jingji tequ*, 63–66.

industry expanded most rapidly in the Shenzhen SEZ. By 1982, Shenzhen tourism ventures had attracted HK$890 million in foreign investment (10.7 percent of total capital construction investment); Zhuhai projects had attracted HK$15.79 (6.5 percent).

Given the large amount of capital investment provided by real estate and tourism ventures, certain Beijing leaders became concerned about the effect of this "capitalist" usurpation of China's sovereignty. Such doubts were raised directly in Beijing during the Guangdong, Fujian, and SEZ Work Conference held between 27 May and 14 June 1981 that produced Central Committee document 1981.27. Critics worried that the SEZs "were just another version of 'foreign concessions' or 'colonies.'"[52] One article reprinted in the local Shenzhen paper reported the existence of "a few comrades [who] maintain a wait-and-see attitude, or have doubts or even a negative attitude toward the trial operations of the SEZs. Some comrades have two kinds of worries: One worry is that the SEZs will become foreign concessions and colonies."[53]

This neocolonialist fear was magnified by an internal government report issued in 1981 by a central government research office, possibly the State Council Economic Research Center. According to one interview with a Shenzhen cadre, "a certain research office issued an internal document that compared the special economic zone to the concessions in old China. Some people even added a note to the document, calling for greater vigilance. What did they want people to guard against? They described our real estate business as selling out the nation's territory. They even used the language that Jiang Qing used during the 'Cultural Revolution.'"[54] Shenzhen had used foreign capital for a large percentage of its development and construction, and because of this some cadres felt that the SEZs would become "'new colonies' that [would be] 'ruled from abroad.'"[55]

Shenzhen and the other SEZs thus became targets of criticism. Guo Yunzhang of the Zhuhai SEZ Management Committee stated that "some comrades fear the SEZs will become 'colonies,' and that Zhuhai will become a 'neighborhood' of Macao." Even the Shekou Industrial Zone, which had been praised by Zhao Ziyang during his 1981 visit, was criticized. One academic asked while visiting Shekou, "In the future, how are you going to be connected to socialism?"[56]

Problems with Entrepôt Trade

The sudden lessening of foreign trade controls in 1979 encouraged Chinese localities to increase their exports with little regard for the dictates of the state export plan. With the increased amount of foreign exchange they retained, these localities in turn imported more expensive durable goods from abroad, through both legal and illegal channels.

Xu Dixin, director of the Chinese Academy of Social Sciences' Institute of Economics and a future president of Shantou University, warned of the consequences by using a negative interpretation of the "eight immortals" phrase: "Every province, especially every SEZ, will consider only their development needs; like 'the eight immortals crossing the sea, each showing their special prowess,' they will consider only themselves, even at the expense of national sovereignty or even the unitary nature of the planned economy. This occurred during the winter of 1979 when many provinces reduced the selling price of Chinese medicines on the Hong Kong market and during the 1980 Spring Guangzhou Trade Fair."[57] Localities, including the SEZs, placed their parochial needs above the state plan and the "national good." This was the core problem faced by the new central-government leadership as it implemented the general economic reforms of the 1980s.

There is a long history of entrepôt trade in Guangdong and Fujian Provinces; the tradition continued through the post-Liberation period.[58] The significant growth of entrepôt trade after 1979 was encouraged by the extraordinary powers of importation accorded to the two provinces and their SEZs by Central Committee documents 1979.50 and 1981.41. These powers were often abused during the early period of the decentralization experiment. According to the Chinese leadership, most of the legal and illegal imported goods flooding the national economy during the early 1980s were funneled through the various coastal ports and the SEZs of Guangdong and Fujian.

Entrepôt trade went on in Guangdong and Fujian throughout the early 1980s. Sometimes overseas Chinese willingly brought or mailed durable goods to relatives living in two provinces; others were "intimidated and bribed" to bring goods in. Local units and individuals subsequently sold the goods at black markets located in the two provinces or the SEZs.

Central Military Commission and State Council document 1980.184 offers a detailed report on illegal importation in Guangdong and Shenzhen between 1979 and 1980. According to the report, the Shantou customs office recorded the importation of "250,000 televisions, over 480,000 radio cassette players, 1,160,000 hand-held calculators, and 180,000 wristwatches. In fact, these amounts are growing monthly. In May of last year [1979], the Shantou Customs counted over 6,000 hand-held calculators sent through the mails. In November of 1979, the number had increased to 38,000."[59]

In other cases, Guangdong and Fujian units acted as middlemen in securing durable goods for customers in other regions of China. One very lucrative import item was foreign automobiles.[60] Automobiles are prestigious items in China. Chinese were very unhappy with domestic car production, which was based on Soviet technology of the 1950s. After production units and localities were granted greater decision-making rights in 1979, they bought more automobiles, especially imported models from abroad. By 1980, domestic automobile production exceeded the state production plan by 77.4 percent; still, more than 20,000 vehicles were imported outside the plan.[61] According to a State Council Office Circular of 20 March 1982, "Between January 1980 and June 1981, different areas illegally purchased over 10,000 vehicles of different types. Most were bought from Guangdong at a high price."[62] One State Planning Commission report issued in 1981 stated that Guangdong had imported "several tens of thousands of automobiles."[63]

The SEZs, particularly Shenzhen, were major partners in this entrepôt trade. Document 1979.50 had specifically allowed the SEZs to import many goods duty-free or at reduced tariff rates. According to document 1980.41, "The machines, equipment, spare parts, raw materials, and other production materials should be allowed to be imported duty-free; in principle, the goods used in daily life should be supplied by the domestic economy. Those necessary items used in daily life, which the domestic economy truly has difficulty supplying, can be imported upon approval and customs duties levied. Some of the items can be imported on a reduced or duty-free basis." Duty-free importation originally was designed as a government support measure to reduce SEZ construction costs. The goods were intended for SEZ consumption, and not to be reexported into the interior economy. According to Central Committee document 1981.27, regular import duties would be levied on those goods that were permitted to be reexported to the interior.

Yet with the high domestic demand for such durable goods and the high cost of SEZ construction, large-scale reexportation to the domestic economy did take place. It can be assumed that entrepôt trade was the fastest growing economic activity of the SEZs and the major source of financing between 1979 and 1982. Net profits earned from entrepôt activities were high. SEZ enterprises and individuals could earn various transaction fees in both RMB and foreign exchange; the entrepôt trade did not require a developed infrastructure nor many skilled workers; and the SEZs, especially Shenzhen, had ready access to Hong Kong and the interior.

The entrepôt trade was carried out on both the small and large scale. Domestic tourists visiting the two provinces and the SEZs were a conduit for transporting imported goods to the interior. While designed to attract Hong Kong tourists and their foreign currency, the SEZs attracted many tourists from the Chinese mainland. According to one Western study, approximately 45 percent of the visitors to the Xilihu resort area in the Shenzhen SEZ were from the interior; one-third of the 300,000 tourists who visited Shenzhen in 1983 were from the interior.[64] Besides visiting the local attractions, domestic tourists in the early 1980s were interested in buying foreign goods; imported goods could be purchased directly in the SEZ at very low prices and transported back duty-free to the interior. The variety of cheap imported goods sold on Zhongying Street in Shatoujiao, located in the Shenzhen SEZ straddling the Hong Kong–China border, and in Shantou's markets became legendary throughout China.[65]

SEZ work units and the representative offices of domestic work units (*danwei*) carried out larger-scale entrepôt trade. Document 1981.27 permitted SEZs to engage in foreign trade: "Under the guidance of the unified state policy, the SEZs can engage in foreign trade. The SEZs can act as an agent for every province, municipality, and [special administrative region] and carry out approved export and import operations, yet not be under the uniform management of the MFT." Often, the SEZ units acted as procurement agents for the durable goods demanded by domestic units. For instance, according to a 1982 report of the Guangdong Party Propaganda Department, "Some collectives and even state-owned units used their foreign exchange to import batches of cloth and ready-made clothes. They then sold them to the interior at a high price and made a great profit. . . . Some people purchased agricultural sideline products at high prices from outlying areas, sold them across [the Hong Kong] border, and earned foreign exchange; some purchased large amounts of industrial goods for resale on the domestic market; some even smuggled goods or dealt in smuggled goods. This greatly corrupted the people's ideology."[66]

In addition, provinces and central ministry departments established representative offices in Shenzhen in the early 1980s, ostensibly to expand exports to Hong Kong and abroad. Document 1980.41 had allowed, "upon approval, some departments and areas [to] station a few people in Shenzhen to investigate the business situation in Hong Kong, Macao, and abroad as well as make contacts with them." However, these representative offices would instead procure imported materials to be reexported to the interior. According to document 1980.184, "Purchasing agents, sent by the Parts and Accessories Department of the Second Ministry of Machinery's Sixth Bureau, linked up with commune members from Chaoyang county and Xiacuo Brigade members from Pinggong Commune to sign a false contract. Under the pretext of procuring woven rubberized tape, they used over RMB 64,800 to purchase 548 electronic calculators and 2 radio cassette players."[67]

Another method was to establish joint ventures to import the durable goods. In 1983, *Renmin ribao* reported the case of Harper Motors. "When Shenzhen Special Economic Zone had just been set up, Harper Motors wanted to use the preferential treatment provided by the Zone to raise car competitiveness in the domestic market. Shenzhen agreed with this and let it come. But subsequently it wanted to dump its cars and invade our domestic market. We could not agree with this, because our country's car industry has had a certain foundation and we cannot give up our car market to foreign countries. In the end, Harper Motors pulled out. In this way, we protected our own car industry."[68]

Yet the most widespread method of entrepôt trade was smuggling. As early as March 1980, the Ministry of Public Security cited Guangdong and Fujian as the centers for smuggling activities.[69] According to document 1980.184, black markets were established "in Guangzhou, Shantou, Foshan, Shenzhen, Haimen, Shanwei, and Fujian Province's Qingyang, Shishi, and Changle. Often there are more than 1,000 people gathered at these places."[70]

Smuggling was not a new occupation in southern China, especially among the fishing peoples of Guangdong and Fujian, who had long engaged in smuggling with the Taiwanese. But the opening policy and the more relaxed atmosphere of 1979 allowed smuggling to flourish.[71] According to document 1980.184, in 1979 the state uncovered 13,423 cases of smuggling involving an estimated RMB 7.31 million in goods.

Compared with 1978, the number of cases increased by 40 percent and the value of the goods confiscated doubled. In Guangzhou alone, the number of smuggling cases was four times the number in 1978. As stated in document 1980.184,

> During the last half of 1979, over 200 Taiwanese fishing vessels entered the areas around Guangdong Province's Shanwei and Haimenzhen alone, smuggling 200,000 watches. . . . From December 1979 to January 1980, Guangdong's Haimenzhen port investigated 12 Taiwanese fishing trawlers. They discovered over 210 liang of smuggled gold, 322 jin of silverware, over 2,490 pieces of silver yuan, 72 radio cassette players, 36 pocket calculators, and 18,650 Taiwanese watches. In January 1980, Shaoguan Municipality uncovered smuggling, profiteering and speculation cases involving over 150 people covering 10 provinces. They seized 124 liang of gold, 39,900 silver yuan, 130 jin of musk, over 500 jin of other expensive medical supplies, 2 jin of agate, and RMB 18,300 in cash.[72]

Chinese smugglers took advantage of the high international prices of gold, silver, Chinese medicine, and musk to purchase durables such as televisions, radios, and calculators.

Larger units, such as "state-owned commercial enterprises, cooperative enterprises," and smaller dealers, such as "communes, streets offices[,] and individual entrepreneurs," were involved in the domestic trading of smuggled goods. In one village near Shantou, two hundred people from an agricultural production team decided to quit working the land and instead trade in foreign goods. Besides local peasants and workers, military personnel, "Party and Youth League members, and the sons and daughters of high officials" trafficked in smuggled goods.

These dealers were clearly attracted by the high profits; the sale price of smuggled goods was reportedly two to ten times the purchase price. There also was a high demand for the goods. Black market traders would sell goods for a lower price than the state retail price; and, naturally, the traders would not demand prior purchase approval from the buyer's unit. Document 1980.184 states, "Cai Jiancheng and three others of Fujian's Anxi county purchased 173 pocket electronic calculators in Fujian at RMB 70 to 90 apiece. On average, they sold them in Sichuan for

RMB 250 apiece. . . . When converted from the Hong Kong price, a 20-inch Japanese Lesheng color television set is worth RMB 623. The procurement price for state-run commercial enterprises, including the levied customs duty, is RMB 1,660. The retail cost is RMB 3,020. Purchased from an individual, the price is around RMB 2,200." Units ranging from universities to state enterprises "used all means possible to penetrate overseas Chinese areas and rush to purchase foreign goods."[73]

The People's Liberation Army (PLA) was among the most active purchasing organizations. Document 1980.184 states,

> To purchase the 'three machines' [televisions, radio cassette players, hand-held calculators], some military units have sent people on special vehicles to purchase the goods; some have used helicopters to transfer the goods; some have exchanged military lumber supplies for the goods; to avoid inspection, some have sealed containers with strips declaring they were "defense materiel"; some even intimidated and bribed their overseas Chinese relatives who were not willing to buy foreign goods. The PLA unit stationed in Guangdong's Haimenzhen numbers over 400 people. Since last July, they have received on average RMB 6,000 in remittances per day to purchase foreign goods. This town has a black market in foreign goods. On average, four or five military vehicles would arrive to buy foreign goods.

Entrepreneurs, including party and government officials, took advantage of the special policies for the SEZs to carry out large-scale smuggling operations, thus transforming Shenzhen into one of the largest smuggling centers on the southeast China coast. The most infamous case of smuggling in the SEZs was uncovered during the fall of 1981. The case of the Shenzhen branch (*Shenzhen fenbu anjian*) was especially sensational because of the involvement of Zhou Zhirong, a "temporary" secretary of the Shenzhen Party Committee.

Zhou Zhirong was responsible for the Shenzhen branch of the China Electronics and Technology Import-Export Corporation. The corporation was a state-owned enterprise established in Shenzhen in May 1980 to carry out import-export activities for the national electronics industry. Under Zhou's direction, the corporation violated management policies, used a large amount of foreign exchange to smuggle goods and avoid tax payments[,] and sought exorbitant profits. According to the initial investigation, for the first nine months of 1981 the branch colluded with people here and abroad. The branch forged documents, smuggled goods[,] and deceived Customs under the planning of the branch's responsible leaders. They smuggled in large amounts of televisions, watches, radio-tape players etc.[,] nine times. The [smuggled] radio-tape players alone amounted to 26,824 sets, avoiding over RMB 12 million in duties. This branch also changed the dates of the contract and broke important rules and regulations. They brazenly violated State Council regulations requiring approval of television and radio-tape player importation after February 1981. They illegally imported 135,000 television sets, 86,500 radio-tape players and 850,000 tape cassettes.[74]

Zhou Zhirong's case and other cases of malfeasance persuaded the leadership in Beijing to intervene in the decentralization process to control the smuggling, profiteering, and speculating activities carried out by the local leadership and the military in Guangdong and Fujian.

The Macro Effects of Entrepôt Trade

The existence of large-scale entrepôt trading, including smuggling, in a decentralized foreign trade environment created several serious macroeconomic problems for the Beijing leadership. First, the desire by localities to buy foreign goods with retained foreign exchange created a competitive market in the command economy that inhibited fulfillment of procurement quotas and exacerbated the inflation rate. To obtain the foreign exchange necessary to purchase imported goods, localities increased the amount of goods they exported. This in turn increased domestic demand for goods for export. As more SEZ work units obtained export privileges, they increasingly competed among themselves and with the state to procure export items. The command economy could not accommodate this new infusion of market-style competition. Competition not only affected state procurement quotas but also created dramatic price fluctuations and set prices below profit margins.

Several examples of this market-style competition are cited in government directives and the open literature. Faced with problems in tea export procurement in 1981, the State Council complained that "in some areas, production units are not strictly carrying out the state plan. Many units have intervened in tea production, forced price hikes and hurried procurement, and competed with the state for raw materials. . . . The tea export plan procurement must be guaranteed; general management is to be given to the National Supply and Marketing Cooperative Central Office and the MFT organs. No other department can intervene."[75] Competition between buyers also caused commodity prices to rise, and the state was unable to afford goods at the inflated prices. An excellent example of this phenomenon was the inflationary price for freshwater pearls in the early 1980s. Suzhou was a major producer of freshwater pearls, which had been a profitable Chinese export. Before 1979 the pearls produced in Suzhou were exported through Shanghai. Starting in 1980, areas and ports outside the region could procure and export the pearls. Competition for pearls drove up the procurement price, which rose from a 1979 average of RMB 406 for half a kilogram to more than RMB 900. As a result the Suzhou Prefecture Foreign Trade Department was unable to obtain them, because it could not pay the higher price.[76]

The rise in export-product procurement prices also exacerbated inflationary tendencies present in the national economy. In 1979 the state raised the procurement price of primary agricultural products, the sales price of agricultural side products, and the salaries and bonuses of staff and workers in China.[77] In April 1980 the Central Committee complained that

some localities, departments and enterprise units have violated pricing policy and pricing discipline without regard for the general good. To increase their profits and issue more bonuses, they indiscriminately enlarged the numbers of commodities whose prices were to be readjusted, [and] arbitrarily raised the rate of readjustment; some adopted improper methods to raise prices, such as changing labels, mixing low-quality and fake goods with regular goods, employing shoddy methods to produce inferior goods, selling seconds at regular prices, and selling less than the quantity specified; some indiscriminately reduced the number of set-price goods and replaced them with goods with a negotiated price. To raise material prices, some units even procured goods at the regular set price and sold them at a negotiated price; some arbitrarily raised the number of public utilities and services requiring fees and raised the fee rates.[78]

Throughout 1980 and 1981 the State Council adopted various measures to control inflation. It strengthened price management, readjusted the negotiated price system, and instituted stricter price controls of certain important industrial goods.[79]

Second, the entrepôt trade threatened native industries. According to the Central Military Commission and State Council opinion issued in document 1980.184, "Currently, the private sales and purchases of imported materials brought in by overseas Chinese, Hong Kong, Macao and Taiwanese compatriots, [and] the smuggling and speculative sale of foreign goods, gold, silver and expensive medicine[,] is very prevalent. In some areas, it is very serious. It has already influenced the sales of certain domestic industrial products. It has caused serious market disruption, and seriously corrupted the ideas of certain cadres, staff, workers, and people. In general, Chinese 'people believe that foreign goods are excellent in quality.'"[80] Purchasing units and individuals thus preferred to buy imported goods, rather than similar goods produced on the domestic market.

General Secretary Hu Yaobang criticized this attitude during his speech to the Central Committee Secretariat on 14 January 1982. He stated, "In my opinion, except those uniformly arranged by the state, no department or locality should be allowed to import consumer goods on an unauthorized basis. Those areas and departments that are currently privately importing consumer goods for themselves are in reality harming national industry. This is disgraceful behavior and the greatest profiteering [crime]. This is not the importation of advanced technology. This is harmful to the nation and the people."[81] Hu Yaobang clearly was aware that Chinese units considered foreign goods to be more prestigious and of higher quality. He was especially concerned that such attitudes would reduce demand for domestically produced goods. This would cause a drop in domestic production, which would lead to unemployment and to greater government outlays for domestic production support.[82]

Third, the desire for imported goods adversely affected the financing and implementation of the domestic development strategy, which was partially financed with overseas-Chinese remittances. Central Military Commission and State Council document 1980.184 stated that "since the sale of foreign goods [on the domestic market] potentially is profitable, many Overseas Chinese and Hong Kong/Macao Compatriots are sending materials instead of currency. This has seriously affected Overseas Chinese remittances."[83] With fewer overseas-Chinese remittances in the bank accounts, the government's access to ready foreign exchange was restricted.

The implementation of the domestic development strategy also was affected. According to Beijing's small-scale ISI strategy, units and localities would finance technical renovations of their industrial structure with imports, using locally retained foreign exchange. Instead, however, units and localities used their retained foreign exchange funds to import consumer goods.

During his speech to the Central Committee Secretariat on 14 January 1982, Hu Yaobang cited the case of Gansu, a very poor province located in western China, to highlight the problems caused by entrepôt trade. In 1981, he said, Gansu earned

> local foreign exchange [totaling] US$15m and retained an amount [totaling] over US$6m. Yet this amount of foreign exchange was not used effectively. Except a minority of areas and cities that imported badly needed equipment and medical equipment, the majority blindly imported things such as watches, bicycles, and sewing machines. These materials were of poor quality, and they were cheated! Besides what has been reported, it is unknown what things have been imported. Look, they don't know that this hard-earned foreign exchange is to be used to import needed equipment, technology, and raw materials, to increase production and earn even more foreign exchange. Instead, they waste it on importing low-quality consumer goods and let the foreigners again leave with profits.[84]

Because foreign exchange funds were diverted to consumer imports, local planners were unable to finance the development of their community or region.

Fourth and finally, the Beijing leadership was apprehensive about the involvement of party and military cadres in smuggling, profiteering, and speculation activities. The leadership had admitted in Central

Committee document 1979.50 that "the development of foreign trade activities is bound to be accompanied by capitalist ideology and a bourgeoisie lifestyle. We must directly address this problem, strengthen our political-thought work, uphold the four basic principles, guard against and resist the corrosive influence of nonproletarian ideology."[85] The leadership was concerned that, indeed, the "peoples' ideas [were being] corrupted," pointing to the recurrence of "gambling, itinerant performers, and prostitutes." As Crane argues, leaders were concerned that the zones would create "'Hong Kong-ization' (*Xiangganghua*); that is, they would be conduits of capitalist exploitation and decadence"[86] People in the SEZs would be enticed by Hong Kong's capitalist system, with its decadence of high living and emphasis on exorbitant consumption—drinking, eating, gambling, and cavorting—that would corrupt the Chinese soul. Everyone would become entrepreneurs (*quanmin jingshang*) and engage in the illegal entrepôt trade and promote a culture of bribery, acting as go-betweens in supply and marketing activities or in construction-contracting activities, and renting out land to outsiders for cultivation. It led to "the old ideas of relying on luck, relying on contacts and connections." And as in the case of the SEZ "temporary" party secretary, Zhou Zhirong of the Shenzhen SEZ, such influences also led to smuggling and the acceptance of bribes.[87]

Learning to Decentralize

The initial phase of China's opening was perhaps the most adventurous yet dangerous period for China on the pathway to adopting its Third Way. Deng Xiaoping, Chen Yun, and the bureaucratic Stalinists agreed that the revolutionary Stalinist approach was moribund and had contributed to a decline in China's economic welfare. Chen Yun convinced the more daring Deng that China could not afford to finance a large-scale ISI strategy, as it had in the past. The bureaucratic Stalinists thus agreed to take a more flexible attitude toward the roles of the international and domestic markets to jump-start China's economic growth. They also agreed to experiment with greater decentralization, in which, in the initial SEZ policy, economic power was decentralized to the provincial and municipal levels, with limited oversight from Beijing.

Between 1979 and 1982 the bureaucratic Stalinists gradually came to see the ramifications of the phrase, "the eight immortals crossing the sea, each showing their special prowess." On the positive side, decentralization invigorated the economy and China's export capabilities. On the negative side, provinces, localities, and individuals placed their parochial needs above the needs of the party and the state. Beijing subsequently took a series of steps to rectify these problems in the early 1980s. The compromise adopted reflected Deng Xiaoping's desire to maintain a more unified coalition of elites, unlike Mao, who destroyed the Yan'an Roundtable. However, in reality Deng's experiences abroad in Russia and the Western economies made him realize that the Leninist NEP approach emphasizing the market would be the key to China's future economic takeoff, especially if international capital could also be harnessed to finance China's domestic growth and technological renovation. The old Stalinist-trained economist Chen Yun would disagree, thus leading an ever-larger gulf of opinion among elites. Deng Xiaoping temporarily mended the growing fissure, but with his adoption of Zhao Ziyang's coastal development strategy in 1984, Deng would once and for all commit to the international Leninist agenda.

CHAPTER THREE

Review and Adjustment of the Experiment, 1981–83

The fourth phase in China's experiment with special economic zones entailed review and adjustment. It was time, as Chen Yun stated in his December 1981 speech, to "summarize experiences." From 1981 to 1983, central government elites continuously reviewed the implementation of the initial experiments; through this process, they learned which policies worked and did not work well. They convened central and regional meetings and conferences, conducted on-site inspections, discussed policy implementation with the relevant bureaucracies and leaders, and so on. When faced with major implementation problems, leaders initiated in-depth policy reviews and ordered mid-course readjustments. Such adjustments could be radical, moderate, or minimal, and they could result in experiment moratoriums or a full-scale implementation of the SEZ experiment nationwide. Disagreements over experimentation could lead to fragmentation among the elites, the severity of which depended on the paramount leader's ability to maintain the coalition. A perceived success could result in the promulgation of that success nationwide and lay the groundwork for new long-term goals for the state.

To review the Guangdong and Fujian decentralization and SEZ experiments, the Central Committee and State Council sponsored a major conference in Beijing in March 1980 (leading to Central Committee document 1980.41) and a second conference in May–June 1981

(Central Committee document 1981.27).[1] Local provincial and SEZ officials reported on the experiments' progress; the Central Committee subsequently promulgated first-order adaptations to correct problems and expand the experiment parameters.

However, first-order policy adjustments could not control implementation problems such as those revealed in the "case of the Shenzhen Branch," which involved a "temporary" secretary of the Shenzhen Party Committee, Zhou Zhirong. Zhou's large-scale smuggling operation was officially reported to "the leading comrades of the Central Committee" on 11 January 1982.[2] According to the Emergency Circular released by the committee, the Standing Committee also discussed the serious economic crimes committed by officials and party members in other provinces, cities, and government departments; the directive specifically mentions Guangdong, Fujian, Zhejiang, and Yunnan.[3] Chen Yun successfully argued for a review of the SEZ policy, stating, "We must summarize the experiences of the SEZs in Guangdong and Fujian and the foreign economic activities of every province. Currently we have not summarized them well."[4]

After 1981 the cohesiveness among the bureaucratic Stalinists deteriorated, resulting in the formation of two elite opinion groups: the international Leninists and the moderate bureaucratic Stalinists, with Deng Xiaoping as paramount leader. Between 1982 and 1983 the moderate bureaucratic Stalinists prevented the expansion of the decentralization and SEZ experiment to the national economy, which they believed would lead to chaos. Deng Xiaoping and the international Leninists proposed an alternate vision. They argued instead for a limited expansion of the decentralization experiment and outward-oriented development, which resulted in the establishment of the fourteen open coastal cities, the economic and technical development zones, and the coastal development areas.[5]

Initial Review and Readjustment: 1980–81

In readjusting the Ten-Year Plan and its ISI strategy, starting in 1979, the bureaucratic Stalinists realized that the central government would require new tools to control the national economy. These tools were an integral component of the decentralization process: localities were given more decision-making powers, and the central government devised new methods to macromanage the economy. The leadership formulated a series of measures to strengthen central bureaucratic supervision and control. In the foreign economic sector, such measures included the reestablishment of the General Customs Administration and the Bank of China (BOC), the establishment of an import licensing system, and the issuance of foreign exchange certificates (FECs).[6]

Yet by time of the Central Committee Work Conference of December 1980, the Beijing leadership realized that the success of these measures was limited, and subsequently they adopted a follow-up series of readjustments. In foreign economic policy, the bureaucratic Stalinists reorganized and strengthened the SIEC as the State Import-Export Administrative Commission (SIEAC) and improved the macromanagement measures in foreign trade and foreign exchange adopted in 1979 and 1980, with a special emphasis on import-export controls and anti-smuggling measures. As a response to the excesses of decentralization, the leadership also tightened party discipline and reaffirmed socialist ideals by promoting what it called "socialist spiritual civilization."

Guangdong, Fujian, and the SEZ leaders also strengthened political ideological work, bureaucratic supervision, foreign trade, and foreign exchange regulations. They established provincial management committees in the four SEZs to comply with central government foreign trade and foreign exchange management measures, including measures to combat smuggling. Finally, they launched their own provincial campaigns for socialist spiritual civilization. During this stage of policy readjustment, the central leadership remained optimistic about the success of the provincial decentralization experiment, including the SEZs. Although problems had occurred, Beijing leaders continued to support provincial management of the SEZ decentralization experiment.

By late 1981, though, the mood of the central leadership had changed. Consistent with the moderate views of bureaucratic Stalinism that he had promoted since the 1950s, Chen Yun was the first senior Chinese leader to voice concern about the effects of decentralization on the planned economy. After Chen Yun reached a compromise with Deng Xiaoping, the Political Bureau initiated a crackdown on illegal economic practices and strengthened general ideological work by promoting the Spiritual Civilization Campaign. In the foreign trade sector, the central leadership established the Ministry of Foreign Economic Relations and Trade (MOFERT), tightened import-export controls, and implemented new foreign exchange laws.

The Central Committee's attitude toward the decentralization experiment also changed as differences emerged among the bureaucratic Stalinists. In addition to his concerns with preserving the guiding role of the planned economy, Chen Yun was very critical of the large scale of the entrepôt trading and smuggling taking place in the two provinces and their SEZs. At his instigation, the State Council implemented three significant measures that profoundly affected the SEZs. First, it imposed a moratorium on new SEZs that would last until September 1987, when the Central Committee approved the Hainan Island SEZ. Second, it undertook a major effort in the SEZs to prosecute economic criminals, rectify the local party structure, and prevent future smuggling and corruption. As part of this effort, a barbed wire fence was erected to completely separate the Shenzhen SEZ from the interior— and its economy.

Finally, Beijing increased its central regulatory powers and took a more active role in supervising the Guangdong and Fujian experiments. In 1982 the central authorities decided not to recentralize the foreign trade system established under documents 1979.202 and 1979.233; they also did not revoke document 1979.50. Instead, the State Council strengthened overall supervision by establishing the Office of the Special Economic Zones, supplanting the authority of the provincial SEZ administrations, with Zhao Ziyang and Gu Mu in charge. The State Council Office and other central government bureaucracies also became more involved in the planning of the SEZs. Most important, Beijing permitted central ministries to invest directly in the zones. This new infusion of domestic capital financed the building of Shenzhen's basic infrastructure, which helped to attract "healthier" FDI that focused on technology-intensive investments.

Stage One: Initial Measures to Control "Chaos,"
1979–80

With its adoption of the readjusted ISI strategy, which included the financing strategies of "opening" to the outside world and decentralizing the foreign trade system, the central government concurrently planned to strengthen central bureaucratic macromanagement of the economy. The promulgation of specific measures undoubtedly was accelerated by the leadership's reaction to the chaotic foreign economic situation of 1979 and 1980 and by trying to control foreign trade losses.[7]

The leadership was especially concerned about the problems of the spring 1980 Guangzhou Trade Fair. To expand exports and earn more foreign exchange, Chinese ministries and units competed at the trade fair to sell to foreign customers. In certain cases, the competition forced Chinese exporters to sell below cost. On 28 May 1980, the former party secretary of Guangdong province Zhao Ziyang submitted a report to the Central Committee, the Party Secretariat, and the State Council on the Guangzhou Trade Fair problems. In a separate opinion, Zhao stated that

> during the past period, there has been much reaction to the problems at the Guangzhou Fair and with importing and exporting. This has created the impression that reforms of the foreign trade structure have caused much confusion. This viewpoint is incomplete and lacks analysis. It must be agreed that over the past year, our foreign trade work has achieved great success. This cannot be separated from the initial reforms carried out since the Third Plenum in the foreign trade structure and the motivating enthusiasm at all levels. It is difficult to avoid problems while carrying out reforms. We need to catch up with problems. For instance, consider the problem of the chemical trade delegation and others at the Guangzhou Fair. If we do our work well, these problems are easy to overcome. We cannot reminisce about the old days of autarky, going on our own, and maintaining a stifling unified control. From now on, we must greatly expand foreign trade. We must resolutely and consistently carry out reform; simultaneously, we must earnestly resolve the problems faced in carrying out the reforms. . . . Foreign trade departments must make an earnest effort and take the initiative to discover and summarize new experiences and methods to strengthen unified management

[while maintaining a policy] of enlivening [foreign export production]. We must promote policies to enliven the economy while avoiding chaos; [unify] management without stifling initiative.[8]

The leadership considered the accelerated adoption of these measures to macromanage foreign trade and foreign exchange transactions to be an integral part of the readjusted development strategy and its policy of decentralization.

Tools for Foreign Trade Macromanagement

One of the first measures adopted was the recentralization of customs management. The General Customs Administration (Haiguan Zong-zhuo) originally was established in 1951 as a centralized bureaucratic unit directly under the central government.[9] Beginning in 1960, customs authority had been transferred to the provincial, municipal, and special administrative region (SAR) levels, and the General Customs Administration was downgraded to the Customs Management Bureau. Because of ineffectual management and the increase of import-export activities at the local levels, the State Council decided to recentralize customs management in 1979; they formally reestablished the General Customs Administration on 9 February 1980.[10]

The new organization, which was directly under the State Council, was responsible for formulating and enforcing all customs regulations and collecting customs duties nationwide. On 29 February 1980 the State Council also approved the establishment of the General Bureau for Import-Export Commodity Inspection (Jinchukou Shangpin Jian-yan Zongju).[11] The General Administration for Industry and Commerce was authorized to investigate all cases of smuggling, profiteering, and speculation.[12] So that the "leadership [would] get the facts" about the foreign trade situation, the State Statistical Bureau Foreign Trade Statistical System was established.[13] In a complementary move, the SIEAC established the State International Balance of Payments Statistical System in 1981; the Guangdong provincial government established its own customs division.[14]

In 1980, the State Council took initial steps to strengthen foreign trade administration and regulations. The most important measure was a new import-export permit system adopted by the SIEAC and the MFT on 3 June 1980.[15] Specific measures were also adopted to prevent illegal exports of antiques.[16] A new import licensing system also was introduced. On 26 August 1980 the SIEAC issued regulations titled "Temporary Measures for Foreign Trade Import Management" and "Temporary Measures for Local Foreign Trade Import Management," which established an import licensing system (*jinkou huowu xukezheng zhidu*).[17] Separate regulations were authorized for processing and assembly operations and compensation trade.[18] To stop large organizations (*shehui jituan*) from importing restricted durable goods, the State Planning Commission revised regulations and established bureaucratic procedures to prevent importation of the most desirable items, such as automobiles, motorcycles, rugs, air conditioners, and tape recorders.[19] Additional regulations were issued that restricted domestic sales of imported materials.[20]

Strengthening Foreign Exchange Macromanagement

The State Council strengthened foreign exchange management in 1979 and 1980 to prevent the squandering, diversion, evasion of controls on, and illegal procurement of foreign exchange. Starting in 1979, the leadership centralized the administration and management of foreign exchange. They reestablished the BOC and the State General Administration for Foreign Exchange Management.[21] In December 1980, the State Council issued the "Temporary Regulations for Foreign Exchange Management," State Council document 1980.311, which outlined "the first comparatively comprehensive and systematic rules and regulations for foreign exchange management since 1949."[22]

The State Council had approved several measures in January 1980 to prevent foreign currency from circulating within the domestic economy. According to a People's Bank of China report, such circulation "was harmful to the state's prestige . . . created a black market, . . . corrupted the cadre and people, . . . [and] created inconvenience to overseas Chinese and foreign guests."[23] The report proposed to reduce the number of Chinese organizations allowed to accept foreign currency and to institute a new authorization system totally controlled by the State Council. To prevent the growth of the foreign currency black market, the Bank of China would issue FECs, which were exclusively for the use of short-term foreign visitors and overseas Chinese.[24]

As a follow-up to document 1979.202 that initiated foreign trade expansion in August 1979, the MFT issued regulations in 1980 concerning the use of foreign exchange earned in nontrade activities. All departments were required to obtain the approval of the state before importing materials using such foreign exchange.[25] Detailed regulations were issued defining the proportion of foreign exchange earned in nontrade activities that could be retained by the localities, the methods used to calculate the retained proportion, and the distribution and accepted uses of that proportion of foreign exchange.[26]

Stage Two: Intermediate Readjustment, 1981

By the end of 1980 the bureaucratic Stalinists realized that the decentralization measures adopted in 1979 had an adverse effect on both the economy and their attempts to readjust the economic plan. Imports in 1980 exceeded exports by US$1.278 billion (see Table A). The state found it especially difficult to control smuggling and profiteering. That year the General Bureau for Industrial and Commercial Administration investigated 280,000 cases of speculation and profiteering and imposed fines totaling RMB 67 million.[27] Such activities "directly threaten[ed] stability and unity, and [were] ruining economic readjustment and stability," the government declared.[28]

At the Central Committee Work Conference held on 16–25 December 1980, the leadership focused on the problems of decentralization and the readjusted ISI strategy. Chen Yun, Zhao Ziyang, Li Xiannian, and Deng Xiaoping called for a renewed attempt to carry out domestic readjustment by reducing spending and inflation.[29] Chen Yun directly voiced his concerns about the "chaotic" foreign trade situation, stating, "Currently the prices on the international market for some Chinese goods have dropped. This is not a normal, necessary drop. To gain foreign exchange, various provinces, cities and departments have lowered the prices. We must research methods to export our goods but not sell cheaply. Essentially, we 'cannot let fertile water escape onto others' property.'"[30] To prevent "fertile water from escaping," measures were implemented in 1981 to strengthen general foreign trade and foreign exchange supervision, regulations, and ideological work. Concurrent measures were adopted to improve SEZ leadership and promote correct party "style."

Strengthen Foreign Trade Macromanagement

To strengthen general foreign trade policy supervision and management, the Central Committee Work Conference in December 1980 assigned the SIEAC for all economic cooperation and aid agreements with foreign countries.[31] On 1 September 1981, the Central Committee and State Council declared the SIEAC was a "comprehensive" department, responsible for the implementation of Central Committee and State Council foreign trade policies and directives. The SIEAC would thereafter supervise all central government trade departments and regional and local trade offices operating in China and abroad.[32]

To carry out this supervision, the Central Committee established the CCP Committee on Foreign Economic Inspection and Discipline (Zhonggong Duiwai Jingji Jilü Jiancha Weiyuanhui) under the SIEAC, and the Central Discipline and Inspection Commission (CDIC). In addition, the SIEAC was directed to reorganize. Chen Muhua was appointed first vice party secretary and first vice chairman of the SIEAC; Zheng Tuobin was appointed SIEAC vice chairman.[33]

Building on the initial measures adopted in 1979–80, the bureaucratic Stalinists strengthened foreign trade and foreign exchange regulations. To guarantee fulfillment of the State Export Procurement Plan and reduce domestic competition for export goods, the State Council issued several specific circulars in 1981 prohibiting the export of certain goods, such as tea, sugar, and tin, outside the plan.[34] To control the legal importation of durable goods, the MFT and the SIEAC issued a follow-up circular on the import licensing system established in 1980. The circular directed that all units desiring to import durable goods first must comply with certain bureaucratic procedures before applying for the actual import permit.[35] These procedures, as stipulated in various government circulars, were designed to prevent the widespread importation of durable goods.[36]

To prevent the illegal importation of durable goods, the leadership adopted more stringent regulations regarding smuggling and profiteering in late 1980 and 1981. In response to document 1980.184, which had detailed the rampant smuggling in Guangdong and Fujian, the General Administration for Industry and Commerce and the General Customs Administration issued the "Circular on attacking smuggling and speculating on the resale of import and export materials" on 30 October 1980. The document clearly specifies the penalties for violators of import regulations, especially those reselling goods on the local markets.[37] The General Administration for Industry and Commerce also issued circulars that forbade the mailing of smuggled goods and restricted the sale of overseas Chinese and Hong Kong products on the domestic market.[38]

After the Central Work Conference of December 1981, the State Council adopted stronger anti-smuggling and profiteering measures, issuing two major directives. To ensure the fulfillment of the state procurement plan for the national economy and foreign trade, the State Council adopted document 1981.3 on 7 January 1981. This directive forbade state-owned units from "forc[ing] up commodity prices" and causing "panic buy[ing]." It also stated: "Industries and mines can sell their goods if they first meet state procurement quotas. Individuals are not allowed to peddle industrial goods if they have not received permission from the industrial and commercial departments in charge." To reduce the resale of foreign goods on the domestic market, document 1981.3 stipulated: "Individuals are not allowed to sell cars, tractors and other large transportation vehicles. . . . Overseas Chinese are only allowed to bring in and send goods for their use and the use of their relatives. They are not allowed to sell these privately at a profit or, if sold according to the state price, to a state organ. Other units and individuals are not allowed to buy or sell them, especially smuggled goods. We must deal severely with those cadre and active duty military personnel engaged in smuggling."[39] The second major directive from the December 1981 work conference is State Council and Central Military Commission document 1981.6, issued in January 1981, entitled "Directive on Resolutely Attacking Smuggling Activities." It is a guide for civilian and military units on how to carry out the nationwide anti-smuggling campaign.

To mobilize provincial and local officials and coordinate efforts between regions and departments, several conferences on the anti-smuggling effort were held. Two meetings of the Conference to Attack Smuggling were convened, focusing on smuggling activities in Guangdong, Fujian, and Zhejiang. Little is known about the first meeting except that it was probably held in early 1981, coinciding with the issuance of State Council document 1981.6.[40] The summary of the second meeting was approved by the Central Committee and the State Council on 3 August 1981. The Central Committee Circular attached to the summary states,

> Since last year [note: referring to 1980], smuggling has run rampant in the three coastal provinces of Guangdong, Fujian and Zhejiang and has spilled over to many areas in the country. The primary reason smuggling has spread unchecked is that there are some leading cadres who do not fully comprehend the perniciousness of smuggling nor the necessity to attack it. In addition, the management system is not strict, political thought work is weak. This gives smugglers at home and abroad an opportunity to collude. . . . [T]he struggle against smuggling is not only an economic but a political struggle. It is a manifestation of carrying out the class struggle. . . . We must carry out a struggle against and deal with severely all illegal elements that support, protect, or sell smuggled goods.[41]

The problem of smuggling was also discussed at the National Conference for Customhouse Leaders. Customs officials were told they must "effectively struggle against all smuggling and illegal behavior that violates the economic readjustment or political stability."[42]

Strengthen Foreign Exchange Oversight

The most important measure taken to prevent the circulation of foreign exchange on the Chinese market was the issuance of foreign exchange certificates (FECs) in April 1980. In one year, the Bank of China issued more than RMB 930 million in FECs. Admitting that FECs were a flawed but necessary tool, the State Planning Commission and SIEAC put out a report on 12 June 1981 suggesting changes in FEC regulations.[43] The leaders asked local governments to carry out greater supervision and management of FECs, especially concerning the pricing of goods and services involved and the prevention of price reductions that would entitle the seller to more FECs.[44] Chinese banks were urged to increase their efforts in FEC recovery and to prevent long-term retention by units (*danwei*) or individuals. The types of transactions carried out by Chinese units that required FECs and the number of units permitted to accept FECs were restricted. The State Council hoped that these measures would limit competition between domestic units for FEC resources.

As a supplement to the "Temporary Regulations for Foreign Exchange Management" adopted in December 1980, circulars were issued in 1981 to prevent foreign exchange violations. State Council document 1981.20 ordered all units to repatriate those funds that had been transferred abroad without prior permission.[45] Regulations issued in August restricted the importing and exporting of foreign exchange, precious metals, and foreign exchange instruments.[46] Units were not allowed to buy imported material from private overseas connections or foreigners using RMB as payment.[47] All units receiving loans from overseas Chinese and foreign lenders were required to obtain prior approval from the BOC.[48] To prevent further foreign exchange violations, the state decided to redistribute the management of foreign exchange among domestic units. A document issued by the State General Administration for Foreign Exchange Controls and the BOC on 17 April 1981 states, "There are some departments and enterprises engaging privately in the buying and selling of foreign exchange. One U.S. dollar is equivalent to four or five renminbi. This must be completely terminated." In redirecting the private selling of foreign exchange, the state realized that there would be "some enterprises and units that received permission to import equipment, spare parts, scientific and research materials, but are unable to arrange within the plan the necessary foreign exchange. In such cases, the Bank of China will redistribute the funds."[49]

The state thus sought legal avenues through which to redistribute foreign exchange among domestic units and to use foreign exchange resources more effectively.[50] To reduce demand for foreign exchange and prevent profiteering and black market activities, the State General Administration offered bonuses to those units that reported foreign exchange violations.[51]

Strengthen Ideological Work

In 1980 the bureaucratic Stalinists realized that the party and its socialist ideal had lost a degree of legitimacy.[52] People's enthusiasm in the 1950s for the socialist objective of rebuilding and revitalizing China had been replaced by the trauma of the Cultural Revolution in the 1960s and apathy in the 1970s. By the early 1980s, the party leadership felt the need to revitalize both the economic system and the country's ideological fervor. This need became apparent to the leaders as they encountered difficulties with decentralization in 1980 and 1981. Now there were two interpretations of the slogan, "The eight immortals crossing the sea, each showing their special prowess." On the one hand, the decentralization of 1979 invigorated the economy, but on the other, the actions taken by units and individuals were not necessarily for the "greater good." The leadership thus undertook to strengthen party discipline and reaffirm socialist ideals.

The CCP had established the CDIC in 1978 under Chen Yun, and the CDIC continued to issue circulars stressing strict party discipline; to investigate "bad practices," such as bribery and using "connections" (*guanxihu*); and to discipline party members.[53] Yet, circulars and investigations had only a limited effect. The leadership realized that there was a more fundamental problem facing the country. In a speech given on 26 November 1980 at a conference discussing internal party rules and norms convened by the CDIC, Hu Yaobang stated,

> As for the country, there is still uneven development in discipline and inspection work. Some departments, provinces, and cities are very good and some are very bad. Why is there a difference? Perhaps there are many reasons, but probably the major reason is whether people dare to do their job.... Think about it. Why are there so many situations in which people shift blame? ... I think that this is a problem not only in our own line of work. I think quite a few comrades in many levels of society also have a problem with their spiritual condition.[54]

The "spiritual condition" was a major topic discussed at the December 1980 Central Committee Work Conference. The leadership had learned that the economic reforms initiated in 1979 required a concurrent renewal of socialist ideological beliefs. As Zhao Ziyang said, "While we construct a high level of material civilization, we simultaneously must construct a high degree of socialist spiritual civilization. Only in this way can we guarantee the long-term development of China's economy and guarantee the socialist direction of material civilization construction."[55]

The leaders thus decided to strengthen political ideological work by promoting "socialist spiritual civilization."[56] They initiated two campaigns, in civilian society and the military, in February 1981.[57] During his July 1981 "Speech on problems on the ideological front," Deng Xiaoping was critical of the portrayal of socialism in a recent film entitled *Sun and Man* (*Taiyang yu ren*), and said that there were many people desiring to depart from the party line and promote bourgeois liberalism.[58] As a response, in August the Propaganda Bureau convened a Conference on the National Ideological Front. Conferees strongly criticized those who had "departed from the Socialist road and the Party leadership and [who] have bourgeois liberal tendencies."[59] Individuals engaged in profiteering, speculation, and smuggling were included among those regarded as bourgeois liberal elements who needed reeducation or incarceration, or both.

The Government Response and the SEZs

The bureaucratic Stalinist response to the perceived chaos in foreign trade was to strengthen the management and regulation of foreign trade and foreign exchange nationwide, and to strengthen political ideology. Guangdong and Fujian had been granted a larger degree of autonomy than other provinces in 1979. But even so their internal policies, including SEZ policies, were affected by the government's response to the chaotic situation.

At the national level, the leadership strengthened foreign trade management by clarifying the powers of the SIEAC. The strengthening of provincial leadership was a major objective of Central Committee document 1981.27, which was produced by the 1981 Work Conference on Guangdong and Fujian Provinces and the SEZs. It declared that provincial leaders were to be "transformed into a collective fighting group with lofty aspirations and great ideals, [who] can seek truth from fact, are unified, and seek economic efficiency." They were "to streamline bureaucratic organizations, [and] abolish swollen bureaucracies, duplication, bureaucratic delays, and all other maladies of bureaucracies. This [was] especially true for the SEZs."

Specifically, document 1981.27 approved the separation of Shenzhen from Bao'an county and the upgrading of its administrative status. As for the other three SEZs, document 1981.27 stipulated the establishment of individual SEZ management committees that would answer to their respective municipal governments. With the appointment of Liang Xiang as Shenzhen party secretary, Wu Nansheng could work full-time on coordinating SEZ activities in the provincial government.[60]

The two provinces also were to comply with the measures adopted nationally to strengthen foreign trade and foreign exchange regulations. Echoing Chen Yun's policy statement at the December 1980 Work Conference, document 1981.27 stressed the need to "uphold a united front toward the outside and carry out the policy of [ensuring] 'Fertile water does not leak onto the other man's land.'" To maintain this united front, document 1981.27 revoked the Guangdong provincial government's right, granted in February 1980, to manage provincial customs affairs. Document 1981.27 stated that Beijing would resume responsibility for "customs management, including customs receipts and the reduction or elimination of duties."[61]

To strengthen export regulations, document 1981.27 forbade the two provinces and their SEZs from going "outside the province to procure export materials at higher prices or monopolize their trading." Exports of planned commodities (such as refined oil and tungsten ore) and goods with foreign export quotas were to be handled by the MFT. To manage exports to Hong Kong, a "consultative system" was established "under the leadership of the Hong Kong/Macao Work Committee and headed by China Resources."[62]

As for the import controls, document 1981.27 stated that import permits were necessary "whenever the two provinces import commodities restricted by the state or whenever units that have not been granted import rights import goods."[63] The provinces were forbidden "to resell to other provinces, municipalities, and SARs those commodities whose importation would contradict the protection of domestic industries.

This is to avoid influencing the normal domestic market order and the healthy economic development." Point 5 of State Council document 1981.6 specifically states that the two provinces were forbidden to reexport to the interior machinery equipment that originally had been imported by those provinces.[64]

Document 1981.27 also called for stronger local management of foreign exchange. Branch offices of the State General Administration for Foreign Exchange Control were opened in each zone. The local governments' management of retained foreign exchange was to include ensuring its proper use. Specifically, they were ordered to ensure that the difference in the cost of a good priced in both RMB and FEC would not exceed 20 percent.

Unlike the previous Central Committee documents concerning the two provinces and the SEZs, document 1981.27 contained major sections on combating corruption and on political ideology work. Echoing the calls of State Council documents 1981.3 and 1981.6 to attack speculation, profiteering, and smuggling activities, document 1981.27 declared that "a protracted struggle must be undertaken against smuggling, tax evasion, domestic and foreign collusion, corruption and graft, harming the public good for self-enrichment, and other violations of law and discipline."[65]

The two provinces thus planned to "organize a maritime smuggling investigation group." The Guangdong Provincial People's Congress adopted provisional rules for the entry and exit of personnel, registration of SEZ enterprises, labor management, and land development in the SEZs.[66] Within the Shenzhen SEZ, the local party committee and the government issued four articles outlining measures to attack smuggling.[67] Document 1981.27 also mentioned for the first time that "the demarcation line between the SEZ and non-SEZ areas must be established in all haste. The People's Armed Border Police units will patrol the line. Signposts must be erected along the SEZ demarcation line and a patrol road built. In necessary sectors, a steel fence should be erected. Customs and the Armed Police should establish joint Inspection Stations along those railroads and roads leading to the non-SEZ areas. The Armed Police will erect sentry posts along pedestrian walkways." It is interesting that the steel fence was planned "in necessary sectors." The partial fence was not intended to isolate Shenzhen;

it was merely to control exchanges with the interior economy. Although such initial controls were ineffectual, Beijing leaders expanded the partial-fence initiative in 1982.

As for political ideology work, document 1981.27 focused on combating sectarian attitudes by reminding the local leadership that "the economic activities of the two provinces are closely related to those of the whole country. The two provinces must pay attention to the entire situation when adopting various types of important economic measures. The two must consider and estimate the influence of the measures on the entire country. This is especially true in foreign economic trade and using the Hong Kong and Macao markets." The Beijing leadership also warned the local leadership not to "overlook the way the influence of the foreign bourgeoisie can seep into our politics and ideology as well as illegal economic activities. We must maintain a clear head and a high degree of alertness. We must prevent surprise attacks from the sugar-coated bullets of the capitalist classes. We must adopt various ways of developing education on a grand scale of the clear-cut upholding of the Four Cardinal Principles."[68]

To "maintain a clear head," document 1981.27 called for launching the Spiritual Civilization Campaign. "To cultivate sound socialist practices," the local leadership would concentrate on propaganda work. Special attention was given to the need "to strengthen propaganda education, improve television broadcast work, and enrich cultural life." And to adhere to Deng Xiaoping's Four Cardinal Principles, the local leadership would also work to improve "the management of public order and prosecute all criminal elements according to the law."[69]

By the summer of 1981 the slogans and methods of the Spiritual Civilization Campaign in Guangdong and Fujian were similar to those used during the Cultural Revolution. The Hong Kong press even reported the compilation of lists of Shenzhen cadres who were "traitors" and "collaborators."[70] In response, the summary of the 1981 Work Conference on the SEZs that produced Central Committee document 1981.27 repudiated outright "the 'leftist' wind of the 'theories of neocolonialism.'"[71] It argued, "Some comrades have questioned: Could the SEZs become concessions? Are they not colonies? The conference believes these questions have no basis. Our special zones are special economic zones, not special political zones. Our country exerts full sovereignty within the entire SEZ structure. This is fundamentally different in nature from the concessions and colonies caused by the Unequal Treaties." However, document 1981.27 was unable to disavow the problems with SEZ policy implementation and criminal economic activities.

In sum, the policies outlined in document 1981.27 were directly influenced by the readjustment of the decentralization policy adopted at the 1980 Central Work Conference. Document 1981.27 conforms to the leadership's initiative to strengthen foreign trade, foreign currency management, and political ideological work nationwide. However, it also shows that the leaders in Beijing were still optimistic about the decentralization experiment and the SEZs. They were convinced they could continue to macromanage foreign trade and allow the two provinces to enjoy great freedom in managing their own foreign trade and foreign exchange. For instance, the national export-permit system was not enforced in the two provinces. According to document 1981.27, those units approved to carry out export activities did "not have to apply for export permits, except in certain regulated cases." The leadership still believed that problems encountered with the decentralization experiment and the SEZs could be solved by "tinkering" with policy regulations.

By late 1981, however, the tinkering measures had proven ineffective. The smuggling and profiteering originating from the two provinces and the SEZs continued unabated. In retrospect, the situation seems analogous to the little Dutch boy discovering he cannot stop the leak in the dike with only his finger.

Stage Three: Chen Yun Makes His Move

By December 1981 certain members of the bureaucratic Stalinists in Beijing were dissatisfied with piecemeal measures taken to resolve the problems of decentralization. As a member of the Standing Committee, chairman of the party's Discipline and Inspection Commission, and a senior economic policy maker, Chen Yun launched a major attack against the excesses of decentralization during that month's Conference of First Party Secretaries from Provincial, Municipal, and Special Administrative Regions, held between December 15 and 23.

In an important speech entitled "Some Views on Economic Work," Chen Yun argued for the continued importance of the state plan. In January 1982 he summarized the speech, stating, "Last December, I spoke of four points. I primarily stressed the strengthening of the planned economy and did not say it did not work."[72] Chen Yun's first point was his concern that decentralization of the agriculture sector would divert production to cash crops, such as tobacco and cotton, that had higher profit margins; this would create procurement problems for lower-profit goods (vegetables and other foods). His second was his concern that the state plan's emphasis on food production was being supplanted by increased construction. Third, he argued for a reassessment of the SEZ policy. And fourth and finally, he argued that construction should be carried out only in accordance with the state plan.[73] Chen revealed that he would work to strengthen the role of the plan in China's economy: "Currently planning is not welcomed! So, in the beginning of this year I am talking to a few of the responsible comrades of the State Planning Commission about this matter. Should the SPC indulge in idle boasting? Or should it be earnest and down to earth? Should we forget past experiences?"[74] With Chen Yun's subsequent initiatives he would reassert the importance of the plan and demonstrate that the market should be a secondary tool to help fulfill the plan (*yi jihua jingji weizhu, shichang tiaojie weibu*).

Because he was concerned about the SEZs' detrimental effect on the state plan, Chen Yun forced a decision on decentralization problems. His first target was entrepôt trade in the SEZs. During a meeting of the Party Standing Committee on 11 January 1982, Chen Yun submitted a brief from the CDIC's report on "criminal economic activities" in the SEZs and other regions in China. According to the Emergency Circular issued by the Standing Committee on 11 January, the brief summarized "the extremely serious criminal smuggling activities by some cadres. Some of them were in responsible leadership positions."[75]

The contents of the CDIC report and the positions adopted by the leadership can only be hypothesized. It is highly probable that the brief described the case of the Shenzhen Party Branch involving Zhou Zhirong, "temporary" secretary of the Shenzhen Party Committee. Zhou's large-scale smuggling operation was probably uncovered in September or October of 1981; it was officially reported to "the leading comrades of the Central Committee" on 11 January 1982.[76] According to the Emergency Circular put out on that date, the Standing Committee also discussed serious economic crimes committed by "some cadres and responsible cadres in other provinces, cities, special administrative regions, and central government departments."[77] The directive specifically mentions Guangdong, Fujian, Zhejiang, and Yunnan provinces.

During the 11 January 1982 meeting of the Standing Committee, several bureaucratic Stalinists strongly criticized the criminal activities and excesses facilitated by decentralization. Chen Yun lobbied for a strong response; he continued to fear the effect of decentralization on party discipline and local leaders' adherence to the state plan. In his December 1981 speech Chen had specifically called for a review of the SEZ policy, stating, "We must summarize the experiences of the SEZs in Guangdong and Fujian and the foreign economic activities of every province."[78] Commenting specifically on the 1981 smuggling case, he stated, "Whatever it is that we are calling 'rectifying the party style,' in the end we just need to rectify party style." It is unclear whether Chen Yun or Hu Qiaomu added, "This is the crucial deciding point for the success or failure of carrying out special policies and lively measures [in Guangdong and Fujian]. If we carry out this struggle, our SEZs and our special policies and lively measures will succeed. If we don't carry out this struggle, we will lose."[79] To combat these threats, Chen Yun argued for the implementation of a Strike Hard Campaign against Economic Crimes. According to Zhao Ziyang, Chen Yun wrote in the margin of the CDIC report that the campaign should make "a hard and resolute strike, like a thunderbolt."[80]

Hu Qiaomu's criticisms were more severe. As Mao Zedong's former secretary, official party historian, and the drafter of many of Mao and Deng's policies, Hu Qiaomu was not opposed to reforms, but he was greatly concerned about their ideological implications, and in the 1980s he often sided with Chen Yun to promote a moderate approach. In his speech to the Guangdong and Fujian cadres on 12 February 1982, Hu argued that they were facing a class struggle against capitalism and its degenerate influences, including smuggling, pornography, and even foreign spies.

In the give and take of our fight against special agents and spies, we are not facing a simple ideological problem. We are dealing with a severe problem with some capitalist countries (including several who established diplomatic relations with China several years ago and say so many nice things) that are carrying out spying activities. Since the Third Plenum, we have brought order from chaos and have made great strides in our socialist construction. However, our management system and measures have not kept up with the changes in economic policy. And our ideological work has not kept up with the changes either. Thus, class struggle continues. Although some people have talked about it continuing for several years, not enough people in the party are paying attention.[81]

According to Hu Qiaomu, China was being attacked on all fronts. From within, China confronted the leftover feudal attitudes of the exploitive classes. Outside of China, capitalist forces constantly attacked China's exterior regions, including the border areas of Guangxi, Yunnan, Tibet, Xinjiang, Inner Mongolia, and in the Northeast.

We are now facing the capitalist classes living in Hong Kong, Macao, Taiwan and abroad. They want to erode and corrupt our ranks, and even talk about the Hong Kong-ization of Guangdong. We must struggle against them. However, except for the small number people with whom we are jointly operating enterprises, the PRC lacks jurisdiction over these people. We cannot use the same methods we used against the national bourgeoisie in 1952. Thus, this is a long-term struggle. [First Party Secretary of Guangdong] Ren Zhongyi just made a statement which I agree with, but I want to make a small revision. He thinks that the high tide of smuggling and corruption has already passed. Perhaps this is so (but one cannot say it is a low tide either). Speaking from a long-term perspective, we cannot see things this way. There could be even higher high tides, unless at this very moment we are extremely clearheaded and adopt very strict measures. If we do not, there will definitely be higher tides. When we get back Hong Kong and Macao, many capitalists will become PRC nationals. Hong Kong is part of the PRC but maintains an older system and is still a free port. As this is one country, two systems, we will not be able to avoid an even more complicated situation from arising. We must be fully prepared. Resolving the Taiwan problem will be a bit further in the future, but we also must be prepared. Actual interaction between Taiwan and the mainland has gradually increased. Guangdong is facing problems dealing with Hong Kong and Macao. Fujian is facing the Taiwan problem. Thus, we can believe that the high tide has passed. In a very long period of history, this struggle will not shrink to nothing. Thus, there are some differences with the struggle of 1952.[82]

Hu was fearful that the Chinese people were sacrificing their spirit and selling their country in praising foreign countries and foreign ways, and that as a result China was facing its highest rate of criminal behavior, which was three times the 1956 rate. Young people were turning a cold shoulder to the party and all types of questionable publications were being printed. But Hu was especially concerned that a new bourgeois class was emerging, just as it had in the Soviet Union during the period of the NEP, when the so-called NEPmen emerged as large-scale urban traders, manufacturers, financiers, and assorted speculators.[83]

Even though the Soviet Union's implementation of the "New Economic Policy" did not last for a particularly long period of time, a new class arose within society, the Nepmen, who emerged as a result of the New Economic Policy. It is fine that afterward Stalin struggled with Bukharin. It is fine that they carried out a cruel form of collectivization against the peasants. These things can be put into context. There were some good points about implementing the New Economic Policy, but not that many. It introduced some inconveniences, as the result of which Stalin turned the policy around and put an end to it. The current problems we are facing are different from Stalin's time. And we certainly cannot use Stalin's methods to resolve the problems. His methods were not appropriate. We do not have the same situation as the Soviet Union, as our opening policy will be carried out in the long term.[84]

Hu Qiaomu made an indirect connection between the emergence of the NEPmen and the corruption carried out by the new bourgeoisie found in the two southern provinces. He advocated not only a rectification of Zhou Zhirong and the Shenzhen party branch that "had become rotten," but also a large-scale campaign against this emerging class of opponents to China's revolution. "We will fail if we do not carry out this struggle on a large scale, carry out only an isolated campaign to rectify the party's style and discipline, or advocate only socialist spiritual civilization."[85] While arguing against an expanded class struggle, which was a mistake in the past, Hu Qiaomu called for a more comprehensive nationwide campaign, which eventually resulted in the Anti–Spiritual Pollution Campaign of October–December 1983, and the Anti–Bourgeois Liberalization Campaign of the late 1980s.

Hu Yaobang concurred with the need to summarize experiences but continued to support the decentralization experiment and its foreign economic reforms. In his major speech on foreign trade delivered to the Central Party Secretariat on 14 January, Hu Yaobang said, "From 1978 to 1980, our foreign economic relations truly made great strides forward, unlike those of the past. Yet there also arose several errors in certain [areas]. In view of this, we must summarize our experience and steadily carry out measures. In addition, we do not want any mistaken views, even the idea of shrinking back and not again daring to develop foreign economic relations. . . . How can we reduce our efforts because of a small number of problems?"[86] However, during the 12 February 1982 meeting with Guangdong and Fujian cadres, Hu Yaobang warned that the threat to party control was reminiscent of ideological threats the party faced in 1937 and 1938.[87]

Zhao Ziyang was more vocal in his support of Chen Yun's position. In his 22 December 1981 speech, Chen Yun made an interesting remark in support of Zhao Ziyang's concern for the entire country, stating, "Some comrades say that after Comrade Ziyang arrived in Beijing, he spoke the Beijing dialect [Beijinghua]. I think this is correct, since Comrade Ziyang is in charge of the whole country."[88] In return for Chen's support, Zhao Ziyang pledged in 29 January 1982 that it was the responsibility of the State Council to "coordinate with the Central Commission for Discipline Inspection and the judicial departments to complete the task."[89] However, Zhao emphasized that the party elites had not initiated a new political campaign. In his speech to the Guangdong and Fujian cadres on 13 February 1982, Zhao Ziyang praised the progress made by the two provinces and their SEZs but reinforced the serious nature of the economic crimes committed in the provinces and the need "to struggle against the strongly corrosive nature of the party and cadre, which is extremely poisonous to the entire society." Education of the cadre "could not be done in a halfway fashion and, especially, treated like 'water off a duck's back.'" Zhao pointedly reminded them that "Chen Yun stated that the number one task for the SEZs was to reassess their experiences." While a political campaign would not be initiated and the two provinces would continue to carry out special policies and flexible measures, he said the provinces "needed to enact legislation to strengthen supervision, investigation, and punishment."[90]

Zhao Ziyang repeated his full support for Chen Yun during a speech to the National Conference on Industry and Communications on 4 March 1982, stating:

> Recently Comrade Chen Yun has made a series of important directives on economic work. He has again emphasized: Our country must ensure the leading role of the planned economy supplemented by market regulation. We must carry out the basic plan of "Number One is to eat; Number Two is construction." He also pointed out the Number One task of the SEZs is to summarize experiences thoroughly. . . . In implementing the opening policy and the enlivening of the domestic economy, we must maintain a clear mind and support, as mentioned above, principles proffered by Comrade Chen Yun. . . . We cannot waver in this correct policy that has already been defined. . . . Since we are opening the economy, it is inevitable that it will bring in some bad things and bad influences of capitalism.[91]

Zhao continued Chen Yun's theme of attacking the "unitism, separatism, and liberalism" that had been caused by the expansion of autonomy. According to Zhao, such tendencies

> weaken and cast aside the unified state plan. They disrupt and divide the unified socialist market. They influence the unity of the nation. Some areas and units do not investigate and solve problems in the interest of the whole nation, but in their interest. In terms of the state, this noncompliance with the unified state plan harms the many and helps the few; it shifts one's troubles onto one's neighbors and harms their interest

for self-aggrandizement; in terms of foreign affairs, by not carrying out unified policies toward the outside we fight among ourselves and let "fertile water leak onto the other man's land."[92]

In his enthusiasm to support Chen Yun, Zhao Ziyang went even further than Chen in certain cases, saying, "Comrade Chen Yun has stated that currently the Number One task of the SEZs is to summarize experiences. As I see it, not only should the SEZs, Guangdong, and Fujian do this, but the entire country is confronted with a problem of summarizing experience."[93] As his later actions revealed, Zhao Ziyang's ideas about the role of the plan and the market differed from Chen Yun's. Yet in 1982 Zhao apparently supported Chen Yun's position for political reasons.

As the newly emerged paramount leader, Deng Xiaoping sought to bridge the growing divide within the bureaucratic Stalinists. Deng was fully supportive of Chen Yun's initiative to control economic crimes and the 1980 Work Conference's initiative to promote spiritual civilization. One month after the 11 January 1982 Standing Committee meeting, he openly agreed with Chen Yun's and Hu Qiaomu's criticism of smuggling and adoption of a bourgeois lifestyle by stating during a meeting with the premier of Morocco,

> We cannot import those decadent things. Since opening, the contacts with the outside will always have an impact. The problem is whether one can understand these influences. One needs a clear head and cannot be taken by surprise. One also must thoroughly resist these influences and adopt effective measures—including legal measures—to eliminate these bad things. On the one hand we must resist the corrupt practices, graft, embezzlement, and bribery of the capitalist world; we also must resist bad practices within society and the harming of others to benefit oneself. On the other, we must promote spiritual civilization. We must teach the later generations to have ideals, morality, to be courteous, disciplined, and to struggle arduously.[94]

Deng took personal responsibility for the decentralization policy, especially SEZ policy. From experience, he understood that these mistakes in the SEZs could devolve into a crisis and threaten the unity of the bureaucratic Stalinist leadership. It was thus in his self-interest to contain the criticism and co-opt Chen Yun by agreeing to some of his demands, such as the temporary cessation of the opening strategy.

Deng Xiaoping made great efforts to deny the similarity between the economic crimes of 1982 and those of 1952. Thirty years before, on 30 November 1951 and 26 January 1952, the Central Committee had issued two directives initiating major campaigns against corruption, waste, and economic crime.[95] Their purpose was to remove corrupt and unreliable bureaucrats (via the Three Antis Campaign) and crack down on illegal economic practices prevalent in the urban economy (in the Five Antis Campaign). Mass meetings were convened to criticize bureaucrats; more than 450,000 enterprises were investigated for illegal economic practices.[96]

Considering his own involvement with the 1952 campaign, Chen Yun was perhaps the first to draw the analogy between those events and 1982, which he did in his brief to the Standing Committee on 11 January.[97] Zhao Ziyang, who had agreed with Chen Yun's position at the time, stated in his speech of 4 March 1982, "The smuggling, profiteering, and corruption and all other criminal activities in the economic sector are much more serious than the 1952 'Three Antis' and 'Five Antis' period."[98] The analogy was drawn again in the Guangdong and Fujian Conference Summary (Central Committee document 1982.17) and in the Central Committee "decision" to attack criminal activities, issued on 13 April 1982.[99] Hu Qiaomu made a direct comparison in his 12 February 1982 speech to the Guangdong and Fujian cadres, arguing that the party in 1952 "had carried out a furious attack on the capitalist class, resulting in saving a large number of party cadres, and putting only a few to death."[100]

Yet in his speech to the Political Bureau on the Central Committee and State Council's April 1982 decision, Deng Xiaoping argued that comparisons between 1982 and 1952 were inappropriate. While agreeing that there were many significant cases of corruption in 1982, the amount of money involved was small, he said. During the Three Antis and Five Antis Campaigns, Deng said, one case involved RMB 560,000; in 1982, none of the cases presented in Chen Yun's 11 January brief involved such a large amount.[101] It appears that Deng was trying to limit the scope of the 1982 anticorruption campaign, which he feared would break apart the Third Plenum consensus reached by the bureaucratic Stalinists and reverse the decentralization experiments.

Based on the decisions reached by the Standing Committee on January 11 and 13, it appears Chen Yun and Deng Xiaoping reached a compromise. Like the Three Antis Campaign, the 11 January Emergency Circular proposed that "smuggling, graft, corruption, and the theft of state property" should be "resolutely resolved" within the party. On 13 January, the Central Committee approved the "Directive on strengthening political and legal work," asking all party members to ensure public order "in a comprehensive way."[102] Deng Xiaoping also spoke on the proposed streamlining of the party and government bureaucracy.[103] Somewhat analogous to the Five Antis Campaign, the assault against economic crimes would be carried out nationwide, with special emphasis on Guangdong, Fujian, Zhejiang, and Yunnan.

In contrast to the 1952 campaigns, the 1982 Emergency Circular stipulated,

> We do not want to launch a denouncement and exposure campaign concerning these matters among all the cadres and masses. We want to avoid the chaos [caused by] unfair accusations and everyone feeling in danger. First we must thoroughly investigate and dispose of current major criminal cases in the economic sphere committed by those responsible comrades; major criminal cases in the economic sphere that were not disposed of or were not dealt with within the past two years also are to be handled. Within the entire country, thorough disposition is to be limited to only 10 to 100 cases. Yet these are to be given wide publicity among the cadres and masses.[104]

The directive recognized that a major campaign would disrupt the reforms. Thus, the 1982 "campaign" was an educational tool to convince "the bad people . . . [to] greatly restrain themselves."

Immediately after the issuance of the 11 January Emergency Circular, the Central Committee initiated three major actions.[105] First, it called a conference of leaders from Guangdong and Fujian, who met in mid-February. Senior leaders of the party, the military, and the provinces attended, including Hu Yaobang, Zhao Ziyang, and Hu Qiaomu.

The Guangdong and Fujian Conference Summary, which was issued 1 March 1982 as Central Committee document 1982.17, called for "the struggle to further assault illegal criminal activities in the economic sector" in Guangdong and Fujian. Second, the Standing Committee of the National People's Congress approved the "Decision to Severely Punish Criminals Who Damage the Economy," on 8 March 1982.[106] This was followed on 13 April with Central Committee document 1982.22, entitled "Decision to Strike Hard against Serious Economic Crimes."[107] Finally, the Central Commission on Discipline Inspection sent 154 midlevel cadres to carry out the campaign nationwide. By the end of 1982, more than 164,000 cases had been uncovered and 86,000 cases brought for judgment; 30,000 people were sentenced, with fines totaling more than RMB 320 million.[108]

To prevent future foreign trade problems, Premier Zhao Ziyang, during his 4 March 1982 speech, proposed to continue the expansion of certain foreign trade rights but "firmly to prevent the mistaken methods of having too many entities dealing with foreign businessmen [duotou duiwai], and competitive price cutting." Adherence to the state plan was mandatory. Units were prohibited from retaining export goods for their own use or selling them on the market. He further suggested that material pricing and taxation should be centralized.[109] Gu Mu added, following his inspection tour of Guangdong and the SEZs, that "to this day, we have found not a single case in which the nation was humiliated or state sovereignty was surrendered. . . . Doubts about whether the SEZs can continue are simply groundless."[110]

Deng and the bureaucratic Stalinists did not cancel the decentralization experiment but instead strengthened their macromanagement of the economy. In foreign economic trade, the leaders desired "to reinforce their control over export/import activities as the uneven development of national, regional, and enterprise efforts became increasingly evident."[111] The State Council strengthened the authority of the SIEAC. To avoid "having too many entities dealing with foreign businessmen," the SIEAC, the MFT, the Foreign Economic Liaison Department and the Foreign Investment Commission of the PRC were combined to form MOFERT. The NPC approved this reorganization of the foreign trade bureaucracy on 8 March 1982.[112] To coordinate and manage foreign trade in the port areas, as suggested by Zhao Ziyang in his 4 March 1982 speech, MOFERT established four offices, in Shanghai, Tianjin, Dalian, and Guangzhou.[113]

Continuing the policies to strengthen export controls, State Council document 1981.179 established eleven categories of goods that were scarce domestically. To limit their exportation, the council required exporters to apply for export permits for those goods.[114] If exporters wished to export regulated goods outside the plan, they were required to obtain approval from the local materials distribution department, the SIEAC, and the SPC. High export duties were also imposed on goods that were in high demand on the domestic market or were exported at a loss to the state.[115]

To avoid the *duotou duiwai* problem and competitive price cutting, the State Council approved the division of export goods into three categories.[116] The first category of twenty-three commodities, all in high demand domestically, would be uniformly managed by the specialized foreign trade import-export corporation under MOFERT or the import-export corporations under the industrial ministries.[117] The second category included 173 commodities for which "management authority overlaps between localities and departments, . . . international competition is fierce, or . . . export quotas, quality and/or quantity restrictions exist."[118] The localities, under the guidance of the MOFERT import-export corporations, could conclude transactions for the goods. All other export goods were contained in the third category. The localities would enjoy "complete control of exporting goods that do not belong to the above two categories."

The import permit system was strictly enforced. In 1982 the state effectively restricted the legal importation of the most desired durables (Table D). The State Council also continued its policy of restricting purchases by large organizations or units.[119] To protect China's domestic industry, State Council document 1982.33 restricted imports of machinery that was manufactured domestically.[120] The importation of synthetic textiles also was prohibited, "to protect the normal development of domestic production."[121] By the time of the September 1982 Conference on Import-Export Permit Management Work, customs leaders boasted that both the export and import permit

Table D
Import Licenses Issued by MOFERT, January 1981–August 1982

Import item	1981	1982 (Jan.–Aug.)
Watches	2,400,000	940,000
Motorcycles	1,083	34
TVs	880,000	150,000
Radio cassette players	610,000	120,000
Cameras	36,315	370

SOURCE: "Guanyu yinfa 'Jinchukou xukezheng guanli gongzuo zuotanhui jiyao' de tongzhi" [Circular on the publication of "The summary of the conference on import-export permit management work"], *Waijingmaoguanchuxuzi* 1982.132, issued by MOFERT on 21 November 1982, in *DJFZH*, 265–76.

systems had "controlled price-cutting competition, stabilized foreign markets . . . [and] prevented blind development of [the] domestic market."[122]

In addition to strengthening foreign trade controls, the state adopted several measures to strengthen its control of foreign exchange. The State Council approved the PBOC's request to strengthen its position as the country's central bank. Although the Bank of China maintained its role in managing foreign exchange, the People's Bank was now responsible for the "overall management of foreign exchange and gold, managing foreign exchange reserves, setting the rate of exchange between the RMB and foreign currencies, and representing the Chinese government whenever it participated in international financial activities."[123] The Central Committee also issued a decision that strengthened previous measures forbidding the circulation and trading of foreign exchange within the country and the depositing of foreign exchange in Hong Kong banks.[124] And newer regulations were introduced in November 1982 to strengthen management of retained foreign exchange earned from trade and nontrade activities.[125]

To increase finance capital, Central Committee document 1982.50 directed the Bank of China to issue more loans for SEZ development. In addition, Hong Kong–Chinese banks and foreign banks could establish SEZ branches and representative offices. A more complete set of economic laws also was promulgated.[126] Most important, restrictions on economic interchange between the domestic economy and the SEZs were relaxed. The domestic sale of SEZ products was permitted if the product: (1) was scarce on the domestic market; (2) had a large percentage of domestically produced components; or (3) was produced by foreign or Hong Kong/Macao businesses using advanced technology and equipment. Central, provincial, and local government enterprises were encouraged to transfer technicians to the SEZs to establish cooperative ventures. As a result, more than five hundred "interregional" enterprises (*neilian qiye*) were established in Shenzhen by 1984, with a total capitalization of RMB 650 million and HK$126 million.

Finally, the Central Committee continued to strengthen the political ideological work initiated in 1980. The theme of the Spiritual Civilization Campaign remained the same. In a conference summary approved by the Central Committee on 28 May 1982, propaganda leaders warned that "in constructing a Socialist Spiritual Civilization, the corrosiveness of capitalist ideology must be checked. . . . We must realize that to struggle against corrosion, we must build Socialist Spiritual Civilization. This is an important part of carrying out the Five Stresses and Four Beauties Campaign. We must teach cadres and youths to fight capitalist corruption and to continue the fight against feudal superstition, gambling, the buying and selling of wives and the kidnapping and selling of women, [and] pornography."[127] The leadership increased its nationwide efforts throughout 1982. In February the Central Committee Secretariat issued the "Report on Deepening the Campaign for 'Five Stresses and Four Beauties.'"[128] The report stipulated that every March would be designated National Civilization and Courtesy Month (Quanmin wenming limao yue). Premier Zhao Ziyang even appeared on television the night before the inauguration of the month-long propaganda event.[129]

Foreshadowing future events, the Central Committee issued in March 1982 the "Regulations strictly Prohibiting the Importation, Reproduction, Sale or Broadcasting of Reactionary, Pornographic, and Obscene Recordings and Tapes."[130] In May, the Ministries of Culture and Public Security issued the "Circular on Prohibiting the Lending of Picture Books and Other Materials from H. K., Macao, and Taiwan." Leaders were particularly concerned that these materials concerning ghosts, sex, and death were flooding the domestic market, especially in southern China.[131]

The Elites' Response and SEZ Policy

Members of the party leadership had been increasingly concerned with the ideological nature and development path of the SEZs. "Some leading comrades" feared that the SEZs would become "'new colonies' that [would be] ruled from abroad." Other leaders worried "that economic criminal activities [would] spread unchecked."[132] By 1982 the leadership agreed that SEZ policy needed to be modified.

The leaders had three possible options. According to an article in *Fujian luntan* in April 1982, they could:

> oppose [the SEZs], to regard them as concessions, as treasonable, or even as the breeding ground for all social evils. [The second option was] to propose setting up special zones that are sealed off, somewhat small in scope, somewhat slow in pace, merely bringing in selectively certain labor-intensive enterprises from Hong Kong or other places, which would then export a small quantity of processed goods, while remaining completely sealed off from the rest of the country, in other words, to establish what one might call "pure export commodity processing zones." Yet another approach [was] to turn the special zones into hubs or centers for economic contacts on a large scale between our country and the world, and to use the special zones to implement our global economic strategy.[133]

In retrospect, it is clear the leadership could adopt only one option. Considering Deng's strong support of the decentralization measures and the SEZs, the first option was not appropriate. Suddenly reducing the size of the Shenzhen SEZ from 327.5 square kilometers to just a few square kilometers was not a practical solution either. Shenzhen had attracted a certain amount of foreign investment capital and was becoming a very visible showcase for the opening policy. Any reduction in size would cause doubt not only among potential foreign investors but also among British negotiators engaged in discussions concerning the future of Hong Kong after 1997. The leadership thus chose to place a moratorium on future SEZ construction and improve the implementation of current SEZ policy.

In his earlier defense of the planned economy, Chen Yun had attacked SEZ policy in his December 1981 speech. He was specifically concerned with preserving the planned economy by restricting the impact of international market forces on China's currency and native industries. He had thus focused on combating SEZs' "economic criminal activities." Rejecting the neocolonialist approach, Chen Yun had adopted a phlegmatic view and called for a general review of SEZ policy.

Chen Yun was thus adamantly opposed to further expansion of the SEZs. Provincial officials, including those from Jiangsu, were envious of the "special policies and flexible measures" granted to Guangdong and Fujian by Central Committee document 1979.50. The new leadership in Beijing had attempted to resolve undue inequality by adopting State Council documents 1979.202 and 1979.233, which allocated greater foreign trade authority to the localities.[134] Beijing had also approved an increase in the number of provincially managed export commodity processing bases and new regulations concerning ECPB management and financing.

But the localities desired even greater autonomy and lobbied to establish their own SEZs.[135] In December 1981, Chen Yun rejected their appeal, stating:

> In the four cities of Shenzhen, Zhuhai, Shantou, and Xiamen in Guangdong and Fujian provinces, experimental SEZs are being run in certain areas (the whole province of Guangdong is not a special zone, the whole province of Fujian is also not a special zone). For now, we can run only these. We cannot increase the number of SEZs. Naturally, many areas also want to carry out processing of foreign goods and equity joint ventures. But we cannot increase the number of SEZs again. We cannot carry out processing of foreign goods at the expense of our own commodities. . . . Provinces like Jiangsu cannot have SEZs. While seeing the beneficial side of SEZs, one also must fully estimate the side effects of the SEZs. For instance: the simultaneous circulation of renminbi and foreign currency is not good for the renminbi. This will harm the renminbi since its value will decrease while that of foreign currency will increase. Speculative activities in the Jiangsu-Zhejiang region have a long history. The activities of bad elements are popular and rampant [remen relu]. Our number one responsibility now is thoroughly to summarize experience.[136]

One month later, in January 1982, Chen Yun added, "In [December], I stated that all areas want to run SEZs and 'open the dike.' If this is allowed to happen, all the foreign capitalists and opportunists within the country will swarm to carry out speculation and profiteering on a grand scale. We cannot let this occur. The number one problem of the SEZs is to summarize experiences."[137]

Consequently, the Guangdong and Fujian Provincial Conference of February 1982 was held in Beijing to assess and improve SEZ policy implementation. According to the conference summary published as Central Committee document 1982.17, only the leaders of these two provinces were invited because "(1) these are coastal provinces bordering Hong Kong/Macao and opposite Taiwan, [and] they are the primary conduits to the interior for smuggling and trafficking in smuggled goods; [and] (2) because these two provinces are carrying out special policies and flexible measures in the economic area, both are running SEZs on a trial basis, and both need to resolve clearly some problems of a policy nature. This is not to say that other provinces and cities (for instance, Zhejiang, Shanghai, Yunnan, Beijing) do not have similar serious problems that must be resolved with great effort."[138] The purpose of the conference, according to Central Committee document 1982.17, was to consider "how to implement more tenaciously and effectively the Central Committee's 'Emergency Circular' and further carry out the struggle to assault illegal criminal activities in the economic sector; how to sum up experiences thoroughly, to straighten out the guiding ideology in foreign economic activities; and how to improve the implementation of special policies and flexible measures and develop the two provincial economies." Document 1982.17 says that these goals would be achieved by, first, reaching a mutual understanding of the problem; second, adopting measures to "assault the illegal criminal activities in the economic sector"; and third, "summing up the SEZ experience."[139]

Everyone agreed that the primary cause of the problems was the failure of political ideological work and management measures "to keep pace" with the reforms. That failure had resulted in the pervasive influence of the "capitalist ideology and bourgeois lifestyle" throughout the country. (Similar to ideas expressed in the 1952 Five Antis Campaign, this lifestyle entailed smuggling, swindling, corruption, graft, and theft of state property.) Thus, the purpose of the entire party was to struggle against these economic crimes and capitalist ideology.

Although the document acknowledges that the "exploiting class" had been eliminated in mainland China, the current struggle was nonetheless part of "a limited class struggle." Therefore, everyone was required to participate fully. As document 1982.17 warned, "This [class] struggle is related to the success or failure of our country's socialist modernization construction. It is related to the prosperity and decline of our party and country. We absolutely cannot treat this matter lightly. Given the specific historical circumstances, this must be a long-term, protracted struggle. It must be revived several times. The whole party must have a complete knowledge about this and a high degree of vigilance. We can never be slack in this struggle."[140] These were prophetic words. The struggle against bourgeois liberalism was revived often during the 1980s, including after the June Fourth Incident in 1989.

The second purpose of the conference was to discuss implementation of the 11 January Emergency Circular "to assault the illegal criminal activities in the economic sector." According to one Hong Kong report, investigators initially sent to Shenzhen "asserted that 80 percent of the cadres there had been corrupted and 80 percent of these corrupt cadres' income was illegal."[141] Yet the circular emphasized that only a few high-level cadres who had committed the most offensive crimes should be prosecuted. Thus, document 1982.17 stated that criminal prosecution would be confined to imposing penalties on "middle- and higher-level cadres (including their relatives) and some units and collectives, and not on the ordinary cadre."

The case of Zhou Zhirong—the Shenzhen party secretary who was accused of large-scale corruption and smuggling—was handed over to the office of the Guangdong procurator. After five months of investigation, Zhou and an accomplice were formally arrested on 30 October 1982, and expelled from the party and their government posts. Zhou reportedly was imprisoned for eleven years and his accomplice received a death sentence, while 575 people in sixty-four different organizations were sanctioned.[142] In addition, the Party Committee of the China Electronics and Technology Import-Export Corporation, Shenzhen Branch, was abolished and replaced with a "temporary small leadership team." The case was then reported in national and local newspapers.[143]

Most cadres underwent political and ideological reeducation. They were required to attend local conferences called by the Shenzhen Party Committee and to study the cadre handbook issued in 1982.[144] In the end, 336 cadres in Shenzhen were transferred and replaced with cadres from all over the country, and all 303 branches of the party in Shenzhen were "rectified." The Old Bao'an cadres, about whom Mayor Liang Xiang had complained, were replaced to "prevent sectarian tendencies ... [and the] forming [of] small bands and groups."[145]

To build a socialist spiritual civilization and eliminate the tendency "of thinking in terms of money" (*xiang qian kan*), Shenzhen Municipality strengthened its propaganda tools by approving the publication of several newspapers and magazines. These included a daily paper (*Shenzhen tequ bao*), a magazine for party members (*Tequ dang de shenghuo*), and a magazine for intellectuals (*Tequ wenxue*). To ensure proper implementation of the Spiritual Civilization Campaign, Zhou Yang, the vice minister of the Propaganda Department, and Wang Zhen visited Shenzhen in February 1982 for an inspection.[146]

As a complement to the measures adopted in Beijing to prevent smuggling, Guangdong and Fujian carried out policies restricting the transfer of smuggled imported materials to the interior. On 17 August 1982 the State Council issued document 1982.111, entitled "Temporary Regulations on Strengthening Commodity Import Management of Guangdong and Fujian Provinces and Preventing the Transference of Smuggled Goods to the Interior."[147] The importation of the most popular durable goods—including televisions, motorcycles, and watches (referred to as "the seventeen imported commodities")—was severely restricted.[148] Only those trade channels approved by the State Council could import such commodities. Their resale to outside units was prohibited unless directly approved by the appropriate State Council department. Any department under the State Council that wished to import these commodities first had to be granted a "seventeen-imported-commodities" transport certificate by the State Materiel Bureau, the Ministry of Commerce, and the Textile Industry Ministry. In addition, inspection was tightened in Guangdong and Fujian's railroad stations, airports, and post offices. To prevent foreign participation in smuggling and corruption, overseas Chinese and Hong Kong and Macao "compatriots" were barred from offering "contributions" (i.e., bribes).[149] Foreign businessmen also were prohibited from smuggling in items while conducting compensation trade and processing and assembly activities.[150]

The most dramatic anti-smuggling measure implemented in the Shenzhen SEZ was the "second line" (*di'er xian*). In addition to the barbed wire fences that already separated Shenzhen from Hong Kong, a second barbed wire fence (the second line) was erected to separate Shenzhen from the interior (Bao'an county). By 1983, six inspection stations and two customs stations had been built, as well as an eighty-kilometer road that paralleled the second-line fence in some places. As previously described, a second line in certain areas had originally been proposed in document 1981.27, which called for the People's Armed Border Police to patrol the perimeter, signposts to be erected in certain areas, and, "in necessary sectors, a steel fence." According to the recommendations in document 1981.27, after the demarcation line was enforced "all production and consumer materials whose import have been approved for SEZ use will be imported duty free. Exceptions include tobacco and spirits, whose duties will be reduced by half from their lowest duty, and some materials whose duties will be levied according to the rules. Goods and materials transported from the SEZ to the interior will comply with the normal import regulations."[151]

Yet because so many smuggled goods had continued to pour across the demarcation line, "assaulting the domestic market," Beijing decided to construct a nearly 109-kilometer-long barbed wire fence to separate Shenzhen from Bao'an. Beijing also decided to allocate RMB 130 million for the project. By 4 February 1982, Shenzhen Municipality had established the Second Line Construction Command Post and had transferred cadres, technicians, and construction personnel to start work on the line; in December 1984, the fence was completed.[152]

Chen Yun had stated in December 1981 that the primary task of the SEZs was to summarize their experience. According to him, "The summary of experiences is a way to add to achievements, overcome shortcomings, and correct mistakes. Only by summarizing experiences can we better implement special policies [and] flexible measures and carry out well the trial operation of the SEZs."[153] "Summarizing experiences" entailed the adoption of measures to strengthen SEZ policy implementation; it did not imply that the opening policy, the decentralization policy, or the SEZ policy was being reconsidered. Document 1982.17 reaffirmed that "it must be clear that the party policy to carry out an 'opening' to the outside and an enlivening of the domestic economy is an unswerving policy adopted in consideration of socialist modernization construction and the international conditions." As Chen Yun pointed out, "There have also arisen many new circumstances and problems that need research and solutions."[154] Additional policies and measures were needed to cope with these "new circumstances."

With the discovery of corruption in the Shenzhen government, specifically the case of Party Secretary Zhou Zhirong, both the provincial and central governments decided that the zones needed closer supervision. On 15 October 1981 the Guangdong Provincial Party established a new Standing Committee of the Shenzhen Municipal Party Committee, composed of cadres transferred from Guangzhou. Liang Xiang, who had replaced Wu Nansheng as first party secretary in March 1981, continued as first party secretary and mayor of Shenzhen.[155] In a related move, the entire Shenzhen municipal government structure was reorganized and streamlined. The number of Shenzhen Standing Committee members and vice mayors was reduced from 19 to 8; the number of municipal government bureaus (*ju*) was reduced from 65 to 32; the number of Shenzhen municipal administrators was reduced from 2,237 to 867.[156]

These measures did not completely satisfy the Beijing leadership. Previously Beijing had entrusted central government oversight to the SIEAC, with specific responsibility assigned to Gu Mu and Jiang Zemin. Besides the occasional visit and the annual conference, the SIEAC did not adopt a highly interventionist role and allowed the Guangdong and Fujian provincial governments to supervise the SEZs. After the issuance of the 11 January 1982 Emergency Circular, the leadership decided to strengthen its direct supervision of the SEZs. In summarizing the experiences of the SEZs, the bureaucratic Stalinists in Beijing agreed to impose a greater degree of macromanagement to balance sectarian tendencies (the negative interpretation of the "eight immortals" phrase) and ensure that SEZ policy would benefit the entire country.

After closing the SIEAC, the State Council reorganized SEZ oversight and opened a separate State Council Office of the SEZs (Tequ

Bangongshi) on 4 June 1982, with Zhao Ziyang and Gu Mu in charge.[157] In a certain sense, recentralization did occur. The mere presence of a central government department dedicated to SEZ affairs, with Gu Mu as leader, naturally reduced the supervisory role of the Guangdong provincial government. The central government thus became more involved with actual government planning and financing.[158]

Yet Deng Xiaoping remained adamant that the decentralization experiment and the opening strategy were sound. The Central Committee did not revoke the previous Central Committee documents concerning provincial decentralization and SEZ policy (documents 1979.50, 1980.41, 1981.27); Articles 3 and 24 of the "Regulations of Guangdong Province's SEZs" allocating SEZ management responsibility to the provincial government also were retained. The top leaders of Shenzhen, including the first party secretary and the mayor, were still transferred from Guangzhou. The Provincial People's Congress continued to approve SEZ rules and regulations. The Guangdong provincial government also organized the first major conference on the SEZs, convened in June 1982. Guangdong and Fujian cadres and academics at the conference discussed both justifications for establishing the SEZs and development strategy.[159] By 30 October 1982, Chen Yun agreed that "the SEZs must be run, and run better[,] by continually evaluating experience."[160]

Guangdong and Fujian were thus allowed to continue the decentralization policies of 1979. After 1982, however, the central government played a more important supervisory role. The two provinces were allowed "to be daring," but only within certain limits. The statement on domestic economic policy that Chen Yun presented on 2 December 1982 aptly described the situation. "From now on," he said, "we will continue to implement the policy of enlivening the domestic economy. We will continue to give full play to the regulatory power of the market. We will also prevent any attempts to disregard the state plan. . . . It is like the relationship between a bird and its cage. You cannot keep the bird in your hand since it will die. You must let it fly. But you can only let him fly inside the cage, otherwise he will fly away."[161] While Mao Zedong rejected Chen Yun's moderate approach to experimentation and reform in the 1950s, Chen Yun was more successful in balancing Deng's *maojin* (rash advance) approach to opening. Yet during the next several years,

Chen Yun would be increasingly unable to preserve the planned economy from the new outward-oriented development strategy.

Coping with New Circumstances

While Beijing did not grant the coastal leaders the same powers enjoyed by Guangdong and Fujian, it is clear that as early as 1982 Zhao Ziyang was developing a coherent national development strategy that envisioned the coastal regions as integrated with the international economy while the interior regions remained protected and gradually developed through the trickling in of technology from the coastal regions. The next step in the process was the promulgation of Central Committee document 84.13, from 4 May 1984, that announced the opening of the coastal regions to foreign investment and the establishment of a form of export-promotion zone, the ETDZs. Eventually, in January 1988, Zhao Ziyang officially announced the coastal development strategy, which was the culmination of the complex learning process that led to China's outward-oriented development.

While the crisis of 1982 interrupted the transition from an inward-to an outward-oriented development regime, elites used the period between 1982 and 1984 to study the problems encountered with the SEZs and decentralization and change their approach. The crisis also brought about a division within the Third Plenum coalition, with the split between international Leninists, like Zhao Ziyang and Hu Yaobang, who favored more market-oriented development, and moderate bureaucratic Stalinists, like Chen Yun, who favored more plan-oriented development. As a paramount leader who valued consensus, Deng Xiaoping finessed the disagreements between these factions to prevent the same cycling of development strategies that dominated the pre-1978 period. He co-opted Chen Yun's criticisms and would not approve the establishment of a new SEZ until 1987; euphemisms for the market economy, such as "market socialism," would be prevalent during this period.

Although Chen Yun had been promoting a bureaucratic Stalinist strategy of moderate, steady economic growth guided by the state plan since the 1950s, he gradually accepted Deng's expansion of the decentralization experiments with market-oriented reforms during the 1980s. As paramount leader, Deng was finally free to promote market-oriented development, about which he had gained a basic understanding when he was in France and the USSR in the 1920s. Just as he had supported Mao's revolutionary Stalinism in the 1950s to promote the Great Leap Forward, Deng now supported the international Leninists, led by Premier Zhao Ziyang, to open the economy to the market and the outside world.[162]

CHAPTER FOUR

Coastal Expansion, 1983–88

As the cohesiveness of the internationalist elite coalition deteriorated after 1981, the leadership in Beijing split into two elite opinion groups, the international Leninists and the moderate bureaucratic Stalinists, with Deng Xiaoping in overall control as paramount leader. Between 1982 and 1983 Deng moderated differences between the two groups by continuing the process of reviewing and readjusting, phase four of the Guangdong and Fujian decentralization experiments. Readjustments included the dramatic construction of "second-line" barriers between the Shenzhen SEZ and Guangdong's Bao'an county. He also approved the one-year Anti–Spiritual Pollution Campaign, starting in spring 1983, to combat Western ideological pollution which in the words of Stuart Schram was intended as a "remedy for the 'crisis of faith'" in the party and to "prevent experiments in democratization from getting out of hand."[1] During this period, the moderate bureaucratic Stalinists successfully prevented the international Leninists from expanding decentralization and the SEZ experiments, which they believed would lead to chaos in the national economy.

Yet Zhao Ziyang and the international Leninists were building an alternate vision in which China would treat foreign trade and investment as "engines" for domestic development. From the very beginning of the decentralization experiment, Zhao Ziyang had envisioned the coastal regions as absorbing foreign investment and producing goods for the international market. More integrated with the international market, the coastal economies would act as "practical laboratories" in which China could experiment with foreign technology and management techniques. Protected from international competition, the interior regions would concentrate on production for domestic consumption, and also implement technical and management renovations based on the coastal experiment.

By 1984 Deng Xiaoping was satisfied with the readjustment of the decentralization experiment and allowed a temporary abatement of the party rectification campaign.[2] Undoubtedly Chen Yun and the moderate critics were deeply offended and would never forgive Deng's protégé General Secretary Hu Yaobang for criticizing their "leftist" influences within the party, and for using the Anti–Spiritual Pollution Campaign to impugn the economic reform agenda. Hu Yaobang had already defended the SEZ initiative in early 1982 against Chen Yun's criticisms by championing the continuation of the experiment.[3] However, Deng temporarily silenced Chen Yun and permitted Zhao's radical expansion of the decentralization experiment.

Moving forward, Deng initiated phase five of the complex learning process, expansion, which included expanding the scope of the decentralization experiments and outward-oriented development to China's entire coast, from Dalian on the Bohai Sea to Hainan and Beihai on the Gulf of Tonkin. Elites in Beijing envisioned Guangdong and Fujian and their SEZs as important experimental hothouses for the coastal and national economic reforms. Having waited five years to participate in the decentralization experiment that began in 1979, the coastal economies now established fourteen open coastal cities, the economic and technological development zones, and three open coastal economic regions (*jingji kaifang qu*) that would be more fully integrated into the global economy. Phase five's expansion eventually included the establishment of China's fifth SEZ and newest province, the island of Hainan.

These initiatives formed the basis of the economic policy Zhao Ziyang outlined in "The strategic thinking concerning China's coastal areas developing an outward oriented economy," approved by Deng Xiaoping on 23 January 1988.[4] Zhao's plan would move China's outward-oriented policies from the experimentation phase into the formal adoption phase and initiate the shift in the 1990s to a consultative economic paradigm (discussed in chapter 5).

The Initial Coastal Development Strategy

As early as the issue of State Council document 1979.202, "Regulations on the Problems of Devoting a Major Effort to Expand Foreign Trade and Foreign Exchange Revenue" in August 1979, elite leaders had envisioned transforming the coastal regions into "a mighty export base . . . [that would] possess advanced technology and favorable production conditions to produce a large quantity of competitive, high quality goods."[5] Beijing, Tianjin, Shanghai, Guangdong, Jiangsu, Zhejiang, and Shandong were specifically ordered to develop more capital-intensive products for export, especially high-quality precision goods. While all areas were given increased plan-oriented incentives to export, only Guangdong and Fujian were allowed to experiment with export special zones—later renamed SEZs. The SEZs were specifically designed to attract foreign investment from the overseas Chinese community, businesspeople from Hong Kong and Macao, and other foreign manufacturers; other "qualified" areas were initially limited to establishing overseas Chinese investment companies.

Document 1979.202 also identified Shanghai's Chongming Island in the Yangtze River estuary as an SEZ, but such a zone was never established. In his memoirs, Zhao Ziyang explains,

> Originally, there were to be more SEZs along the coastal regions, including around Shanghai and in Zhejiang province. But Chen Yun said those areas were not to establish SEZs. This region, as Chen Yun put it, was famous for its concentration of opportunists who would, with their consummate skills, emerge from their cages if given the slightest chance. The Research Office of the Secretariat directed by Deng Liqun also collected material that attempted to prove that the SEZs would degenerate into "foreign concession zones." At one point, these criticisms were widespread, a result of the influence of Chen Yun and Deng Liqun.[6]

Just as Chen Yun had stopped the development of Fujian's second SEZ, Langqi on the Min River estuary near the provincial capital of Fuzhou, Chen Yun's objections killed the Shanghai SEZ proposed on the Yangtze

River. Regional leaders had thus focused on gaining greater decision-making authority and not on establishing their own SEZs.

One month later, in August 1980, the State Import-Export Commission released State Council document 1979.233, "The Report of the Beijing, Tianjin, and Shanghai Export Work Conference."[7] To overcome inefficiency and bureaucratic obstacles, the SIEC suggested that the local trade bureaus and the MFT form a partnership to manage the local import-export corporations; the municipalities could formulate their foreign trade procurement and export revenue plans as well as export, via the local import-export corporation, less important and lower volume export goods. The three cities could approve compensation trade, technology, and equipment imports valued at US$3 million. A second Beijing, Tianjin, and Shanghai export conference in 1980 focused solely on plan-oriented reforms and incentives to increase exports.[8] As 22 percent of total national export revenue was derived from these three municipalities in the late 1970s, Beijing was willing to provide the three cities with only very limited foreign economic autonomy.

Regional leaders had lobbied Beijing to expand the Guangdong and Fujian decentralization experiment and grant their areas increased decision-making authority in domestic and foreign economic activities. These requests coincided with Central Committee and State Council discussions concerning problems in implementing an economic readjustment of the Ten-Year Plan and formulating the Sixth Five-Year Plan. The timing of the regional requests was ill-fated, as Beijing leaders were also dealing with mounting economic crimes within the two southern provinces, a situation that had exacerbated the growing rift between Chen Yun's moderate view and Deng's more rash approach to China's opening.

As the newly appointed premier, Zhao Ziyang recognized the need to provide an intellectual justification for enlarging the coastal decentralization experiment, whose original purpose in the early 1980s was to discover alternate ways to finance China's ISI development. As the Guangdong party leader in the 1950s and 1960s, Zhao Ziyang had seen the development potential of the coastal economy.[9] Overseas Chinese remittances from Hong Kong and Southeast Asia established schools and improved infrastructure in the province in the 1950s, and overseas Chinese capital built twenty-one enterprises in Guangdong that produced 130 different products, worth RMB 71 million, between 1955 and 1956.[10] In the early 1960s the Central Committee approved Zhao's request to expand the Importation of Materials to Develop Export Industries (*Yijin yangchu*) program for processing imported goods for reexport, which contributed to Guangdong's economic recovery following the Great Leap Forward. Reminiscing on this time, Zhao stated, "I believed strongly back then that there was a huge potential in foreign trade for the coastal regions. Our system and policies had suffocated it. It wasn't for lack of opportunity, or because it had been impossible, but rather because it had not been permitted."[11] When he was appointed party secretary of Sichuan in 1975, Zhao successfully experimented with market economic reforms that reenergized the moribund Sichuan economy in the mid- to late 1970s.[12] Strongly supported by Deng and Chen Yun, Zhao continued to implement his visionary outlook, which eventually resulted in the coastal development strategy and a transition to a cooperative economic paradigm.

Premier Zhao Ziyang outlined his long-term development vision in an important speech to the State Council in April 1981.[13] Zhao discussed in detail nine different economic problems that China's leaders must consider when formulating their new economic policies, including the need to produce more consumer goods; to readjust the traditional emphasis on heavy industry; to conserve energy—especially oil; to fully utilize older infrastructure; and to emphasize market and administrative mechanisms to encourage growth. Among the problems he identified, Zhao described the fifth one as "Finding a reasonable division of labor between the coastal and interior areas to bring into play their strengths." Zhao argued that while the world in the 1980s was talking about the "north-south dialogue," China was dealing with a difference between its developed eastern coastal economy and backward western economy. China's leaders had to create a division of labor in which each area could use its strengths to accelerate the country's development.

In thinking about the future role of the coastal areas, Zhao "wondered what would happen if the coastal regions were all oriented toward developing export-oriented industries."[14] He initially focused on the top urban economic centers—such as Shanghai, Tianjin, and Guangzhou—which the State Council had started to address with State Council documents 1979.233 and 1980.145. Zhao argued that these coastal urban areas should be further opened so they could more easily follow the development pathway taken by Japan, South Korea, and Singapore. Citing the foreign trade promotion and export-processing strategies employed since the early 1960s to earn foreign exchange, such as the *Yijin yangchu* program, Zhao argued that these areas initially should import the raw materials and various components needed to process goods for export. Then, by gradually increasing the domestic content of such exports, China would be able to increase employment and foreign exchange reserves. The government would facilitate the areas' connections with the international marketplace by enacting policies to encourage their exports, including establishing more foreign trade export bases, specialized factories, and workshops to produce higher-quality export items at lower manufacturing costs. Zhao and China's leaders had accumulated two decades of experience using such export-promotion strategies and thus appreciated how they could increase foreign exchange reserves and promote higher levels of management and technology expertise.

As for the underdeveloped interior economy, Zhao argued that it should increase production of traditional exports while concurrently developing new exports. With its abundant natural resources and large market, the interior economy had improved its basic infrastructure over the preceding three decades and could now increase the country's overall productive capacity. As the coastal economy transitioned away from its traditional emphasis on heavy industry toward producing more sophisticated export goods, the country would establish a division of labor in which the interior economy would assume responsibility for producing goods needed by the domestic economy, which would cause the urban coastal cities, such as Shanghai, Tianjin, and Qingdao, to stop expanding their production of cotton textiles, for example. Said Zhao, "You don't want one side to eat both the coarse and refined grain. . . . [L]et others have their fill as well."

Zhao was concerned that the interior economy might monopolize the supply of raw materials, such as tobacco and cotton, which would prevent supplies from reaching the coastal factories producing well-known brands. More sensitive to Chen Yun's objections than Hu Yaobang was, Zhao argued that the interior economy must be developed in a planned and gradual fashion. It must continue to provide raw materials and goods to the coastal economy in accordance with the plan; once those planned targets were met, then the coastal and interior economies could discuss the disposition of excess materials and goods.

Several months later, while discussing coastal development during a meeting of the Central Party Secretariat in July 1981, Zhao again invoked the Hong Kong, Taiwan, and Singapore development model that combined exports and imports by engaging in export processing and assembly. While Guangdong and Fujian were developing along a separate path, the coastal areas had to discover how to carry out fundamental structural reforms.

> I told a Shanghai comrade that Shanghai enjoyed the best conditions to be primarily outward-oriented. The Shanghai area, with more than 100 million people, can truly revitalize the front lines of foreign trade. . . . Foreign trade reforms cannot be uniformly imposed. I suggest that of all the coastal cities, we first relax restrictions on Shanghai and Tianjin, especially by giving them more decision-making powers in export processing and assembly, production and marketing, domestic and foreign trade. I suggest that Shanghai become a Western clothing trust [tuolasi], process imported materials for export, and do its own production and marketing. Shanghai-brand Handkerchiefs has already established a company that combines manufacturing and trade.[15]

Zhao realized that while the coastal economy was developing at a faster rate, it was the interior economy that had the greatest potential for growth. Thus, he believed, interior industrialists needed to realize their potential by studying the example of coastal industry, such as Shanghai's comparatively advanced levels of management and technological know-how. Because of its history, Shanghai and other coastal urban economic centers had always been more developed and accumulated more management and technical knowledge, through which they achieved greater production efficiency than the rest of China. "Shanghai's average gross domestic product per person was US$1,600, while Tianjin averaged US$900 and Beijing US$1,000. Shanghai profits rates topped 57.6 percent, which was over double the amount earned in Beijing and Tianjin, over four times the rate earned by Guangzhou, and six times [that] earned by Wuhan."[16] Zhao argued that if everyone could be as efficient as Shanghai, the production and profit rates of the national economy would double.

Coinciding with the U.S. Reagan administration's implementation of supply-side or "trickle-down" economics, which reduced taxes on high-income earners with the expectation that the benefits would trickle down to the lower-income citizens, Zhao proffered a geographical "trickle-down" strategy for China's economic and technological transformation.[17] Naturally China should study the most advanced technology from abroad, Zhao determined, but at the same time it needed to decide which technology was most appropriate for China's level of development. Zhao was aware that foreign analysts had argued that countries in the developing world should import not the most advanced technologies but only the technology appropriate for that country's level of development, so that it could be absorbed and utilized efficiently. Some Chinese elites had learned this lesson while establishing ISI projects since the 1950s. Zhao applied this argument to the relationship between China's coastal and interior economies. While Shanghai had the ability to absorb advanced foreign technology, interior economies should focus on already existing technologies available in the coastal areas; they did not need to purchase advanced technology from abroad. Zhao thought it far more appropriate for the interior economies to improve their production capacity by absorbing and adapting existing technology and experiences as they came to them from Shanghai. Thus he asked the State Planning Commission and other bureaucracies to establish programs to send leaders, managers, and technicians from the interior economies to Shanghai and other coastal cities, where they could choose from what Zhao described as providing a never-ending smorgasbord of technological and managerial methods appropriate for the domestic Chinese palate.

Finally, Zhao Ziyang suggested that the coastal and interior economies should establish various forms of economic exchange, including jointly managed firms, technology and personnel transfer agreements, and consulting services. Zhao realized that China's underdeveloped production and distribution system meant that Shanghai and the coastal economies were producing various goods for the coastal markets but were unable to supply the interior markets. After two decades of semi-autarkic strategies, especially the Third Front during the 1960s and 1970s, China's distribution system was provincially oriented, with goods produced in one area nearly impossible to find outside that home province, no matter how well they were made.[18] In effect, each province had implemented an ISI strategy, but instead of developing an independent production base to substitute for imports from abroad, many provinces had established production bases to substitute for imports from other provinces.

Zhao thus argued that coastal industries could provide the technology to jointly manage industries with interior companies, which would provide the industrial site, labor, and raw materials. They also could negotiate various technology transfer agreements, such as the one that existed between two textile manufacturers located in Shanghai and Yichang, Hubei's second largest city, located on the Yangtze River. The Shanghai business provided personnel with expertise in design, equipment installation, and management for a two-year period, and in return received a portion of the Yichang manufacturer's profits during that time. The Shanghai textile concern guaranteed that 80 percent of the Yichang factory's textiles would be first-quality goods within the first year of operation. The third method of economic exchange was consulting: industries could plan the transfer of talented personnel from the coastal economy to the interior, including retired workers who have years of valuable experience—which had been a practice promoted by the state since the 1950s to transfer Han people to Xinjiang and the west.[19] In this way, coastal economies could provide consulting services through which interior areas could gain managerial and technical advice on how to develop their economy.

Readjusting the Coastal Development Strategy: 1982

The leaders of nine coastal areas—Beijing, Tianjin, Shanghai, Liaoning, Hebei, Shandong, Jiangsu, Zhejiang, and Guangxi—met with leaders of the State Planning Commission, the State Economic Commission, the SIEAC, and the ministries of finance, foreign trade, and communications in November 1981. The leaders undoubtedly hoped that their areas, too, would enjoy the preferential policies granted to Guangdong and Fujian.

Two months later, with the Emergency Circular of 11 January 1982, Deng Xiaoping agreed with the moderate bureaucratic Stalinists to implement a two-year reassessment of the coastal experiment and institute the socialist Spiritual Civilization Campaign. Several days after the January 1982 Political Bureau meeting and Hu Yaobang's speech on foreign economic relations, the Central Committee and State Council issued "The Summary of the Conference of Nine Provinces, Cities, and Special Administrative Regions on Foreign Economic Trade Work."[20] Deng had agreed with Chen Yun that they needed to consolidate control and examine the problems encountered with Guangdong and Fujian's decentralization experiment. Only once they had learned how to overcome these problems would the elites then consider granting the coastal regions greater decision-making authority. Zhao Ziyang thus had to delay his vision for coastal development.[21]

Analysis of the Central Committee's summary attached to the coastal conference circular clearly indicates the impact of the 1982 crisis on elites' attitudes toward expanding decentralization. Building on previous themes of developing foreign trade and the coastal economy, the committee wrote:

> Conditions must be ripe to approve the implementation of self-managed foreign trade, in establishing local fiscal responsibility and assuming responsibility for profits and losses. We especially wish to emphasize that the more initiative is inspired at all levels, the greater the superiority of the socialist system and planned economy will manifest itself to be; this will strengthen unity, coordination, and management, and maintain a united front to the outside. Every managing organization must adopt effective measures to rectify quickly problems that harm our country's reputation and allow "fertile water to drain onto other's land."[22]

This is an interesting reaffirmation of the superiority of the planned economy and Chen Yun's views of economic development, especially the reference to his May 1961 speech concerning the management of foreign trade.[23]

During the ensuing two years of evaluation and readjustment of the decentralization experiment, elites tightened their macromanagement of domestic and foreign economic policy. The country also underwent the Sturm und Drang created by the Anti–Spiritual Pollution Campaign. Anecdotal evidence suggests local provincial governments, as in Guangzhou, remained dissatisfied with the slow pace of decentralization and continued to pursue decentralization privileges.[24]

Readjustment and Spiritual Pollution: 1982–84

During the fourth phase, readjustment, Beijing elites approved a few important initiatives to strengthen coastal exports and the SEZ investment climate. While unable to expand the decentralization experiment to the entire Chinese coast, the Central Committee's coastal conference circular of 15 January 1982 instructed provincial leaders to increase their percentage of reprocessed finished goods to 50 to 60 percent of total foreign trade exports. Noting that 45 percent of China's industrial enterprises were in these eleven provinces, cities, and autonomous regions, elites put a renewed emphasis on renovating the medium- and small-scale industrial enterprises using foreign technology. Along with the newly empowered Liaoning province, Beijing, Tianjin, and Shanghai's authority to approve technology and equipment imports was increased from US$3 million in imports to US$5 million; the other coastal entities were granted the right to import equipment and technology valued up to US$3 million. Furthermore, the coastal leaders were instructed to promote greater integration with the interior regions (*jingji lianhe*). The coastal areas would "transfer production technology in a planned way to the interior. This included production technology, production manuals, technological secrets, and the dispatch of skilled technicians to provide instructions." Most important, the leadership declared that "Beijing, Tianjin, Shanghai, and the important municipalities in the coastal areas must provide goods targeted for foreign markets. Interior factories, for the most part, will target the needs of the domestic market."[25] In December 1982, the National People's Congress approved the State Council's decision to open the port cities of Nantong and Zhangjiagang, on the Yangtze River, to foreign ships.[26]

Beijing also approved the geographical expansion of the Zhuhai SEZ in 1983, but, as mentioned, no major Central Committee or State Council work conference was convened on the provincial decentralization experiment and the SEZs.[27]

Four days after the Central Committee and State Council approved the promulgation of document 1983.11 that outlined the economic development of Hainan Island, they also put forward one of the first innovative expansions of SEZ policy since January 1982.[28] While promising the utmost discretion so that Taiwanese investors would not be prosecuted by the government of the Republic of China, the State Council issued document 1983.57, granting special privileges to Taiwanese investors in the SEZs.[29] Taiwanese-invested enterprises—whether 100 percent Taiwanese-owned, joint ventures, or other cooperative arrangements—that planned to be in operation over a ten-year period would enjoy tax-free status for the first four years and a 50 percent discount from the fifth to the tenth year; for five years, they would not be required to pay land-use fees. Most important, these Taiwanese-financed companies were granted partial access to the domestic Chinese market—30 percent of any goods produced by Taiwanese-invested entities that used imported materials or advanced technology could be sold in China. Finally, any Taiwanese entity that invested in the older industries located in the older urban areas of Zhuhai, Shantou, and Xiamen would be allowed to import materials tax free from abroad and would be taxed at a rate of only 15 percent. The nascent coastal strategy had always envisioned the use of overseas Chinese investment and investment from Hong Kong and Macao. But State Council document 1983.57 was a major step toward promoting greater economic integration with the Taiwanese economy and establishing a new Greater Chinese economy.

However, the Anti–Spiritual Pollution Campaign of 1983 briefly interrupted new innovations in Zhao Ziyang's coastal development strategy. Elites instigated a series of ideological campaigns focused on the impact of "unhealthy" political and economic influences on the perceived legitimacy of communist ideology.[30] Following the suppression of the Democracy Wall movement in 1979, Hu Qiaomu, Deng Liqun, and moderate bureaucratic Stalinists had promoted a campaign against bourgeois liberalism at the December 1980 work conference in order to "suppress opinions on the subject of political system reform" and to

focus on the "elimination of the influence of feudalism."[31] This an-
nouncement had coincided with the Political Bureau's decision to accuse
Hua Guofeng of "having committed 'leftist' mistakes and others, but
not mistakes of political lines" and to announce his resignation.[32] With
the Emergency Circular of January 1982, they once again saw an opportunity to expand their campaign against "spiritual pollution."[33]

Deng Xiaoping shared Chen Yun's concern about an ideological
"weakening" within the state. During his speech to the Second Plenum
of the Twelfth Party Congress on 12 October 1983, Deng Xiaoping noted
that "within the Party, there still are quite a few important problems that
have yet to be cleared up or resolved," including remaining "leftist" problems from the Cultural Revolution, the more recent problems of crimi-
nality, and "spiritual pollution" and the corrosive influence of bourgeois
ideology, which posed an ominous threat to the party and the state.[34]
With the apparent support of Chen Yun, Deng Liqun expanded the campaign to attack all aspects of the reforms promoted by Hu Yaobang and
Zhao Ziyang, including the decentralization experiment and the SEZs.

Initiating Phase Five: Deng's First *Nanxun*

In a demonstration of his absolute authority as paramount leader, Deng
pushed aside objections from his close cohort, Chen Yun, for whom he
retained a high degree of respect. Deng unilaterally ended the phase
four readjustment process, including the campaign against spiritual
pollution, to initiate the fifth phase of the decentralization experiment:
expansion. Deng never embarrassed Chen Yun or attacked him like
Mao had attacked Zhou Enlai and Chen Yun for opposing his vision
of rash advance—*maojin*—in 1958.[35] Mao Zedong had readily dis-
mantled the Yan'an Roundtable to enact his revolutionary Stalinist
vision of the Great Leap Forward. As paramount leader, Deng did not
dismantle but "selectively" ignored the Third Plenum consensus of 1979
to enact Zhao Ziyang's vision of a socialist market economy that combined ideas of bureaucratic Stalinism and the NEP.

Deng's 1984 decision to disregard Chen Yun's concerns about the
decentralization experiment was no doubt influenced by two interre-
lated deadlines. Deng fully understood that Central Committee/State

Council document 1979.50 had approved the implementation of the Guangdong and Fujian decentralization experiment for only five years. By the end of 1984, leaders in Beijing had to decide whether to extend the experiment for another five years.

Deng also faced a self-imposed deadline regarding Hong Kong, which he considered extremely important to Chinese sovereignty and its reputation abroad.[36] Deng thus directly challenged British prime minister Margaret Thatcher on 24 September 1982 by announcing that China would take back Hong Kong—not just the New Territories but also Hong Kong Island and Kowloon—by 1997: "This of course won't happen today, but within one or two years China must formally announce Hong Kong's return."[37] Although in November 1983 the Thatcher government conceded that there would not be a British government presence in Hong Kong after 1997, the two sides continued negotiating into 1984. Deng Xiaoping and Zhao Ziyang had agreed that the successful implementation of the Guangdong and Fujian decentralization experiment was directly connected to the successful reunification of Hong Kong, Macao, and Taiwan with the mainland. They viewed the Shenzhen SEZ as an intermediary between capitalist Hong Kong and the mainland's command economy. To demonstrate how this would work, and to pacify British negotiators as well as Hong Kong citizens and capitalists, Deng enunciated the "one country, two systems" principle as it would apply to Hong Kong in discussions with Hong Kong businesspeople in June 1984.[38] Almost two years to the day after Deng had laid down his ultimatum to Prime Minister Thatcher, negotiators signed the draft of the Sino-British Joint Declaration, which was officially signed on 19 December 1984.[39] Deng was realizing his vision of a reunified, more market-oriented China; Hong Kong was to be integrated into the Chinese economy and would act as an engine of trade and development.

In 1984 Deng also entrusted Zhao Ziyang and the international Leninists to expand Zhao's strategy of coastal development. Deng ended the Anti–Spiritual Pollution Campaign and reenergized the provincial decentralization experiments.[40] He approved the nationwide expansion of an agricultural responsibility system, expanded state-owned enterprise reforms, approved another five years for the Guangdong and Fujian decentralization experiment and their SEZs, expanded the decentralization experiment to each of the coastal provinces, and agreed to the reunification with Hong Kong.[41] According to Zhou's memoirs,

> In 1985, taking things a step further, we eliminated the mandatory procurement program in agriculture, and basically became market oriented, freed from the planned economy, with the exception of a few products like cotton. The emergence of township and village enterprises, private manufacturing and commercial enterprises, joint ventures and solely owned foreign enterprises—all of these were set up outside the planned economy. Together they formed an economic sector that responded only to market forces. . . . [T]he other important aspect was the reduction of the planned economic sector. The change was not instantaneous. Instead it began with a small number of minor changes, but it gradually involved bigger changes. Policies and measures were introduced to shift more power to lower levels of administration and expand the autonomy of enterprises. To reform economic planning, there was a gradual reduction of direct planning, an expansion of indirect planning, a reduction in material resources allocated by the state, and an expansion of the types of quantities of products that were traded by SOEs themselves. . . . In addition, we also introduced a contract scheme for enterprises and pricing reform. All of these measures played strong ancillary roles while the market sector continued to grow.[42]

As paramount leader, Deng had the ability to "launch sudden, surprising, and dramatic personal initiatives."[43] With his first official visit to the south—or *nanxun*—in 1984, Deng initiated phase five to facilitate Zhao Ziyang's international Leninist vision of Chinese development.

During the Chinese Spring Festival from 24 January to 5 February 1984, Deng, along with Yang Shangkun and Wang Zhen, carried out a widely publicized visit to Shenzhen, Zhongshan, Zhuhai, and Guangzhou.[44] After the festival Deng and Wang Zhen continued on to Xiamen, where Deng urged quicker development. In Shanghai, he visited the Baoshan Iron and Steel complex that he had promoted under Hua Guofeng's New Great Leap and praised its use of foreign technology and innovation. They returned to Beijing on 16 February.[45] Assuming personal responsibility for the opening strategy and the zones, Deng inspected the decentralization experiment to evaluate the criticisms that the zones were hotbeds of bourgeois liberalism and corruption.

After listening to Shenzhen mayor Liang Xiang explain during his visit that Shenzhen's industrial output had doubled between 1982 and 1983, and subsequently inspecting the building site of China's largest skyscraper to date—the city's fifty-three-story International Trade Building—Deng reportedly stated, "After seeing all of this, I now fully understand" (*Kanjianle, wo dou kan qingchule*). Remarking that Shenzhen had recently succeeded in restoring order and that even Hong Kong refugees were beginning to return to China, Deng sought to defuse the impact of the recent spiritual pollution campaign. Deng guaranteed Shenzhen's future by writing, "The development and experience of Shenzhen has proven that our policy of establishing the SEZs is correct"; he wrote a similar, more cogent inscription for Zhuhai, which Deng described simply as "good."[46]

Reporting back to the Beijing elite on 24 February, Deng stated,

> On this visit to Shenzhen, I had the impression of an area of *amazing development*. The speed of Shenzhen's construction is very fast, especially in Shekou. The reason is that we gave them a bit of autonomy, and they could take responsibility for projects under US$5 million. Their slogan is, "Time is money, and efficiency is life." When Shenzhen builds a building, it only takes a couple of days to build one floor and in just a few days a whole building is completed. The workers all came from the interior of China. Yet the reason they work efficiently is because they have implemented a contract system, where benefits and penalties are clearly delineated.[47]

He encouraged the physical expansion of the Xiamen SEZ and said Beijing should even consider making it a "free port." In addition, Deng made one of the most quoted statements to be found in all subsequent Chinese writings, "Spiritual civilization comes from material civilization" (*Jingshen wenming shi cong wuzhi wenming laide ma*):

> The SEZs are windows to the outside world. They are windows of technology, they are windows of management techniques, they are windows of knowledge, and they are windows of foreign policy. From the SEZs, we can import technology, acquire knowledge, and master management techniques. Management is a means of knowledge. The SEZs have

become our base for the opening, and not just economic opening but also in the training of personnel, which is very beneficial for us. Also, they are a way for us to expand our influence abroad. I have heard it said that Shenzhen's public order has improved, and that the people who escaped to Hong Kong are now returning. One of the reasons is the vast improvement of employment opportunities, [also] an increase in salaries and the rise in material standards of living. In effect one can see that spiritual civilization comes from material civilization . . . right![48]

Deng's 1984 *nanxun*, or tour of the south, to visit the SEZs was an instantaneous hit across the country. Books for sale at the Beijing Wangfujing Xinhua Bookstore extolled Deng's trip as if he were Moses parting the Red Sea so his people could venture forth to seek the truth.[49]

Deng's promotion of Yuan Geng's Shekou slogan "Time is money, efficiency is life" encapsulated his view that one could simultaneously build spiritual civilization while making money. During the thirty-fifth anniversary of the founding of the People's Republic, in October 1984, Deng's support for the new reforms was put on display for the entire world to see. Standing on the reviewing stand at the Tiananmen Gate where Mao had blessed hundreds of thousands of Red Guards during the Cultural Revolution, Deng and the revolutionary elites first admired the symbols of China's strength as demonstrated by its goose-stepping soldiers, trucks towing China's ICBMs and MRBMs, and China's Soviet-era fighter-bombers flying along Chang'an Avenue. The demonstration of China's modernizing military was followed by a massive parade of groups and floats celebrating China's history and achievements, especially its more recent agricultural and industrial reforms.

Yet there was one unforgettable float from the Shenzhen SEZ's Shekou Industrial Zone that drew attention, as it displayed just twelve large Chinese characters, representing "*Shijian jiu shi jinqian, xiaolü jiu shi shengming*" (Time is money, efficiency is life). A multitude of highly spirited young people spontaneously danced around this ideologically risky float, which had a great impact on the Chinese spectators. Onlookers broke into genuine applause for the enthusiastic youths and the ideas represented by the float. They were celebrating both a genuine end to the Cultural Revolution and the country's passionate embrace of economic change.[50]

Ten months after Deng Xiaoping's first *nanxun*, Zhao Ziyang visited Guangdong in November 1984 to investigate the current state of the decentralization experiment and to discuss with the provincial party committee how Guangdong, the Pearl River Delta area, and the Shenzhen and Zhuhai SEZs could play a larger role in promoting national economic reforms. After remarking on the great improvement in Guangdong's living standards since his visit in 1982, Zhao praised the province's social order and "spiritual manner." Like Deng, Zhao highly applauded the speed with which buildings and various infrastructure projects in the Pearl River Delta area had been completed.

In addition to learning about local infrastructure construction methods, Zhao was particularly impressed by Guangdong's price reforms, which the Third Plenum of the Twelfth Central Committee had decided were the key to reforming China's national economy.[51] To establish a plan-guided economy rather than a plan-directed one, China needed to establish a rational pricing system that could influence industrial production decisions and yet not bring about wide-scale inflation. Praising Guangdong's experimentation with the reforms, Zhao remarked,

> You all in Guangdong have some good experiences dealing with pricing reforms. Because there had been an increase in the people's income, people have had a greater ability to absorb the pricing reforms. The other day we were talking about the price of vegetables in the Guangzhou marketplace being completely free to fluctuate. In Beijing, vegetable prices would have risen by 30 percent and this would have been very problematic. However, in Guangzhou there really wasn't a big problem. When it comes to economic structural reform, we must follow what Comrade Xiaoping has stated. First carry out reforms in a certain local area, and should they succeed, expand the area of implementation. Take one step at a time. Take a step, look, and take the next step. If you take a step that results in something good, then take the next step. If there are any missteps, then make some changes and proceed ahead. Comrade Xiaoping's words are very important. We currently are undergoing the experimentation-implementation phase in our economic structural reforms. The [1984 Third Plenum] "Decision" put forward the road to reform but did not provide concrete details. In the end, we can know the path only through implementation, understanding of problems, and

reimplementation. In our reforms, Guangdong is in an excellent position to provide experience from which the whole country can learn. That includes negative experiences. The case of the opening up of the Guangzhou vegetable market is an excellent example. All the SEZs and the coastal areas must provide the country with their experiences in opening and reforming the economy.[52]

Zhao Ziyang subsequently promoted the strategy that Guangdong and the coastal areas should link their efforts to import capital, knowledge, and technology (*waiyin*) for developing China's infrastructure and modernizing its industries with those domestic enterprises that use both domestic and foreign inputs (*neilian*) to manufacture goods for the domestic and export markets. To help link domestic industries with foreign advanced technology and management techniques, the *waiyin neilian* enterprises could filter (*guolü*) or sift through (*shaixuan*) various technologies and management techniques and select those most appropriate for adoption in the interior economy. While based in the SEZs and the coastal areas, they would be given authority to cross provincial and ministerial barriers to promote domestic economic development. Perhaps influenced by the past, Zhao's approach seems similar to the three-fronts concept of development used during the previous decades to describe economic planning: the first and second importation fronts would be the SEZs and the coastal provinces, while the third front, in this case, would be the interior economy.[53]

Following his discussions with party leaders in Guangzhou, Zhao traveled to Shenzhen, where he spoke to party and municipal leaders on 27 November 1984. In his speech, Zhao reiterated Shenzhen's long-term goals: "(1) to be a 'window' [to bring foreign technology, management techniques, and so on into China], and (2) to provide experience to aid the country's reforms." Reflecting on the past two years of party rectification and the Anti–Spiritual Pollution Campaign, Zhao stated,

The SEZs must pay special attention to building both a material and spiritual civilization. The building of a socialist spiritual civilization is very important. Is it true that once people become wealthy spiritual civilization declines? I don't think so. Japanese social practices are far better than America's, which are just awful. Hong Kong's social practices are not any better. Singapore is a bit better. They promote Confucianism and emphasize respect for one's parents. For material civilization the Singaporeans study the West, but they also preserve Eastern culture. We want to catch up to the developed countries by importing foreign technology from the developed Western capitalist countries. However, we absolutely cannot transfer everything from Western countries. We cannot promote feudal morality but must preserve and carry forward the Chinese civilization and its fine traditions.

Zhao commiserated with party leaders and recognized that they "had suffered patiently but never wavered."[54]

Four days after Zhao Ziyang returned from inspecting Guangdong, Gu Mu traveled to Fujian, to hold more detailed talks with Guangdong, Fujian, and various Beijing ministerial officials about the progress made during the five-year SEZ experiment, and the role that Zhao Ziyang envisioned the zones would play in fulfilling the Third Plenum's economic reform plans. These were preparatory discussions for the upcoming Joint Conference on Opening the Coastal Cities and the SEZs, to be held in Fuzhou on 10 January 1985. The conference resulted in State Council document 1985.46, a circular about the "Conference Summary on Continuing Guangdong and Fujian's Carrying Out Special Policies and Flexible Measures in Foreign Trade Activities," approved on 28 March 1985. As "practice had proved that this decision was completely correct," State Council document 1985.46 authorized another five-year continuation of the experiment first approved in Central Committee/State Council document 1979.50. However, unlike the earlier document, document 1985.46 placed even greater emphasis on the success of the provincial decentralization experiment, as it "not only has a great importance for the economic development of the two provinces and the nation, but also will have a very positive influence on stabilizing Hong Kong and completing the greater task of uniting all of China."[55]

The conference document lists the two provinces' major accomplishments, including bringing in US$1.7 billion in actualized foreign investment, which represented 43 percent of China's total actualized foreign investment between 1979 and 1984. At the conference, members agreed that the central government in Beijing would (1) allow the provinces to continue to formulate their own economic plans; (2) loosen its oversight of the foreign investment approval process; (3) grant the provinces more approval rights to upgrade industrial technology; (4) continue to implement the fiscal retention scheme for Guangdong and the fiscal support scheme for Fujian; (5) allow the provincial branches of the PBOC to provide low-interest loans for capital construction and to roll over any unused credit to finance technological innovations; (6) allow the provinces to establish new financial institutions and to issue foreign bonds, and give greater authority to the Guangdong International Trust and Investment Corporation and Fujian's Investment and Enterprise Holdings Corporation; (7) increase from 25 to 30 percent the amount of foreign exchange that could be earned and retained by provinces from commodity exports; (8) expand the categories of export products that could be managed by the province, and outline procedures for the SEZs to report the import of restricted goods; (9) loosen border controls on well-known foreigners, people from Hong Kong, and overseas Chinese visitors and their luggage; and (10) give greater attention to developing direct trade and investment from Taiwan.

Although Deng had ended the 1983 Anti–Spiritual Pollution Campaign and its attempt to purge those behind the reform experiments, the moderate bureaucratic Stalinists continued to criticize the experiment, if in a more tempered tone. Attempting to influence the State Council as it deliberated extending the decentralization experiment, Hu Qiaomu visited the Xiamen SEZ in March 1985. Hu publicly praised the zone, its comprehensive development, and its role in promoting growth within the southern Fujian area. But his criticisms in general echoed other leaders at the time: Hu pointed out the need to develop economic relations with the interior areas and institute comprehensive plans for zonal development; stated that the SEZs should not establish industries that could compete with China's existing light industry, such as television and electric fan manufacturing; advocated encouraging overseas Chinese investment from Southeast Asia and expanding China's existing economic relationship with the Middle East; insisted that SEZs should follow existing rules and regulation; and said they ought to export more goods to the Hong Kong market to counter the inflow of foreign goods from Hong Kong.[56]

Yet, while he accepted Deng's desire to complete the "first stage of party rectification," Hu argued that the party needed to continue to rectify the disciplinary problems that still plagued both party and state. Foreshadowing the 1987 campaign against bourgeois liberalization, Hu was critical of the "bad customs and habits" that had arisen within Fujian and the country during the national reform process. Reviving his concerns about the "NEPmen" and bourgeois attitudes of 1982, Hu primarily criticized the new "focus on money in every activity" (*yiqie xiang qian kan*). The phrase itself was a play on an existing political slogan, "Focus on the future in every activity," with the term "future" replaced by its homonym in Chinese, "money." Hu was concerned that Chinese people and the party were more concerned about building a capitalist world than a socialist world.

> Socialist enterprises obviously need to make money, but the "focus on money in all activities" is definitely not a socialist concept. . . . [T]he problem is with "in all activities," which implies that everything from one's soul to the body's every sinew must focus on money. Then what is the difference between socialism and capitalism? We want to develop a commodity economy, which isn't the same as recognizing or tacitly accepting "focusing on money in all activities." Communist Party members, government departments, socialist enterprises must without hesitation promote the concept of serving the people and enriching the nation with all their hearts so that we can quadruple the GVIAO by 2000.[57]

As for bad habits, Hu questioned why those in government and business enterprises were spending their money on Western suits. He criticized the revival of the old and wasteful habit of sponsoring large weddings with large processions of cars, renting large guest halls that could hold dozens of tables full of guests, and wasteful spending on flowers. And he was concerned about the return of prostitution, which had been so prevalent before 1949. Not wanting to impugn the steadfastness of the Chinese people, Hu appears to argue that the prevalence of prostitution was the result of "foreigners coming here and we try to satisfy their needs. But this doesn't mean that we can satisfy everything. We not only absolutely cannot satisfy their desires for such bad things as prostitution and gambling but must strictly forbid it and must never soften our position."[58]

Hu Qiaomu's criticism of Fujian's "bad customs and habits" and the focus on making money did not influence the State Council's decision to grant the five-year extension to the coastal experiment. After all, Deng Xiaoping had given his personal approval to the decentralization experiment in 1984, which resulted in its expansion along the entire Chinese coast. However, Hu's criticisms would be revived in two years and again would threaten the international Leninist vision of decentralizing the Chinese economy and opening to the outside world.

The SEZs as Experimental Hothouses

With the initiation of the fifth phase of the complex learning process, the international Leninists needed Guangdong, Fujian, and their SEZs to play key roles in experimenting with a variety of domestic and foreign economic policy reforms. The coastal and national economies would eventually learn from their successful efforts and implement their own economic reforms.

Often, foreign analysts were critical of Shenzhen's ability to attract foreign investment and to develop the *waiyin neilian* enterprises. They said the SEZs were too isolated and lacked the required infrastructure, skilled workers, technicians, and managers. While enjoying certain benefits, the zones were still subject to certain restraints from the domestic command economy.[59] Many newly built industrial complexes throughout Shenzhen in the mid-1980s remained vacant, while the occupied factories were run by foreign and Hong Kong investors who were in Shenzhen to take advantage of low-cost land and labor and the absence of intrusive bureaucratic regulations. Shenzhen's most popular industries in the mid-1980s were simple processing and assembly operations that supplied Western markets with products like simple electronic items, Cabbage Patch dolls, and silk flowers. Academics argued that such simple operations had little beneficial spillover for the Chinese economy besides raising the salary level of unskilled workers.[60]

Such foreign criticisms were joined by internal ones . . . not from those who were worried only about "bad customs or habits," but from

those concerned that the SEZs were not attracting foreign investment. On 30 September 1986, deputy chairman of the State Planning
Commission Zhu Rongji met with a delegation from the [Hungarian]
Newspaper Publishing Company. When discussing the SEZs, Zhu
stated, "We have just started the initiative in Shenzhen, and obviously
it is not running smoothly. Newspapers published in Hong Kong only
give news about what is going wrong in the SEZs. We had the hope that
these zones would attract an abundance of foreign capital, but instead
mainly domestic capital is accumulated here. We had hopes that these
zones would focus on exports, but our hopes regarding exports have
not been fulfilled so far."[61] The following year Zhu Rongji would be
appointed mayor of Shanghai; his leadership there—which transformed Shanghai into a modern, vibrant city—eventually led to his
appointment as premier from 1998 to 2003.

The criticisms of Zhu and others were perhaps unfair, as the zones
were undergoing a fundamental transformation in the 1980s. Shenzhen,
no longer the sleepy fishing village of the late 1970s, was becoming a
modern industrial center with expanded road networks and port facilities, telecommunications, and modern housing complexes that attracted
talented couples from the interior, who after years of living apart could
finally live together as a family, in decent housing and employed in the
same city. Many were drawn by Shenzhen's proximity to Hong Kong and
the Hong Kong investment that was fueling industrial development in
Shenzhen, Dongguan, and the entire Pearl River Delta. The influx of
domestic investment, as well, and talented cadres created growth in several key economic sectors, including tourism, processing and assembly
operations, management training, and telecommunications. Various
tourist hotels, resorts, and tourist sites were established throughout the
zone to attract foreign capital from weekend visitors from Hong Kong.
Industrial managers from the SOEs attended Shenzhen-based consulta-
tion and training centers to study Shenzhen management techniques.
Shenzhen University, having hired academics from some of the top national universities and a substantial number of foreign experts from
Hong Kong and abroad, trained a new cadre of students aiming to become proficient in English, new technology, and management skills.[62]

Chinese leaders were most pleased with the foreign-financed enterprises from Taiwan, Japan, and the United States that built electronic

assembly operations in Shenzhen, including the Hon Hai Precision Industry Company—better known as Foxconn—established in 1988. Taking advantage of the preferential treatment given to Taiwanese investors as provided by State Council document 1983.57, this Taiwan-based multinational corporation initially opened a small assembly operation in Shenzhen that made use of inexpensive Guangdong workers who were bussed into the SEZ. In subsequent years, the Foxconn operation morphed into a huge, self-contained industrial complex located in Shenzhen's Longhua Science and Technology Park that assembled products for customers from all the major electronics manufacturers, ranging from Apple to Vizio. Their operations expanded into China's interior by establishing production centers in Zhengzhou, Wuhan, Beijing, Tianjin, and Guangzhou.[63] Foxconn and other multinational operations contributed to raising employment levels and training a new cadre of more technologically proficient workers.

Although it employed Chinese workers in high-tech industries, Hon Hai did not represent Zhao Ziyang's vision of a *waiyin neilian* enterprise. Instead corporations such as ZTE, Huawei, and Tencent, established in Shenzhen in the 1980s and 1990s, embodied Zhao's vision.[64] ZTE was founded in 1985, and within thirty years it would be one of the top ten global producers of smartphones. Huawei was established two years later, in 1987, and would grow to become the world's largest manufacturer of telecommunications networks and equipment in 2012.[65] While these manufacturers emerged as two of China's most prominent industrial leaders during the ensuing three decades, their rise was accompanied by various controversies. The U.S. House of Representatives Permanent Select Committee on Intelligence issued a report in 2012 claiming that Huawei had a very close working relationship with the CCP, the PLA, and the state.[66] The United States accused ZTE of establishing shell companies to ship illegal routers, microprocessors, servers, and other controlled items to the Iranians and North Koreans between 2010 and 2016. In March 2017, the U.S. secretary of commerce announced that ZTE had agreed to pay up to US$1.19 billion in civil and criminal penalties.[67] These accusations and penalties attest to the phenomenal growth of China's electronics industry, which, like other industries around the world, received strong support from the state.

Initially, Huawei's Shenzhen plants produced simple telecommunications products such as digital watches, telephones, and phone
switches. Eventually, with government contracts from the Ministry of
Posts and Telecommunications and the PLA, and US$10 billion in
export financing from the China Development Bank, Huawei used reverse engineering, ingenuity, in-house R & D, and hard work to develop
and market worldwide everything from the telecommunications network hardware to computer chips and smartphones.[68] According to
Huawei's founder Ren Zhengfei, the company's goal was "to develop
the national industry, not to set up joint ventures with foreign companies, to closely follow global cutting-edge technology, to insist on
self-development, to gain domestic market share, and to explore the
international market and compete against international rivals."[69] Huawei also relied on technical cooperation agreements with Chinese industries and universities in the interior economy and with large
multinationals, although cooperation with foreign multinationals is
not a high priority because of their unwillingness "to transfer their
most advanced core technologies to a Chinese partner over whom they
do not have management control."[70]

These new SEZ companies—Huawei and Foxconn—would inspire
the development of other indigenous SEZ firms, such as Tencent Hold-
ings, established in Shenzhen in 1998 by a Shenzhen University graduate, Ma Huateng. Two decades later, Tencent would become one of
the world's largest Internet companies, owing to its instant messaging
service Tencent QQ, WeChat, and a plethora of online games and services. The SEZs also became the testing ground for various economic
and management reforms that eventually would be adopted by the
coastal and interior economies. The very first Chinese labor contract
was signed in 1982 at the Bamboo Grove Hotel.[71] The Law of the PRC
on Economic Contracts Involving Foreign Interests promulgated on
March 1985 was first implemented a year beforehand in Shenzhen; the
regulations concerning technology import contracts promulgated in
May 1985 were first tested in Shenzhen in February 1984.[72]

Perhaps one of the zones' most important contributions was the
testing of the State Council's "Twenty-two Articles," promulgated in
October 1986 to encourage greater foreign investment throughout
China.[73] Of fifteen articles that mandated specific improvements in the

investment environment, fourteen had already been tested in the Shenzhen SEZ. The most successful of the articles tested involved reductions in land-use fees (Article 4); preferential access to short-term revolving lines of credit (Article 6); elimination of taxes on remitted profits (Article 7); preferential tax treatment after tax holidays (Articles 8, 9, 10); exemption from the Consolidated Industrial and Commercial Tax for export products (Article 11); elimination of import permits for inputs required to produce export goods (Article 13); and the regulation of local foreign exchange, which included the establishment of "foreign exchange adjustment centers" (Article 14). SEZ officials estimate that the state conducted more than 200 experiments with various reform measures in the Shenzhen SEZ, which thus has clearly fulfilled its role as an experimental laboratory.[74]

The success of the readjusted SEZ policy was symbolized by the motto of Shenzhen's Shekou Industrial Zone, "Time is money, efficiency is life," and by Deng Xiaoping's 24 February 1984 description of the SEZs as windows of technology, management, knowledge, and foreign policy. The SEZs continued to encounter problems and to undergo policy reviews and readjustments from 1985 to 1987.[75] Yet Deng and Zhao were satisfied with the SEZ policy and guaranteed a five-year extension, giving Guangdong and Fujian the right to carry out "special policies and flexible measures" until 1989.[76] Deng also agreed with Zhao's plan to expand the decentralization experiment to China's coastal economy after 1984, and with the establishment of a new SEZ encompassing all of Hainan Island in 1987.

Expanding the Experiment:
The Fourteen Open Coastal Cities

After returning from his first *nanxun*, Deng put forward several policy initiatives on 24 February 1984, including the expansion of the opening to various Chinese coastal ports and Hainan. Sensitive to Chen Yun's concerns, Deng made it clear that "these places would not be called SEZs, but could enjoy many of the SEZ policies."[77] The Party Secretariat and the State Council planned a conference for the coastal municipality from 26 March to 6 April to analyze Deng's comments and determine the next steps in opening China's coastal regions. Having visited Tianjin and Dalian in early March in preparation for the conference, Gu Mu suggested that the coastal cities were part of the old state planned economy, with old infrastructure and old ideas.[78] Perhaps reflecting on his experience overseeing the four SEZs since 1979, Gu Mu wisely suggested that each coastal city needed to formulate its economic development plan, which would be submitted to Beijing for approval.

Hu Yaobang and Zhao Ziyang—together with leaders from various government ministries, the NPC, and the PLA general staff—met in Zhongnanhai to discuss Deng's views with leaders from eight coastal municipalities (Tianjin, Shanghai, Dalian, Yantai, Qingdao, Ningbo, Wenzhou, and Beihai), the four SEZs (Shenzhen, Zhuhai, Shantou, and Xiamen), and the Hainan Administrative Region (HAR), as well as provincial officials from Liaoning, Shandong, Zhejiang, Fujian, Guangdong, and the Guangxi Autonomous Region. A summary of the conference was issued on 4 May 1984 as Central Committee document 1984.13, which expanded the coastal experiment by creating a chain of fourteen open coastal cities.[79] But document 1984.13 is more significant than that, as it builds on Zhao Ziyang's 1981 coastal development strategy by providing a blueprint for the expansion of the coastal experiment beyond Guangdong and Fujian provinces to include all the coastal provinces and Hainan Island.

While the document constantly reaffirms the correctness of Deng Xiaoping's vision of the opening policy, in its last paragraph it also invokes Chen Yun. Document 1984.13 argues that policy makers must

> comply with remarks [made by] Comrade Chen Yun to "Liberate our thinking, seek truth from fact, continue our explorations, and do a solid job." We must combine great drive and earnest orderliness to initiate a new stage of using foreign capital and importing advance technology. We must race against time and quickly overcome the backward nature of our economy, technology, and management skills. We must struggle to realize the strategic goals proposed at the Party's Twelfth Congress.[80]

Two years before, Chen Yun had stopped further expansion of the decentralization experiment by insisting that the SEZs should "summarize their experiences." Document 1984.13 marks the official end of that reflective period and the beginning of a new expansion phase in the experiment.

In his opening speech, Gu Mu made it very clear that in deference to Chen Yun's dictum, the open coastal cities would not become SEZs, despite what several Western and Chinese scholars mistakenly proclaimed.[81] Local authorities would need to raise their own funds, adopt prudent measures in opening and yet be on the forefront of economic growth, and focus on training a new generation of bureaucratic leaders while instilling a sense of integrity and ideological firmness. The provincial leaders of Jiangsu, Fujian, and Guangdong successfully lobbied for the inclusion of their key coastal cities during the meeting, and it was agreed that some of the cities would establish ETDZs.[82] At the conclusion of the conference, Deng Xiaoping and Li Xiannian appeared with the conference members for a group photo; when Gu Mu reported on the meeting to Chen Yun on 23 April, he stated that he "was all for the decision and stressed the importance of summing up the experience as the work went along."[83]

The Central Committee and State Council issued document 1984.13 on the auspicious date of May fourth, which was 65 years after the May Fourth Movement of 1919 that was a major political and sociological turning point in Chinese history.[84] The circular clearly stated that this was the result of Deng's 24 February 1984 comments following the first *nanxun*. The policy, it said, would be an effective tool in "their race against time to overcome as soon as possible the backward nature of China's economy, technology, and management." Entrusting the implementation to Gu Mu and the State Council SEZ Office, Deng and the other key leaders made it clear that those cities that had the best management expertise, technological know-how, and infrastructure should be the first to develop. Foreign technology, capital, and management experience would be primarily absorbed by the SEZs, gradually utilized by the fourteen open cities and the "Large Open Coastal Economic Zones" established in the Yangtze and Pearl River Deltas as well as southern Fujian, and from there, disseminated into the interior economy.[85]

The leaders hoped that, while attracting foreign investment, the cities would also renovate their older industries, implement plans that would take advantage of their specific strengths, and share their experiences with the interior economies. They recognized that because the coastal cities possess

> a relatively favorable geographic position [and] enjoy a good economic base and good economic management and technological expertise, [they] are bound to be the first to progress forward. While taking advantage of foreign capital, technology and markets, these coastal cities must first carry out technical transformation of older industries. . . . [T]hey also must implement small and intermediate projects that require little investment and enjoy a high turnover rate with high profits. This will enable the coastal cities to accumulate a greater amount of savings more quickly. They thus can aid the entire country by providing financial and material support, as well as qualified personnel. They also can share with the interior regions their accumulated experiences of dealing with the outside world.[86]

Along with Guangdong, Fujian, and the SEZs, the coastal cities would be integrated into the international economy and act as "gatekeepers," regulating the flow of international goods and ideas into the domestic marketplace. And in deference to Chen Yun, the conference leaders declared that "everyone must unceasingly summarize their experiences and progress forward in a sound manner."[87]

As in the initial opening policy outlined in Central Committee document 1979.50, Beijing would not provide large amounts of investment capital, but would offer the fourteen open cities FDI incentives somewhat like those already enjoyed by Guangdong and Fujian, including lower tax rates on FDI projects and foreign access to the domestic market. To operate a more market-oriented economy, the Central Committee also advised that the leaders of the fourteen open cities should "consult the successful reforms of the SEZs and gradually implement their competitive bidding system in basic construction, contract responsibility system, labor contract system, cadre hiring system, floating wage system, various management responsibility systems, etc. They also can establish trade centers, adopt an enterprise bidding system for equipment and material acquisition, invigorate commodity circulation and reform the banking system according to State regulations."[88] To make themselves more competitive on the international marketplace, the coastal cities adopted the most successful of the SEZ reforms. They were granted similar approval rights over foreign-investment projects, the retention and use of foreign exchange, and the ability to attract technologically advanced industries by granting tax-free importation of advanced technology and implementing a reduced tax rate or a temporary tax holiday for foreign-invested enterprises. The Central Committee had already accorded similar rights to the HAR in its document 1983.11. The committee also made it abundantly clear that coastal leaders had to study the experiences of the SEZs and adopt various innovations in decision-making authority that the SEZs had successfully tested, in such areas as the examination and approval of foreign-invested companies, the entry and exit of foreigners and Chinese nationals, the competitive bidding process, and so on.

The Real Problems of Transforming Old into New

Unlike Deng, with his enthusiastic *maojin* approach to development, Zhao Ziyang shared with Chen Yun a deeper understanding of the complexity of reforming China's economy. He thus held a less sanguine view of the coastal-zone cities, especially Shanghai, as catalysts for domestic economic reform.[89]

In 1981 Zhao praised Shanghai as an efficient, up-to-date, production dynamo that "enjoyed the best conditions to be primarily outward-oriented."[90] But during the interim period of review and adjustment, Zhao and leaders in Beijing began to see the serious problems facing coastal cities, especially Shanghai. Between July and December 1984, Zhao authorized extensive studies and convened a research conference on devising a new development strategy for Shanghai. When he and Yao Yilin inspected the city in early December, Zhao realized that despite Shanghai's positive attributes and its important economic role, the city faced real difficulties. He concurred with city officials that the national economy was siphoning too much capital from Shanghai; as a result, Shanghai was suffering from insufficient housing stock, an outdated transportation system, large municipal debts for infrastructure projects, and serious pollution problems. The cost of importing raw materials and energy was expanding exponentially, and the city had seen a substantial drop in industrial production for certain goods. Reflecting Shanghai's new development strategy, Zhao Ziyang argued that its industries needed to undergo a basic transformation; the city had to renovate its old industries and establish new ones. Zhao also argued that Shanghai had to develop its tertiary industries, reviving its role as the country's premier financial center, its food and beverage industries, tourism, and its commercial sectors. However, this could not be accomplished until Shanghai's crumbling infrastructure was modernized. "If you do not have electricity, roads, and the commodification of land, then there is no way one can develop," Zhao declared.[91]

On 29 December 1984, Zhao Ziyang submitted his "Report to Central Leaders on the Transformation and Revitalization of Shanghai" to Hu Yaobang, Deng Xiaoping, Chen Yun, and the members of the Party Secretariat and the State Council Standing Committee.[92] Zhao Ziyang proposed to raise the percentage of Shanghai's retained financial revenue for the next six years from 13.2 percent to 23.2 percent, which was less than the 25 percent proposed by Shanghai's leaders but still a substantial increase. From 1985 to 1990, Beijing would continue to allocate US$300 million a year to Shanghai for importing foreign technology; not only could those funds be rolled over to the next fiscal year, but Beijing would also allocate a similar amount in renminbi, as loans, for foreign technology procurement. Zhao proposed that the retention rate for foreign exchange revenue should be increased to 25 percent, while the proportion of foreign exchange revenue that could be earned by *Yijin yangchu* industries and the various enterprises that were processing imported materials for export should be increased from 30 percent to 70 percent.

Although Shanghai's problems were more complicated than those of the other coastal cities, they all shared the same problems of outdated technology, lack of electricity, lack of foreign capital and investment, underdeveloped transportation and communications systems, older ways of bureaucratic thinking, inefficient industries, and so on. To help remedy this situation, Zhao continued to promote his 1981 idea: linking domestic industries with foreign advanced technology and management techniques—the *waiyin neilian* enterprises—which now were to be established in the fourteen open coastal cities.[93] He hoped that the coastal cities could be a model for economic reform, and that their experiences would eventually be absorbed and copied by urban centers in the interior.[94]

In his memoirs, Zhao Ziyang recalls visiting Shanghai in the mid-1980s and realizing that the Pudong rice fields on the east bank of the Huangpu River, opposite old Shanghai, would be an excellent area for urban expansion. As in the early 1980s with the SEZs, however, the state lacked the capital to finance the infrastructure needed to develop the Pudong New Area. In 1987 Zhao met with an American structural engineer, Lin Tung-Yen, who was born in Fuzhou, China, and had graduated from the University of California, Berkeley. Lin had founded T. Y. Lin International in San Francisco in 1953, a firm that specialized in providing planning, design, engineering, and construction services to countries around the world. Lin proposed that Shanghai could develop Pudong by renting the land for thirty to fifty years; foreigners would supply the development capital, and China would not need to establish a new SEZ or any ETDZs. Zhao reports that there were two major obstacles to developing Pudong and Shanghai: "One was that it was a critical region, and the other was Chen Yun's attitude"; Chen Yun believed that in "dealing with regions such as Shanghai and Zhejiang, one must proceed with caution, because people in these areas were especially skilled and familiar with capitalist behavior."[95] Just as he had stopped the development of the Shanghai SEZ on Chongming Island in 1979, Chen Yun fought against the acceleration of Shanghai's development in the 1980s. Only after 1992, when Deng Xiaoping finally broke with the moderate bureaucratic Stalinists during his second *nanxun*, would General Secretary Jiang Zemin, the former mayor and party secretary of Shanghai, focus on implementing the new "socialist market economy" and accelerating Shanghai's development, marked by the myriad of tower cranes that dominated the city's skyline in the 1990s.

Among the most interesting models approved by document 1984.13 were the ETDZs. Located within or on the periphery of the established coastal cities, these processing zones were designed not only to attract high-technology investment but also to provide such products to the interior economy and to "disseminate management knowledge of new techniques, technologies and science" to the rest of the municipalities and the surrounding coastal and interior regions. Not all cities would be allowed to develop ETDZs, a restriction that resulted in behind-the-scenes haggling and politicking. But their establishment heralded the first of several new initiatives to introduce smaller export processing zones in both the coastal and the interior economies.

Allowed to retain fiscal revenues and to import machinery and equipment duty-free during their first five years of operation, the ETDZs relied on the local municipality, Chinese–foreign equity joint ventures, cooperative ventures, and foreign-invested enterprises as their primary sources of development capital; interestingly, some also would be allowed to carry out entrepôt trade. Yet the ETDZs were different from the SEZs. Their major purpose was more specialized, as document 1984.13 put it, because they were to concentrate on "develop[ing] new technologies and high-grade products. This will increase export receipts and provide new materials and critical components and parts to the interior regions; it also will disseminate management knowledge of new techniques, technologies and science."[96] The central leadership designed the ETDZs to be much smaller and less complicated than their SEZ cousins, the largest of which—Hainan—covers China's second largest island. Thanks to their ability to rely on skilled technicians and development capital from the adjacent municipalities, many of the ETDZs quickly established themselves as competitive rivals of the SEZs for foreign investment.

Besides the ETDZs, in the late 1980s the State Council approved another new type of export-processing zone with a program called National Industrial Development Zones for New and Advanced Technology (NIDZNATs). First approved on an experimental basis in the Zhongguancun area in Beijing in 1988, these scientific industrial parks were granted "national" status in 1991. They were located in twenty-one major Chinese cities and in the Shenzhen, Xiamen, and Hainan SEZs and the Shanghai and Dalian ETDZs. According to the 1991 State Council decrees, NIDZNATs were charged with increasing the country's technological production levels and strengthening its international competitive strength, especially in such areas as microelectronics, aeronautics, laser technology, biological and material sciences, energy resources, ecosystems, and medicine.[97]

While document 1984.13 presents a comprehensive view of coastal development, several sections are devoted to the SEZs and the Hainan Administrative Region. Although it acknowledged Chen Yun's dictum to "summarize experiences," it also directed the SEZs to import advanced technology, especially for knowledge-intensive projects, and to "assimilate these experiences, bring forth new ideas, and transfer them to the interior." Given Deng Xiaoping's admiration for the Shekou Industrial Zone experiment, the SEZs were to "popularize" the Shekou model and eliminate "the old conventions." In addition, document 1984.13 gave the older urban areas surrounding the Shantou and Zhuhai SEZs the same rights and privileges accorded the fourteen open coastal cities, and expanded the Xiamen SEZ to include the entire island of Xiamen. As for Hainan, local party and military authorities were ordered to focus on specific infrastructure projects, such as improving Haikou's airport, telecommunications, roads, and so on.

Finally, and most important, the document began to open up the Chinese economy to the international marketplace. The Central Committee recognized that FDI was the primary financial tool fueling coastal development and acknowledged that

> one important reason why foreign businesspeople come to China is because we have a market of 1 billion people. They are very much attracted by this potential market. It will be difficult to use foreign capital and import technology if distinctions cannot be made and there is a total emphasis on exports. The leading comrades of the Central Committee have repeatedly stated that this problem must be resolved. Limited access to internal markets can be allowed in exchange for needed advanced technology. All foreign businesspeople who truly provide advanced technology, techniques, and equipment can be allowed limited access. A set proportion of their goods can be sold internally. Internal sales of products that are scarce on the domestic market and must be imported can also be sold in order to substitute for the imports. "Foreign goods" [yanghuo] produced in the coastal areas can substitute for imported foreign goods. Some products that are available on the domestic market yet are lacking in quality and variety can be also sold domestically at an approved appropriate level. This will encourage the improvement of domestically produced products. We assuredly must protect our industry and promote continuous development. However, we cannot call for protection of those products that have backward technology and poor quality. This would defeat the purpose of development.[98]

This is truly an amazing if not path-breaking passage. The Central Committee recognized that the inwardly oriented development path of the previous thirty years was moribund and had resulted in products of "backward technology and poor quality." In document 1984.13 the Central Committee argues instead for an outward-oriented development strategy that would not open all of China to the vicissitudes of the international marketplace but would allow foreign investors and foreign products access to the domestic market. Of course, such access was to be monitored and controlled; the Central Committee entrusted the State Economic Commission, the Ministry of Commerce, MOFERT, and the State Planning Commission to formulate new rules and regulations to control foreign penetration. Yet this passage, and this document, were the keys that opened China to the outside economy, and eventually promoted China's partial integration with the world economy.

To explore the benefits of decentralization and foreign investment, many of the open coastal cities initiated a series of conferences, starting in 1984, to put forward their definitive development plans. The State Council subsequently issued a variety of circulars and official letters approving plans to open to the outside world, to build necessary infrastructure, and to allow local officials to travel abroad. The State Council also approved detailed plans to establish the fourteen cities' ETDZs, including laws and regulations regarding land usage, administrative management, preferential treatment, technology imports, taxation, cooperation with domestic industries, enterprise registration procedures, salary schedules, and dealing with foreign-invested enterprises (FIEs).[99]

Coastal Development: SEZs and the Wenzhou Model

Beginning in the mid-1980s, Deng Xiaoping, Zhao Ziyang, Wan Li, and other international Leninists promoted economic growth in the coastal areas based largely on the experience of the SEZs. However, leaders also promoted a more ambitious model, Wenzhou.

Wenzhou has become famous for its "back-alley banking" system, which financed Wenzhou's vibrant private-sector economy, and for its family-owned businesses, which acted as a catalyst for domestic economic growth in the same way that small and medium-size firms became the backbone of Taiwan's economic growth.[100] The economic hub of southern coastal Zhejiang province, Wenzhou was designated as one of the original fourteen open coastal cities, and its "Report and Request for Instructions on the Plan to Further Open Wenzhou Municipality to the Outside World" was approved by the State Council on 14 March 1985. The State Council stated that Wenzhou should become "an important industrial, foreign-trade port city and window to opening up foreign trade relationships."[101]

However, Wenzhou, unlike many of the other coastal cities whose infrastructure had been built up during the semicolonial era by European, American, or Japanese colonial powers, lacked the basic infrastructure they enjoyed, as the city's report recognized. The State Council agreed that Wenzhou had to first improve its basic infrastructure and bring about a technological transformation by entering into exchange agreements with domestic and foreign firms. The state and the military thus agreed to finance the construction of a civilian airport, which was first completed in 1990 and later transformed into Wenzhou Longwan International Airport in 2013.[102] To improve telecommunications, the state and military also established a coaxial cable network between Hangzhou, Wenzhou, and Fuzhou. The Seventh Five-Year Plan included the building of a hydroelectric dam and a dock capable of handling ten thousand tons. Nevertheless, in the end the State Council decided not to include Wenzhou in the first group of fourteen economic and technological development zones established between 1984 and 1988 because of its underdeveloped infrastructure. After Deng Xiaoping's first *nanxun*, the State Council approved a second group of ETDZ proposals that included the Wenzhou ETDZ.[103]

Beijing and local Zhejiang officials directly supported Wenzhou's growth, according to Liu.[104] To help Wenzhou overcome its poor infrastructure, Vice Premier Wan Li supported Wenzhou's promotion of private businesses, local markets, and private investment, just as he had supported the decentralization of agriculture by instituting the household responsibility system in Anhui in 1977. Premier Zhao Ziyang, who had also championed decentralized control of agriculture while guiding Sichuan's development in the 1970s, joined Wan Li to support

Wenzhou not only as an open coastal city but also its designation as an experimental reform zone in September 1987.[105] The Shanghai Party Committee's newspaper *Jiefang ribao* coined the phrase "Wenzhou model" and supported greater economic interaction between the two cities. And Wenzhou party elites, especially those at the lower levels, often protected private businesses because they were engaged in business themselves.[106]

Creating the Open Coastal Economic Regions

A less appreciated aspect of Zhao's coastal development strategy was the establishment of the open coastal economic regions. This crucial strategy linked the SEZs, the open coastal cities, and the surrounding provinces to form a larger coastal development strategy. The approach fostered the remarkable growth of Dongguan in the Pearl River Delta and impressive economic growth in the Yangtze Delta cities.[107]

Initially confined to the coastal regions, the concept evolved in the early 1990s into the National-Level Open Development New Areas (Guojiaji Kaifang Kaifa Xinqu), the first of which was the Pudong New Area established on 4 May 1990.[108] The State Council would eventually establish these new areas in the fourteen open coastal cities, including the Binhai New Area in Tianjin (2009), the Nansha New Area in Guangzhou (2012), the Xihai'an New Area in Qingdao (2014), the Jinpu New Area in Dalian (2014), and the Fuzhou New Area (2015). Reflecting Jiang Zemin's and Zhu Rongji's adoption of a new western development strategy (*Xibu dakaifa*) in the late 1990s, Chongqing established the Liangjiang New Area in 2010, the Lanzhou New Area was founded in 2012, Xi'an and Xianyang established the Xixian New Area (2014), Guiyang and Anshun established the Guian New Area (2014), Chengdu and Meishan established the Tianfu New Area, and Kunming established the Dianzhong New Area.[109] After Premier Wen Jiabao promoted a "Revitalization Plan for Northeast China's Older Industrial Base" ("Zhenxing dongbei laogongye jidi") in 2003, new areas were also established in Harbin (2015) and Changchun (2016). In 2004 Wen announced a development plan for China's central regions, "The Plan for Central

China's Emergence" (Zhongbu Jueqi Jihua). Hunan's Changsha municipality established the Xiangjiang New Area (2015) and Nanchang, the Ganjiang New Area (2016). Besides the Pudong New Area, the second most celebrated new area is Xiong'an New Area, announced in April 2017, which will encompass 2,000 square kilometers and link the cities of Beijing and Tianjin with the rest of Hebei province.[110]

From 1964 to 1973, the Maoist Third Front strategy for economic development had emphasized interior economic development, which included transferring industrial production and investment from the militarily vulnerable "First Front" coastal regions.[111] With the exception of Shanghai and its environs, China's coastal areas had been made into military buffer zones and were starved of major infrastructure investment and industrial development. By the 1980s, the Pearl River Delta area existed in a "bubble" of time, even though it lay in close proximity to Hong Kong and was the ancestral home to myriad Chinese people living in Hong Kong and throughout the world.[112] Travel through the Pearl River Delta, such as from the Shenzhen SEZ to the provincial capital of Guangzhou, was an arduous journey of four hours. After leaving downtown Shenzhen, with its new skyscrapers, high-rise apartment buildings, and foreign-invested companies, buses crossed the "second line" separating Shenzhen from the rest of the Pearl River Delta and entered the bustling world of reforming rural China. They had to slowly make their way up the river on a two-lane road congested with other noisy buses, Jiefang trucks carrying live chickens or scrap metal, farmers bringing produce to market with their tractors or ox-driven carts, and the ubiquitous bicyclists carrying everything including the proverbial kitchen sink. The chaos of activity on the road was echoed throughout the delta area, where one also had to wait long hours in line for ferries at river crossings where there were no bridges.

Despite the lack of infrastructure, the delta areas of the mid-1980s were economically well off, as local farmers benefited from the agricultural reforms of the early 1980s. On their contracted land, farmers made a profit growing rice, raising livestock, and working in small township and village enterprises. The communities in the Pearl River Delta were a testament to the success of agricultural decentralization, because farmers could afford to build new three-story homes, with television antennas and comfortable furniture. There was little air pollution, and there were banana plantations and beautiful fields of green rice. Terraced hills now overgrown with vegetation stood as a reminder of where, a decade earlier, peasants had been forced to put into practice Mao's dictum of "learning from Dazhai" by constructing rice terraces in inappropriate and difficult terrain.

The towns along the Yangtze River Delta areas of Jiangsu, Zhejiang, and Shanghai Municipality's western counties also enjoyed agrarian prosperity owing to decentralization policy. While Shanghai was considered the country's most important economic hub even during the Maoist Third Front period, the rural environs around Shanghai in the Zhejiang and Jiangsu areas enjoyed a much higher rate of industrialization than similar areas in the Pearl River and Minnan Deltas.[113] Although more geographically challenged by the mountainous areas of southern Fujian province, and by its military "First Front" status because it faced Taiwan, the triangular area between the Xiamen SEZ, Zhangzhou, and Quanzhou also had a strong agricultural sector. Quanzhou had been especially important in the history of Chinese foreign trade, as this very cosmopolitan city had sent its ships to engage in extensive maritime trading beginning in the Song Dynasty (960– 1279), but it had been reduced to a smaller provincial cousin of Xiamen by the nineteenth century.[114] However, like the Pearl River Delta, the Xiamen and Minnan areas had great potential to attract foreign investment from the large number of overseas Chinese who originated from the area, including most of the Minnan Chinese who had immigrated to Taiwan starting in the late 1600s.[115]

While rural industry in the Yangtze Delta was relatively developed, the Pearl River and Minnan Delta areas were more typical of the regions around China's other large coastal cities, which remained in a 1970s-time bubble of low technology, poor communications, and cautious but ambitious local party leaders. The state had established export processing bases in the delta areas of the Yangtze and Pearl Rivers in the early 1960s, but cities such as Foshan were still producing low-cost electrical household goods and porcelain for the export market. Besides the young women who went to work in labor-intensive industries in Shenzhen, the "second line" effectively separated Shenzhen from the rest of

Bao'an, Dongguan, and the other cities on the Pearl River. There were thus two "bubble" economies: the outward-oriented economy of Shenzhen, with its economic ties to Hong Kong, Taiwan, and their market economies; and the inwardly oriented economy of the Pearl River Delta, which provided foodstuffs and labor to Shenzhen, but produced little else.[116]

As the former Guangdong provincial party leader, Zhao Ziyang understood the economic potential of the Pearl River Delta and the coastal regions. As early as 1981 Zhao had sought to link the SEZs and the coastal cities with the industrial potential of their surrounding delta regions. By tapping into the coastal economies, China could attract even more investment from abroad and eventually transmit its technology and know-how to the interior economies. Looking back, one can trace the evolution of the coastal economic policy, beginning with Zhao Ziyang's leading investigations to the coastal regions and his submission of a letter of request (*qingshi*), continuing with Deng Xiaoping's discussion of the *qingshi* and Zhao's convening a State Council conference, and culminating in the Central Committee's approval of the final document establishing the coastal economic regions. Beginning in the mid-1980s, elites began the process of integrating all of China's coastal economies not only with the domestic economy but also with the international markets.

First Stage: Request for Instructions

Zhao Ziyang and State Council members initially visited Guangdong, Shanghai, and Jiangsu and talked with local provincial leaders about coastal economic reforms. After returning to Beijing, Zhao submitted two documents to the party leaders on 29 December 1984, addressing them directly to Hu Yaobang, Deng, Li Xiannian, and Chen Yun; the members of the Party Secretariat; and the State Council's Standing Committee. Zhao's first document was his report on the transformation and revitalization of Shanghai. The second document was a request for instructions on whether to implement a new experiment to establish open coastal economic regions in the Pearl River Delta of Guangdong province and the Yangtze River Delta around Shanghai, Jiangsu, and Zhejiang provinces. If successful, Zhou argued, the experiment would be expanded to the Jiaodong Peninsula in Shandong, and the Liaodong Peninsula in Liaoning. These coastal regions would link the individual open coastal cities, from Dalian in the north to Beihai in the south and the four southern SEZs, to form a coherent integrated coastal economy. "We would have three different levels of opening. One level is the four SEZs; another level is the fourteen open coastal cities; the other level is the Open Coastal Economic Regions. We would want them to implement different types of policies. As for the two Open Coastal Economic Regions, we can use the policies allocated to the fourteen open coastal cities as a guide and give certain rights (a bit less than those given the open cities), that would be drawn up by the State Council Office for the SEZs, and approved by the State Council for implementation."[117] Zhao envisioned these areas breaking down barriers and facilitating greater economic exchange. The coastal areas would aggressively adopt market economy reforms and have the capacity to attract and develop foreign investment, advanced technology, and efficient management techniques from abroad. Once they adapted such technology to China's needs, they would gradually introduce advanced technology and methods to the interior economies, thus promoting more comprehensive growth nationwide.

To achieve his vision of an integrated coastal economy, Zhao Ziyang realized that the State Council would need to implement these reforms in a step-by-step fashion.

> Our initial idea is first to open up the Yangtze River Delta: Shanghai and its counties; Jiangsu's Zhangjiagang and the three cities of Zuzhou, Wuxi, Changzhou with their twelve counties; Zhejiang province's Jiaxing, and its five areas of Jiashan, Haining, and Haiyan counties, and Tongxiang and Pinghu municipalities. In the Pearl River Delta, we first open the two municipalities of Foshan and Jiangmen, and the eleven cities and counties of Zhongshan, Panyu, Zengcheng, Nanhai, Shunde, Xinhui, Taishan, Kaiping, Bao'an, Doumen, and Dongmen.[118]

It is unclear why Zhao Ziyang did not include the Fujian SEZ and the Fuzhou Open City in his initial proposal. The Xiamen SEZ was slower to develop than the other SEZs, and Fujian was a poor province receiving central government subsidies. Whatever the case, Gu Mu rectified the omissions.

Second Stage: Elites Respond to the Request

According to a footnote on Zhao's request, on 1 January 1985 Deng Xiaoping asked Gu Mu, the director of the State Council Office of the SEZs, for his opinion concerning Zhao's request for approval of the new open coastal economic regions. When Gu Mu cautiously responded with an uncommitted answer, Deng enthusiastically stated, "I think it is great to link together these coastal areas." Emboldened by Deng's attitude, Gu Mu stated, "This afternoon, Comrade Ziyang came to talk to me about the request. I was thinking of proposing that we add another delta area, the Minnan Delta encompassing Quanzhou, Zhangzhou, and Xiamen. That way, Guangdong will have the Pearl River Delta, Shanghai will have the Yangtze River Delta, and Fujian will have the Minnan Delta." Deng responded, "That is great! Let's also add the Minnan Delta."[119] Having been approved by Deng, the State Council issued a directive that approved the convening of an in-depth conference to discuss and put forward specific policies to enact the Open Coastal Economic Regions.

Third Stage: Convening a State Council Conference

Zhao Ziyang convened the Conference on the Yangtze River, Pearl River, and Minnan Xiamen-Zhangzhou-Quanzhou Delta Areas in Beijing at the end of January 1985. Provincial party, government, and military leaders from Jiangsu, Shanghai, Zhejiang, Fujian, and Guangdong attended, along with Hu Yaobang, Hu Qili, and Gu Mu, and other party and State Council officials. They spent a week (25–31 January) discussing the Central Committee and State Council directives, Deng's comments on the new coastal regions, and specific policies to enact the regions. On the last day, Zhao gave the concluding speech, and the conference summary was submitted to the Central Committee and State Council.

In his closing speech, Zhao Ziyang emphasized that the leadership's long-term strategy was to open not just the SEZs and the fourteen coastal cities but the entire coastal region. While acknowledging that some areas were upset that they were denied greater decision-making power, Zhao argued that most attendees agreed with the overall policy of opening the coastal areas. He pointed to foreign commentators who described Deng Xiaoping's concept of "socialism with Chinese characteristics" as encompassing the opening policy and economic reforms: "Our reforms have transformed our former closed economy to an open economy, from being closed to the outside world to being open, from being sealed off from one another within China to opening up barriers within the country. We want to develop a socialist commodity production and exchange and cannot close the country to outside interaction. We must open the economy and must reform our previous closed economic model. Thus, the economic reforms and the opening are inseparable."[120] Explaining that they lacked a concrete blueprint for the reforms and opening, Zhao argued that Chinese party leaders and policy experts were guided by Third Plenum strategies adopted at the Eleventh and Twelfth Party Congresses. They were experimenting constantly with new approaches, accumulating knowledge, reassessing their strategy, and moving ahead with new and improved measures, or as Deng had stated, striving "to take one step forward, and observe a bit the consequences" to avoid big mistakes.

Ever since Central Committee document 1979.50 approved the decentralization experiment with Guangdong and Fujian and their SEZs, leaders of other coastal and interior areas had argued for equal treatment. Provincial and municipal leaders had renewed their requests during the 1984 conference that resulted in Central Committee document 1984.13 establishing the fourteen open coastal cities and had actively lobbied for the inclusion of their municipalities.[121] Thus in his concluding speech, Zhao stated that he was especially aware that certain leaders were dissatisfied (bu guoyin) with the slow pace of the opening strategy. While the entire coastal region might eventually be opened, Zhao argued, the country must first gain experience opening up the three delta regions. If after analyzing the results the leadership was satisfied, Beijing would open the entire coastal region from north to south. Most important, Zhao recognized that the interior economies were upset because the coastal areas, which already enjoyed better infrastructure and opportunities to grow, were not being granted equal or greater decision-making rights. He argued that China would completely fail if the areas were opened all at once. While the interior economy could carry out foreign trade and investment activities, the coastal economies, specifically the three coastal regions, were better prepared and able to engage with the international market. As Zhao argued that the opening had to proceed "from small to large areas," he also warned the coastal areas that they would be responsible for expanding their exports and earning foreign exchange, strengthening their management of state-owned enterprises and local government, judiciously using foreign exchange to purchase foreign technology, and controlling black-market activities, such as the buying and selling of foreign exchange.

At the end of the conference, on 31 January 1985, organizers submitted "The Yangtze River, Pearl River, and Minnan Xiamen-Zhangzhou-Quanzhou Delta Areas Conference Summary" to the CCP Central Secretariat and members of the Standing Committee for their review and approval. The conference members proposed nine initiatives.

1. The State Council would grant certain cities and county governments (Suzhou, Wuxi, Foshan, Dongguan, Bao'an, and so on) the decision-making power to approve projects worth up to US$5 million in foreign investment for the technical renovation of older industries and to establish newer industries. For these projects the state would not finance the production of goods; localities would have the capacity to repay all project loans.[122]

2. The State Council ministries and the provincial and municipal governments would aggressively support and give priority to the technological transformation of key export-oriented industries and enterprises by facilitating financing, importing machinery and technology, providing technological guidance, and so on. Until 1990, there would be tax-free importation of technology and equipment not available domestically, and seeds, livestock, or any good needed to develop agricultural export-processing industries.

3. There would be a 20 percent discount on the enterprise income tax for foreign joint ventures, jointly managed enterprises, and wholly foreign-owned enterprises; provincial and municipal governments would need to determine whether they would reduce

or eliminate such taxes. Tax discounts would also be granted to foreign-invested, export-oriented agricultural, forestry, livestock, or breeding facilities. There would be a 15 percent enterprise income tax applied to any foreign-invested project involving power production, communications, port facilities, technology- or knowledge-intensive projects, any foreign-invested production operation valued over US$30 million, or any long-term investment project.

4. The following items could be imported tax free for joint ventures, jointly operated enterprises, and 100 percent foreign-owned enterprises located in the open coastal economic region: equipment and building materials used in building an export-oriented venture; raw materials, components, spare parts, and packaging materials used to manufacture goods for export; imported transportation and office equipment; household goods and transportation used by foreign businesspeople and staff. Goods produced for export by these FIEs would be exempt from export tariffs and the value-added portion of the consolidated industrial-commercial tax.[123] However, if any of this material was used to produce goods for the domestic market, domestic taxes would be levied.

5. Beijing would gradually provide the coastal regional provincial, municipal, and county governments with greater decision-making authority to manage their foreign trade exports. They would determine the costs of foreign exchange conversion, be responsible for profits and losses, and work with MOFERT to arrange matching funds and all the necessary permits. Those located in the Pearl River Delta would establish local companies to manage the export of livestock and fresh foods and would take financial responsibility for carrying out the trade directly with Hong Kong. Jiangsu, Zhejiang, Fujian, and Guangdong provincial governments were also permitted to establish foreign trade companies to export local products and to establish offices abroad.

6. The Bank of China would provide foreign exchange loans at preferential rates for those projects holding the greatest potential to earn foreign exchange that could be used to import foreign technology, equipment, and necessary first-rate goods. Profits earned by the SOEs from the invested project would be used to repay the loan, and only after repayment would the enterprise income tax be levied. Collective enterprises would repay the loans according

to the normal procedures. Any foreign exchange earned would first be used to repay the loans, after which a portion could be retained by the SOE or collective.

7. Guangdong, Fujian, Zhejiang, and Jiangsu would select several islands in the ocean or sandbars in the river as isolated areas in which to establish farms for experiments with improved varieties of imported seeds or livestock that could be introduced into the country. They would enjoy a five-year tax holiday once they began to make a profit.

8. As the regions needed large amounts of infrastructure investment and government resources were limited, the leaders agreed to use innovative means to harness the capital held by the Chinese people. So long as they received approval from the provincial government and the PBOC, the regions could issue bonds and stocks.

9. The regional officials would be given the same preferential treatment as the fourteen open coastal cities in arranging to travel abroad on business.

Beijing entrusted the provincial governments to oversee the macromanagement of the open coastal economic regions and thus prevent duplication of production projects; investments using foreign capital and technology, complying with the MOFERT export quota and permit system; and imports of goods, especially those restricted by the government. The provincial governments were required to use every means to ensure that the state's laws and regulations were enforced, from carrying out political-thought education to using the legal system. Beijing's leaders wanted Guangdong to continue to regulate and control all trade with Hong Kong and specifically restricted the role of individual entrepreneurs, who wished to sell their goods directly to Hong Kong. Mindful of the problems encountered by the Shenzhen SEZ in the early 1980s, the conference summary stated that the provinces were responsible for strengthening controls on currency speculation and profiteering, bribery, smuggling, black-market activities, and the transport and distribution of pornography. They were to be particularly alert to enterprises and organizations that became involved in these illegal activities, especially those importing goods tax free for resale to the domestic economy. Such activities were taking place at that very moment in Hainan, on a wide scale.

Despite all of the possible problems that the new coastal economic regions might encounter, the conference members ended their report by stating that the regions "would make an even larger contribution to building socialist modernization," echoing the call of the April 1979 work conference to implement a new party line.[124]

Fourth Stage: Approval of the Official Document

The Central Committee and State Council subsequently issued Central Committee document 1985.3 on 28 February 1985, which reinforced the major themes of the coastal economic regions being transformed into "trade, industrial, and agricultural production areas that will develop export processing, and expand production of agricultural and other materials used for export processing."[125] The economic regions would use imported technology and new management techniques to ensure the production of high-quality exports that would increase foreign exchange earnings. At the same time, the regions would build economic connections with the interior economies, "mutually develop material resources and jointly produce famous-name goods, exchange personnel and technology that will help the interior economy to develop, and become a window to expand foreign economic connections."[126] In order that "proper procedures [would] be adhered to for propaganda purposes," Zhao Ziyang asked Gu Mu to talk to the right people concerning the approval of the National People's Congress.[127]

Beginning in 1985 the open coastal economic regions became magnets for investment from Hong Kong, Taiwan, and elsewhere as more and more businesses moved their production facilities to mainland China. In turn, the coastal regions used their decision-making power and foreign exchange profits to build infrastructure and restructure their economies to attract foreign investment. These areas are now crisscrossed by superhighways, airports, cargo terminals, railroad lines, and advanced communications networks. Within a fifteen-year period, Central Committee document 1985.3 transformed the Yangtze and Pearl River Delta regions into the most advanced, prosperous, and productive areas in China.[128]

The Circuitous Road to the Hainan
Special Economic Zone

After returning from his first *nanxun*, Deng made it clear in his 24 February 1984 talk that "it will be an amazing victory if we can rapidly develop Hainan."[129] While Deng used the term "rapidly" (*xunsu*) instead of *maojin*, the term Mao used in the late 1950s to promote the Great Leap, it was clear that Deng wanted Hainan's development to be put on the fast track. Unfortunately, fast-tracked policies can have accidents—and in this case, it involved cars.

Located in the South China Sea and comparable in size to Taiwan, Hainan Island was a beautiful but very poor area of Guangdong Province. As the previous party secretary of Guangdong, Zhao Ziyang had long considered the problem of Hainan, which was the final geographical component in his vision of coastal development. The tropical paradise suffered from decades of low capital investment from the provincial capital, Guangzhou, and an economy dominated by the PLA that managed military bases, various production industries, and agricultural farms. Visitors to Hainan today, with its modern skyscrapers, first-class hotels, and an agricultural sector transformed by large dams and irrigation systems, have little concept of the poverty of the pre-1980s period. Hainan's development has been phenomenal, and in large part because of Zhao Ziyang and the island's party administrator, Lei Yu, both of whom suffered politically for their vision.[130]

In 1985, the journey from the provincial capital of Guangzhou to Hainan—at first on a rickety old bus replete with live chickens and loud music—was an agonizing two-day trip spent in long lines waiting for ferries to cross the waterways of the Pearl River Delta and Leizhou Peninsula. However, as passengers neared Hainan, the physical environment changed because Hainan's leaders had plowed profits from their illegal entrepôt trade activities into building up the island's infrastructure. After waiting with farmers and businesspeople on a sandy shore at Leizhou's Hai'an Port, passengers boarded a newly imported Norwegian hydrofoil, which whisked everyone to the more modern port of Haikou. As the island's economic center, Haikou was bustling with activity. Newly built high-rise buildings were intermixed with the ochre-colored stucco buildings of the past. Hundreds of brand-new imported Japanese cars were parked behind fenced holding lots; a few months earlier they already would have been transshipped to mainland ports for waiting Chinese customers.

The next step was to board a new air-conditioned bus heading to Sanya in southern Hainan. It was a three-hour journey with views that were breathtakingly beautiful. A newly built road wove its way along the sandy coastal regions and through the lush, tropical, mountainous interior to the pristine southern port of Sanya, with its large community of Hui and Miao people wearing their traditional blue head scarves. Fishermen disembarked from boats filled with *longxia*, or dragon shrimp. In the town, businessmen in automobile showrooms displayed the newest Japanese imported vehicles. Sanya was a small but busy commercial fishing port situated next to the Yulin Naval Base, in the 1980s the home port of China's diesel submarine fleet that patrolled the South China Sea.[131] There were very few tourist facilities, and only an occasional Australian or Hong Kong tourist could be seen swimming at Sanya's white sandy beaches. Yet things were changing. A vacation villa complex—which was formerly used by Mao Zedong's wife, Jiang Qing, and located in Sanya's Luhuitou district—was installing newly imported Western toilets and showers to suit the occasional tourist as well as the foreign technicians working on offshore gas exploration projects. Traveling around the southern part of the island, visitors might see PLA outposts where soldiers were busy planting crops or manning missile emplacements on offshore islands, children in ragged clothes played on the dusty dirt roads, and groups of farmers gathered around small television sets to watch kung fu videos imported from Hong Kong. The road to the Li and Miao Autonomous County area took travelers past endless green rice fields that yielded three crops a year.

Officially, Hainan was administered by the Administrative Region office in the Guangdong provincial government, but unofficially it was dominated by the PLA. Beijing had designated the island a strategic agricultural producer of rubber following the imposition of the United Nations embargo on trade with China in 1951.[132] In a 1957 letter to the Central Committee and Mao, Zhu De argued that Hainan should be developed as an export base, as it was rich in mineral resources, grew a variety of cash crops, enjoyed abundant marine resources, was positioned near international shipping lanes, and was close to the excellent port facilities in Hong Kong. By taking advantage of Hong Kong and Macao, China could still export Chinese and Hainan goods throughout the world, Zhu De said, implying that by going through the Hong Kong entrepôt, China could bypass any international embargo or sanctions.[133] Yet Hainan remained in an investment freeze as the Third Front strategy of the 1960s sacrificed China's exterior coastal areas and directed most economic investment to the strategically safer interior economies. The PLA dominated the coastal areas such as those on Hainan, where the military made investment decisions in the military sectors but not in civilian sectors.

In his report to the Central Work Conference in November 1978, Xi Zhongxun had argued that Beijing should turn the old revolutionary base of Hainan into a key development area. Not only did the island produce tropical products like bananas and hemp, but it also had 165,000 acres of prime agricultural land that could be developed on its western coast, which was sheltered from typhoons and enjoyed a frost-free climate with plenty of sunshine. Unfortunately, however, the area was also one of the island's poorest and most arid regions. Xi thus argued that the state should build a dam on the Changhua River. An irrigation system would transform the region so that farmers could grow food to supply Hainan and raise cattle on modern farms.[134] Although Xi was unable to persuade Beijing or Guangdong to invest in the dam project, planning proceeded in Hainan. Nine years later, in 1987, Hainan completed a resettlement plan for more 20,000 people who would be displaced by damming the river; in 1992, Hainan received a World Bank loan for US$67 million to help finance the US$197 million project; and sometime after 2000, the Hainan Provincial Electric Power Company completed the Daguangba Dam, a power generating station, transmission lines, and 170 kilometers of irrigation canals. Daguangba is Hainan's largest dam, providing water to irrigate more than 31,000 acres in the most arid part of the island.[135]

According to State Council document 1980.202, which approved a June-July 1980 conference report on Hainan's development, the PLA had taken primary responsibility for developing the island's

infrastructure and transforming the island into China's main producer
of rubber and other major tropical products, such as coffee and pepper.[136] Yet during this early period, the report said,

> there was not enough experience in land planning: barren mountains
> and uncultivated lands were indiscriminately assigned to communes
> and production brigades with large populations and small land holdings;
> after the state agricultural farms were established [note: by the PLA],
> there were many organizational changes between the state farms and the
> communes. After the PLA Production and Construction Corps were
> established, they crudely expanded their lands without following proper
> procedures. Thus, there are many remaining problems. From its initial
> stages, the state farm-commune conflict was never resolved in a timely
> or decisive fashion. Their attacks on lawless people who instigated the
> destruction of state property were ineffectual, resulting in continued
> illegal acts, such as severely bruising rubber trees.[137]

Literally on the front line of China's defenses against the outside world,
Hainan's development also had been determined by the inwardly oriented regime's goal of self-reliance—in this particular case, China's
need for natural rubber.

Unfortunately for the Hainan economy, this inward strategy had
a devastating impact on the island's development. Document 1980.202
blamed the state-owned logging operations that used slash and burn
techniques for reducing the area of Hainan's natural forests from 25 percent of the island in 1949 to 13.6 percent in 1980. The PLA state farms
had assimilated the communes during the Cultural Revolution; while
the local governments eventually regained control of the land, the PLA
state farms retained those lands on which rubber trees had been planted.
As a result of this one-sided development, the indigenous population
was "relatively poverty-stricken; there [was] little fiscal revenue available to local authorities, who lack[ed] the ability to develop production." When this impoverishment led to large-scale violence against
the PLA state farms, the State Council immediately promised that Beijing and Guangzhou would transfer 225 million kilos of grain to Hainan
from 1981 to 1985. Adhering to Chen Yun's dictate during the disaster

of the Great Leap Forward, that "the most dangerous situation is not to have food," the State Council realized that a more comprehensive solution for Hainan's development had to be devised.[138]

State Council document 1980.202 was the first step toward opening Hainan to both the domestic and the international economy. In addition to providing grain supplies, subsidizing grain and petroleum prices, and instituting other domestic economic-development initiatives, Beijing promoted a greater role for Hainan in the international economy, stating that "Hainan's foreign trade primarily will focus on exports to Hong Kong. We must allow Hainan to enjoy a bit more autonomy. Shenzhen and Zhuhai's methods in foreign economic activities can be used as a reference; we thus can give Hainan jurisdictional control. Hainan can be allotted a bit more foreign exchange that has been earned in foreign trade and other foreign exchange receipts, which have exceeded the planned remittal base figure. This will benefit projects that import production inputs for the *Yijin yangchu* program."[139] The central government allowed Hainan's state farms, communes, production brigades, and other economic entities to link with units inside and outside Guangdong province to establish joint ventures; leaders specifically suggested that Hainan use overseas Chinese capital to develop large-scale cattle farms to produce meat for domestic consumption and for export. While these were only initial steps toward opening, it is interesting that local cadres were instructed to learn from "Shenzhen and Zhuhai's methods in foreign economic activities."

Three years later, the Central Committee and the State Council followed up with a far more extensive plan to develop Hainan, issuing Central Committee document 1983.11 on 1 April 1983.[140] The previous December, Zhao Ziyang issued a written comment (*piyu*) to Gu Mu concerning Hainan.[141] While Zhao firmly stated that Hainan could not be an SEZ and was still under the direct control of Guangdong province, he said Beijing could provide the island with more autonomy. He instructed Gu Mu to gather together key cadres to research the Hainan problem, and suggested that Beijing could provide some investment funds to help with the island's development. Zhao Ziyang, General Wang Zhen, Hu Yaobang, and Gu Mu subsequently took part in a series of inspections, conferences, and discussions with local leaders in late winter and early spring of 1983 concerning Hainan's progress since the issuance of State Council document 1980.202. While the focus in 1980 had been on the tension between the PLA and the communes, document 1983.11 provides far more detailed instructions on the opening of Hainan Island. It reaffirms document 1980.202's emphasis on Hainan's role as a supplier of tropical products such as rubber, the need to provide more agricultural inputs, such as fertilizer, and the importance of reforestation. However, document 1983.11 states that "the two weakest links in Hainan's economic development are its backwards transportation system and lack of energy resources."[142] The State Council thus pledged to lay fifty kilometers of railroad track between Lingtou and Basuo, improve the port facilities in Haikou, and draw up plans to build a deep-water port at Yangpu.

In the spirit of the decentralization experiment outlined in Central Committee document 1979.50, which established the SEZs, the Central Committee agreed to give Hainan greater autonomy. By October 1984, the island was officially designated the Hainan Administrative Region (HAR). As such, it was to be treated as a separate planning entity within Guangdong's planning system. With certain limitations, HAR could "undertake all capital construction projects in which it can arrange for capital, the raw materials, fuel and power, transport, commodity marketing, foreign exchange, etc."[143] HAR was permitted to retain all revenues above the fixed provincial quota it was required to pay and it would continue to receive a provincial subsidy, which would be increased by 10 percent for a three-year period. In addition, the PBOC agreed to make HAR an annual loan of RMB 50 million, at a low interest rate, while the BOC would loan it US$50 million in foreign exchange for the next five years. In addition, HAR was permitted to institute a floating wage system and to allow individual farmers and businesspeople to engage in various new contract positions to improve HAR's infrastructure. Finally, the state encouraged outside provinces and production units to invest in Hainan, or in the SEZ parlance, *neilian qiye*. "Alliances within and outside Hainan must be energetically developed. Interior areas, especially those from developed areas, must be encouraged to establish or jointly run factories, agricultural farms, or tourist industries on Hainan. The military based on Hainan and the central government/provincial enterprises, especially the Hainan iron mines, agricultural reclamation, and the overseas Chinese agricultural farms, are important assets for developing Hainan; by using various types of economic associations, they can participate in Hainan's development thorough their financial, technical, managerial, and administrative expertise."[144]

Such arrangements were very similar to the decentralization policies enunciated in Central Committee document 1979.50, with one major exception. Deng Xiaoping had agreed with Chen Yun's December 1981 declaration that no new SEZs were to be established "for now." Thus, document 1983.11 clearly states that "leading comrades of the Central Committee have directed that Hainan should not become a special economic zone." Yet the document's underlying argument is clear. "While guaranteeing the Administrative Region's market supply, we can vigorously expand exports and gradually increase the export proportion of industrial and mineral commodities. By both bringing into full play Hainan's strengths and using the international market, there will be a large increase in Hainan's foreign economic activities in a couple of years . . . [with the] safe energetic use of foreign exchange, the importation of advanced technology, the development of import/export trade, tourism, and the opening to the outside world."[145]

In terms of foreign investment, the HAR was granted the authority to establish various types of foreign joint ventures to exploit the island's mineral resources and to develop its capital and technical infrastructure, so long as the projects were valued under US$5 million. To entice foreign investment, foreign joint ventures, cooperative arrangements, and wholly foreign-owned ventures would enjoy tax-free status during the first two years in which they made a profit; a 15 percent rate would be charged for subsequent years. A tax holiday on remitted joint-venture profits was granted, and for those foreign businesspeople without offices in the HAR, a 10 percent reduction in income tax would be levied on their stock dividends, interest, rent, and copyright fees. To promote investment in the agricultural and cattle industry, something first promoted in document 1980.202, fees would not be charged for any imported equipment, seeds, or breeding cattle.

In terms of import-export authority, the HAR could export domestically produced goods once it had met all state and provincial quota requirements, including those goods to be exported through the Guangdong provincial foreign trade corporation; it was also allowed to manage its export trade in Hong Kong through the auspices of the Yuehai Corporation. As for imports, the HAR was given far-ranging authority, which would turn out to be the source of Hainan's problems in the mid-1980s. Specifically,

> The Hainan Administrative Region can authorize the import of needed agricultural and industrial production materials for production and construction. Locally retained foreign exchange can be used to import certain scarce consumer goods (including those on the seventeen state-restricted import commodities list). This will enliven the market and guarantee supplies for tourism and materials bought with overseas Chinese remittances. The use and sale of the above-mentioned imported materials and commodities are restricted to the Hainan Administrative Region and cannot be resold outside the Administrative Region. Strict approval procedures must be instituted for those commodities on the restricted import list. A biannual report must be submitted for the record to the Guangdong People's Government and the State Economic Commission detailing the amount, sales, and utilization of these restricted materials.... [C]onstruction materials and equipment and materials for the operation of tourist ventures that are joint equity ventures or collaborative ventures can be imported duty-free.[146]

As for foreign exchange, the HAR was entitled to retain all foreign exchange earned above the export plan for five years. Although it would be responsible for any losses, the HAR was granted the privilege to keep "all foreign exchange retained from reprocessing, assembly, or compensation trade, tourist foreign exchange, remittances from overseas Chinese and compatriots from Hong Kong and Macao, and donations made with foreign exchange."[147] To help increase tourism and trade, both the Civil Aviation Administration and the State Economic Commission were entrusted to upgrade HAR's air- and seaport facilities. Central Committee document 1983.11 ends by promising that everyone would "struggle to make Hainan a beautiful and rich Treasure Island possessing a high degree of material civilization and socialist spiritual civilization." While giving obeisance to Chen Yun's "no SEZ" dictum and the ideological campaign, the international Leninists initiated a new experiment in the nascent coastal development strategy.

According to Gu Mu's 16 December 1985 report from the SEZ Office, issued as State Council document 1985.142, Hainan was estimated to have achieved a total 1985 GVIAO value of RMB 36.5 billion, which was a 90 percent increase over its 1980 GVIAO.[148] Gu Mu claimed that this impressive increase in economic growth was a result of the two Central Committee and State Council documents that guaranteed the island's development. Agricultural-sector growth came in part from to the addition of 25,000 acres of land primarily devoted to rubber trees, which increased the production of dry natural rubber by 90 percent between 1980 and 1985. Hainan authorities had also increased the amount of cultivated acreage devoted to sugarcane, coconuts, pepper, and southern Chinese medicinal herbs to 37,000 acres, and reforested 86,500 acres. Farmers' income rose from RMB 139 in 1980 to RMB 340 in 1984.

Economic growth also depended on state and provincial infrastructure investment. From 1983 to 1985, the governments invested in twenty-four large-scale construction projects, eleven of which involved the energy and transportation sectors. They upgraded the port facilities in Haikou, Sanya, and Basuo, built a railroad from the western ports of Basuo to Lingtou, and rebuilt the civilian airports in Haikou and Sanya. At the same time, Guangdong authorities improved the local education system, including the 1983 establishment of Hainan University in Haikou, which coincided with the establishment of Guangdong's Shenzhen University in the Shenzhen SEZ. In 1983 and 1984, foreign investors had signed contracts worth more than US$200 million and had invested US$100 million.

Between 1983 and 1985, Beijing and Guangdong sent to Hainan sixty-one delegations that approved a combined total of RMB 320 million in construction loans; RMB 64 million in direct aid to areas that were "older, had various minorities, were on the border, and poor"; RMB 150 million in low-interest loans; and another US$100 million in foreign exchange. Guangdong alone invested RMB 70 million in Hainan and provided RMB 30 million in loans and subsidies.

Financing Hainan's Infrastructure
through Illegal Imports

Despite such investment and impressive economic advancement, Hainan's industrial growth recovered in 1984 after six straight years of negative growth. Hainan's 1984 annual fiscal revenue was RMB 300 million, which was only 1.4 times what it was the previous year. Lei Yu and local officials decided to use more flexible means to finance the building of the island's infrastructure.

Beginning in mid-1984, the HAR government used its authority granted in Central Committee document 1983.11 to import restricted items, including 90,000 cars, motorcycles, and various types of electronic equipment, that were then resold on the mainland for a tremendous profit. HAR authorities used some of these profits to finance the construction of Hainan's infrastructure.

> Of the first batch approved, 2,300 vehicles arrived in the first half of 1984 and 13,000 came in July, but by September, when higher officials called a firm halt, over 80,000 had been approved.... When Lei Yu, clearly acting on orders from higher provincial officials, finally went to the docks to stop boats [that were] carrying vans from Hainan to the mainland, he nonetheless encountered powerful local resistance. Even after the clampdown was ordered from above in September, over the next two weeks local officials, still consumed by desire, approved the import of 8,900 more vehicles in clear defiance of the order.... They had used over US$1 billion of China's hard-won currency, and not only was there a shortage of hard currency for further purchases, but profiteering had ballooned out of control and attracted national and even international attention.[149]

The Hainan car scandal also implicated the Shenzhen SEZ, as Hainan middlemen had traveled to Shenzhen and other locations to trade RMB for hard currency. These transactions were particularly easy in Shenzhen because Hong Kong dollars functioned as a de facto currency in the zone and decentralization had reduced official supervision. The foreign exchange obtained was used to buy foreign goods, which were then resold in China for markups as high as 300 percent. Profits were pocketed by local Hainan units, including party, media, and government offices. This was later characterized as the largest foreign exchange scam in the history of the People's Republic.[150]

According to State Council document 1985.142, the Central Commission for Discipline Inspection and the Guangdong Party Committee held five different meetings of the party's expanded standing committee to investigate the Hainan "car incident." The State Supply Bureau was tasked with financing and disposing of 57,422 confiscated vehicles, the debt for which included various interest rates and other transaction costs.[151] However, collecting the RMB 400 million owed on the vehicles was difficult, as some had been resold three or four different times, and profits had often been used for such projects as building dormitories or repairing roads. The Ministry of Finance thus decided to provide RMB 100 million to help Hainan pay off the vehicle debt; during Zhao Ziyang's visit to Hainan in February 1986, this amount was raised by another 50 million.[152]

At the national level, the State Council strengthened its financial and commerce controls by issuing document 1985.38, entitled "The Decision on Strengthening Foreign Currency Management," on 13 March 1985.[153] Between December 1984 and March 1985, foreign exchange reserves dropped from US$14.4 billion to US$11.3 billion.[154] The State Council accused certain localities and offices of illegally using their retained foreign exchange by exchanging it for renminbi and depositing it in their bank accounts. Other localities and offices illegally sold foreign exchange and FECs. As this had a hugely detrimental impact on the CCP and the state, the State Council reassumed control of foreign exchange by establishing a foreign currency quota for all provinces and municipalities directly under the central government. The PBOC and its local foreign exchange management offices managed the quota and strengthened foreign currency management procedures. Units desiring to use foreign exchange had to work within their allotted quota. They were forbidden to buy or sell foreign exchange or even allow the local use of foreign exchange.

The State Council on 13 March also issued the "Circular on Firmly Prohibiting Profiteering on Local Resale of Goods."[155] Referring to the Hainan problem, the State Council argued that a few units and individuals had illegally profited from the resale of steel, automobiles, color televisions, and other valuable imported durable goods, which often changed hands several times, with prices constantly increasing. To stop such trade, the State Council ordered that only state-owned trading organizations could deal with sales of key production materials and consumer goods that were in high demand. Units and individuals were forbidden to engage in trade profiteering, to raise prices on goods that had fixed state prices, and to use false contracts and invoices. The State Council also ordered all government agencies to investigate and resolve any illegal activities found within their organizations, resolve tax evasion cases, and impose disciplinary measures against any individual involved in such activities. The State Council issued another circular in April prohibiting the importation of color TV production lines, with special attention given to the SEZs and the ETDZs. Future TV import projects would be handled in Beijing, according to the state plan.[156] A notice was issued on 15 June that restricted the importation of all refrigerators unless approved by MOFERT or the Ministry of Light Industry.[157] In October, the State Council prohibited all military units, schools, and industrial enterprises from importing expensive vehicles until 1987. Beijing would manage all vehicle imports, starting in 1986.[158] The State Council also approved plans to strengthen smuggling checkpoints set up in dock areas, train stations, and along key transport arteries in the three southeastern coastal provinces, including Guangdong and Fujian. The report stated that, between 1980 and 1984, authorities had investigated more than one million cases of smuggling and issued RMB 300 million in fines.[159]

However, such tightening of centralized control failed to satisfy some delegates attending the Chinese People's Political Consultative Conference (CPPCC), 25 March to 25 April. The conference, which had to be extended in order to reach a consensus on a variety of issues, was the scene of acrimonious debate on zonal policy. The critique of Hainan was being applied to Shenzhen. Some delegates charged that Shenzhen was filled with "carpetbaggers" taking advantage of the rest of the country.[160] The third session of the Sixth National People's Congress was meeting at the same time as the CPPCC in Beijing. In his government work report presented on 27 March 1985, Zhao Ziyang stated that the government was resolving a variety of unhealthy tendencies, "including the careless issuance of bonuses, goods, and subsidies, the sharp increase of material prices to gain high profits, using one's authority to buy and resell scarce goods for a profit, winning friends by gift giving, to give and take bribes, and other unhealthy tendencies."[161] To prevent further criticism, Deng Xiaoping addressed the problems the next day during his meeting with the vice president of the Japanese Liberal Democratic Party. Deng admitted that problems with implementing the economic reforms were inevitable and expected (*meiyou shenma liaobuqi*). But he reaffirmed that he would boldly go forward with the reforms while reviewing policy implementation at regular intervals to "correct every wrong step immediately." He agreed with foreign commentators that China had already progressed so far in its opening that it could not go backward. In fact, Deng stated that "China might open up further in the future."[162] Thus, the criticism of Hainan and the SEZs died down.

To "wrap up" (*baofu*) the problem in November 1985, Gu Mu stated that the party was faced with three major issues. Many cadres had not been involved in the incident yet were troubled by the implications of the investigations on their future and wanted to transfer out of Hainan. On the other hand, there were more than 700 cases of cadres who were guilty of corruption, and more than 2,000 cases under investigation. Finally, the state had to settle between RMB 500 and RMB 600 million in debts and creditors' rights. The state also had to dispose of more than RMB 1 billion in illegally imported goods. Complicating the situation, there were two hurricanes in September and October 1985 that left 171 people dead, collapsed 18,365 buildings, destroyed more than 100 bridges and 224 kilometers of roads, downed 300 kilometers of electrical lines, and destroyed 169 reservoirs.

Considering the investigations and economic problems faced by Hainan, the State Council issued a notice on 7 December 1985 that strengthened the import management regulations for Fujian and Guangdong, which included Hainan. Under the new rules, the provinces and SEZs had to comply with new regulations in order to import twenty-four types of durable goods, including automobiles, electronic calculators, televisions, stereos, VCRs, washing machines, refrigerators, cameras, watches, air-conditioning units, and copying machines. None of the items could be sold to buyers in other provinces; they could be used only within the provinces that imported them, the SEZs, and

Hainan. The foreign exchange needed to buy these goods had to be raised internally. All transportation units and the post offices had to enforce the new regulations. Imports of vegetables, fruits, and seafood were also prohibited, unless they were to be used by top hotels, joint-venture restaurants, or foreign aircraft and ocean-going vessels.[163]

In the end, the State Council decided to continue to implement Hainan's expanded authority as outlined in Central Committee document 1983.11, and even to expand economic policies to encourage Hainan's development. Hainan cadres again were to concentrate on developing the island's abundant resources, and were ordered to draw up an extensive economic development plan by 1986 that would take into account a joint plan drawn up by the State Planning Commission and Japan, with the suggestions of Go Keng Swee (Wu Qingrui), the former deputy prime minister of Singapore and an economic adviser to the Chinese State Council, and a Malaysian agricultural economist based at the World Bank. The report reemphasized developing Hainan's tourist industry in a planned and coordinated manner. Gu Mu also asked that a more scientific approach be taken to develop Hainan's tropical crops, including the importation of foreign varieties. And he asked the state and province to work together to expand the 1,300 industrial enterprises on the island. Gu Mu emphasized the document 1983.11 directive, "To use the opening to the outside world to promote island development." He argued that Hainan had already implemented several joint investment projects from Singapore, the United States, and Japan to develop better tropical products, including palm oil, coffee, new coconut products, pineapples, bananas, and shrimp. In the future, Go Keng Swee suggested, Singapore would be interested in establishing a modern hog-raising operation. Although the situation was "still not ripe," in the future Hainan could allow wholly foreign-owned ventures and be given greater responsibility for its fiscal affairs and foreign investment.

On 14 February 1986 Zhao Ziyang led a delegation of party leaders—including Hu Qili, Tian Jiyun, and Qiang Xiaochu, secretary of the Central Discipline and Inspection Commission—on a tour of eight different Hainan counties and two cities during a ten-day inspection trip. Zhao addressed a conference of leading Guangdong party, government, and military cadres, including the Guangdong party leader, Lin Ruo, and the new Hainan administrative district party leader, Yao Wenxu.[164] As a top Guangdong party leader himself in the 1950s and 1960s, Zhao was fully qualified to remark on Hainan's economic progress during the 1950s and how much it had progressed since 1980. In tackling the Hainan car incident, Zhao offered a positive interpretation of events in order to move forward. He said that all Hainan cadres should learn from previous mistakes, noting "one fell into the pit, but one can [still] gain knowledge" (*chi yi qian, zhang yi zhi*). Implying that the moderate bureaucratic Stalinists should not use the problem to attack Hainan or the opening, Zhao stated, "This is a temporary problem, and so long as the comrades in Hainan resolve the issue, then it is not difficult to resolve."[165] He then added,

> Because the opening of Hainan and its development is a nationwide task, it is one that must be taken up by everyone. The comrades in Hainan have already absorbed this lesson, and those who seriously broke the law and party discipline have already undergone party discipline, political discipline, and legal discipline. We are all working together to make sure that the development of Hainan is not hindered by the car incident. This was just one event. I have already stated that we cannot make the punishment and legal sanctions against those who made mistakes also apply to the several millions of people living in Hainan. Because the central and Guangdong governments are okay with this outcome, we must make an all-out effort to help Hainan with its problems.

Referring to the central government's partial financing of the debt owed after Hainan's car incident, Zhao argued that this was the only way to help Hainan recover economically. Zhao argued that Hainan would have to take partial responsibility for the debt as a lesson that had to be learned, and that the central government lacked the funds to finance the entire debt. Zhao then returned to Gu Mu's report and emphasized that the Beijing and Guangdong governments needed to help Hainan financially and administratively, so it could return to the development path.

While his February 1986 speech envisioned Hainan as a key component of the coastal development strategy, it would be almost two more years before Zhao opened a conference, in December 1987, on establishing the new Hainan province and China's newest and largest special economic zone. During the interim period, CDIC first secretary Chen Yun and Deng Xiaoping agreed that the Hainan corruption cases had been resolved successfully. Beijing and Guangdong authorities used this period to rebuild the island after the devastating series of natural disasters and to transform the Hainan bureaucracy and local bureaucrats to serve the national interest and not local self-interest. Eventually, Beijing established a preparatory committee to study the establishment of a new Hainan province and SEZ.

The core reason for Zhao's delay undoubtedly was the discussion on political reform initiated in spring 1986. Subsequently, Hu Yaobang resigned, on 4 January 1987, and Zhao Ziyang was appointed acting general secretary until the Thirteenth Plenum. Eventually Li Peng was appointed premier (see chapter 6). As Zhao Ziyang wrote,

> My activities in 1987 can be divided into two major phases. From January to April, when I had just succeeded Yaobang as [acting] general secretary, I took on the designated task of waging a nationwide Anti-Liberalization Campaign. Most of my energy and concentration was focused on figuring out how to prevent the campaign from overreaching, to control and limit the "left wing" who were hoping to use the campaign to oppose reform. This "left wing" struggle was opposed to the principles set forth at the Third Plenum [in 1978]. The second phase ran from May until the beginning of the 13th Party Congress [in October], I reemphasized reform, tried to prevent a swing to the left, and opposed ossified thinking—all with the preparation for the 13th Party Congress in mind.[166]

Deng realized that Li Peng had limited economic policy experience and a penchant for the model of the Soviet Union, where he had studied for several years. Deng thus decided that "for the time being, after taking the post of general secretary, Zhao will continue to manage economic affairs and continue to head the Central Economic and Financial Leading Group."[167]

Before the opening of the Thirteenth Party Congress in September 1987, Zhao set forth his vision for Hainan's development in a meeting with the leader and vice leader of the Hainan Provincial Preparatory

Committee: the future Hainan party secretary, Xu Shijie, and the future governor, Liang Xiang.[168] The State Council had already been drawing up new policies and regulations concerning the province and the SEZs. The Preparatory Committee and the State Council SEZ Office were ordered to draw up separate versions, which would be reconciled by the State Council. Following State Council approval, Zhao intended to submit the new plans to the National People's Congress for its approval in 1988.

Zhao Ziyang thus established the guidelines for the committee's policy formulations. He told them to make Hainan into a "first-class experiment for comprehensive national organizational reforms."[169] As Zhao was preparing to aggressively promote the separation of the party and the state at the upcoming Thirteenth Party Congress in October, he argued that the new provincial SEZ should be something entirely different from the normal Chinese provinces and SEZs.[170] Zhao wanted a clear separation between Hainan's Communist Party and its government, and also between the Hainan Communist Party and its industries. "We can make the party and government organizations much smaller, while enlarging the economic entity. Several development companies can be established that have greater management powers. But the government will not interfere. We want to establish a small government, but [a] large society."[171]

As "America and Canada were both developed from the East to the West," Zhao directed that Hainan should be gradually developed by focusing first on the coastal regions and then on the interior areas.[172] Zhao suggested that Hainan establish development corporations separate from the government; they could be foreign joint ventures or 100 percent foreign-owned ventures. The companies would be granted legal authority to develop specific parcels of land. As for development capital, Hainan would primarily rely on Hong Kong and Macao investments but would also welcome investment from other Chinese provinces. To attract investors from Hong Kong and Macao, Zhao stated that Hainan's primary financing source was its control of property rights. Having obviously learned about the Hong Kong government's methods of financing government operations through its land sales, Zhao suggested that foreign companies should enter into long-term transferable land leases from the government, ranging from thirty to fifty years at various rates, to develop real estate. Such land rights could be used as security to procure foreign mortgages.

Finally, Zhao was very concerned about Hainan's lack of qualified technical personnel. He instructed Xu Shijie to put special effort into attracting technicians from the mainland and from the group of Chinese students returning from their overseas studies. To attract such personnel, Zhao argued that Hainan should arrange to build better housing. If Hainan could offer technical experts good jobs and decent accommodations, it would be able to attract people living on the mainland to transfer to Hainan. As the former Shenzhen party secretary and mayor, Liang Xiang fully understood this technique. Shenzhen spent large amounts of money to build excellent accommodations where mainland families, often formerly divided by work-unit assignments in different cities, could reunite and live the "good life." However, Zhao Ziyang clearly stated that the city government should not use the same methods to attract party or government personnel. The technicians were the key to Hainan's technical transformation.

From 8 to 11 December 1987, the State Council convened a conference in Haikou, Hainan, that was attended by sixteen State Council departments, the Hainan Provincial Preparatory Committee, various leading Guangdong party officials, representatives from Hong Kong–based Chinese enterprises, and the Xinhua News Agency, which during British colonial rule acted as China's de facto government representative in the Crown colony. The State Council approved the conference report in document 1988.24, issued on 14 April 1988, which approved the establishment of China's largest SEZ in Hainan and established Hainan as a separate province.[173] The document promised to provide Hainan "with even more flexible policies" so that "within three to five years, Hainan would catch up to the national economic levels, and by the end of the century reach the levels of the other most advanced economically developed areas in the country, and set its sights on catching up with the other Southeast Asian developed economies and other regional areas."[174] Hainan would use foreign capital, especially from Hong Kong, Macao, and Taiwan, to develop its infrastructure (ports, airports, roads, railroads, coal mines, electrical generation plants, hydroelectric plants, and so on) in a gradual fashion, starting in the island's coastal areas and gradually moving toward the interior. Investors from outside the country's borders (*jingwai*) who invested more than 25 percent in a specific industry could enjoy the favorable tax treatment accorded to foreign-invested enterprises. With approval of the PBOC, foreign banks and other foreign financial organizations could be established on Hainan to help invest in Hainan's future. Foreign-invested enterprises would enjoy the same treatment accorded to the fourteen open coastal cities and the SEZs for tax abatement schemes and other investment incentives. Hainan was permitted to establish its own foreign trade companies to export Hainan goods abroad. Having encountered problems with entrepôt trade and duplication of imports, Hainan could import goods necessary for its development, but only in accordance with State Council regulations designed to prevent import duplication and other import problems.[175]

As a newly established province, Hainan would gradually receive more decision-making powers from Beijing. In the short term, the provincial government was to work with the Xinhua News Agency's Hong Kong office to provide travel documents for Hong Kong investors and travelers. With a couple of exceptions, Beijing would gradually cede management control of its SOEs based in Hainan. The Hainan government would have the right to approve basic construction projects and technological renovation projects valued under RMB 200 million. However, Hainan's autonomy would be restricted in certain areas, and it would need permission for various economic activities, such as the construction of factories that use controlled imports to produce goods to be sold in the interior economy. To subsidize Hainan's development, Beijing agreed to give a set amount of money every year, from 1988 to 1995. During this time period, Beijing would allocate 550,000,000 *jin* of grain annually to Hainan to supplement its food resources and allow it to concentrate on producing its tropical crops.

The National People's Congress approved the establishment of Hainan as a separate province and as a special economic zone on 13 April 1988. The State Council issued document 1988.24 on 14 April 1988. Hainan now entered a new period of accelerated development; it would become known for its beaches, the Bo'ao Forum for Asia that promotes regional economic integration, and as a logistical base to support China's activities in the South China Sea.

Nanxun as the Catalyst for the Third Way

China's opening to the outside world was a learned process. Elites had learned that the inwardly oriented regime of the 1950s to 1970s had reached its limits, and that a new experiment for development was needed. The adoption of Central Committee document 1979.50, which initiated decentralization with Guangdong and Fujian provinces and the SEZs, was the first experiment. Problems that arose with implementation engendered a split of the post-GLF coalition into two factions, the international Leninists and the moderate bureaucratic Stalinists; these two opinion groups differed on the roles to be played by the state and the market. Yet the crucial catalyst for initiating the Third Way was Deng Xiaoping's promotion of Zhao Ziyang's coastal development approach of outward-oriented development, which harnessed FDI and foreign technology to accelerate China's domestic growth.

With his first *nanxun* in 1984, Deng Xiaoping approved the initial decentralization strategy involving Guangdong and Fujian and allowed Zhao Ziyang to pursue his vision for China's coastal development. Zhao successfully established the fourteen open coastal cities with the passage of Central Committee document 1984.13, the open coastal economic regions with Central Committee document 1985.3, and the Hainan SEZ with State Council document 1988.24. The next chapter examines how Zhao Ziyang successfully formulated and enacted his coastal development strategy.

CHAPTER FIVE

Initiating China's Third Way

Ten years had passed since Hua Guofeng began opening China to the outside world by sending hundreds of State Council and institutional delegations abroad to learn how the world had changed in the years after the People's Republic of China was established. Contrary to Mao's inward-focused revolutionary Stalinist approach, the delegations discovered that China might use foreign knowledge from outside to achieve its long-term goals of building a strong national defense, developing a self-sufficient economy, and guaranteeing the party's hegemony over the state, the economy, and the people. Hua Guofeng and Zhao Ziyang had taken part in this great adventure, traveling to Eastern Europe and Iran in August 1978, where they were inspired by foreign technologies and management techniques. Hua Guofeng subsequently accelerated China's large-scale ISI program and approved small-scale experiments with the household contract system, compensation trade, cooperative production, the use of commercial loans for smaller projects, and borrowing money from foreign governments and international financial institutions under preferential interest rates. Hua also revived the 1950s policy of welcoming overseas Chinese investment and allowed foreign businesses to establish joint ventures.

However, Chen Yun reminded his colleagues in 1980 that the international marketplace was dangerous and advised caution, as "foreign capitalists are capitalists."[1] The shared view was that there were foreign capitalists who "sincerely hope to cooperate with us and use legitimate methods to do business" and those who would "resort to dishonest means or even means in violation of China's sovereignty—such as swindle [sic], bribery, smuggling, infiltration, and espionage—to harm . . . the Chinese people and corrupt Party members, cadres and other people."[2] While Chen Yun should not be criticized as a xeno-phobe, as he had long promoted interaction with the world economy, he did convince Deng Xiaoping that China's huge foreign indebtedness caused by the New Great Leap would lead to economic disaster. This threat of economic crisis initiated phase one of the learning process in China's experiment with decentralization, and brought about the end of Zhou Enlai's approach of large-scale ISI development, promoted by Premier Hua Guofeng.

Yet this crisis did not initiate another simple learning cycle like those China had been through several times since the 1950s, whenever the bureaucratic Stalinists held power. Instead, the reaction led to a far deeper level of complex learning, in which key leaders recognize the inherent contradictions between previously held ideas and reality and shift their long-term goals and policies. The Chinese elites realized that their inward-oriented strategy to achieve self-reliance was increasingly ineffective and expensive. They thus experimented with the outward-oriented export-led strategy that eventually became China's Third Way of development. Leaders continued to pursue the long-term goal of a strong national defense but changed their goal of a self-reliant economy to an economy fueled by export-led growth; they reduced the party's control over the economy while maintaining and adapting its hege-mony over the state and the people.

Deng Xiaoping continued and expanded Hua's experiments with the bureaucratic Stalinists' development model II. Since his visits abroad—to France in May 1975, to Japan in October 1978, and to Singa-pore in November of 1978—Deng had enthusiastically supported the New Great Leap Forward. But after listening to Chen Yun's counsel, he approved a comprehensive readjustment of Hua's large-scale ISI pro-gram. While carrying out the phase two readjustment of the economy, Deng simultaneously initiated phase three with his approval of several decentralization experiments outlined in Central Committee docu-ment 1979.50. Leaders in Guangdong and Fujian learned how to use their new economic decision-making powers to control their provincial economies, while leaders in the new special economic zones learned to use domestic and FDI and foreign management techniques to build the SEZs. Chinese businesspeople and farmers learned to take advantage of the loosening controls in the command economy to initiate new ventures and earn profits. Implementation problems were inevitable, and Beijing thus continuously had to review and readjust the decentralization experiments (phase four), a process that culminated with Deng's inspection of the southern coastal region's experiment during his first *nanxun*, in 1984. Satisfied with the experiment's relative success, Deng initiated phase five and expanded the opening of China's coastal economy to the international market by establishing the fourteen open coastal cities, the open coastal economic regions, and the Hainan SEZ. Having approved the accession process for joining the General Agreement on Tariffs and Trade (GATT) and the promulgation of Zhao Ziyang's outward-oriented coastal development strategy in 1988, Deng initiated phase six in China's shift from an inward-oriented goal of self-reliance to an outward-oriented goal of export-led growth.

This sectoral paradigm shift continued through the 1990s. Deng and the bureaucratic Stalinist elites had learned through experimentation that they could enliven the economy by relinquishing a certain degree of party control and increasing the role of domestic and international market forces. The implementation of export-oriented economic policies began to unshackle the coastal economy from the state plan and initiated an economic boom that lasted for decades. China thus became a post-totalitarian state in which the elites altered the economic paradigm to allow limited economic pluralism but kept and adapted their Stalinist political and social paradigm so that ideology became less pervasive, China grew less reliant on mobilization campaigns, and its new leaders were less charismatic and more technocratic. In this way, the CCP elites maintained the party's hegemony while promoting impressive economic growth.

Chinese elites had progressed beyond their inward-oriented view that the purpose of foreign capital and technology was to transform China into a strong and self-reliant economy. Like their counterparts in the East Asian "miracle economies" of South Korea and Taiwan in the late 1950s and 1960s, the second generation of international Leninist

elites, led by Zhao Ziyang, embraced a more outward-oriented Weltanschauung, believing that the international economy could become
an engine for domestic development.[3] Leaders determined that China
would engage in export-led growth in the coastal areas while they
protected the interior economy from the international marketplace
as it gradually moved away from its inward-oriented ISI legacy. By the
1990s, it was this change in thinking that resulted in the establishment
of China's new post-totalitarian state, in which elites adapted the
Stalinist political and social paradigm of the 1950s while shifting to a
consultative, outward-oriented economic paradigm.

This chapter analyzes the initial transition to phase six with Deng's
approval of the GATT accession process and Zhao Ziyang's coastal
development strategy that envisioned export-led growth for the coastal
regions while continuing the ISI path for the interior economy. Although the moderate bureaucratic Stalinists attempted to prevent the
completion of phase six during the period immediately following the
June Fourth Incident at Tiananmen, Deng reignited the transition in
1992 with his second *nanxun*.

Initiating GATT Accession

Searching for ways to finance China's readjusted ISI strategy in the late
1970s, Chinese leaders arranged to establish large lines of credit and
official loans from foreign governments and international organizations. After listening to the Gu Mu delegation's report on their five-
week tour of fifteen European cities in May–June 1978, Deng Xiaoping
had argued that China should take advantage of the Europeans' willingness to invest in China and to provide preferential loans.[4] Thus, by
the end of 1979 China had arranged for approximately US$7 billion in
export credits from France, US$5 billion from Great Britain, US$2 billion from Japan, US$2 billion from Canada, and US$1 billion from Italy.[5]
Initially, U.S. vice president Walter Mondale offered to loan China
US$2 billion. In his July 1980 letter to Deng Xiaoping, Hua Guofeng,
Li Xiannian, and Chen Yun, Zhao Ziyang argued that the U.S. interest
rate of 8.75 to 9.25 percent, which was what the United States normally

charged other nations, was high compared with interest rates offered by other capitalist countries. With President Jimmy Carter running for reelection against the Republican nominee Ronald Reagan, Zhao argued that China should continue to argue discreetly for better loan terms and try to avoid any political entanglements.[6] In the meantime, China successfully applied for a US$1.5 billion loan at a 3 percent rate from the Japanese Overseas Economic Cooperation Fund to finance major construction projects, including two major projects that survived the readjustment of Hua's Ten-Year Plan, the Daqing Petrochemical Company complex and the Baoshan Steel complex.[7]

However, leaders in Beijing realized that the most advantageous way to finance development would be to join the international financial institutions—the International Monetary Fund (IMF), the Asian Development Bank (ADB), and the International Bank for Reconstruction and Development, or World Bank. To take advantage of the IMF's short-term loans to overcome balance-of-payments difficulties, China joined the IMF in 1980 and received a short-term loan to finance its 1981 foreign exchange shortfall. China also rejoined the World Bank in 1980 and successfully applied for a long-term US$800 million loan in 1981.[8] Zhao Ziyang reported on the progress of China's economic reforms to a visiting World Bank vice president on 16 July 1980 and presciently described China's future path of development:

> After two years of reform, China has achieved very good results. From now on, we will not waver and will resolutely carry on with reforms. Of course, we are undergoing the initial stages of reform, and every small reform is a small revolution. It appears that China will be undergoing a long-term reform process. We have a saying in Chinese, "Feeling the stones while crossing the river." This is to say that in part we implement policy and summarize our experiences, and in part [we] move forward in a set direction. Gradually our reforms will move forward, impacting all aspects of life.[9]

In remarking on China's use of foreign capital and how long-term loans from the World Bank would benefit China's development, Zhao Ziyang said,

During the past several years, we did not seriously consider using foreign capital, primarily because we lacked experience in this area. We needed time to discover how to use foreign capital and achieve better results. Everyone knows one needs to repay loans. If the loan is not effectively used, then China's credit will be affected. We do not want this to happen. Of course, as China gradually accumulates more experience, we will use greater amounts of foreign capital. This raises another issue. We have a major problem in implementing modernization. We lack basic infrastructure, especially in our transportation systems, energy resources, telecommunications, port facilities, and urban infrastructure. Everyone knows this is a prerequisite for industrialization and other activities.[10]

The State Council already had approved the Ministry of Petroleum's request of June 1980 to sign agreements with Japanese and French oil concerns to explore jointly for petroleum in the Bohai Sea and the northern part of the South China Sea.[11] Zhao argued that China should stop borrowing capital for the coal or petroleum projects. Instead, he said China should borrow from institutions like the World Bank to finance long-term infrastructure projects, such as hydroelectric dams and other energy resources, transportation projects, port facilities, telecommunications, and education.

With U.S. acquiescence, the PRC assumed a seat at the Asian Development Bank in 1986 and agreed that Taiwan could retain its seat under the name Taipei, China.[12] After the coastal development strategy was approved in early 1988, China received ADB funding and technical assistance for developing its coastal infrastructure—including building bridges in Shanghai, railroads in Guangdong, and facilities to produce all-steel radial tires in Qingdao—and it received technical assistance to improve the State Statistical Bureau and the National Environmental Protection Agency. By the late 1980s Chinese officials were using preferential loans to develop large-scale infrastructure projects designed to enhance China's outward-oriented economic development rather than self-reliance.

Chinese elites also understood the cost of membership in the international financial institutions, which required China to reveal its internal financial secrets to foreign international institutions. As Zhao had pointed out in July 1980, China had learned that in exchange for accepting foreign scrutiny and guidance, global economic institutions could provide low-interest foreign loans—and valuable advice to help transform China's moribund economy. Thus, starting in the 1980s, China's elites consciously decided not only to give up some control of the command economy but also to give up a degree of national sovereignty to the international financial institutions.

However, leaders in Beijing also realized the limitations of financing China's development solely through foreign loans. Just as Chinese elites had increased foreign exports to finance their ISI-based self-reliance strategy in the 1950s, 1960s, and 1970s, leaders in the 1980s focused on export-led growth when considering how to implement their outward-oriented development strategy. The key prerequisite for this new strategy was to join the GATT.

As a command economy, the PRC was not eligible to join the GATT or its successor organization, the World Trade Organization (WTO). While the European community and the United States granted China most-favored-nation status in 1979, China did not enjoy full GATT membership privileges, such as nondiscrimination against its goods, services, and intellectual property; reciprocity of treatment; international norms in trade commitments, trade dispute resolution, and so on. The U.S. president, in accordance with the Jackson-Vanik amendment to the Trade Act of 1974, determined annually whether to grant China normal trade-relations status. Unfortunately, this waiver process often degenerated into an annual battle between the Congress and the U.S. administration concerning China's human rights record, especially after the June Fourth Incident at Tiananmen Square in 1989.

Chinese elites realized that GATT membership would eliminate many nations' protectionist barriers and would avoid the annual U.S. congressional battle over granting China normal trade relations. They also hoped to entice foreign investors who, in the late 1980s, were looking for new areas in Asia to invest in, owing to growing production costs in some Asian and Latin American economies. By attracting FDI, China could implement its outward-oriented development strategy and use the international marketplace as an engine to accelerate domestic growth.

According to Scott Harold and others, Zhao Ziyang initiated a detailed discussion concerning China's future role in the GATT following the Twelfth Party Congress of September 1982.[13] In December 1982 the Ministry of Foreign Economic Relations and Trade—along with the Ministries of Foreign Affairs and Finance, the State Economic Commission, and the State General Administration of Customs—submitted a joint report to the State Council arguing that China should "reassume" its membership in the GATT as a developing economy. According to Li Lanqing, the report "noted that China's trade with the GATT's members had been rising as a result of its reform and opening policy, accounting for approximately 80 percent that of China's total trade."[14] The State Council approved the "Request for Instructions concerning China's Participation in GATT" on 25 December 1982.[15] To avoid the complicated accession process, the leadership hoped to regain China's former position as a contracting party to the short-lived International Trade Organization, the progenitor of the GATT, and to be treated as a developing economy. Chinese observer delegations thus were sent to GATT meetings and to visit with GATT members from Eastern European economies, such as Yugoslavia (1966) and Hungary (1973).[16] China had a contentious trading relationship with various countries, especially the United States, involving its textile exports.[17] "Its participation in the MFA [Multifiber Arrangement] was rather tense, as PRC negotiators engaged in extremely tough bargaining to keep a generous share of textile quotas."[18]

In January 1986 Zhao Ziyang personally thanked GATT director general Arthur Dunkel for his cooperation in helping China gain GATT observer status, and he informed Dunkel of China's intention to resume its membership in the GATT. Zhao framed the request as reflecting the needs of China's opening strategy. "China's policy of opening to the outside world has been developing in a broad and in-depth manner. This policy cannot be reversed. If China can resume its membership in the GATT, it will further expand its trade relations with other GATT members. From the standpoint of developing China's foreign trade, China not only wants to expand its exports but also wants to increase imports. Driven forward by its economic structural reforms, China will reduce discrepancies with most other GATT members in certain areas, such as in foreign trade organization, prices, and exchange rates."[19] Zhao Ziyang subsequently established a small coordinating leadership group to undertake research on the GATT reaccession issue. Ambassador Qian Jiadong of the Chinese Permanent Mission with the United Nations in Geneva formally presented China's request on 10 July 1986.[20] In February 1987 China submitted to GATT a 300-page memorandum of its foreign trade structure, which initiated a give-and-take process of negotiations, including side consultations with the United States. Over the next fifteen years, China adapted its foreign trade system, including export promotion strategies such as the SEZs, to meet GATT/WTO norms.[21]

After having achieved GATT observer status, Chinese negotiators finally achieved full membership in 2001 after years of arduous negotiations. Since that time China has used its impressive economic power to effect changes in the WTO, and the WTO has also had profound effects on its 143rd member, as China has been required to adhere to international norms of foreign trade behavior and market economy principles. To a certain extent, Chinese bureaucratic fiat has given way to a more transparent legal system, which according to WTO norms must be consistently applied and must not discriminate against foreigners. With the reduction or elimination of tariff and nontariff barriers and other protectionist policies, Chinese industrial, agricultural, financial, and service sectors were thrust into a very competitive global marketplace. Its Darwinian effects forced the closure of many state-owned enterprises, thus ruining the livelihood of millions of workers and intensifying social unrest. Stymied by conservative elites, bureaucracies, and regional interest groups over the past several years, reformist leaders such as Premier Zhu Rongji have tried to use the economic crisis created by international competition to merge, privatize, or close China's remaining 75,000 SOEs. While retaining control over enterprises related to national security and maintaining the state's ability to guide development, China's reformist elites looked toward fully marketizing the economy. They hoped that international competition would enable changes that they were unable to realize on their own.

The GATT thus became a vital component of China's new outward-oriented, export-led development strategy. But China first had to shift from its previous, inward-oriented, self-reliance strategy.

The Shift to Outward-Oriented Development

In January 1988 Deng Xiaoping approved Zhao Ziyang's coastal development concept. By the spring, Beijing leaders had issued a set of official documents and speeches that mapped out China's new development strategy for the twenty-first century, marking the beginning of the shift to a new consultative economic paradigm with an outward-oriented development strategy.

Not surprisingly, the inward-oriented thinking of Zhou Enlai and Chen Yun still influenced the bureaucratic Stalinists. This thinking had guided three decades of ISI strategies, characterized by the "156 Projects" with the Soviet Union, the Four Modernizations vision put forth in 1964 and renewed in the Four-Three Plan of 1973, and the Ten-Year Plan of 1978. In the view of the bureaucratic Stalinists, the international marketplace was an effective tool for acquiring the technology to make China a strong, self-sufficient economy. However, neither Zhou nor Chen ever envisioned China as major player in the international market.

Zhao Ziyang had been developing his ideas on the coastal development strategy while he was working in Guangdong province in the 1950s and 1960s, when he said, "I had come to believe that it would be beneficial to allow the coastal regions to utilize international trade to develop their full potential."[22] Beginning with his speech to the State Council in April 1981, Zhao had argued for a "reasonable division of labor between the coastal and interior areas to bring into play their strengths" and argued that the coastal regions should be fully engaged in exporting abroad. These themes were again the focus of his July 1981 speech to the Central Party Secretariat, when he promoted the development of the coastal provinces, whose economic and technological transformation would accelerate domestic economic growth. While the moderate bureaucratic Stalinists' criticisms slowed the evolution of the coastal strategy between 1982 and 1984, Deng's enthusiastic support for the SEZs and coastal opening during his first *nanxun* in 1984 reenergized coastal development. Deng put forward several policy initiatives on 24 February 1984 that eventually resulted in the passage of Central Committee document 1984.13, which established the fourteen open coastal cities; Central Committee and State Council document

1985.3, which established the open coastal economic regions; and State Council document 1988.24, establishing Hainan as a province and China's largest SEZ. Instead of fearing the hostile international marketplace, the international Leninists regarded the international market as a potential partner in development whose capital and technology could renovate and grow the Chinese economy.

During his interactions with GATT officials and with Chinese scholars in the mid- to late 1980s, Zhao increasingly appreciated the development path taken by many of the newly industrialized economies such as South Korea, Hong Kong, and Taiwan, which had pursued export-led growth since the early 1960s that accelerated their domestic industrial development. A decade had passed since Zhao Ziyang had accompanied Hua Guofeng to Romania, Yugoslavia, and Iran in August 1978 and become fascinated with Yugoslav management techniques. The experience of the subsequent ten years had expanded Zhao's worldview, as he worked to replace the Chinese elites' traditional long-term goal of self-reliance with a vision of export-led growth for the coastal economy, retaining the inward-oriented ISI strategy for the interior economy.

As Western scholars were publishing research on the export-led growth model in the mid- to late 1980s, Chinese scholars developed their own version, "the strategy of the great international economic cycle of development" (*guoji da xunhuan jingji fazhan zhanlüe*).[23] Fewsmith states that during the Thirteenth Party Congress, Zhao became interested in the theory put forward by two economists, Wang Jian and Pei Xiaolin, associated with the State Planning Commission.[24] Their approach fit seamlessly into Zhao's existing views of the beneficial impact of the coastal development strategy on China's domestic development. He also fully agreed with their emphasis on the township village enterprises (TVEs) based in rural areas, smaller, more agile producers that were able to adapt more quickly to the demands of the international marketplace than the older SOEs.[25]

In his concluding speech to the Central Work Conference of 5 November 1987, Zhao analyzed the global economy,

> where the reduction in value of the U.S. dollar has increased the value of the Japanese yen, [and] the South Korean and Taiwan currencies. This provides a real opportunity for some of China's coastal areas, such as

Pearl River Delta area adjacent to Hong Kong, the southern Fujian Delta Area and Zhejiang adjacent to Taiwan. Currently there is a new and greater opportunity. Hong Kong has received large numbers of orders, but there is not enough Hong Kong labor, not enough factory space or production capability.[26] They cannot handle it. So, they have turned around and gone outside of Hong Kong to the Pearl River Delta area. As the situation in the Taiwan Straits improves, Taiwan capital and commodity orders will be calling upon our Fujian comrades.[27]

In September 1985, the finance ministers of France, West Germany, the United Kingdom, and Japan had met in New York to sign the joint agreement known as the Plaza Accord, which resulted in significant appreciation of the Japanese and Western European currencies relative to the depreciated U.S. dollar. Thereafter, to compete with South Korean manufacturers, Japanese multinationals had begun moving some of their production facilities offshore to South Korea and Taiwan, especially in precision instrument manufacturing, electrical machinery, industrial machinery, "notably photographic and optical equipment, consumer electronics, semiconductors and integrated circuits, and computers and peripherals," as well as textiles, apparel, and transportation equipment.[28] Zhao predicted that, as local production costs increased in those countries, Japanese corporations and others would start to look to China—which they did, especially after China joined the WTO in 2001.[29]

To lure multinational companies looking for lower-cost production areas, Zhao argued, China must transform its thinking about economic development strategy:

Recently Comrade Wang Jian, who is an associate researcher at the State Planning Commission, suggested that we fully utilize our abundant labor force strengths in the countryside to expand labor-intensive commodity exports. The foreign exchange earned will help build basic infrastructure, which will help us to develop to the next stage of capital-intensive industrialization. We thus would be taking the road of the great international economic cycle development strategy. I think this viewpoint makes sense. Currently, a large proportion of the global market is made up of labor-intensive products. Our country's greatest resource is our labor asset, which is located mostly in the large agricultural areas. It is not just that we have a large population, but our superiority lies in low labor costs. If we raise the quality of our workforce, including its technological and management levels, then we will possess tremendous competitive strength. There are too many people living on too little land in China's coastal areas. Natural resources are not plentiful. If we do not take this road, it will be very difficult to enrich the area.[30]

Zhao concludes his speech to the work conference promoting his vision of the role China would play in the future global economy.

It is completely possible that in the future, China's coastal areas will primarily be dominated by the TVEs, which will rely on low-cost labor with low wages to produce labor-intensive products. They will dominate the international market. First, starting with the coastal areas, the TVEs could produce a very large percentage of China's exports. Medium and small industries occupy a substantial percentage of the total exports in global economies, including the developed ones. This is the situation in Western Europe, Japan, and the United States. To meet this new situation, we must research this question of strategy. In the future, there could be two types of TVEs in the coastal area. One type [would use] low-cost labor to produce labor-intensive goods for export. Another type would earn foreign exchange through agricultural endeavors. Both types of TVEs would exist at the same time. This could truly transform the coastal areas and possesses great potential. We already have gained some experience through experimentation. From now on, we need to pay attention to this issue and conduct some in-depth research.[31]

Zhao subsequently took specific steps to attract investment to China's coastal regions. Starting in autumn 1987, he visited Fujian, Guangdong, Zhejiang, and Jiangsu provinces to rally support for his outward-oriented economic development strategy. He also spoke to a variety of central government ministries on his new coastal development strategy, which could affect 100–200 million people living in the coastal areas.[32] After gaining support, Zhao presented the new development approach to Deng and the senior leaders in January 1988.

Suzhou Work Conference, November 1987

In his first move to gain provincial support, Zhou called a work conference in Suzhou to discuss what the Jiangsu and Zhejiang leaders
thought about his proposals for an outward-oriented economy. On
26 November 1987 Zhao told the assembled cadres that starting with
the open coastal economic regions of the Yangtze and Pearl River Delta
areas, he wanted to "throw [*shuai dao*] the coastal areas into the international market, [where they] would rely on the international market
to develop."[33] If China were to develop the entire coastal area, including
the urban and rural areas, it would drain domestic sources of financing
and raw materials, leading to the strangling of the interior market's
growth. Zhao said that 70 to 80 percent of those living in the coastal
areas would be engaged in the outward-oriented economy, including
"importing materials from abroad—exporting finished goods to make
foreign exchange—and then importing materials again."[34] The coastal
economies would "have a ready cash flow to enable them to import and
export large amounts of goods [*dajin dachu*]."[35] As domestic supplies
were tight, coastal dependence on the international market would relieve the pressure on domestic raw materials and capital. This would
"lessen the contradiction between [the coast and] the central and western areas of China, whose economies undoubtedly would be swept
along in the development of the coastal areas."[36] As the former provincial leader of the Third Front province of Sichuan in the 1970s, Zhao
was very aware of the unbalanced nature of China's development. Since
the early 1980s, he had consistently argued that the coastal economy
had to rely on foreign resources to overcome the disruption of domestic
supplies by the growing coastal economy.[37] He made this argument
again in Suzhou.

To implement an outward-oriented economy, Zhou argued, China
needed to have certain external conditions, including a peaceful international environment, a long-term opening policy, and the ability to
export freely to capitalist countries. Within China, other conditions
were necessary. The first was low labor costs, which China had in abundance in the 1980s. The second was industrial infrastructure. In contrast to the older and moribund SOEs, Zhao focused on the TVEs,

stating that they could use their advantages in labor to engage in labor-intensive industries for exports. The TVEs could easily establish a more sophisticated manufacturing structure that would produce high-quality goods, using sophisticated technology and management techniques. According to Huang, the majority of these TVEs were privately owned and concentrated in several coastal provinces, although they were dwarfed by the SOE-dominated urban coastal economy.[38]

However, Zhao thought that the most important hurdle confronting the outward-oriented economy was the export trade system dominated by foreign trade corporations.

> The opening of foreign trade management would be beneficial for the TVEs and for a business. If they wanted to import some materials or export some materials, they could make automatic arrangements. They wouldn't have to wait half a year, but only one or two months before the good is imported or exported. If the coastal areas cannot enjoy such an environment or conditions, then they won't be able to develop their foreign trade. The reform of the foreign trade structure involves many complicated problems within our country and cannot be resolved by early morning. But we are working toward this direction to resolve the problem. We must resolve this problem now, and everyone has an opinion. Let's list them down, so I can take this back to Beijing for further discussion.[39]

As a result of the decentralization of the foreign trade system, according to Lardy, the original 12 foreign trade corporations set up in 1979 became 800 different organizations by the mid-1980s, and there were even more provincial-level organizations. Many of these new corporations encountered various problems and were unable to meet their contractual obligations.[40] Zhao admitted that China had yet to develop a plan to tackle the reforms of the corporations, but he maintained that the key would be decentralizing the corporations' decision-making powers over foreign trade and deciding who would take responsibility for all profits and losses.

One of the most interesting insights into Zhao's vision of an outward-oriented economy came in his explanation of China's current state of development.

In development theory, there are two ways of discussing the problem of outward-oriented economy: one is called import substitution and one is called export-led. What is import substitution? A country borrows foreign exchange to develop its domestic industry to reduce its imports from abroad. Examples include Mexico, Brazil, and various other Latin American countries; also, a couple of countries in Eastern Europe. Our country, China, is still following this method. Examples of export-led countries include Japan, Korea, and Taiwan. . . . Although their situations are completely different, those taking the road of import substitution, of borrowing foreign exchange to develop their industry, are frequently not doing as well as the export-led types. This is what the economists have described. However, we must start from a realistic viewpoint. I am afraid that our country will implement both methods of development. In some areas, the country still needs to build heavy industry. Other areas can produce exports on a large scale. Basically, developing countries have two types of strategies: import substitution and export-led. Those that carry out an export-led strategy focus on light industrial products, while those focusing on import substitution focus on heavy industrial products.[41]

Zhao was describing the changing Chinese economy of the 1980s. The interior economy was an older economy based on ISI and primarily focused on heavy industry.[42] This was the China of the 1950s, with large steel complexes and petrochemical plants. Leaders needed to borrow foreign exchange to modernize this older manufacturing sector and satisfy domestic industrial needs. But the new economy would be based in the coastal areas, which would invest in light industrial production that would be integrated into the international marketplace. Profits from these exports would allow the coastal areas to develop more quickly, which would gradually trickle down to the interior, ISI-led domestic economy.

Xiamen SEZ Inspection, December 1987

When visiting the Xiamen SEZ in December 1987, Zhao Ziyang challenged the SEZ leaders to expand their outward-oriented initiatives and let each SEZ become "more open, operate more dynamically, attract more foreign capital, expand its exports." He went on to urge leaders to "do a better job of promoting our development of an outward-oriented economy, become even more involved in the international market, so that it will have an even greater ability to attract foreign capital." He concluded, "According to my view, I do not see this as a problem."[43] He urged leaders to research the establishment of bonded warehouses so that the SEZs could use temporary storage to facilitate foreign trade. Zhao also argued that the zones should become involved in international finance, stock markets, bond markets, and futures markets, although in a very slow and managed fashion.

Zhao believed that Beijing could approve the establishment of free trade zones (FTZs), in which all manufacturing would take place within the zone, for reexport without paying a customs fee. As the primary problem was to secure the zone to prevent goods from entering the domestic economy, Zhao proposed that the first FTZ should be established in Hainan, followed by Xiamen and then Shenzhen. However, China's first FTZ was established in Shanghai in 2013, followed by FTZs in Fujian, Guangdong, and Tianjin in 2015. China's first official stock markets were established in Shanghai and Shenzhen in the early 1990s.[44]

"Report on the Coastal Development Strategy," January 1988

Although Zhao had gained support from various coastal provincial party leaders during his November–December 1987 inspection trip of the open coastal areas, he still had to overcome objections from the moderate bureaucratic Stalinists in Beijing.

During the Thirteenth Party Congress in November 1987, Chen Yun and Li Xiannian, who had been the most critical of Zhao Ziyang's market-oriented reforms, retired from the Political Bureau Standing Committee. Premier Li Peng and Vice Premier Yao Yilin assumed their positions on the Standing Committee and represented the second generation of moderate bureaucratic Stalinists. Zhao Ziyang could rely on committee member Hu Qili to support his outward-oriented development, and Qiao Shi became the "swing voter" in the five-person

Political Bureau.[45] However, as Zhao Ziyang told General Secretary Mikhail Gorbachev of the Soviet Union during his fateful visit to Beijing in May 1989, "On issues of importance, the Party still needs Deng Xiaoping to be at the helm. Since the 13th Party Congress, whenever we deal with major issues, we always inform Comrade Deng Xiaoping and seek his guidance."[46] The Standing Committee also consulted Chen Yun on all major economic decisions.[47]

According to Zhao's memoir, the newly appointed premier Li Peng and vice premier and chair of the State Planning Commission Yao Yilin feared that any special treatment of the coastal areas would exacerbate China's overheated economy and high inflation.[48] Zhao countered that "the issue was mainly about overinvestment, belated returns on investment, or investments that yielded low returns. In addition, consumption funds were huge, causing an overabundance of currency in circulation."[49] Zhao argued that the state did not need to invest large amounts of capital in the coastal areas, which produced products in high demand and would not cause localized scarcities. In his November 1987 Suzhou talk, Zhao had stressed that an outward-oriented strategy for the coastal areas would lessen the contradiction between the coastal and interior economies, as the coastal areas would be more dependent on international sources of revenue and supplies. Zhao was also critical of Li Peng's restrictive macroeconomic policies, which were inhibiting coastal economic growth.[50] According to Fewsmith, after the conclusion of the Thirteenth Party Congress and Li Peng's appointment as acting premier, Zhao, as the head of the Central Finance and Economy Leading Group, was less influential over policy formulation than Li Peng. Zhao thus focused on promoting the new coastal development strategy and "maintain[ing] the initiative in economic policy."[51]

In his January 1988 report on "The Problem Concerning Coastal Economic Development Strategy," Zhao began by analyzing the state of the international economy, which had presented China's coastal economy with an "advantageous opportunity."[52] According to Zhao, labor-intensive production had shifted from the United States to Japan, then to Taiwan/South Korea/Hong Kong/Singapore. He predicted that the recent turmoil in the international markets would translate to economic retrenchment and a reduction in international market capacity. However, China's export economy would not be affected, as it focused on middle- and low-value exports. With the increase in value of the Japanese yen and the New Taiwan dollar, investment in labor-intensive production was rising again and the Chinese coastal economy had an excellent chance to attract new foreign investment. He warned China's leaders that they could not miss another excellent opportunity (*liangji*) and must treat the problem with urgency (*jipogan*). This line of argument, which Zhao had used in his previous speeches to the work conferences and on investigatory trips, intrigued Deng, who in his comments used the line, "We cannot lose this opportunity."

Zhao laid out his vision in the report by expanding on many of the themes he had raised during previous work conferences and meetings. Instead of focusing just on the Pearl River, Yangtze River, and Minnan Delta areas, he expanded the coastal development areas to include the Shandong and Liaodong Peninsulas. Those regions would also engage in outward-oriented development, and act as catalysts for central and western Chinese development. Because resources were limited, Zhao argued that it would be preferable to concentrate development in the coastal region, which would allow China to demonstrate that "socialism with Chinese characteristics" could bring about real economic growth and facilitate reunification with Hong Kong and Taiwan. Zhao again focused on the coastal areas' competitive strengths, such as the ability to handle labor-intensive production; plentiful coal for power; and vast supplies of construction materials (stone and sand), for export as well as for building new facilities. The coastal areas needed to focus on labor-intensive and knowledge-intensive production, areas in which China would continue to enjoy a competitive edge for the near future. China's bountiful coal resources could provide electricity to coastal industries. And its abundant construction materials would make China a formidable exporter of those commodities. China's interior could also develop its agricultural products for export. The SEZs and the medium-size coastal cities could develop various high-technology industries, including computer software.

In his memoir, Zhao recalled that the conflict between the richer coastal and poorer interior economies had been exacerbated by the increasing prices that interior economies charged for resources to the coastal economies. "Since the inland provinces had become unwilling to sell their resources cheaply to coastal provinces, the conflict between inland and coastal regions had intensified. Therefore, transforming the coastal regions into an export-oriented economy was a major and critical issue."[53] To prevent further conflict, the coastal regions would be integrated with the international economy and become less dependent on domestic capital and materials. He called this plan *liangtou zaiwai* ("positioning both ends outside the country"), which he explained as

> positioning the two ends of the production process (raw materials and selling on the market) on the international market. If the reprocessing industries in the coastal areas solely relied on domestically procured raw materials, their progress would most certainly be inhibited by major shortages. We can't say that our natural resources and raw materials are very limited, but in relationship to our population they are not plentiful. We can never again talk about "a land of bountiful goods" and be intoxicated with self-satisfaction. It will not get us anywhere if we keep going down the same road, as the conflict between the coastal and interior areas for raw materials will become increasingly acute.[54]

Furthermore, the coastal economies would not rely on foreign loans but would welcome various types of foreign-invested enterprises. According to Pearson, by the end of 1988 around 77 percent of all foreign-invested enterprises in China were located in the coastal provinces, especially in those with "'open coastal cities' (Guangdong, Fujian, Jiangsu, Liaoning, Zhejiang, Shandong, and Hebei), or in the municipalities of Tianjin and Shanghai."[55] Kueh has argued that Zhao's *liangtou zaiwai* strategy was a two-pronged one: for the coastal areas, Zhao was rejecting ISI development while embracing export-oriented development; for the interior economy, Zhao was retaining inward-oriented development.[56] Zhao explicitly advocated for this form of dual-track development at the November Suzhou work conference. It appears to have been more of an early transition phase leading to a comprehensively outward-oriented economy.

In his report, Zhao again emphasized the importance of reforming the foreign trade structure so that the coastal economies could engage directly in the international market. For thirty years, Zhao had described the system as "everyone eating from the same big rice bowl."

Unfortunately, the structural reforms initiated in 1985 were ineffectual and only perpetuated the same problems of the past. Quoting Deng, Zhao said that foreign trade officials "must have the guts, and not be afraid to take risks [*mao fengxian*]." Interestingly, Zhao clearly stated that he is not promoting "rash advance," or *maoxian zhuyi*, which Mao and Deng promoted in the 1950s during the Great Leap Forward.[57] He reminded the leadership of his Thirteenth Party Plenum report, in which Zhao argued that China's foreign trade system should "take responsibility for its profits and losses, loosen control of operations, link production with trade, and promote an agency system." Zhao now added the necessity to "have a united position in dealing with the outside world."[58] To achieve these goals, Zhao said that Beijing should not increase funds for financing trade losses and should ensure that goods can be easily exported and imported. More decision-making power should be given to the localities, he asserted, so that local firms could retain a greater amount of earned foreign exchange, which would be used as circulating funds to finance future foreign trade transactions. Beijing could also establish an insurance-risk fund for those engaged in agricultural and sideline-product production.

Looking back later, Zhao explicitly criticized the centralized planned economy, which had "made the entire nation develop in a uniform manner so the strengths of the coastal regions could not be utilized. Neither the inland nor the coastal regions could develop at a fast pace." Such uniformity had stifled growth, he said, and transformed the booming Shanghai economy of the 1930s into a "rundown [economy that] had fallen far behind Hong Kong, Singapore and Taiwan."[59] To rectify this, Zhao outlined specific policy prescriptions for each actor engaged in the coastal foreign trade: the industries, the managers, the technicians, and the workers.

Coastal Industries

Zhao argued that leaders still needed to implement the industrial reforms promulgated since 1986. "Local cadres consider large and medium-size enterprises as tigers and lions, and small enterprises as monkeys. They suggest that Beijing allow the tigers to come down from the mountains, loosen restrictions on the lions, and free the monkeys to climb the trees."[60] The central government needed to loosen bureaucratic restrictions on local enterprises that dominated China's industrial economy. Zhao's highest expectations focused on the TVEs or the "monkeys," which were far more nimble and could be highly competitive in the international marketplace. As they had yet to earn enough foreign exchange, Zhao argued that the TVEs should rely on their relative strengths and export enough goods that they could accumulate the capital to buy foreign technology to increase production. In addition, he argued that they needed to study the Taiwan model, which was also composed of small industries.

Coastal Industrial Management

Zhao characterized previous industrial management practices as too lax, resulting in poor-quality products, chaotic financial management, and an inability to manage supplies that had led to frightening losses. Zhao argued that foreigners were surprised by the sophisticated nature of China's industrial facilities but appalled by their management practices.[61]

To improve China's industrial management practices, Zhao suggested that the coastal industries should institute a contract system, which would strengthen the power of the industrial managers; managers in turn should lay off underutilized workers and openly advertise for the personnel they did need. Zhao discovered during his discussions with Shenyang factory managers that workers would not listen to managers who lacked the power to discipline workers. Workers were more responsible when they understood that their future was tied to the welfare of a well-managed factory. Some of the factories had implemented a collective risk system (*jiti fengxian banfa*) and contract bidding, so that workers would receive bonuses and other benefits for superior work. Zhao said each of the coastal industries should experiment with specific management systems that would be most suitable to their situation.

Zhao argued that foreigners should manage the foreign-invested enterprises, especially those that were wholly foreign-owned enterprises. Joint ventures and collaborative ventures could allow foreign management or follow international management practices, including hiring workers on the open market and dismissing workers in accordance with contracts and regulations. In this way, the coastal enterprises would resemble their counterparts in the international marketplace and not the old-style "joint-management" structures, by which Zhao was referring to party and state-plan interference in enterprise management. He emphatically denied that China would lose its sovereignty (*sangshi zhuquan*) under the new management style. Instead, he argued, the hiring of foreign managers was a prevalent practice in the international marketplace, including in Japan, the United States, and Great Britain.[62] The boards of foreign corporations primarily hired the most capable managers, with almost total disregard for their nationality. Zhao mentioned that the Wuhan Diesel Engine Enterprise, which was state owned, had hired a very successful foreign manager (*yang changzhang*).[63] As outsiders, foreigners could more easily eliminate older management practices and introduce newer, more stringent methods; improve the production of goods to meet international quality and technological standards; entice more foreigners to invest in China; and improve the quality of Chinese workers.

Coastal Industrial Technology

Zhao argued that China possessed a technological base that surpassed that of other developing countries but had not been fully realized, owing to past policies and structural reasons.[64] The coastal regions should therefore implement a contract management responsibility system to promote competitive companies that would pay more attention to technological improvements. To adopt new technologies to improve export production, coastal enterprises needed to send technicians abroad to learn about the most appropriate new technologies. He called on technical experts to change their minds about not wanting to work for the smaller industries such as the TVEs. Zhao argued that such jobs were not a demotion in status but would allow the technicians to introduce newer technologies more easily than if they were working for larger SOEs.

Zhao also argued that research organizations needed to reduce their dependence on the state and rely on profits gained from increased production. Competition would increase their productivity. He agreed that this might result in a system that favored short-term results. For long-term research, he said units could depend on the local or central government for funding. Zhao encouraged individual researchers, research institutions, and schools to start their own knowledge-intensive companies to develop their technology in the commercial marketplace.[65]

Coastal Industrial Workers

Although China's workers could survive on low wages, Zhao said, their productivity was low because of insufficient training and poor management. He argued that firms needed to increase local wages, increase training, and improve employee management practices.

At the end of his report, Zhao Ziyang returned to the politically sensitive issue of developing an advanced coastal economy that was increasingly different from its interior domestic counterparts. Zhao argued that because of the cultural difference between economies of the coast and interior, the entire national economy could not be developed simultaneously. China could not wait for the interior economy to catch up; if it did, it would lose the opportunity to attract the foreign investors currently looking to relocate their production centers. However, as the coastal economy took off, Zhao said Beijing would implement several measures to prevent a deepening of the "contradiction" between the coastal and interior economies. The coastal economy would implement the *liangtou zaiwai* strategy of "positioning both ends outside the country." By relying on the international economy for most of their production inputs, coastal industries would lessen competition for supplies on the domestic market and stabilize domestic prices for production inputs. The coastal economies would not be taking out foreign loans to finance their operations but would depend on foreign-invested enterprises to provide the necessary development funds to renovate existing factory sites and equipment. Those physical sites would make up the Chinese partners' contribution to the joint ventures and lessen their need for domestic loans and investment. Renovations of older industries would not just involve the physical plant but would also facilitate the introduction of new management and personnel reforms. As for the smaller businesses and factories that had been operating at a loss, Zhao suggested that the state could sell them off to collectives and individuals who could then turn them into profitable enterprises. The sale of such assets and land rights would allow the state to recover some of its investment, which could then be used for buying new technology and equipment. Local coastal governments could use the same method in selling older housing sites to accumulate capital to build new housing. Zhao concluded,

> In sum, the development of the coastal areas must be implemented following the thoughts outlined above. The plan must rely on policy, on good mechanisms, on the strengths of "positioning both ends outside the country" and depending on the individual to develop. The plan cannot look to the state to provide financing and cannot be developed at the expense of the interior economy. The plan cannot just push aside the interior economy but must bring it along in development and help the interior economy to develop. This will make a major contribution to stabilizing the economy of the entire nation. If we follow this path, we can find a pretty good resolution to the various contradictions.[66]

Reactions to the Coastal Development Strategy

Deng Xiaoping had approved the Guangdong and Fujian decentralization experimentation in 1979, enthusiastically reaffirmed his support during his first *nanxun* in 1984, and advocated the 1984 and 1985 expansion of the decentralization experiment to the entire coastal areas. Deng Xiaoping "immediately" approved (*pishi*) Zhao Ziyang's report on 23 January 1988, stating, "I completely agree. We especially must act boldly and accelerate its implementation. By all means we cannot lose this opportunity."[67]

However, some leaders and academics were critical of the new development strategy in 1988. Chen Yun did not overtly criticize Zhao's plan, although he most definitely supported Li Peng and Yao Yilin's concern that the plan would "overheat" a national economy in which price reforms and trade decentralization had already fueled domestic inflation.[68] Inflation was a major problem in 1988, and people worried about the value of their savings as prices rose by 18.5 percent.[69] Chen Yun was mostly concerned about the strategy of *liangtou zaiwai, dajin dachu*, "positioning two ends on the outside, and importing a large amount to export a large amount." Zhao later wrote, "I understood his fears: If we agreed to import raw materials but then our products could not be exported abroad, how would we balance our foreign currency? But while his concern was understandable, the real question was, If we have such favorable conditions and if the four Asian Tigers had managed it, why couldn't we? Why wouldn't we be able to compete?"[70]

Chinese academics involved in the planning process argued in 1988 that that the Asian-miracle economies that had implemented an outward-oriented development strategy were much smaller than China. Zhao responded,

> This issue should have been considered in this way: as long as the products are a good quality and low in cost, they will find their place in the market. Markets are not frozen or a fixed size, where once you had taken your share, there would be no more. Certainly, there was no vacuum in the international market and no commodity that the international market was lacking. The issue was market share: how much you took up and how much I took up. The total volume would grow with world economic development and growth. However, market share is variable and depends on competition. That is why developed countries had stopped producing labor intensive products and adjusted their industries. Once the emerging economies took off, their own labor costs rose, and they gradually lose their advantage. For example, Japan moved its labor-intensive production to the four Asian Tigers, but now the Asian Tigers have lost their advantage on this front. A country like China has the advantage of enormous labor resources. There is no need to worry about the future. Once the first step is taken, we can take a second and then a third. As long as we start exporting labor-intensive products, we would accumulate capital and more advanced technologies, and we could then compete internationally on capital- or technology-intensive products.[71]

Finally, China's central and western leaders objected to the coastal development strategy because they believed it would increase the "contradiction" between the richer coastal provinces and the poorer interior ones that had become more acute ever since document 1979.50 and the decentralization experiment with Guangdong and Fujian.[72] Zhao argued in his memoir that the economic boom of the coastal economies had provided jobs for workers in the interior economies. As the coastal economies prospered and their cost of production rose, "the laws of labor-intensive production would also apply within the country and shift to places where labor was even cheaper."[73] Zhao had envisioned a dynamic process that would not just trickle down, but would gradually bring the entire economy into the global economic marketplace. In the short term, he acknowledged, one area—the coastal area—would develop first. But as production costs grew in the coastal area, FIEs and Chinese companies would move to the less developed areas of the interior economy and use their cheaper production inputs. Thus, in the long term, the entire country would grow and became more fully engaged in outward-oriented development.

Implementing the Strategy

Having received Deng's blessing on 23 January 1988, the Political Bureau approved the coastal development strategy, and Li Peng presented the new strategy in his work report to the National Peoples' Congress on 25 March 1988.[74] In addition to document 1988.24 establishing Hainan as the fifth SEZ and as a new province, the State Council proceeded to issue several official documents on implementing the coastal development strategy, first addressing the expansion of the open coastal economic regions, reforming the foreign trade system, and implementing several regulations concerning outward-oriented development.

Three days after Deng's 23 January approval, the State Council issued a letter approving the expansion of the Minnan open coastal economic region in Fujian Province to include Putian, Quanzhou, Zhangzhou, and Fuzhou.[75] On 18 March 1988 the State Council issued document 1988.21, which expanded the geographical areas of the open coastal economic regions to include Tianjin Municipality and various cities in Hebei, Liaoning, Jiangsu, Zhejiang, Fujian, Shandong, and Guangxi.[76] The council issued another document on 28 June 1988 approving Guangdong province's expansion of the original Pearl River Delta area to include most of Guangdong's coast, from Shantou in the north to Zhanjiang on the Leizhou Peninsula.[77]

The State Council subsequently initiated a series of work conferences, including a conference on reforming the foreign trade structure. On 30 January 1988 Zhao Ziyang had met with the various leaders of the foreign trade corporations and the industrial and trading companies.[78] After congratulating them on their hard work in the initial efforts at decentralizing and enlivening the foreign trade system, including in implementing a new contract system, he urged the leaders to continue to strengthen and improve the reforms. He then focused on new changes for the 50,000 cadres working within the foreign trade system, and subtly warned leaders to adapt to reforms and be supportive of the new outward-oriented strategy. According to Zhao, the pre-1978 foreign trade structure was suited to centralized a bureaucracy that was completely divorced from production and marketing concerns and imported or exported only a limited number of goods. With the pivot toward an outward-oriented economy and the decentralization of the foreign trade structure, those engaged in foreign trade exchanges would have to assume full responsibility for all profits and losses, and no longer rely on the state's largesse whenever contracts cannot be met. The foreign trade system had to develop more sophisticated management techniques, and fully understand the needs of commodity production and trade.

Zhao argued that the foreign trade corporations should be reorganized like the large Japanese and South Korean trading companies. In the mid-1950s the Japanese established the *sogo shosha*, or general trading companies, which engaged in international trade and were involved in everything from raw material procurement to sales and transportation.[79] Zhao hoped that China could establish such "transnational corporations" (*kuaguo gongsi*), which would adopt the contract system, compete for business, and be internationally rather than domestically focused. MOFERT subsequently issued new regulations on 21 May 1988 that reorganized the foreign trade corporations by decentralizing operations to promote outward-oriented development.[80]

At an early March 1988 work conference involving the coastal provinces, areas, and municipalities, Zhao spoke about the two key issues

China faced in implementing the coastal economic development strategy.[81] He first acknowledged that there were skeptics abroad "who [believe] that China just can't pull it off and say those methods of the Mainlanders just do not work." Zhao embraced this criticism by arguing that China's first key obstacle was to adapt to the international marketplace through new policies and regulations and improved attitudes toward work. The government needed to change the current rules and regulations regarding foreign trade, the banks, and foreign exchange management. The second obstacle was the need to organize China's technological capabilities to help the coastal economies compete in the international marketplace.

To overcome these two obstacles to coastal development, the State Council issued document 1988.22 on 23 March 1988, outlining new regulations to support the new outward-oriented development strategy.[82] Under certain circumstances, FIEs could now bypass the central planning system to obtain their production supplies and foreign exchange. The central government expanded the power of the coastal provincial governments, open cities, and SEZs to approve FIEs.[83] The document facilitated the renovation of older production sites by foreign investors, and coastal provinces and cities were permitted to establish their own foreign trade corporations. Beijing gave key coastal provincial cities the right to approve the importation of materials and equipment needed to reprocess goods for export and would no longer require import certificates. The state allowed enterprises engaged in reprocessing to establish various types of business ventures to facilitate importation of production materials, and they were free to use foreign exchange to procure such items. They did not pay import duties on goods for reprocessing, or various other import or export tariffs. The General Customs Administration was directed to formulate new regulations to establish bonded warehouses. Administrators were empowered to oversee the implementation of the new system, and to prevent enterprises from "importing large amounts, and exporting small amounts" or "only importing and not exporting."

The Bank of China and local entities would establish special accounts in which coastal localities and firms could deposit retained foreign exchange and other accounts for foreign exchange circulating funds that could be used to facilitate foreign trade transactions. If the coastal localities lacked the foreign exchange to establish such a circulating funds account, then the state would provide a certain amount of foreign exchange. Foreign exchange adjustment centers, or "swap centers," would be established in various coastal cities.[84] The coastal areas were permitted to organize a risk fund for exporting industries, to help those encountering problems owing to international market fluctuations. Export-oriented industries could also raise funds to arrange their own container ships, as well as rail, air, or canal transportation.

In addition, the state made it easier for businesspeople and foreigners working in the coastal regions to obtain renewable visas for one year. Although it did not provide specific regulations on the issue, the state encouraged the coastal areas to adopt measures that would encourage technicians to work in the smaller industries, especially the TVEs. It also placed a moratorium on the establishment of new development zone, or export processing zones, because coastal areas were to concentrate on renovating their existing enterprises. As for development zones areas already under construction, the state ordered that they should be small and financed by the local government. On 3 July 1988 the State Council also issued document 1988.41, which clarified the incentives for Taiwanese businesspeople to invest in the mainland, including the simplification of entry procedures, the issuance of identification documents, and legal protections and benefits accorded to Taiwanese-invested enterprises and other investments.[85]

In early December the State Council convened a conference to study the implementation of the coastal development strategy and to assess the growth in coastal investments and foreign trade as outlined in State Council document 1988.22.[86] Zhao Ziyang spoke at the conference about the successes in and obstacles to realizing outward-oriented development in the coastal areas, and the necessity to readjust the coastal economy so that it could become more competitive internationally.[87] The council issued the formal conference summary on 13 January 1989 as document 1989.5, in which it praised the progress achieved by the coastal areas and urged them to expand Zhao's outward-oriented *liangtou zaiwai* development strategy, "'positioning both ends outside the country' to increase export revenue and increase supplies in order to alleviate the temporary problems experienced in the domestic economy."[88]

Domestic Inflation and the Moderate Stalinists

By early 1989 Zhao Ziyang and the international Leninists were engaged in an ongoing debate with the moderate Stalinists on the proper strategy to deal with the "temporary problem" of domestic inflation. Premier Li Peng and Vice Premier Yao Yilin had readjusted the economic reforms in fall 1988, mandating a "sudden severe freezing of prices, a transferal of the power of approval for foreign trade activity back to the central level, an effort, as in the past[,] to guide economic behavior through setting quotas and norms in the capital, a closing off of credit, large cuts in currency issuance, a scaling back of capital construction targets, and the cancellation of projects already conceived."[89] By January the moderate Stalinists had reasserted central control over foreign trade corporations by readjusting the export-permit management system to prevent the export of certain raw materials and agricultural goods that had exacerbated the domestic inflation rate.[90] They strengthened restrictions on the local importation of automobiles, major appliances, and televisions and other electronic consumer goods.[91] And they issued new regulations to guarantee the transference of foreign exchange profits to the central government.[92]

The disagreements between the international Leninists and moderate Stalinists went beyond differences over the new outwardly oriented development paradigm and the proper policy to overcome growing inflation. Zhao Ziyang was proposing to transform the Stalinist political paradigm. Zhao's failure to convince Deng Xiaoping and the other leaders resulted in his house arrest after the June Fourth Incident, where he would remain until his death on 17 January 2005.[93]

Conclusion

Spillover and the Stalinist Paradigm

Beginning in 1949, the comprehensive Stalinist paradigm guided China's elites in their long-term goals to build a strong national defense, develop a self-sufficient economy, and solidify the party's hegemony over the state, the economy, and the people. The Stalinist elites thus established a totalitarian party-state in which the Communist Party used Marxism-Leninism–Mao Zedong Thought as the single organizing ideology to dominate and mobilize Chinese citizens.

Following the death of Mao in 1976, Deng Xiaoping, who chose to become a post-totalitarian leader, worked cooperatively with the first generation of Stalinist elites in forming the post-1978 Third Plenum consensus. They agreed to place their primary focus on China's economic growth, while also adapting and strengthening the existing Stalinist political and social paradigm. As the paramount leader, Deng respected and sought to balance differences of opinion among the elites on economic development strategies, yet he retained the right to make all final decisions. Although his efforts at accommodation resulted in the tightening and loosening *fang shou* dynamics of policy delays and implementation adjustments, the process did not devolve into the cyclical policy iterations of previous decades that had suppressed sustained economic growth.[1] Instead, the Third Plenum consensus encouraged a continuous process of complex policy learning and the adoption of the outward-oriented consultative economic paradigm.

Deng's Third Plenum consensus also preserved and adapted the Stalinist political and social paradigms first established in the 1950s. Following the tumult of the Democracy Wall movement in the late 1970s, the first generation of Stalinist elites reached an implicit agreement to maintain the party's hegemonic role in the state and society. However, ideas that spilled over into society from experimentation in the 1980s often challenged the party's hegemonic role by empowering new non-party actors and thus planting the seeds for a new Chinese civil society.[2] Spillover is an unavoidable result of sectoral paradigm experimentation and is one of the transaction costs of policy reform. The ruling elites may determine that spillover has positive effects they can use as a catalyst for simple or complex learning in other policy sectors. They also may determine that it has negative effects that must be contained or eliminated.

During the 1980s, the second generation of leaders harmonized economic experimentation with China's Stalinist political and social paradigms by reducing the role of the party in political and social policy. Deng Xiaoping and other first-generation revolutionaries supported Hu Yaobang's attempts to counteract Mao's revolutionary Stalinist approach of normative ideological development.[3] This less ideologically oriented approach to government was subsequently reinforced with the June 1981 publication of the "Resolution on Certain Questions in the History of Our Party since the Establishment of the PRC," and later by an unsigned editorial that appeared in the 7 December 1984 edition of the party's primary newspaper, *Renmin ribao*.[4] The original editorial stated, "One cannot expect the works of Marx and Lenin written in their time to solve today's problems," and this was later corrected to read "to solve all of today's problems." Reflecting the comments of Party General Secretary Hu Yaobang, the editorial created quite a political uproar in Beijing and signaled a new round of political reforms.[5] In summer 1985 Hu Yaobang argued that "outdated theories must be rejected . . . [and] the latest achievements of all humanity must be incorporated into [the Marxist canon]."[6]

A year later, on 28 June 1986, Deng Xiaoping initiated a discussion to promote political and legal reforms when he described the fight against corruption and illegal activities. Deng suggested that preparations should be made to discuss the relationship between the party and the government at the upcoming Thirteenth Party Congress in 1987.[7] Hu Yaobang subsequently encouraged a vigorous intellectual discussion, beginning in the spring of 1986, that questioned the continued relevance of Mao Zedong Thought and Deng's Four Cardinal Principles, which had strengthened the intimate party-state relationship. Deng Weizhi argued in *Jiefang ribao* on 21 May 1986 that multiparty elections should be held in China, and the vice chancellor of the University of Science and Technology in Anhui province, Fang Lizhi, encouraged students to take to the streets to argue for greater democracy in China.[8]

Zhao Ziyang met with Hu Qili, Tian Jiyun, and Bo Yibo on 18 September 1986 to discuss the next steps toward promoting new political reforms. On 23 September, Deng Xiaoping approved their proposal to form the Central Political Structural Reform Research and Discussion Group, which established an office to analyze domestic and foreign political reforms.[9] Their goal was to provide the Standing Committee with a tentative plan for political structural reforms that could be pproved at the Seventh Plenum of the Twelfth Party Congress and subsequently included in Zhao's report to the Thirteenth Party Congress in October 1987. Starting at their first meeting on 7 November 1986, Zhao Ziyang focused on the importance of separating the party from the state, empowering the National People's Congress, and redressing the relationships among the Political Bureau's Standing Committee, the Political Bureau, the Central Committee, and the Secretariat to give the Central Committee a more supervisory role over the Political Bureau.[10] Zhao also promoted freer elections, empowering workers to have a real say in the governance of SOEs, and streamlining the country's bureaucracy.[11]

Anticipating objections from the elites, Zhao Ziyang recognized that "many of our comrades have several reservations concerning the separation of party and the state. One reason is that they have not learned through experience the good aspects of separating the party and the state. If we talk more about its positive aspects, then there will be fewer reservations. I am hoping everyone will discuss the good points of party-state separation during the Party Congress meeting."[12] Deng had consistently fought against spiritual pollution, bourgeois liberalization, and Western-style democracy since suppressing the Anti-Rightist

Movement in 1957; he had crushed the Beijing Spring by ending the Democracy Wall movement of 1978–79 and approved the Anti–Spiritual Pollution Campaign in 1983. Deng strongly believed this struggle should continue until 2050.[13] He and other members of the old guard were concerned in fall and winter 1986 that Hu Yaobang had lost control of the political reform debate. The questioning of the party's ideological foundation spread from the ideological circles in Beijing to various universities around China, resulting in a series of student demonstrations in December 1987, starting at the University of Science and Technology in Hefei and spreading east to Jiaotong and Tongji Universities in Shanghai, north to Peking University, and south to the campus of Shenzhen University.[14] As a result, the first generation of bureaucratic Stalinists believed Hu Yaobang had violated one of their sacred rules by questioning the party's hegemony and its ideology.[15] When Hu objected to clamping down on the student demonstrators, Deng Xiaoping and the bureaucratic Stalinists forced Hu to submit his resignation letter as party leader, on 4 January 1987; the leaders issued document 1987.3, listing six reasons for Hu's resignation, and attached Hu's self-criticism.[16]

Zhao Ziyang became acting general secretary and immediately implemented the Anti–Bourgeois Liberalization Campaign. In one of his first speeches as acting general secretary, during the Chinese New Year celebration on 29 January 1987, Zhao Ziyang made it clear by directly quoting Deng Xiaoping that he had learned from Hu's mistakes:

"In a large country such as China, if you did not have the leadership of the Communist Party, the country would be split up into pieces [*sifen wulie*] and there would be a total failure." He has very explicitly stated, "The key to persevering with the Four Cardinal Principles is to insist on the leadership of the party." Only the leadership of the Communist Party will stabilize the entire country, focus the people's determination and power, and carry out reform and construction.[17]

Economic reformers, especially in the coastal regions, feared a greater retreat from the decentralization initiatives, which would have had a devastating impact on the coastal cities and the SEZs.[18] Starting with his Chinese New Year speech, Zhao emphasized that the Anti–Bourgeois Liberalization Campaign was to be a short-term policy and that the country would continue to implement the economic reforms, as Deng had not altered the fundamental emphasis on economic reform first enunciated at the 1978 Third Plenum.[19]

With the strong support of the first generation of moderate bureaucratic Stalinists, including Chen Yun and Li Xiannian, Li Peng eventually was appointed the new premier.[20] Li was the first true technocrat appointed to the office, and as a reliable party apparatchik he enjoyed the full trust of the first-generation leaders. Those first-generation elites instructed the new general secretary, Zhao Ziyang, and Premier Li Peng to renew the Anti–Bourgeois Liberalization Campaign, which resulted in party expulsions and criticisms; with the subsequent issuance of Central Committee document 1987.4, mass-media personnel accused of liberal bourgeois tendencies were removed from their positions.[21]

General Secretary Zhao continued to follow Deng's instructions to enact economic and political reforms, a blueprint for which would be presented at the November 1987 First Plenum of the Thirteenth Party Congress.[22] When the campaign against bourgeois liberalism threatened to spill over to the economic decentralization experiments, Zhao received Deng's approval to contain the campaign.[23] In his 29 January 1987 speech, given at the New Year's celebration of the Communist Youth League (CYL), Zhao had stated,

Are there some comrades and friends who fear that the Anti–Bourgeois Liberalization Campaign might have a negative impact on reforms and construction? "The Report from the Expanded Central Committee Political Bureau" has already been formally published. The various urban and rural, domestic and foreign policies will not change. Comprehensive reforms will not change. Opening to the outside world will not change. Enlivening the domestic economy will not change. Policies remain unchanged regarding our respect for intellectuals and personnel. Not only will these policies not change, but we will work even harder to do better. . . . The one who spoke the earliest, the most, and the most profound words concerning the reforms, opening, enlivening the economy is Deng Xiaoping. The one who spoke the earliest, the most, and the most profound words concerning the Four Basic Principles and against bourgeois liberalization is also Deng Xiaoping.[24]

Zhao had intentionally spoken to an organization closely allied with Hu Yaobang, who had been deposed as party general secretary two weeks earlier. Zhao reminded all the CYL members that Deng remained the paramount leader and that everyone should follow Deng's directives. But Zhao's major fear was not opposition from CYL members. In his memoir, he argues that some of the first generation of bureaucratic Stalinists elites

> were attempting to use the Anti-Liberalization Campaign to oppose reform. An appropriate response needed to be made in order to influence public opinion; otherwise it would be difficult for the 13th Party Congress to support reform. I was prepared to give a speech about it. Deng completely supported my idea. On May 12, 1988 [actually, 13 May 1987], I spoke to comrades working in the area of theory and ideology. I said that after the implementation of the Anti-Liberalization Campaign, the general climate had changed; therefore, the campaign could be brought to a close. The tasks going forward would mainly be in the field of education. I also said that the disturbance caused by liberalization was temporary, while the disturbance caused by leftists was long-lasting and fundamental. I listed many mistaken leftist comments in the theoretical and ideological arena opposing reform. [25]

Deng Xiaoping accepted Zhao Ziyang's suggestion to close the Policy Research Office of the Central Party Secretariat, which under Deng Liqun had become one of the most important party agencies to oppose the reforms. Deng also approved the closure of the CCP theoretical journal *Red Flag* in June 1988.[26] Hu Qili replaced Deng Liqun as director of the party's ideology and propaganda policies; Deng Liqun, who had close ties to Chen Yun and Li Xiannian, did not get enough votes to gain a seat on the Political Bureau for the Thirteenth Party Congress in 1987, or to join the Standing Committee of the Central Advisory Commission.[27]

Believing that he still had Deng's support, Zhao Ziyang issued his Work Report to the Thirteenth Party Congress, promoting a larger role for the market in regulating China's economy.[28] China was still in the primary stage of socialism, as had been formally acknowledged in the "Resolution on Certain Questions in Our Party's History since

the Founding of the PRC" in 1981.[29] However, for the economic reforms to succeed, Zhao argued that the party had to implement fundamental political reforms, including separating the party and the state,
decentralizing power, enacting bureaucratic and personnel reforms,
strengthening the rule of law, and enhancing the role of the people by
allowing a greater role for representative organizations and nongov-
ernmental organizations.[30]

In a 14 October 1987 speech, "On Separating the Party and the
State," given at a preparatory meeting of the Central Committee before
the opening of the Thirteenth Party Congress, Zhao had said that many
socialist countries had been discussing reforming their political structures "in order to overcome the corrupt practices when the party and
state are not separated and to fully utilize state organizations." Such a
separation had to take place at all levels, from the Central Committee
to the provinces, cities, counties, townships and villages, and within
enterprises. Only by separating the party and the state, argued Zhao,
could the party truly strengthen its political control over the state,
extract itself from the administrative morass of day-to-day affairs of
the state, and oversee policy implementation instead of implementing
policy itself.[31]

To achieve these goals, Zhao Ziyang revitalized the Leading Group
for the Reform of the Political Structure and established the Political
Structure Reform Office. The Institute of Marxism-Leninism–Mao
Zedong Thought and the Chinese Academy of Social Sciences' Institute
of Sociology established the Study Group on China's Political Structural Reform, which published various studies. In August 1988 Zhao
initiated the process of eliminating the party core groups, which had
been established after 1949 to impose hegemonic control over the local,
provincial, and national government bureaucracies, monitor any malfeasance, and ensure implementation of the party's general line. The
party core groups were the CCP's most important tool for maintaining
the party-state and regulating all experimentation with the comprehensive Stalinist paradigm.[32]

Despite Zhao's call to reduce the hegemony of the party during the
Thirteenth Party Congress, the first generation of bureaucratic Stalinist elites retained their Third Plenum consensus norm in promoting
economic reforms but preserved party hegemony. After 1987 it appeared

that Zhao Ziyang would be dealing with a new Political Bureau. Virtually all of the first generation of bureaucratic Stalinist elites retired from their seats, including Deng Xiaoping, Chen Yun, Li Xiannian, and Peng Zhen; they were replaced by a new generation of technocratic leaders, including Li Peng, Hu Qili, and Jiang Zemin. However, according to Zhao Ziyang, the Political Bureau's Standing Committee was required to consult with Deng Xiaoping concerning all important political matters and with Chen Yun on all important economic matters. The first generation thus thwarted Zhao Ziyang's attempt to eliminate the party-state, which would have signaled a fundamental change from the Stalinist political paradigm and initiated a more comprehensive third-order paradigm change. Deng and the elder bureaucratic Stalinists believed that Zhao held seriously dangerous ideas that would threaten the party's rule, such as when he admitted on Chinese television on 19 May 1989 that the youth were China's future and the leadership "was already old, and do not matter anymore [*women yijing laole, wusuowei le*]."[33] And as Zhao's memoir would later demonstrate, Deng was correct about Zhao's strongly held belief in fundamental democratic reforms.[34]

Deng needed to contain the negative costs of spillover from the decentralization experiments, maintain party hegemony, and strengthen elite cooperation to ensure that political turnover and policy adjustments did not have a negative impact on economic paradigm experimentation. If economic policy adjustments expanded into cross-sectoral policy areas, the entire economic reform experiment could be discredited. In the worst case, the Third Plenum consensus would dissolve and the ruling elite coalition would be replaced by a new coalition, which would eliminate the experiments and introduce their own approach.[35] Although just such a cyclical policy process had dominated the dynamics among elites before 1979, Deng Xiaoping had worked to avoid its repetition, and to maintain his coalition, at times by adjusting policy implementation, as demonstrated by his promotion of the Anti-Spiritual Pollution Campaign of 1983–84 and the Anti-Bourgeois Liberalism Campaign in 1987, and at times by dismissing recalcitrant modernizers, such as Deng Liqun and Hu Yaobang in 1987—and Zhao Ziyang in 1989.[36]

Zhao's attempted loosening of the party's political hegemony was reversed after the June Fourth Incident and his subsequent house arrest, when the new general secretary, Jiang Zemin—complying with the wishes of Deng Xiaoping and the moderate Stalinists, including Chen Yun, Li Xiannian, and Yang Shangkun—reinstated and strengthened party controls. In the fall of 1989 the moderate Stalinists further promoted the recentralization of economic controls by restricting the autonomy of regional foreign trade corporations, strengthening Beijing's foreign trade controls, enacting production incentive schemes to regulate exports, and, in December, devaluing the renminbi to increase exports.[37] However, while working with Deng and the moderate Stalinists, Jiang Zemin gradually emerged as an international Leninist. Jiang promoted Zhao Ziyang's more pluralized policy-making process, which included the various State Council offices, the leadership small groups, the Central Committee Policy Research Office, think tanks, and various provincial governments. Jiang also allowed businesspeople to become members of the Communist Party.[38] Without mentioning Zhao Ziyang, Jiang embraced the new economic paradigm and adapted Zhao's coastal development strategy. As Zhao says in his memoir, "After June Fourth, the strategy was no longer mentioned by name, but it has continued. It was because of the sustained development of the coastal economy that the nation reached large export volumes in just a few years and foreign reserves grew to a huge amount. It was all because of having taken this path, was it not? Of course, after June Fourth, no one could talk about this strategy as a policy, which undermined even more active implementation of this strategy."[39]

In his 29 September 1989 speech celebrating the fortieth anniversary of the founding of the PRC, Jiang Zemin declared, "The Central Committee and State Council have already announced various economic reform policies, measures, and basic policies concerning the SEZs and coastal development areas, which we must continue to implement and gradually improve. We must continue to carry out pilot schemes and experimental programs and summarize experiences for those experimental reforms already approved and areas that are currently undergoing comprehensive reform experimentation."[40] Although the State Council circular attached to the annual review of the SEZs in 1990 emphasized the need "to build both a material and spiritual civilization and uphold the four basic principles, strengthening political work, guaranteeing the correct political path," the document strongly supported the "outwardly oriented economy" of the zones.[41] One week later, on 2 June 1990, the Central Committee and the State Council issued Central Committee document 1990.100 approving the development and opening of Pudong, which at the time was mostly rice fields located on the eastern bank of the Huangpu River in Shanghai. As the former mayor and party secretary of Shanghai, Jiang had warmly embraced Zhao Ziyang's coastal development strategy and Lin Tung-Yen's suggestion in 1987 to develop Pudong. However, Chen Yun had stopped the plans for a Shanghai SEZ in the 1980s and the development of Pudong (see chap. 4). Now, as party general secretary, Jiang made Shanghai's economic development the new national priority; according to document 1990.100, this was an "important step" in promoting China's opening, and all ministries and areas were to support this new coastal development initiative.[42]

In his 26 November 1990 speech commemorating the tenth anniversary of the establishment of the Shenzhen SEZ, Jiang praised Deng Xiaoping for promoting the zones and then praised each of the SEZs for their ability to harness foreign investment to accelerate domestic economic growth. He furthermore stated, "This year the Central Committee and State Council also approved the development and opening of the Pudong New Area, which is a long-term strategy for our country's economic development. This will fully utilize the economic, scientific, and technical strengths of Shanghai and the rich coastal areas along the Yangtze River. This marks a new chapter in China's opening to the outside world."[43] In addition to envisioning a new leading role for Shanghai in China's coastal development, Jiang expanded the coastal strategy in the 1990s by introducing his western development strategy, a plan to overcome the income inequality between coastal and interior economies by establishing large investment projects in China's western regions, including Chongqing.[44]

Taiwanese investors were undeterred by the June Fourth Incident in 1989 and flocked to China to take advantage of the new Taiwanese investment reforms put in place the year before; the Chinese joke in the early 1990s was that the "Taiphoon" was blowing. However, international financiers and businesspeople remained cautious, as the bureaucratic Stalinists were reversing the economic decentralization reforms of the 1980s and openly criticizing foreign influences for corrupting "China's material and spiritual civilizations." To demonstrate to domestic elites and foreign businesspeople his commitment to China's opening and the reforms, Deng embarked on his second southern tour (*nanxun*) and visited Wuchang, the Shenzhen and Zhuhai SEZs, and Shanghai during January and February 1992. In a series of speeches and meetings that eventually were broadcast throughout China, Deng countered the conservatives among the bureaucratic Stalinists by stating that the zones and reforms that he had initiated were a success.[45] Deng ended all questions regarding the 1980s decentralization experiments, allowing Jiang Zemin and Premier Zhu Rongji to implement new policies consistent with the consultative economic paradigm and reengaging in difficult negotiations with the United States concerning China's entry into the GATT.[46] GATT accession would require dramatic adaptations in China's command economy system and a greater integration with the world economy.

After China joined the GATT in December 2001, the PRC was opened to greater domestic and international competition that resulted in mergers, privatization, and closures among China's 75,000 SOEs. However, reformist elites' dreams of marketizing the economy have yet to be achieved. China's largest companies are state-owned, such as the China National Petroleum, Sinopec, and the State Grid Corporation, and are ranked in the top five companies listed in *Fortune* magazine's top five hundred firms for 2019.[47]

Deng Xiaoping's second *nanxun* was his last major public political act before his death in 1997. He had gained an understanding of market economies during his work and study experiences in Europe and the Soviet Union under the New Economic Policy in the 1920s. Although Mao had made him responsible for overseeing the Great Leap Forward in the late 1950s, Deng rejected Mao's radical normative economic strategy by 1961 and joined with Liu Shaoqi, Zhou Enlai, and Chen Yun in adopting NEP-style ideas about using market-oriented, remunerative measures to help China recover from the economic failures of Mao's GLF and the Cultural Revolution. Deng Xiaoping appointed Zhao Ziyang and other international Leninists to experiment with a new Third Way of development that promoted outward-oriented policies, including a greater role for the market and the establishment of the SEZs. This was not a comprehensive paradigm shift, however. Starting in the 1990s, Chinese elites shifted to a new consultative economic paradigm but kept and adapted the Stalinist political and social development paradigm. Deng and subsequent leaders continued to pursue the goals of building a strong national defense, developing limited integration with the international economy, and guaranteeing the party's continued control over the state, the economy, and the people.

Since 1949, the ability of the PRC leadership to experiment with economic policies and learn from mistakes has played a crucial role in China's eventual adoption of outwardly oriented development. This Third Way of development is enabling China to challenge the United States for world economic hegemony.

Citation Abbreviations

The following abbreviations are used when these works are cited in the notes.

DJFZH   Zhejiangsheng Sifating and Zhejiangsheng Duiwai Jingji Maoyiting, *Duiwai jingji falü zhengce huibian*

DXPWX   Deng Xiaoping, *Deng Xiaoping wenxuan, 1975–1982*

DXPWX-3   Deng Xiaoping, *Deng Xiaoping wenxuan, di san juan* [vol. 3]

GJGFX   Hanshou Xuexi Ziliao Bianjizu, *Gongye jingji guanli fagui xuanbian*

LXNLCJM   Li Xiannian, *Li Xiannian Lun caizheng jinrong maoyi, 1950–1991*

MZDWJ   Mao Zedong, *Mao Zedong wenji*

RZJSH   Bo Yibo, *Ruogan zhongda juece yu shijian de huigu*

SJTN   Shenzhen Jingji Tequ Nianjian Bianji Weiyuanhui, *Shenzhen jingji tequ nianjian*

SQYZWX   Zhonggong Zhongyang Wenxian Yanjiushi, *Sanzhong quanhui yilai zhongyao wenxian xuanbian*

XZ   Huang Zhenzhao and Chen Yu, *Xiwang zhichuang*

YCKTGWX   Guowuyuan Tequ Bangongshi and Guowuyuan Bangongting Mishuju, ed. *Yanhai chengshi kaifang he tequ gongzuo wenjian xuanbian*

YJFZDWX   Gong'anbu Zhengce Falü Yanjiushi, *Youguan tong jingji fanzui zuo douzheng de wenjian xuanbian*

ZELJJWX   Zhonggong Zhongyang Wenxian Yanjiushi, *Zhou Enlai jingji wenxuan*

ZELNP   Zhonggong Zhongyang Wenxian Yanjiushi, *Zhou Enlai nianpu (1949–1976)*

ZJTN   Xianggang Zhongguo Jingji Tequ Nianjian Bianjibu,
           Zhongguo jingji tequ nianjian
ZRGJD   Fang Weizhong, *Zhonghua Renmin Gongheguo jingji dashiji
           (1949–1980)*
ZRGJFX   Zhongguo Shehui Kexueyuan Faxue Yanjiusuo, *Zhonghua
           Renmin Gongheguo jingji fagui xuanbian, 1979.10–1981.12*
ZRGJGD   Dangdai Zhongguo de Jingji Guanli Bianjibu, *Zhonghua
           Renmin Gongheguo jingji guanli dashiji*
ZZYWJ   Zhao Ziyang, *Zhao Ziyang wenxianji (1980–1989)*

Notes

Important Actors

1 Teiwes, *Politics at Mao's Court.*

2 Teiwes and Sun, "China's Economic Reorientation," 165, 183.

3 Zhao, *Prisoner of the State*, 93.

4 Bachman, *Chen Yun and the Chinese Political System*, 297.

5 Pantsov and Levine, *Deng Xiaoping*, 26–28.

6 Barnett, "Soviet Commodity Markets," 329–52; Sutton, *Western Technology and Soviet Economic Development*; Pantsov and Levine, *Deng Xiaoping*, 38–39.

7 Vogel, *Deng Xiaoping*, 25.

8 Bachman, "Differing Visions," 310–11.

9 Chung, "CEP of the Utopian Project," 157.

10 Teiwes and Sun, "China's New Economic Policy," 1.

11 Tong, *Fengyu sishinian*, 2:358.

12 Mao Zedong, "Dui zhongyang guanyu ziliudi deng wenti de zhishi de piyu xiugai he daini de buchong zhishigao" [A supplementary directive to the written comments that were revised and drafted by others concerning the Central Committee's directive on private plots and other problems], in Mao, *Jianguo*, 8:305–8.

13 Li Xiannian, "Jiajin fazhan dazhong chengshi jiaoqu de fushipin shengchan," in *LXNLCJM*, 1:361.

14 Li Xiannian, "Yinianlai," *LXNLCJM*, 1:335.

15 Li Xiannian, "Kefu dangqian jingji kunnan" [Overcoming current economic problems], in *LXNLCJM*, 1:448–49.

16 Li Xiannian, "Guanyu liangshi wenti de yifeng xin" [A letter on the grain problem], 30 July 1961, to Mao Zedong and the Central Committee, which approved and transmitted the letter on 2 August 1961, in *LXNLCJM*, 1:469–70.

17 Li Xiannian, "Yiju xinqingkuang zuohao waimao gongzuo" [Do a good job in foreign trade work in accordance with the new circumstances], speech to the National Foreign Trade Planning Conference, 26 September 1963, in *LXNLCJM*, 2:151; Li Xiannian, "Yinianlai," 335; Reardon, *Reluctant Dragon*, 105–28.

18 Li Xiannian, "Yiju xinqingkuang zuohao waimao gongzuo," *LXNLCJM*, 2:148–49; Li Xiannian, "Zhengque chuli neiwaimao de guanxi" [Correctly resolve the relationship between domestic and foreign trade], 30 May 1961, in *LXNLCJM*, 1:456.

19 Li Xiannian, "Jiben jianshe yao jizhong liliang da jianmiezhan" [Capital construction must concentrate its powers to fight a war of annihilation], speech to an expanded meeting of the Small Leading Group of the National Planning Conference, 21 February 1973, in *LXNLCJM*, 2:270–72.

20 Chen Yun, "Liyong," in Chen Yun, *Chen Yun wenxuan*, 3:224.

21 Teiwes and Sun, "China's Economic Reorientation," 171.

22 Zhao, *Prisoner of the State*, 92.

23 *ZRGJGD*, 381.

24 Teiwes and Sun, "China's Economic Reorientation," 175, 179.

25 Zhao, *Prisoner of the State*, xviii–xix.

26 Guangdong Nianjian Bianji Weiyuanhui, *Guangdong nianjian*, 1987, 225.

27 Zhao Ziyang, "Duiwai jingji maoyi lingyu de sixiang yao jiefang" [We must liberate our thinking in foreign economic trade area], speech to the Central Party Secretariat, 27 and 30 July 1981, in *ZZYWJ*, 1:200.

28 Zhao, *Prisoner of the State*, 134–35.

Introduction

1 The concept of long-term goals is based in Western theories of rational choice and not the current Chinese idea of "core interests." See Deng and Wang, *Eyes of the Dragon*.

2 For a more detailed analysis, see Reardon, *Reluctant Dragon*.

3 Pye, "How China's Nationalism Was Shanghaied," 124–30; Bernstein, "Introduction," 7–14; Lüthi, *Sino-Soviet Split*, 19–23.

4 Blyth, *Great Transformations*.

5 Lowenthal, "Development vs. Utopia." For more on this approach, see Reardon, *Reluctant Dragon*, chap. 1.

6 Brinton, *Anatomy of Revolution*, 207; Kotkin, *Stalin*, 1:487.

7 Cheremukhin et al., "Was Stalin Necessary," 9.

8 Kotkin, *Stalin*, 1:571, 663, 676, 737.

9 Kotkin, *Stalin*, 1:668–73; Bernstein, "Introduction," 8.

10 Li, Hua-Yu, "Instilling Stalinism," 109; 112–14.

11 Hofheinz, "Autumn Harvest Insurrection," 37–87; Mao, *Mao's Road to Power*; Heilmann, "From Local Experiments to National Policy," 5–7.

12 Lüthi, *Sino-Soviet Split*, 27.

13 Mao Zedong, "Zai Chengdu huiyi de jianghua" [Speech at the Chengdu Conference], 9 March 1958, in *MZDWJ*, 7:371; Mao Zedong, "Tong Sulian zhu Hua dashi Youjin de tanhua" [Discussion with Soviet ambassador Yudin], 22 July 1958, in *MZDWJ*, 7:393; Kampen, "Wang Jiaxiang, Mao Zedong," 713.

14 Friedman, "Maoism," 161.

15 Li, Hua-Yu, "Instilling Stalinism," 114.

16 Mao, "Zai Chengdu huiyi de jianghua," *MZDWJ*, 7:370.

17 Schram, "Mao Zedong a Hundred Years On," 132.

18 Mao Zedong, "Reading Notes," in Mao, *Miscellany of Mao Tse-Tung Thought*, 291.

19 Li, Hua-Yu, "Instilling Stalinism," 121–23; Bernstein and Li, *China Learns*, 1–26; Hou, "'Get Organized,'" 169–70; Walder, *China under Mao*, 25–27. Also see Watson, *Mao Zedong and the Political Economy*.

20 Pantsov and Levine, *Mao*, 366; Wheatcroft, Davies, and Cooper, "Soviet Industrialization Reconsidered," 264–94.

21 Zhou Enlai, "Guanyu muqian xingshi de baogao" [Report on current conditions], presented on 29 December 1955 to the National Conference of Factory and Mining Managers, in *ZELNP*, 1:531–32.

22 Li, Hua-Yu, *Mao and Economic Stalinization*, 3–4, 61–94; Lüthi, *Sino-Soviet Split*, 22–23.

23 Fewsmith, *Dilemmas of Reform*, 64–65.

24 Pantsov and Levine, *Mao*, 366–67; Pantsov and Levine, *Deng Xiaoping*, 156.

25 Hou, "'Get Organized,'" 172.

26 Hou, "'Get Organized,'" 172–76; Bernstein, "Introduction," 9–10; Li, Hua-Yu, *Mao and Economic Stalinization*, 32–34.

27 Zhonggong, *Liu Shaoqi nianpu*, 2:204.

28 Liu Shaoqi, "Guanyu xin Zhongguo de jingji jianshe fangzhen" [Plans for the economic construction of the new China], June 1949, in Liu Shaoqi, *Liu Shaoqi*, 148; Zhu Yuanshi, "Liu Shaoqi yijiusijiunian mimi fang Su," 74–89.

29 Conquest, *Great Terror*, 18–22.

30 Pantsov and Levine, *Deng Xiaoping*, 172.

31 Mao Zedong, "Tong Sulian zhu Hua dashi Youjin de jianghua" [Discussion with Soviet ambassador Yudin], 22 July 1958, in *MZDWJ*, 7:386; Shi Zhe, "'Zhongsu youhao tongmeng huzhu tiaoyue' qianding shimo," 52–57; Liu Shaoqi, "Zhongsu liangguo zai Xinjiang sheli jinshu he shiyou gongsi wenti" [The problem of establishing Sino-Soviet metal and oil joint venture companies in Xinjiang], report submitted to Mao Zedong on 2 January 1950, in Liu Shaoqi, *Liu Shaoqi*, 150–51.

32 *ZELNP*, 1:257–58; Lüthi, *Sino-Soviet Split*, 38; Pantsov and Levine, *Mao*, 390–91.

33 Mao, "Zai Chengdu huiyi de jianghua," *MZDWJ*, 7:370–71.

34 Hou, "'Get Organized,'" 182–83.

35 Li Fuchun, "Diyige wunian jihua de fangzhen he renwu" [Direction and mission of the FFYP], presented to the Second Session of the First NPC on 5 July 1955, in Li Fuchun, *Li Fuchun xuanji*, 133–48. Also see *RZJSH*, 1:284–307; Sutton, *Western Technology*.

36 Mao Zedong, "Duli zizhude gao jianshe" [Using self-reliance to build China], 17 June 1958, in *MZDWJ*, 7:380.

37 Lowenthal, "Development vs. Utopia."

38 Davies, "Changing Economic Systems," 19.

39 Lüthi, *Sino-Soviet Split*, 22–23; Trotsky, *Revolution Betrayed*, 114.

40 *ZELNP*, 1:115. For more on Arkhipov, see Radchenko, *Unwanted Visionaries*, 44–48.

41 *ZELNP*, 1:130–31.

42 Kong, "Transplantation and Entrenchment, "157–60.

43 Pantsov and Levine, *Deng Xiaoping*, 156–57.

44 Balassa, *Process of Industrial Development*, 18–22.

45 Kong, "Transplantation and Entrenchment," 160–62.

46 "Guanyu 1952 nian xuanpai fu Su liuxuesheng gongzuo de baogao" [Report on sending Chinese students to the Soviet Union for study in 1952], in *ZELNP*, 1:214; Reardon, *Reluctant Dragon*, 56–57.

47 *RZJSH*, 1:472.

48 Mao Zedong, "Summing-Up Speech at 6th Expanded Plenum of 7th Central Committee," September 1955, in Mao, *Miscellany of Mao Tse-Tung Thought*, 17; Pantsov and Levine, *Deng Xiaoping*, 160–62; Teiwes, "Establishment and Consolidation," 45–50.

49 *RZJSH*, 1:484; Pantsov and Levine, *Deng Xiaoping*, 165–76.

50 *RZJSH*, 1:485–90; Vogel, *Deng Xiaoping*, 124.

51 Tong, *Fengyu sishinian*, 2:349–50.

52 Mao Zedong, "Talk Opposing Right-Deviation and Conservatism," presented on 6 December 1955, in Mao, *Miscellany of Mao Tse-Tung Thought*, 28.

53 *RZJSH*, 2:808–9.

54 *RZJSH*, 1:522. Also see *ZELNP*, 1:524; MacFarquhar, *Origins*, 1: 30–32; *RZJSH*, 1:466–67; Walder, *China Under Mao*, 154.

55 Lowenthal, "Development vs. Utopia."

56 Lüthi describes Mao's post-1955 economic policies as akin to revolutionary Stalinism of the late 1920 and early 1930s. See Lüthi, *Sino-Soviet Split*, 27, 72, 74, 78, 80, and 84.

57 Mao Zedong, "Duli zizhude gao jianshe" [Using self-reliance to build China], 17 June 1958, in Mao, *Mao Zedong wenji*, vol. 7, 380.

58 Lüthi, *Sino-Soviet Split*, 41–42; Friedman, "Maoism, Titoism, Stalinism," 159–214.

59 *ZELNP*, 1:587.

60 Reardon, *Reluctant Dragon*, 60–75.

61 Reardon, *Reluctant Dragon*, chap. 2.

62 Moltz, "Divergent Learning," 303.

63 *RZJSH*, 2:522.

64 Zhou Enlai, "Diyige wunian jihua de jingyan he jiaoxun" [The experiences and lessons to be learned from the First Five-Year Plan], *ZELJJWX*, 278–328.

65 *ZELJJWX*, 295.

66 Qing, "Eisenhower Administration and Changes"; Zhongguo Duiwai Jingji Maoyi Nianjian Bianji Weiyuanhui, *Zhongguo duiwai maoyi nianjian*, sec. 4, 18, 19, 58, 67.

67 *ZELNP*, 2:205.

68 Zhou Enlai, "Guanyu Xianggang wenti" [Concerning the Hong Kong problem], *ZELJJWX*, 354.

69 *ZELNP*, 2:31.

70 Lin Jinzhi, *Huaqiao huaren yu Zhongguo geming*, 478–84.

71 Guangdong Nianjian Bianji Weiyuanhui, *Guangdong nianjian, 1987*, 225.

72 Tong, *Fengyu sishinian*, 2:389.

73 "Guanyu zhixing duiwai maoyi jihuazhong cunzai wenti de qingshi baogao" [The report and request of instructions concerning existing problems in carrying out

the foreign trade plan], approved by the Central Committee 18 March 1959, in *ZELJJWX*, 397.

74 "Lizheng wancheng dangnian duiwai maoyi de shougou he chukou renwu de jinji zhishi" [Emergency directive to exert utmost effort to meet foreign trade procurement and export responsibilities], issued by the CCP Central Committee and the State Council on 26 October 1959, in *ZRGJGD*, 131.

75 Li Xiannian, "Liangnian yilai guomin jingji tiaozheng gongzuo qude juda chengjiu" [The two years of readjustment work pays off with tremendous achievements], presented to the NPC on 5 August 1963 and approved/transmitted by the Central Committee 11 August 1963, in *LXNLCJM*, 2:134.

76 *ZELNP*, 2:382.

77 Reardon, *Reluctant Dragon*, 119–28.

78 *ZELNP*, 2:577–78.

79 This process took decades. See Zhao Ziyang, "Sanxian jianshe tiaozheng gaizao shouxian yao zhiding guihua" [In readjusting and transforming Third Front construction, we must first establish a plan], 20 November 1983, in *ZZYWJ*, 2:241–44; Zhao Ziyang, "Sanxian qiye tiaozheng bixu gao junmin jiehexing"[Readjustment of Third Front Industries must take an integrative nature], 16 August 1984, in *ZZYWJ*, 2:447–50.

80 Zhou Enlai, "Xiang sige xiandaihua de hongwei mubiao qianjin" [Forging toward the magnificent goal of the Four Modernizations], a portion of the Government Work Report presented to the first meeting of the Fourth NPC on 13 January 1975, in *ZELJJWX*, 652.

81 Tan, Yao, and Li, *Waimao fuchi*, 70.

82 Chen Yun, *Chen Yun Wenxuan*, 3:217–18.

83 *ZELNP*, 3:621.

84 *ZELNP*, 3:583, 636–38; Yu Shicheng, *Deng Xiaoping yu Mao Zedong*, 269–75.

85 *ZELNP*, 3: 680–81.

86 Reardon, *Reluctant Dragon*, chap. 5; *ZRGJGD*, 270; *ZRGJD*, 496–98.

87 Chen Donglin, "Chen Yun yu 70 niandai," 2:1102; *ZRGJD*, 560.

88 "Guanyu dali kaizhan niuzhuan qiye kuisun, zengjia yingli gongzuo de tongzhi" [Circular on emphasizing the turnabout of industrial losses and increasing profits], issued by the State Council 8 July 1977, in *ZRGJGD*, 305.

89 Vogel, *Deng Xiaoping*, 193.

90 Guo, "Dimensions of *Guanxi*," 84, 89–90.

91 Vogel, *Deng Xiaoping*, 198–204, 229–40.

92 Zhou, "Xiang sige xiandaihua de hongwei mubiao qianjin," *ZELJJWX*, 652–53.

93 Hua, "Report."

94 "Guanyu Shanghai xinjian gangtiechang de changzhi xuanze, jianshe guimo he youguan wenti de qingshi baogao" [Report and request for instructions concerning the site selection and construction scale of Shanghai's new steel mill], approved by the State Council on 11 March 1978, in *ZRGJD*, 597.

95 Li Xiannian, "Zai zhongyang gongzuo huiyishang de jianghua" [Speech to the Central Work Conference], in *SQYZWX*, 1982, 117.

96 Hasan, "Yugoslavia's Foreign Policy," 87–88.

97 Halpern, "Learning from Abroad," 80–83.

98 Hasan, "Yugoslavia's Foreign Policy," 88.

99 Li, Lanqing, *Breaking Through*, 67.

100 Pantsov and Levine, *Deng Xiaoping*, 336.

101 Teiwes and Sun, "China's New Economic Policy," 15.

102 Teiwes and Sun, "China's New Economic Policy," 15; Li, *Breaking Through*, 53.

103 Teiwes and Sun, "China's New Economic Policy," 15.

104 *ZELNP*, 3:518–19; Chen Yun, "Liyong guonei fengfu laodongli shengchan chengpin chukou" [Use China's abundant labor to produce finished products for export], in Chen Yun, *Chen Yun wenxuan*, 3:224; Li, *Breaking Through*, 52–55; Vogel, *Deng Xiaoping*, 221–27.

105 Vogel, *Deng Xiaoping*, 189–90.

106 Hasan, "Yugoslavia's Foreign Policy," 88.

107 For example, see Zhao Ziyang, "Bixu jizhong zijin baozheng zhongdian jianshe" [We must concentrate our capital to guarantee important construction], 17 March 1983, in *ZZYWJ*, 2:42–47; Zhao Ziyang, "Xiongyali de jingji gaige zhide yanjiu he jiejian" [The Hungarian reforms deserve to be researched and borrowed from], 23 July 1983, in *ZZYWJ*, 2:131–41. Also see Hong, "Provincial Leadership and Its Strategy," 384–85; Shambaugh, *Making of a Premier*, chap. 6; Halpern, "Learning from Abroad," 82–83.

108 Halpern, "Learning from Abroad," 85–98.

109 Chen Yun, "Zai caijing," *SQYZWX*, 1982, 172, 173. According to the Two What-evers approach, the party-state would "resolutely uphold whatever policy decisions Chairman Mao made, and unswervingly follow whatever instructions Chairman Mao gave." *Renmin ribao*, 7 February 1977.

110 UN Development Programme, "First Country Programme for the People's Republic of China."

111 *ZRGJD*, 605; *ZRGJGD*, 319.

112 Crane, *Political Economy*, 25.

113 Li Xiannian, "Zai Guowuyuan Wuxuhui shang de jianghua" [Speech to the State Council Ideological Discussion Conference], 9 September 1978, in *LXNLCJM*, 1:368–81.

114 Li, *Breaking Through*, 55.

115 For a detailed discussion of this period, see Vogel, *Deng Xiaoping*, 221–27.

116 Vogel, *Deng Xiaoping*, 226.

117 Deng Xiaoping, "Gaoju Mao Zedong sixiang qizhi, jianchi shishi qiushi de yuanze" [Raise high the banner of Mao Zedong thought, uphold the principle of seeking truth from fact], in *DXPWX*, 123.

118 For greater in-depth analysis of Deng's views in the late 1970s, see Teiwes and Sun, "China's New Economic Policy"; Teiwes and Sun, "China's Economic Reorientation," 163–87.

119 Li, *Breaking Through*, 56–60.

120 Vogel, *Deng Xiaoping*, 299.

121 Li, *Breaking Through*, 61.

122 Vogel, *Deng Xiaoping*, 301, 308.

123 Zhao, *Prisoner of the State*, 92.

124 *ZRGJD*, 603.

125 Chen Yun, "Tiaozheng," *SQYZWX*, 1982, 76–77.

126 Chen Yun, "Zai caijing," *SQYZWX*, 1982, 172, 173.

127 Long, *Liyong waizi gailun*, 253, 288, 300; Kokubun, "The Politics," 19–44; Davie and Carver, "China's International Trade," 27; Zhao Ziyang, "Jinnian jingji xingshi he 'liuwu' jihua shexiang" [Tentative ideas about this year's economic situation and the '6.5' economic plan], report delivered to the Political Bureau on 2 September 1980, in *ZZYWJ*, 1:79–88.

128 Chen Yun, "Jingji xingshi yu jingyan jiaoxun" [The economic situation and the lessons from experience], in *SQYZWX*, 1982, 606; Hua, "Report"; *ZRGJD*, 505.

129 *ZRGJD*, 505, 605–6.

130 "Guanyu dali kaizhan niuzhuan qiye kuisun, zengjia yingli gongzuo de tongzhi" [Circular on emphasizing the turnabout of industrial losses and increasing profits], issued by the State Council on 8 July 1977, in *ZRGJGD*, 305.

131 "Guanyu dongjie ge danwei cunkuan de jinji tongzhi" [Emergency circular on the freezing of each unit's bank accounts], issued by the CCP Central Committee on 28 October 1976, in *ZRGJGD*, 297; "Guanyu jianjue yasuo he yange kongzhi shehui jituan goumaili de qingshi baogao" [Report and request for instructions on strictly reducing and controlling the buying power of social groups], issued by the SPC et. al and approved by the State Council 28 March 1977, in *ZRGJGD*, 300; "Guanyu jinyibu zuohao huanwai gongzuo de baogao" [Report on further improving foreign aid work], submitted by the MFT on 23 August 1977 and approved by the CCP Central Committee on 25 September 1977, in *ZRGJGD*, 307.

132 "Quanguo jieyu ranliao, dianli jingyan jiaoliu huiyi jiyao" [Summary of the Conference on Conserving Fuel and Energy], issued by the State Council on 9 April 1977, in *ZRGJGD*, 301; "Quanguo tielu gongzuo huiyi jiyao" [Summary of the National Work Conference on the Railroads], issued by the CCP Central Committee 22 February 1977, in *ZRGJGD*, 299–300; "Quanguo jiben jianshe huiyi jiyao" [Summary of the Conference on Capital Construction] and the accompanying circular issued by the State Council on 3 April 1977, in *ZRGJGD*, 301; "Guanyu pizhuan quanguo yejin gongye gongzuo huiyi jiyao de tongzhi" [Circular on the approval and issuance of the National Conference on the Metallurgical Industry], issued by the State Council 15 April 1977, in *ZRGJGD*, 302.

133 "Guanyu jinnian yilai waimao shougou jihua zhixing qingkuang he wenti de baogao" [Report on problems in fulfilling the foreign trade procurement plan since the beginning of this year], issued by the SPC and MFT and approved by the State Council on 15 May 1977, in *ZRGJGD*, 303–4; Li Xiannian, "Jiji zengjia chukou," 310–11.

134 Chen Yun, "Guanyu dangqian jingji wenti de wudian yijian" [Five points regarding current economic problems], in *Chen Yun wenxuan*, 3:235–38.

135 Chen Yun, *Chen Yun tongzhi*, 118.

136 Chen Yun, "Dui jingji gongzuo de jidian yijian" [Some views on economic work], presented on 22 December 1981 at the Conference of First Party Secretaries from

Provincial, Municipal, and Special Administrative Region Party Committees, in *SQYZWX*, 1058.

137 Chen Yun, "Dui jingji gongzuo," *SQYZWX*, 1057–58.

138 Chen Yun, "Dui jingji gongzuo," *SQYZWX*, 1059.

139 For the actual documents, see Reardon, *Reluctant Dragon*, 194–99.

140 Li Xiannian, *Li Xiannian zhuan*, 1071.

141 "Guanyu jianli chukou shangpin shengchan jidi de qingshi baogao" [Report and request for instructions on establishing an export commodity production base], submitted by the MFT and approved by the CCP Central Committee 30 June 1960, in *ZRGJGD*, 143. See also translation in Reardon, *Reluctant Dragon*, 229–30.

142 Friedman, "Maoism," 165.

143 Malle, *Economic Organization of War Communism*, 495–514.

144 Malle, *Economic Organization of War Communism*, 453–54.

145 Bernstein, "Introduction," 7–8.

146 Davies, "Changing Economic Systems," 8.

147 Malle, *Economic Organization of War Communism*, 455.

148 Reardon, *Reluctant Dragon*, 53. For a discussion of Chinese understanding of the NEP, see Heilmann, "From Local Experiments," 17–18.

149 Dittmer, *Liu Shao-chi*, 11, 15.

150 Friedman, "Maoism," 165.

151 Vogel, *Deng Xiaoping*, 23–25.

152 Pantsov and Levine, *Deng Xiaoping*, 38–39.

153 Reardon, *Reluctant Dragon*, 35–36.

154 Pantsov and Levine, *Mao*, 478–80; Shambaugh, "Deng Xiaoping," 465–66.

155 Directive drafted by Liu Shaoqi for the Central Committee on 30 March 1950, in Zhonggong, *Liu Shaoqi nianpu*, 2:246.

156 Lin Jinzhi, *Huaqiao huaren yu Zhongguo geming he jianshe*, 478–84.

157 *ZRGJD*, 532; Deng Xiaoping, "Guanyu fazhan gongye de jidian yijian" [A few ideas on industrial development], in *DXPWX*, 28–41.

158 *ZRGJGD*, 296; *ZRGJD*, 559–60.

159 Bruton, "Reconsideration of Import Substitution," 903–36.

160 Chen Yun, "Jingji xingshi yu jingyan jiaoxun" [The economic situation and lessons from history], in *SQYZWX*, 563.

161 Malle, *Economic Organization of War Communism*, 453.

162 Oi, "Fiscal Reform and the Economic Foundations," 102–3.

163 Childs, *Sweden*; Macmillan, *Middle Way*.

164 Giddens, "Socialism and After"; Giddens, *Third Way and Its Critics*, chap. 1.

165 Niall Dickson, "UK Politics: What Is the Third Way?"

166 Naughton, *Growing Out of the Plan*, 311.

167 Truex, "Consultative Authoritarianism and Its Limits," 6; He and Warren, "Authoritarian Deliberation," 269–89.

168 Teets, *Civil Society under Authoritarianism*, 44.

169 Teets, *Civil Society under Authoritarianism*, 5.

170 Cheng and White, "Elite Transformation and Modern Change," 12–6; Cheng and White, " Thirteenth Central Committee," 393–98.

171 Chen Yun, "Jingji xingshi yu jingyan jiaoxun" [The economic situation and lessons from experience], in *SQYZWX*, 601.
172 For an interesting critique of the famous *The East Asian Miracle Report* from the World Bank that states that the East Asian "miracle" did not offer a new third way of development, see Amsden, "Why Isn't Everyone Experimenting?" 631.
173 "Zhongguo gongchandang zhongyang weiyuanhui guanyu jianguo yilai dang de ruogan lishi wenti de jueyi" [Resolution on certain questions in the history of our party since the founding of the PRC], 27 June 1981, in *SQYZWX*, 788–849.
174 George and Bennett, *Case Studies and Theory Development*, 206. Also see Collier, "Understanding Process Tracing," 823–30. For a recent example in China studies, see Kuo, "Chinese Religious Reform," 1053.
175 See, for instance, Chun, "China's Museums Rewrite History."
176 For a detailed discussion of official Chinese documents, see Reardon, *Reluctant Dragon*, 217–25.

Chapter One

1 Linz and Stepan, *Problems of Democratic Transition*, chap. 3.
2 For a comprehensive analysis of the domestic decentralization strategy, see Naughton, *Growing Out of the Plan*.
3 Mishler and Rose, "What Are the Origins of Political Trust?" 30–62; Mishler and Rose, "Generation, Age, and Time," 822–34; Reardon, *Reluctant Dragon*, 184–85.
4 Haggard and Kaufman, *Politics of Economic Adjustment*; Brooks and Kurtz, "Capital, Trade," 703–20; Domínguez, *Technopols*, 199.
5 Bachman, "Differing Visions," 300–301; Cheng, "Modernization of Chinese Industry," 37; Brown, "China's Program of Technology Acquisition," 165–68.
6 Chen Yun, "Tiaozheng," *SQYZWX*, 1982, 76–77.
7 Long Chucai, *Liyong waizi gailun*, 232; *ZRGJD*, 496–97, 506.
8 Deng Xiaoping, "Uphold the Four Cardinal Principles," 30 March 1979. The Four Cardinal Principles are to promote the socialist path, the people's democratic dictatorship, the leadership of the Chinese Communist Party, and Mao Zedong Thought and Marxism-Leninism.
9 Deng Xiaoping, "Jianchi sixiang jiben yuanze" [Uphold the Four Cardinal Principles], in *DXPWX*, 144–70; Deng Xiaoping, "Remarks on Successive Drafts of the 'Resolution on Certain Questions in the History of Our Party since the Founding of the People's Republic of China,'" 22 June 1981, in *Selected Works of Deng Xiaoping, Volume 2 (1975–1982)*. Accessed 26 April 2017. https://dengxiaoping works.wordpress.com/2013/02/25/remarks-on-successive-drafts-of-the-resolution -on-certain-questions-in-the-history-of-our-party-since-the-founding-of-the -peoples-republic-of-china/.
10 Teiwes, "Paradoxical Post-Mao Transition," 72.
11 Baum, *Burying Mao*, 144–48; Twelfth National Congress, "Constitution of the Communist Party (1982)."

12   Deng Xiaoping, "Zai zhongyang guwen weiyuanhui di yici quanti huiyishang de jianghua" [Speech at the First Plenary Session of the Central Advisory Commission of the Chinese Communist Party], 13 September 1982, in *DXPWX-3*, 7.

13   Guo Xuezhi, "Dimensions of *Guanxi*," 83–84.

14   Li Xiannian, "Zai zhongyang gongzuo huiyishang de jianghua" [Speech to the Central Work Conference], in *SQYZWX*, 109, 121.

15   Lieberthal and Oksenberg, *Policy Making in China*, 169–268; Zhonggong Renminglu, *Zhonggong renming lu*, 305; Fewsmith, *Dilemmas of Reform*, 87–90; Ju, "'New Economic Group,'" 192–97.

16   Chen Yun, "Tiaozheng," *SQYZWX*, 1982, 74–79; Fewsmith, *Dilemmas of Reform*, 62–68; Li Xiannian, "Zai zhongyang," *SQYZWX*, 109, 112–17; Zheng, Han, and Zheng, *Zhongguo jingji*.

17   World Steel Association, *World Steel in Figures 2014*; Zhang and Kim, "Chen Yun's Role," 46–47.

18   Li Xiannian, "Zai zhongyang," *SQYZWX*, 130; "Guanyu banfa 'Jixu yinjin he shebei jinkou gongzuo zhanxing tiaoli' de tongzhi" [Circular on the issuance of "The temporary regulations on technology and equipment importation"], State Council document 1981.12, issued 21 January 1981, in Zhongguo Renmin Yinhang Bangongshi, *1981 Jinrong guizhang zhidu xuanbian*, 2: 311–14.

19   Li Xiannian, "Zai zhongyang," *SQYZWX*, 124–25.

20   Long Chucai, *Liyong waizi gailun*, 232.

21   *ZRGJD*, 496–97; *ZRGJGD*, 270.

22   Li Xiannian, "Zai zhongyang," *SQYZWX*, 123–25.

23   Chen Yun, "Jingji xingshi yu jingyan jiaoxun" [The economic situation and lessons from experience], in *SQYZWX*, 601.

24   For more detail, see Reardon, *Reluctant Dragon*, chap. 7.

25   "'Guangdong shengwei, Fujian shengwei guanyu duiwai jingji huodong shixing texu zhengce he linghuo cuoshi' de liangge baogao" [The approval and transmittal of the "Two reports of the Guangdong and Fujian Provincial Committee concerning the implementation of special policies and flexible measures in foreign trade activities"], Central Committee document 1979.50, issued by the Central Committee and State Council on 15 July 1979, translated in Reardon, "China's Coastal Development Strategy (I)," 19–44.

26   "Ping Lin Biao de 'Zhengzhi bianfang'" [Criticizing Lin Biao's Strategy of "Political Frontier Defense"], in *Jiefang junbao*, 15 October 1978.

27   For instance, see Wang Dao'nan, "Shekou gongyequ," 24–26; Liu Yuezhou, "Shenzhenshi chuanghui"; Zhang Suiqiang, "Zhiqing taogang yanjiu," 128–35; Schoenhals, "Cultural Revolution on the Border," 27–54.

28   Sun Ru, *Qianjinzhong de Zhongguo jingji tequ*, 12–13.

29   Xi Zhongxun, "Guangdong de jianshe ruhe dagan kuaishang" [How to go all out for Guangdong's construction and quickly develop], 8 November 1978, in Xi, *Xi Zhongxun wenxuan*, 274–85.

30   For instance, see "Guanyu jiji zhengqu qiaohui de yijian" [An opinion on actively fighting for overseas Chinese capital], State Council document 78.29, cited in Zhongguo Renmin Yinhang Jihuasi, *Lilü wenjian huibian*, 674.

31 Xi, "Guangdong de jianshe ruhe dagan kuaishang," 284–85.

32 Liang Wensen, *Zhongguo jingji tequ*, 188. In Daoism, each of the eight immortals embodied different qualities of prosperity, longevity, and good fortune. The term also refers to the eight elders, who were from the second generation of Chinese leaders, including Deng Xiaoping, Chen Yun, and Li Xiannian.

33 *Renmin ribao*, 18 January 1985.

34 Liang Xiang, "Construction and development in the Shenzhen Special Economic Zone," *Foreign Broadcast Information Service—China*, 24 January 1986, P1.

35 Chan, Chen, and Chin, "China's Special Economic Zones," 95–96.

36 "Guanyu baozheng tongyi guojia caizheng jingji gongzuo de tongzhi" [Circular on guaranteeing the state unified financial and economic work], issued by the CCP Central Committee on 3 March 1950, in *ZRGJD*, 14.

37 "Guanyu huafen zhongyang yu difang zai caizheng jingji gongzuoshang guanli zhiquan de jueding" [Decision to designate administrative authority to the central government and the localities in financial and economic work], issued by the Political Affairs Council on 4 May 1951, in *ZRGJD*, 47–48.

38 Li Xiannian, "Zai zhongyang," *SQYZWX*, 140.

39 Li Xiannian, "Zai zhongyang," *SQYZWX*, 142, 143.

40 Hu Qiaomu, "Guanyu shehui zhuyi shiqi jieji douzheng de yixie tifa wenti" [Some problems with the wording of socialist class struggle], in *SQYZWX*, 38–42.

41 Deng Xiaoping, "Jiefang sixiang, shishi qiushi, tuanjie yizhi xiangqiankan" [Liberate thinking, seek truth from facts, unite and look to the future], in *DXPWX*, 142.

42 "Guanyu dui yuan gongshang yezhe de ruogan juti zhengce de guiding" [Several specific policy regulations regarding former industrialists and businesspeople], submitted by the United Front Department et al. and approved by the CCP Central Committee on 17 December 1979, in *ZRGJGD*, 371.

43 Deng Xiaoping, "Yikao lixiang erkao jilu caineng tuanjie qilai" [Only by first relying on the ideal and then relying on discipline can we become united], in *DXPWX-3*, 98–99; Deng Xiaoping, "Zai Zhongguo gongchandang quanguo daibiao huiyishang de jianghua" [Speech at the National Meeting of Representatives of the Chinese Communist Party], in *DXPWX-3*, 141–47; Peng Kehong, "Gongtong fuyu de biyou zhilu," in Zhonggong Zhongyang Shujichu Yanjiushi Lilunzu, *Diaocha yanjiu*, 466–76.

44 For more background on the new leadership's ideas on economic structural reform at that time, see Chen Yun, "Jihua yu shichang" [Planning and market], in *SQYZWX*, 68–71.

45 Li Xiannian, "Zai zhongyang," *SQYZWX*, 141–42. According to Deng Liqun, the use of the market as a regulatory tool was proposed by Chen Yun and first mentioned publicly by Li at the April Work Conference.

46 Li Xiannian, "Zai zhongyang," *SQYZWX*, 140.

47 Li Xiannian, "Zai zhongyang," *SQYZWX*, 140.

48 Li Xiannian, "Zai zhongyang," *SQYZWX*, 143; *ZRGJGD*, 171.

49 The government experimented with many different fiscal decentralization methods between 1976 and 1979. See Wang and Zhu, *Jingji tizhi gaige shouce*, 844–45;

ZRGJGD, 297; Donnithorne, "New Light," 97–104. Then, between 1979 and 1980, two methods were adopted. On the first, see "Guanyu shixing 'Shouzhi guagou, quan'e fencheng, bili baogan sannian bubian' caizheng guanli banfa de tongzhi" [A circular on financial administrative procedures for "linking local expenditures and revenues, sharing total revenues between local and central authorities at fixed ratios and holding rations unchanged for a three-year period"], issued by the State Council on 13 July 1979, in *ZRGJGD*, 348. The second method is outlined in "Guanyu shixing 'Huafen shouzhi, fenji baogan' caizheng guanli tizhi de tongzhi" [Circular on the trial regulations on the implementation of the "System of dividing revenue and expenditure between the central and local governments and holding each responsible for balancing their budgets' fiscal administrative system"], State Council document 1980.33, adopted on 1 February 1980, in Zhonghua Renmin Gongheguo Caizhengbu, *Caizheng guizhang*, 11.

50 World Bank, *China: External*, Annex 1; Wu Wutong, *Duiwai maoyi*, 54; Tan, Yao, and Li, *Waimao fuchi*, 174–78; Li Xiaoxian, *Duiwai maoyi yuanli*, 40; Guojia Jingji Tizhi Gaige Weiyuanhui, *Zhongguo jingji*, 759–61.

51 "Duiwai maoyi bixu tongyi duiwai de jueding" [Decision that there must be unified trade abroad], issued by the CCP Central Committee during the last ten days of August 1958, in *ZRGJGD*, 116, and Guoji Maoyi Wenti Bianjibu, *Zhongguo Duiwai*, 444.

52 Li Xiaoxian, *Duiwai maoyi yuanli*, 40–41.

53 For a concise description of the prereform foreign trade corporation system, see Oborne, *China's Special Economic Zones*, 35–38.

54 Li Xiaoxian, *Duiwai maoyi yuanli*, 41–42.

55 *Beijing Review*, 6 April 1981, 21, as cited in Halpern, "Learning," 95.

56 Reardon, *Reluctant Dragon*, chap. 7.

57 "'Duiwai maoyi jinkou guanli shixing banfa,' 'Duiwai maoyi difang jinkou guanli shixing banfa' de tongzhi" [Circular on the issuance of "The trial procedures for foreign trade import administration" and "The trial procedures for the localities concerning foreign trade import administration"], Maojinguanzi 1980.383, issued by the MFT et al. on 26 August 1980, in *DJFZH*, 339.

58 "Guanyu kaifang Changjiang gangkou sheli haiguan jigou de qingshi" [Request for instruction for opening customs offices along the Yangtze River], approved by the State Council on 28 March 1980, in *ZRGJGD*, 382; Zheng, Han, and Zheng, *Zhongguo jingji*, 6.

59 "Guanyu xiada difang duanqi waihui daikuan zhibiao de tongzhi" [Circular on the issuance of the target for short-term foreign exchange loans for localities], Yinzhongwuzi 1979.943, issued by the Bank of China et al. on 26 June 1979, in Zhongguo Renmin Yinhang Jihuasi, *Lilü*, 668; Tan, Yao, and Li, *Waimao fuchi*, 92, 98; "Chukou shangpin waihui liucheng shixing banfa" [Trial procedures for the retention scheme of foreign exchange derived from export commodities] and "Guanyu feimaoyi waihui liucheng shixing banfa" [Trial procedures for foreign exchange derived from nontrade activities], attached to State Council document 1979.202, in *GJGFX*, 4, 440–48; Caizhengbu Waihui Waishi Caiwusi, *Feimaoyi waihui*, 83.

60 "Guanyu jinyibu kaizhan gongye gaizu shidian gongzuo de tongzhi" [Circular on further developing the industrial reorganization work at the pilot projects], issued by the State Economic Commission on 16 September 1979, in *GJGFX*, 2:1–28.

61 *Caimao zhanxian*, 5 August 1980, cited in Zhang Zerong, *Zhongguo jingji tizhi gaige*, 206–7.

62 On State Council document 1979.233, see Reardon, "China's Coastal Development Strategy (I)," 39–42.

63 "Guanyu zai Jing, Jin, Lu de bage qiye jinxing qiye guanli gaige shidian de tongzhi" [Circular on experimenting with enterprise administration reform in eight enterprises located in Beijing, Tianjin, and Shanghai], issued by the State Economic Commission et al. on 25 May 1979, in Hanshou Xuexi Ziliao Bianjizu, *Gongye jingji guanli fagui xuanbian* [Collection of industrial economic management laws], 1:239–46; Wang and Zhu, *Jingji tizhi*, 827; Zhang Zerong, *Zhongguo jingji tizhi gaige*, 144, 154; Li, Xu, and Wu, *Shehui zhuyi gaigeshi*, 544.

64 "Zhongguo Yinhang quanguo fenhang jingli huiyi jiyao" [Summary of the National Conference for Managers of the Bank of China], issued by the State Council on 4 August 1980, in *ZRGJGD*, 395–96.

65 Shanghai Shehui Kexueyuan, *Shanghai jingji*, 723–26. For information on Tianjin's foreign trade corporation, see Gu Shutang, *Tianjin jingji gaikuang*, 281–86.

66 For more on the various export promotion strategies, such as using imports to promote exports (*Yijin yangchu*), see Reardon, *Reluctant Dragon*, 83.

67 "Guanyu Shanghai wanju hangye shixing gongmao heyi de qingshi baogao" (Report and request for instructions for carrying out the amalgamation of industry and trade of Shanghai's toy industry), submitted by the Shanghai Municipal Revolutionary Committee et al. and approved by the State Council on 18 August 1979, in *ZRGJGD*, 354–55; Shanghai Shehui Kexueyuan, *Shanghai jingji*, 754–55.

68 *ZRGJGD*, 354–55; Shanghai Shehui Kexueyuan, *Shanghai jingji*, 754–55.

69 Reardon, "China's Coastal Development Strategy (I)," 38. The fiscal administration system outlined in Central Committee document 1979.50 was a hybrid of the *shouzhi guagou* (linking local expenditures and revenues) and *huafen shouzhi, fenji baogan* (dividing revenues and expenditures between central and local governments and holding each responsible for balanced budgets) experimental methods, which were adopted between 1979 and 1980.

70 Reardon, "China's Coastal Development Strategy (I)," 19–21.

71 "Guanyu gaige haiguan guanli tizhi de jueding" [Decision to reform the customs administration structure], issued by the State Council on 9 February 1980, in *ZRGJGD*, 378. The "Decision" established a separate customs office (*fenshu*) in Guangdong, controlled by the Guangdong provincial government. Also see Zhang Zerong, *Zhongguo jingji tizhi gaige*, 196.

72 "Guanyu wozhu Xianggang Zhaoshangju zai Guangdong Bao'an jianli gongyequ de baogao" [Report on Hong Kong China Merchants' Steam and Navigation Company establishing an industrial zone in Bao'an county], submitted by the Guangdong Revolutionary Committee and the Ministry of Communications on 6 January 1979 and approved by Li Xiannian on 31 January 1979, in *SJTN*, 1984: 232.

73 Li, Lanqing, *Breaking Through*, 93; Xinhua, "The birth of an important decision," *Foreign Broadcast Information Service—China*, 18 June 1984, K3.

74 Deng Xiaoping, "Guanche tiaozheng," *DXPWX*, 322.

75 Chen Yun, "Dui jingji gongzuo de jidian yijian" [Some views on economic work], in *SQYZWX*, 1057.

76 For an excellent analysis of the commissions during this period, see Li, *Breaking Through*, 99–110.

77 Besides his duties as chairman of the SIEC and the SFIC, Gu Mu was a member of the State Council Finance and Economy Commission; in 1980, he was made a secretary of the Central Committee Party Secretariat. See Zhonggong Renminglu, *Zhonggong renming lu*, 313; Xianggang Zhuanshang Xuesheng Lianhui, *Jingji tequmian*, 98.

78 "Guanyu wozhu Xianggang Zhaoshangju," in *SJTN*, 1984, 232; Huang and Chen, *Xiwang zhichuang* 1, 124, 125; Xiong and Xu, *Shekou shouce*, 46.

79 Renmin Ribaoshe Gongshangbu, *Zhongguo duiwai kaifang*, 917; *SJTN*, 1985: 616; Zhuhai Jingji Nianjian Bianji Weiyuanhui, *Zhuhai jingji*, 273; Central Committee document 1979.50, translated in Reardon, "China's Coastal Development Strategy (I)," 19–44.

80 See *ZJTN*, 1983: 365; Central Committee documents 1980.41, 1981.27, and 1982.17, in Reardon, "China's Coastal Development Strategy (I)," 45–95.

81 Jiang Zemin, "Shezhi jingji tequ, jiakuai jingji fazhan" [Setting up the economic zone, and accelerating economic development], 21 August 1980, in *Jiang Zemin wenji*, 1:1–4.

82 Zhonggong Renminglu, *Zhonggong renming lu*, 160; Zhongguo Renmin Cidian Bianjibu, *Zhongguo renming dacidian*, 106; Zhuhai Jingji Nianjian Bianji Weiyuanhui, *Zhuhai jingji*, 274; *ZJTN*, 1983: 383; Li, *Breaking Through*, 79–85.

83 "Guanyu chongfen liyong Xianggang Zhaoshangju wenti de qingshi," approved by the CCP Central Committee on 12 October 1978, cited in *XZ*, 150.

84 *XZ*, 147–52.

85 Li, *Breaking Through*, 73–74.

86 *Shenzhen fengcai*, July 1–2, 1986.

87 "Guanyu wozhu Xianggang Zhaoshangju," in *SJTN*, 1984: 232.

88 Li, *Breaking Through*, 75.

89 On the discussion in Beijing, see Li, *Breaking Through*, 77–79.

90 *XZ*, 12; Chen and Xue, "Xiwang zhichuang," *Renmin ribao*, 15 September 1987; Zhonggong Shenzhen Shiwei, *Shenzhen tequ fazhan*, 136.

91 The original right of administration was granted by "Guanyu wozhu Xianggang Zhaoshangju," in *SJTN*, 1984: 232. After the passage of document 1979.50, Guangdong, Shenzhen, and CMSN amended the agreement on 18 November 1979 by signing "Guanyu jingying Shekou gongyequ de neibu xieyi" [Internal agreement on the operations of the Shekou Industrial Zone], cited in *XZ*, 128.

92 Nantou authorities of the Shenzhen SEZ refused to collaborate with the Shekou Administration Committee to install communications between two areas. Chen and Xue, "Xiwang zhichuang," *Renmin ribao*, 15 September 1987.

93 Li, *Breaking Through*, 79–85.

94 Li, *Breaking Through*, 85–86.

95 *Shenzhen Daily*, 14 July 2008.

96 *DXPWX-3*, 51–52.

97 Operated by the Overseas Chinese Enterprise Company, the Guangming Farm in Bao'an is also accorded SEZ preferential treatment. The farm employed many Vietnamese refugees who arrived in the late 1970s and 1980s. See *SJTN*, 1985: 117–18; Shenzhenshi Duiwai Xuanchuanchu and Xianggang Xinwanbao, *Zhongguo jingji tequ*, 135–42.

98 "Guangdong, Fujian liangsheng huiyi jiyao de pishi" [Comment on the "Summary of the Conference on Guangdong and Fujian Provinces"] Central Committee document 1980.41, translated in Reardon, "China's Coastal Development Strategy (I)," 45–58.

99 "Guangdong, Fujian liangsheng he jingji tequ gongzuo huiyi jiyao" [Summary of the Guangdong, Fujian and SEZ work conference], Central Committee document 1981.27, issued by the Central Committee and the State Council, translated in Reardon, "China's Coastal Development Strategy (I)," 59–79.

100 "'Guangdong, Fujian liangsheng zuotanhui jiyao' de tongzhi" [Circular promulgating the "Summary of the Guangdong, Fujian provincial conference"], Central Committee document 1982.17, translated in Reardon, "China's Coastal Development Strategy (I)," 81–95.

101 "Guanyu Guangdong, Fujian liangsheng jixu shixing teshu zhengce, linghuo cuoshi de huiyi jiyao de tongzhi" [Conference summary on continuing Guangdong and Fujian's carrying out special policies and flexible measures in foreign trade activities], State Council document 1985.46, issued on 28 March 1985, in *YCKTGWX*, 1:82–87.

102 Central Committee document 80.41, in Reardon, "China's Coastal Development Strategy (I)," 56.

103 Central Committee document 80.41, in Reardon, "China's Coastal Development Strategy (I)," 51–52.

104 See *ZJTN*, 1983: 365; Central Committee document 1980.41, 45–58.

105 Vogel, *One Step Ahead*, 314–17; Lai, Hongyi, *Reform and Non-State Economy*, 132, 138; Li, *Breaking Through*, 121.

106 *ZJTN*, 1983: 389. During this early period, the Xiamen SEZ existed only on paper. Analysis of the SEZ administration practices in the post-1982 period thus is more worthwhile.

107 Zhonggong Renminglu, *Zhonggong renming lu*, 849–50; Guangdong Nianjian Bianji Weiyuanhui, *Guangdong nianjian*, 1987, 83–90.

108 *ZJTN*, 1984: 232; *XZ*, 124.

109 *ZJTN*, 1983: 381; *SJTN*, 1985: 616.

110 Zhonggong Shenzhen Shiwei Zhengce Yanjiushi, *Diaocha yanjiu*, 6.

111 Wu Nansheng was first appointed as a member of the Standing Committee of the Guangdong Provincial Party in May 1977 and was appointed as a vice secretary in September 1977. He was made full secretary in December 1978 (Zhonggong Renminglu, *Zhonggong renming lu*, 262, states that appointment was made in

April 1978); he retained the post until 1985. See Guangdong Nianjian Bianji Wei-yuanhui, ed. *Guangdong nianjian, 1987*, 84–85.

112 *SJTN*, 1985: 617; *ZJTN*, 1984: 331.

113 *ZJTN*, 1983: 365.

114 Li, *Breaking Through*, 113–21; *ZJTN*, 1983: 366.

115 *ZJTN*, 1983: 332, 368; Zhuhai Jingji Nianjian Bianji Weiyuanhui, *Zhuhai jingji*, 274. Zhuhai and Shantou established individual administration committees on 14 November 1981 and 16 December 1981, respectively. The Xiamen SEZ Admin-istration Committee was established on 26 November 1980. See *ZJTN*, 1984: 332; Zhuhai Jingji Nianjian Bianji Weiyuanhui, *Zhuhai jingji*, 275; *ZJTN*, 1983: 370, 389.

116 "Zhonghua Renmin Gongheguo Guangdongsheng jingji tequ tiaoli" [Regulations of Guangdong province on special economic zones], approved at the Fifteenth Session of the Standing Committee of the Fifth NPC on 26 August 1980. English translation in *SJTN*, 1985: 201–7.

117 "Guanyu shouquan Guangdongsheng, Fujiansheng renmin daibiao dahui ji qi changwu weiyuanhui zhiding suoshu jingji tequ de gexiang danxing jingji fagui de jueding" [Resolution concerning the authorization of the people's congresses and their standing committees of Guangdong province and Fujian province to formulate various specific economic regulations for their respective special eco-nomic zones], adopted at the Twenty-First Session of the Fifth NPC Standing Committee on 26 November 1981. English translation in *SJTN*, 1985: 208.

118 *ZJTN*, 1983: 366; Zhuhai Jingji Nianjian Bianji Weiyuanhui, *Zhuhai jingji*, 273, 274.

119 Liang Wensen, *Zhongguo jingji tequ*, 190–91.

120 Tan, Yao, and Li, *Waimao fuchi*, 136–37.

121 Li, *Breaking Through*, 87–91.

122 "Guanyu dui Yue jinxing ziwei fanji, baowei bianjiang zhandou de tongzhi" [Circular on fighting the Vietnamese in self-defense and in defense of our bor-ders], issued on 14 February 1979, in *SQYWX*, 64.

123 Li, *Breaking Through*, 87–91; Zhonggong Shenzhen Shiwei, *Shenzhen tequ fazhan*, 190; *ZRGJD*, 617.

124 "Guanyu Bao'an Zhuhai liangxian waimao jidi he shizheng jianshe guihua shexiang de pifu" [Approval of the planned construction of the two foreign trade bases and cities in Bao'an and Zhuhai], issued by the State Council on 23 March 1979, in *ZJTN*, 1983: 381; Zhuhai Jingji Nianjian Bianji Weiyuanhui, *Zhu-hai jingji*, 273; *SJTN*, 1985: 615.

125 Li, *Breaking Through*, 91–92.

126 Li, *Breaking Through*, 93.

127 Guangdong People's Government Office, "Guanyu shiban Shenzhen, Zhuhai, Shantou chukou tequ de chubu shexiang" on 5 May 1979 in Renmin Ribaoshe Gongshangbu, *Zhongguo duiwai kaifang*, 917.

128 Barson, "Special Economic Zones," 464; Central Committee document 1980.41, Reardon, "China's Coastal Development Strategy (I)," 45–58.

129 Li, *Breaking Through*, 95. For fascinating details on the approval of Central Committee document 1979.50 see 95–99.

130 Jao and Leung, *China's Special Economic Zones*, 22.

131 *ZJTN*, 1983: 366.

132 *ZJTN*, 1983: 365–66.

133 Central Committee document 1980.41, in Reardon, "China's Coastal Development Strategy (I)," 45–58; Li, *Breaking Through*, 110–11.

134 Zhonggong Shenzhen Shiwei, *Shenzhen tequ fazhan*, 16; also see Liang Wensen, *Zhongguo jingji tequ*, 98.

135 In 1983, the Guangdong Provincial Government submitted "Guanyu shedang tiaozheng Zhuhai jingji tequ qucheng fanwei de baogao" [Report on properly adjusting the Zhuhai SEZ area], requesting the State Council to expand the Zhuhai zone from 6.8 to 15.16 square kilometers. On 29 June 1983 the State Council approved the measure, issuing "Guanyu tiaozheng Zhuhai jingji tequ qucheng fanwei wenti de pifu" [Approval of adjusting the Zhuhai SEZ area], Guohanzi 83.117, in *YCKTGWX*, 1:112. In 1984 the Guangdong Provincial Government submitted "Guanyu tiaozheng Shantou jingji tequ qucheng fanwei de qingshi baogao" [Report and request for instructions on readjusting the Shantou SEZ district area] to the State Council, requesting that it expand the Shantou zone from 0.2 to 52.6 square kilometers. Approving the request, the State Council issued "Guanyu tiaozheng Shantou jingji tequ qucheng fanwei wenti de pifu" [Approval to readjust the Shantou SEZ district area], Guohanzi 84.167, on 29 November 1984; see *YCKTGWX*, 1:112–13.

136 "Guanyu Xiamen jingji tequ shishi fang'an de pifu" [Approval of implementing the plans for the Xiamen SEZ], State Council document 85.85, issued 29 June 1985, in *YCKTGWX*, 1:113–16.

137 This was the original emphasis of the Guangdong provincial report contained in Central Committee document 1979.50, which stated, "Construction of the three special zones also must be accomplished in stages, with the initial primary focus on grasping Shenzhen's construction."

138 Also see Li, *Breaking Through*, 134–40.

139 Central Committee document 81.27, in Reardon, "China's Coastal Development Strategy (I)," 72–73.

Chapter Two

1 Liu and Zou, *Duiwai kaifang zhengce wenda*, 44.

2 Zhongguo Duiwai Jingji Maoyi Nianjian Bianji, *Zhongguo duiwai maoyi nianjian, 1984*, IV6.

3 During my first research trip to the Shenzhen SEZ, in spring 1985, a researcher from the Shenzhen University SEZ Economic Research Institute criticized the reliability of SEZ statistics. The researcher stated that the local SEZ officials did not possess an understanding of statistics and were too concerned with "policy considerations." Although more attention was paid to SEZ statistical work in the 1980s, it is prudent to regard all SEZ data with caution.

4 For more statistical information on the period from 1979 to 1984, see *SJTN*, 1985: 581–614.

5 Li, Lanqing, *Breaking Through*, 141.

6 For a summary in English of this period, see Davie and Carver, "China's International Trade," 29–31.

7 Liu and Zou, *Duiwai kaifang zhengce wenda*, 44–45.

8 "Guangdong, Fujian liangsheng huiyi jiyao de pishi" [Comment on the "Summary of the Conference on Guangdong and Fujian Provinces"], Central Committee document 1981.27, translated in Reardon, "China's Coastal Development Strategy (I)," 78.

9 Reardon, "China's Coastal Development Strategy (I)," 62.

10 Reardon, "China's Coastal Development Strategy (I)," 78.

11 "Guanyu shouquan Guangdongsheng, Fujiansheng renmin daibiao dahui jiqi changwu weiyuanhui zhiding suoshu jingji tequ de gexiang danxing fagui de jueding" [Decision to delegate legislative authority to the Guangdong and Fujian Provincial People's Congresses and their standing committees to formulate various individual laws for the SEZs], issued by the NPC Standing Committee on 26 November 1981 and effective 1 January 1982, in Zhongguo Shehui Kexueyuan, *Zhonghua Renmin Gongheguo jingji fagui xuanbian*, 512.

12 Zhonggong Shenzhen Shiwei Bangongting, *Shenzhen tequ fazhan*, 191.

13 *ZJTN*, 1983: 367; *ZJTN*, 1984: 233, 234, 331; *ZJTN*, 1983: 617.

14 Po, "Shenzhen lingdaoceng," 54; Zhonggong Shenzhen Shiwei Bangongting, *Shenzhen tequ fazhan*, 190–92; Shenzhenshi Renmin Zhengfu Bangongting, *Shenzhen jingji tequ*, 3; fieldwork, interview, Shenzhen, September 1986.

15 Po, "Shenzhen lingdaoceng," 190–92; "Construction and development in the Shenzhen Special Economic Zone, *Jingji ribao*, 11 December 1985, as translated in *FBIS—China*, 24 January 1986, P1.

16 Zhonggong Shenzhen Shiwei Changwei, *Shenzhen tequ jingji*, 9, 15.

17 Yuan Geng, "Xuexi Shekou de fangfa, ba woguo de yan'anxian liyong qilai" [Study Shekou's methods, let them be used in China's coastal areas], given on 9 February 1983, in *XZ*, 21.

18 During my research in 1986, I was asked by a local shopkeeper in Nantou if I was from Japan, although I am a six-foot-four, brown-haired, blued-eyed foreigner. Fieldwork, interview, Nantou, Shenzhen, August 1986.

19 Fieldwork, interview, Zhuhai, September 1987.

20 Shenzhenshi Renmin Zhengfu Bangongting, *Shenzhen jingji tequ*, 2.

21 Minzhengbu Xingzheng Quhuachu, *Zhonghua Renmin Gongheguo*, 195.

22 *Ta kung pao*, 27 February 1981.

23 Zhongguo Renming Cidian Bianjibu, *Zhongguo renming dacidian*, 338; Zhonggong Renminglu, *Zhonggong Renming lu*, 635; Vogel, *Canton*, 166; Guangdong Nianjian Bianji Weiyuanhui, *Guangdong nianjian*, 1987, 90.

24 Lai, "SEZs and Foreign Investment," 77–78.

25 "Liang Xiang to Be Transferred to Hainan," *Cheng Ming*, translated in *FBIS—China*, 5 March 1985, W3.

26 Crane, *Political Economy*, 52–55.

27 Dong Yun, "Ta zhuyi xiqu waimian," 4.

28 Xinhua," The Birth of an Important Decision," *FBIS-China*, 18 June 1984, K3.

29 Yuan Geng, "Xuexi Shekou de fangfa, ba woguo de yan'anxian liyong qilai" [Study Shekou's methods, let them be used in China's coastal areas], 9 February 1983, in *XZ*, 3. For more information on the personnel system in Shekou, see *XZ*, 50–58.

30 Jinan Daxue Jingji Xueyuan Jingji Yanjiusuo, *Zhongguo jingji tequ yanjiu*, 85.

31 *ZJTN*, 1984: 233; *XZ*, 46.

32 *XZ*, 128–30.

33 *SJTN*, 1986: 238. For a detailed account of Zhao's directive to implement the Shekou model, see Zhuhai Jingji Nianjian Bianji Weiyuanhui, *Zhuhai jingji nianjian*, 275; Zhonggong Shenzhen Shiwei Bangongting, *Shenzhen tequ fazhan*, 194.

34 Sun Ru, *Qianjinzhong de Zhongguo*, 40–41.

35 Chu, "Population Growth," 132–33.

36 "Shenzhen's Zou Erkang on successes, problems," *Ta Kung Pao*, 26 July 1985, translated in *FBIS—China*, 1 August 1985, W1.

37 "Guanyu qieshi jiaqiang xindai guanli yange kongzhi huobi faxing de jueding" [Decision to earnestly strengthen credit administration and strictly control currency issuance], issued by the State Council on 29 January 1981, in *ZRGJFX*, 305.

38 "Guanyu jiaqiang jiben jianshe jihua guanli, kongzhi jiben jianshe guimo de ruogan guiding" [Several regulations concerning the strengthening of administration of the capital construction plan and restricting its scale], issued by the State Council on 3 March 1981, in *ZRGJFX*, 3.

39 "Guanyu pingheng caizheng shouzhi, yange caizheng guanli de jueding" [Decision to balance the fiscal budget and strictly manage fiscal affairs], issued by the State Council on 26 January 1981, in *ZRGJFX*, 211.

40 "Guanyu qieshi jiaqiang," *ZRGJFX*, 305.

41 "Guanyu jiben jianshe tingjian huanjian xiangmu shanho gongzuo de ruogan jueding" [Regulations on the stoppage or slowdown of capital construction projects], issued by the State Capital Construction Control Commission, State Planning Committee, et al. on 20 January 1981, in *ZRGJFX*, 316; "Guanyu jiaqiang jiben jianshe jihua guanli, kongzhi jiben jianshe guimo de ruogan guiding" [Several regulations concerning the strengthening of administration of the capital construction plan and restricting its scale], issued by the State Council on 3 March 1981, in *ZRGJFX*, 3.

42 Deng Xiaoping, "Guanqie tiaozheng fangzhen, baozheng anding tuanjie" [Fully carry out readjustment plans, guarantee stability and unity], in *DXPWX*, 322.

43 Li, *Breaking Through*, 124–26.

44 "Construction and development in the Shenzhen Special Economic Zone, *Jingji ribao*, *FBIS-China*, 24 January 1986. Most probably, the prohibition of other domestic Chinese investment was justified on ideological grounds.

45 "Guangdong, Fujian liangsheng huiyi jiyao de pishi" [Comment on the "Summary of the Conference on Guangdong and Fujian Provinces"], Central Committee document 1980.41, translated in Reardon, "China's Coastal Development Strategy (I)," 56.

46 Jinan Daxue Jingji Xueyuan Jingji Yanjiusuo, *Zhongguo jingji tequ yanjiu*, 137.

47 Reardon, "China's Coastal Development Strategy (I)," 74–75.

48 *SJTN*, 1986: 247.

49 Jinan Daxue Jingji Xueyuan Jingji Yanjiusuo, *Zhongguo jingji tequ yanjiu*, 137.

50 Li, *Breaking Through*, 126–28.

51 Zhu Jianru, *Zhongguo zuida*, 135–41; *SJTN*, 1985: 620; Yeh, "Planning," 125.

52 Li, *Breaking Through*, 150.

53 Xu, Mao, and Wu, "Guanyu jingji tequ jianshezhong de jige wenti."

54 Luo, "The Shenzhen 'Earthquake,'" 9–13.

55 Chen and Xue, "Xiwang zhichuang"; Xu, "Jiji wending, banhao jingji teque," 2–6.

56 Chen and Xue, "Xiwang zhichuang."

57 Xu, *Zhongguo*, 115.

58 For instance, see Fairbank, *United States and China*; Kung and Ma, "Autarky," 509–34.

59 "Guanyu jiaqiang dui Huaqiao, Gang'ao, Taiwan tongbao jinkou wupin guanli he daji zousi, touji daoba huodong de baogao" [Report on strengthening management of imported materials from overseas Chinese, Hong Kong Macao and Taiwan compatriots and attacking smuggling, engaging in speculation and profiteering activities], State Council document 80.184, State Council and Central Military Commission document 1980.184, translated in Reardon, "China's Coastal Development Strategy (II)," 12.

60 On this period, see Harwit, *China's Automobile Industry*.

61 "Guanyu kongzhi qiche shengchan, jinkou he gaijin fenpei banfa de zhanxing guiding" [Temporary regulations on restricting automobile production and importation and improve methods of distribution], Jizong 1981.195, issued by the State Planning Commission et al. on 4 April 1981, in *DJFZH*, 1077.

62 "Guanyu jixu kongzhi shehui jituan goumaili de baogao" [Report on continuing to restrict institutional purchases], Guobanfa 1982.25, submitted by the State Planning Commission et al. and issued as a State Council Office Circular on 20 April 1982, in Zhongguo Shehui Kexueyuan Faxue Yanjiusuo, *Zhongguo jingji guanli*, 2:907.

63 "Guanyu jinkou xiaoqiche de chuli he zuojia wenti de baogao de tongzhi" [Circular on the report on handling the imported car problem and its pricing], State Council Office document 1981.81, submitted by the State Planning Commission and transmitted by the State Council Office on 14 October 1981, in Zuo Chuntai and Song Xinzhong, *Zhongguo shehui zhuyi caizheng jianshi*, 117.

64 Fong, "Tourism," 82.

65 Shenzhenshi Renmin Zhengfu Bangongting, *Shenzhen jingji tequ*, 12; *XZ*, 23; Wang Wenyang, *Jingji tequ*, 31; Jinan Daxue Jingji Xueyuan Tequ and Shenzhenshi Kexue Jishu Xiehui, *Zhongguo jingji tequ yanjiu*, 182–85.

66 Wu Qunce, Qu Chifeng, and Zheng Weibiao, "Tequ jingji," 364.

67 Reardon, "China's Coastal Development Strategy (II)," 12.

68 Ding Xueliang, "Earnestly carry out reforms, eliminate influence of vestiges of feudalism," *Renmin ribao*, 23 August 1983, as translated in *FBIS—China*, 30 August 1983, K7.

69 "Guanyu jianjue daji zhongda zousi he touji daomai jinkou wuzi fanzui huodong de lianhe tongzhi" [Joint circular on firmly attacking large smuggling and speculating on the resell of imported materials activities], issued by the Ministry of Public Security, the General Customs Administration, and the General Administration for Industry and Commerce on 15 March 1980, in *YJFZDWX*, 128; Central Committee document 1980.41 also states: "The two provinces have reported that currently smuggling activities are extremely serious and that they must seriously attack and earnestly resolve the problem." See Reardon, "China's Coastal Development Strategy (I)," 52.

70 Reardon, "China's Coastal Development Strategy (II)," 14.

71 "Guanyu zhizhi zai duiwai jingji huodong zhong weizhang huodong de tongzhi" [Circular on restricting activities that break rules and regulations in foreign economic activities], issued by the Shenzhen Municipal Revolutionary Committee on 13 October 1979, as cited in *SJTN*, 1985: 616.

72 Reardon, "China's Coastal Development Strategy (II)," 12–14.

73 Reardon, "China's Coastal Development Strategy (II)," 15.

74 *ZJTN*, 1982: 294. For a general description, see *ZJTN*, 1982: 293–96; 1981: 137–41.

75 "Guanyu jiaqiang chaye gongzuo de tongzhi" [Circular on strengthening tea work], issued by the State Council on 24 April 1981, in *ZRGJGD*, 422.

76 Guoji Maoyi Wenti Bianjibu, *Zhongguo duiwai maoyi wenti yanjiu*, 191.

77 For agricultural price increases, see "Guanyu tigao mianhua shougou jiage he (qijiu) jiu hao dianbao baozheng miannong kouliang gongying de tongzhi" [Circular on raising the cotton procurement price and the 1979 number 9 cable on guaranteeing grain supplies to cotton farmers], issued by the State Council on 27 February 1979, in Wang and Zhu, *Jingji tizhi gaige shouce*, 340; "Guanyu tiaozheng liangshi he youzhi youliao tonggou jiage de tongzhi" [Circular on readjusting the general procurement price for grains and oils], issued by the Ministry of Commerce et al. on 11 April 1979, in Wang and Zhu, *Jingji tizhi gaige shouce*, 340; *ZRGJGD*, 330, 360; Wang and Zhu, *Jingji tizhi gaige shouce*, 836; *Renmin ribao*, 31 October 1979. On salary hikes and associated measures, see "Guanyu zhigong shengji de jixiang juti guiding" [Several specific measures on raising the salary grades for staff and workers], issued by the State Council on 25 October 1979, in *ZRGJGD*, 366; "Guanyu tigao zhuyao fushipin xiaojia hou fagei zhigong fushipin jiage butie de jixiang juti guiding" [Several specific regulations on distributing subsidies to staff and workers for agricultural side-products after their prices have been raised], issued by the State Council on 17 October 1979, in *Zhonghua Renmin Gongheguo caizheng shiliao*, 161; *Renmin ribao*, 31 October 1979.

78 "Guanyu jiaqiang wujia guanli, jianjue zhizhi luanzhangjia he bianxiang zhangjia de tongzhi" [Circular on strengthening price administration, and firmly preventing indiscriminate price inflation and covert inflation], issued by the Central Committee and the State Council on 8 April 1980, in *ZRGJFX*, 38.

79 "Guanyu yange kongzhi wujian, zhengdun yijia de tongzhi" [Circular on strictly controlling material prices and rectifying discussed prices], State Council document 1980.295, issued by the State Council on 7 December 1980, in *ZRGJFX*,

43; "Guanyu zhonggong chanpin jiage de jixiang zhanxing guiding" [Temporary regulation on pricing of heavy industrial products], issued by the State General Administration for Material Prices on 18 June 1981, in *ZRGJGD*, 432; "Guanyu gongye shengchan ziliao shichang guanli zhanxing guiding" [Temporary regulations on industrial production material market administration], State Council document 1981.120, issued on 8 August 1981, in Guojia Wuziju, *Wuzi guanli falü huibian*, 130.

80 "Guanyu dangqian duiwai jingji maoyi ruhe wei guomin jingji tiaozheng fuwu de baogao" [Report on how the current foreign economic trade serves the national economic readjustment], submitted by the SIEC and approved by the State Council on 3 June 1981, in *ZRGJGD*, 430.

81 Hu Yaobang, "Guanyu duiwai jingji guanxi wenti" [Problems concerning foreign economic relations], speech to the CCP Secretariat Conference on 14 January 1982, in *SQYZWX*, 1121.

82 Feuchtwang and Hussain, *Chinese Economic Reforms*, 320.

83 Reardon, "China's Coastal Development Strategy (II)," 15.

84 Hu Yaobang, "Guanyu Duiwai," in *SQYZWX*, 1111–22.

85 "'Guangdong shengwei, Fujian shengwei guanyu duiwai jingji huodong shixing texu zhengce he linghuo cuoshi' de liangge baogao" [The approval and transmittal of the "Two reports of the Guangdong and Fujian Provincial Committee concerning the implementation of special policies and flexible measures in foreign trade activities"], Central Committee document 1979.50, issued by the Central Committee and State Council on 15 July 1979, translated in Reardon, "China's Coastal Development Strategy (I)," 21.

86 Crane, *Political Economy*, 36–37.

87 Wu Qunce, Qu Chifeng, Zheng Weibiao, "Tequ jingji," 362–66.

Chapter Three

1 "Guangdong, Fujian liangsheng huiyi jiyao de pishi" [Comment on the "Summary of the Conference on Guangdong and Fujian Provinces"], Central Committee document 1980.41, issued on 16 May 1980; "'Guangdong, Fujian liangsheng he jingji tequ gongzuo huiyi jiyao' de tongzhi" [Circular promulgating the "Summary of the Guangdong, Fujian and SEZ Work Conference"], Central Committee document 1981.27, issued by the Central Committee and the State Council on 19 July 1981, translated in Reardon, "China's Coastal Development Strategy (I)," 45–58, 59–79.

2 "Jingji tongzhi" [Emergency circular], issued by the CCP Central Committee on 11 January 1982, translated in Reardon, "China's Coastal Development Strategy (II)," 21–23.

3 This possibly included the bribery and smuggling case of Yu Tianzhang, which involved more than a hundred people in nine provinces, cities, and SARs, and RMB 28,500. See Si, *Guoneiwai dashiji*, 21.

4   Chen Yun, "Dui jingji gongzuo de jidian yijian," [Some views on economic work], in *SQYZWX*, 1059.

5   On the opening of the fourteen coastal cities, see "Yanhai bufen chengshi zuotanhui jiyao" [Summary of the conference of some coastal municipalities], Central Committee document 1984.13, issued on 4 May 1984, in Reardon, "China's Coastal Development Strategy (I)," 49–66. On opening the coastal regions, see "Changjiang, Zhujiang sanjiaozhou he Minnan Xia Zhang Quan sanjiao diqu zuotanhui jiyao de tongzhi" [Circular promulgating the "Summary of the Yangtze, Pearl River Delta and Xiamen, Zhangzhou, Quanzhou Delta Area in Southern Fujian"], Central Committee document 1985.3, in *YCKTGWX*, 74–81.

6   Lin and Schramm, "China's Foreign Exchange Policies," 246–80.

7   Zhao Ziyang, "Jinnian jingji xingshi he 'liuwu' jihua shexiang" [Tentative ideas about this year's economic situation and the "6.5" economic plan], report to the Political Bureau delivered on 2 September 1980, in *ZZYWJ*, 1:83.

8   Zhao Ziyang, "Dui waimao tizhi gaigezhong yixie wenti de yijian" [Views regarding several problems encountered while reforming the foreign trade structure], in *ZZYWJ*, 1:43. Also see Zhao Ziyang's speech on domestic economic reforms presented on 16 March 1980 at the expanded meeting of the Sichuan provincial committee, reprinted in Zhang Zerong, *Zhongguo jingji tizhi gaige*, 190.

9   "Zhonghua Renmin Gongheguo zhanxing haiguanfa" [The temporary customs law of the PRC], approved by the Government Administration Council of the Central People's Government of the PRC on 23 March 1951, in *ZRGJGD*, 20.

10 *ZJTN*, 1981, 137–41; Li Xiaoxian, *Duiwai maoyi yuanli*, 302–12.

11 "Guanyu gaige jinchukou shangpin jianyan guanli tizhi de tongzhi" [Circular on reforming the Import-Export Commodity Inspection Administration structure], State Council document 1980.57, issued 29 February 1980, in *ZRGJGD*, 379; "Guanyu quanguo shangjianju juzhang huiyi de baogao" [Report on the national conference for commodity inspection bureau chiefs], issued by the State General Administration for Commodity Inspection on 29 April 1981, in *ZRGJFX*, 32; also see Wang Zhengming, *Sanzhong quanhui yilai*, 122.

12 "Guanyu chachu touji daoba anjian de jige wenti de lianhe tongzhi" [Joint circular on several problems in investigating and resolving profiteering and speculation cases], issued by the General Administration for Industry and Commerce et al. on 25 January 1980, in *YJFZDWX*, 143.

13 "Guanyu benfa 'Duiwai maoyi yewu tongji zhidu' de tongzhi" [Circular on the publication of the foreign trade statistical system], Maozongtongzi 1980.764, issued by the MFT et al. on 18 November 1980, in *DJFZH*, 361.

14 "Guanyu jianli guoji shouzhi tongji zhidu de tongzhi" [Circular on establishing the state international balance-of-payments statistical system], Jinchuzongzi 81.046, issued by the SIEAC et al. on 2 September 1981, in Zhongguo Renmin Yinhang Bangongshi, *1981 Jinrong*, 355. On Guangdong's customs division, see "Guanyu gaige gaiguan guanli tizhi de jueding" [Decision to reform customs administration structure], issued by the State Council on 9 February 1980, in *ZRGJGD*, 378; Zhang Zerong, *Zhongguo jingji tizhi gaige*, 196.

15 "Guanyu chukou xukezheng zhidu de zhanxing banfa" [Temporary measures for the export permit system], issued by the SIEAC et al. on 3 June 1980, in *DJFZH*, 239; "Guanyu chukou shenqingshu ji xukezheng deshi he youguan wenti de tongzhi" [Circular concerning problems with export applications and permit forms]. Maochuqizi 1980.423, issued 21 August 1980, in *DJFZH*, 353.

16 "Guanyu jiaqiang lishi wenwu baohu gongzuo de tongzhi" [Circular on strengthening protection of historical objects], issued by the State Council on 17 May 1980, in *YJFZDWX* 88; updated on 20 April 1981 by "Guanyu jiaqiang anquan cuoshi fangzhi wenwu shiqie de yijian" [An opinion on strengthening security measures to protect against the theft of historical relics], issued by the State Bureau for Historical Relics et al. on 20 April 1991, in *YJFZDWX*, 90.

17 "Guanyu 'Duiwai maoyi jinkou guanli shixing banfa' 'Duiwai maoyi difang jinkou guanli shixing banfa' de tongzhi" [Circular on the issuance of "The Trial Procedures for Foreign Trade Import Administration" and "The Trial Procedures for the Localities concerning Foreign Trade Import Administration"], Maojinguanzi 1980.383, issued by the SIEAC et al. on 26 August 1980, in *DJFZH*, 339.

18 "Dui jiagong zhuangpei he zhongxiaoxing buchang maoyi jinchukou huowu jianguan he zhengmianshui shishi xice" [Detailed regulations for the supervision of the import and export of materials needed by processing/assembly operations and small and medium-size compensation trade operations and the levying or elimination of duties], issued by the SIEAC et al. on 6 March 1980, in *YJFZDWX*, 116.

19 "Guanyu xiuding 'Shehui jituan goumai zhuanxing kongzhi shangpin de guiding' de tongzhi" [Circular on revising the "Regulations on Institutional Groups Purchasing Specialized Restricted Items"], Konggouzi 1980.4, issued by the SPC et al. on 3 April 1980, in Zhonghua Renmin Gongheguo Caizhengbu, *Caizheng guizhang*, 80; "Guanyu shehui jituan goumaili guanli banfa" [Administration methods for organizational purchasing], Konggouzi 1980.13, issued by the State Council Small Group on Finance and Trade et al. on 17 November 1980, in Zhonghua Renmin Gongheguo Caizhengbu, *Caizheng guizhang*, 86.

20 "Guanyu dui toujidaoba fenzi liyong youbao jidi shangpin juti chuli banfa de buchong tongzhi" [Supplementary circular on the specific measures to deal with profiteers and speculators using the mails to send commodities], issued by the General Administration for Industry and Commerce et al. on 4 December 1980, in *YJFZDWX*, 132; "Guanyu guanche zhixing Guowuyuan tongzhi yange kongzhi wujia, zhengdun yijia ying zhuyi de jige zhengce wenti de tongzhi" [Circular on fully complying with the State Council's circular on strictly controlling material prices and rectifying discussed prices], issued by the Ministry of Commerce on 9 December 1980, in *ZRGJFX*, 46l.

21 "Guanyu gaige Zhongguo Yinhang tizhi de qingshi baogao" [Report and request for instructions in reforming the structure of the Bank of China], submitted by the PBOC and approved by the State Council on 13 March 1979, in Wang and Zhu, *Jingji tizhi gaige shouce*, 847; *ZRGJGD*, 331–32.

22 "Waihui guanli zhanxing tiaoli" [Temporary regulations for foreign exchange administration], State Council document 1980.311, issued by the State Council on 18 December 1980, in *DJFZH* 397.

23 "Guanyu weihu renminbi tongyi shichang jinzhi waibi zai guonei shichang liu-
tong de baogao" [Report on protecting a unified market for the renminbi and
prohibiting the circulation of foreign exchange in the internal market], submitted by the PBOC and approved by the State Council on 5 January 1980, in
ZRGJGD, 374. Also see Zheng, Han, and Zheng, Zhongguo jingji, 70; Renmin
ribao, 27 January 1980.

24 "Waihuijuan huanjuan zhanxing guanli banfa" [Temporary administration procedures for foreign exchange certificates], issued by the BOC on 19 March 1980,
in DJFZH, 472. For date of actual issuance, see "Guanyu jiaqiang waihuijuan
huanjuan guanli gongzuo de baogao" [Report on strengthening foreign exchange certificate administration], State Council document 1981.100, submitted
by the SPC et al. on 12 June 1981, in Zhongguo Renmin Yinhang Bangongshi,
1981 Jinrong guizhang, 242.

25 "Guanyu gebumen shiyong feimaoyi waihui liucheng jinkou wuzi de tongzhi"
[Circular on every department's use of retained foreign exchange gained from
nontrade activities to import materials], Maojinguanzi 1980.491, issued by the
MFT on 23 August 1980, in DJFZH, 467.

26 "Guanyu yinfa 'Feimaoyi waihui liucheng shishi xice' de tongzhi" [Circular on
publishing the "Detailed regulations for retained foreign exchange earned from
nontrade activities"], Huizongzi 1980.869, issued by the State General Administration for Foreign Exchange Administration et al. on 29 September 1980, in
DJFZH, 443; "Guanyu pianzhi feimaoyi waihui yijiubayi niandu shouzhi jihua
he yijiubaling niandu shouzhi juesuan de tongzhi" [Circular on the formulation
of the 1981 revenue and expenditure plan for foreign exchange earned from
nontrade activities and the final accounting for 1980 revenues and expendi-
tures], Caiwaizi 1980.389, issued by the Ministry of Finance on 5 December 1980,
in Zhonghua Renmin Gongheguo Caizhengbu, Caizheng guizhang, 599.

27 "Xiang Guowuyuan de huibao tigang" [Outline of the report to the State Council],
submitted by the General Bureau for Industrial and Commercial Administration
and approved by the State Council on 27 June 1981, in ZRGJGD, 435; ZRGJFX, 63.

28 "Guanyu jiaqiang shichang guanli daji touji daoba he zousi huodong de zhishi"
[Directive on strengthening market regulation and attacking speculation, prof-
iteering, and smuggling activities], State Council document 1981.3, issued by the
State Council on 7 January 1981, in ZRGJFX, 16.

29 Chen Yun, "Jingji xingshi yu jingyan jiaoxun" [The economic situation and lessons
learned from experience], in SQYZWX, 601–7; Zhao Ziyang, "Guanyu tiaozheng
guomin jingji de jige wenti" [Problems in readjusting the national economy], in
SQYZWX, 608–26; Deng Xiaoping, "Guanche tiaozheng fangzhen, baozheng
anding tuanjie" [Implement the policy of readjustment, ensure stability and
unity], in DXPWX, 313–33.

30 Chen Yun, "Jingji xingshi," SQYZWX, 605.

31 "Guanyu tong xifang guojia jingji hezuo you guojia jinchukouwei guikou guanli
de tongzhi" [Circular on readjustment of the SIEAC administration over state
economic cooperation with Western countries], issued by the Office of the State
Council on 26 December 1980, in ZRGJGD, 409.

32 These departments and agencies included the State Commission for the Control of Foreign Investment, the Ministries of Foreign Trade and Foreign Economic Relations, the State General Administration for Foreign Exchange Control, the BOC (and the PBOC), the General Customs Administration, the General Administration for Commodity Inspection, China International Trust and Investment Corporation, and the Committee to Promote International Trade.

33 "Guanyu jiaqiang duiwai jingji maoyi gongzuo tongyi lingdao he guikou guanli de jueding" [Decision to strengthen unified leadership of foreign economic trade and direct administration], issued by the Central Committee and the State Council on 1 September 1981, in *ZRGJGD*, 443.

34 "Guanyu jiaqiang shitang shougou diaofa gongzuo, yange kongzhi xiaoshou de tongzhi" [Several regulations regarding state industrial enterprises carrying out on an experimental basis the substitution of the profit-turnover scheme with a taxation scheme], issued by the State Council on 20 March 1981, in *ZRGJGD*, 418; "Guanyu jiaqiang cha'ye gongzuo de tongzhi" [Circular on strengthening tea production], issued by the State Council on 24 April 1981, in *ZRGJGD*, 422; "Guanyu jiaqiang xi de chanxiao guanli he jianjue zhizhi luancai lanwa xikuang ziyuan de jinji tongzhi" [Emergency circular strengthening the production and sales of tin and firmly preventing the indiscriminate mining of tin resources], issued by the State Council on 8 April 1981, in *ZRGJFX*, 388.

35 "Guanyu dui jinkou guanli shixing banfa gebie wenti zhanxu xiugai de tongzhi" [Circular on temporary revisions for various problems with the trial methods for import administration], Maojinguanzi 1981.293, issued by the MFT et al. on 18 August 1981. This is an update of "Guanyu 'Duiwai maoyi jinkou guanli shixing banfa' 'Duiwai maoyi difang jinkou guanli shixing banfa' de tongzhi" [Circular on the issuance of "The Trial Procedures for Foreign Trade Import Administration" and "The Trial Procedures for the Localities concerning Foreign Trade Import Administration"], Maojinguanzi 1980.383, issued by the MFT et al. on 26 August 1980, in *DJFZH*, 339.

36 The importation of durable goods had to comply with "Guanyu jianjue daji zousi huodong de zhishi" [Directive on resolutely attacking smuggling activities], State Council and Central Military Commission document 1981.6, issued in January 1981; directives issued by the Commission on Machinery (Jixiehui) in 1981; and other directives, as cited in *YJFZDWX*, 150. After the supervisory organization issued a document approving the importation, the unit would submit the approval to the MFT or the local Foreign Trade Administration to obtain the import permit. Once the good was imported, the General Customs Administration would inspect and approve it.

37 "Guanyu fabu 'Daji zousi, touji daomai jinchukou wupin de tongzhi' de tongzhi" [Circular on the publication of "The Circular on Attacking Smuggling and Speculating on the Resale of Import and Export Materials"], issued by the General Administration for Industry and Commerce et al. on 30 October 1980, in *YJFZDWX*, 125.

38 "Guanyu dui toujidaoba fenzi liyong youbao jidi shangpin juti chuli banfa de buchong tongzhi" [Supplementary circular on the specific measures to deal

with profiteers and speculators using the mails to send commodities], issued by the General Administration for Industry and Commerce et al. on 4 December 1980, in *YJFZDWX*, 132; "Guanyu guanche zhixing Guowuyuan tongzhi yange kongzhi wujia, zhengdun yijia ying zhuyi de jige zhengce wenti de tongzhi" [Circular on fully complying with the State Council circular on strictly controlling material prices and rectifying discussed prices], issued by the Ministry of Commerce on 9 December 1980, in *ZRGJFX*, 46l.

39 "Guanyu jiaqiang shichang guanli daji touji daoba he zousi huodong de zhishi" [Directive on strengthening market regulation and attacking speculation, profiteering, and smuggling activities], State Council document 1981.3, issued on 7 January 1981, in *ZRGJFX*, 16; see also *YJFZDWX*, 77.

40 "Yunyong falü wuqi, daji zousi huodong" [Use the law as a weapon to attack smuggling activities], *Zhongguo fazhibao*, 1 May 1981.

41 "Di-er'ci daji zousi gongzuo huiyi jiyao" [Summary of the second work conference on attacking smuggling], approved by the Central Committee and State Council on 3 August 1981, in *ZRGJGD*, 440; Si, *Guoneiwai dashiji*, 78; *Renmin ribao*, 29 August 1981.

42 "Guanyu quanguo haiguan guanzhang huiyi de baogao" [Report on the national conference for customhouse leaders], submitted by the General Customs Administration and approved by the State Council on 2 September 1981, in *ZRGJGD*, 443.

43 State Council document 1981.100, in Zhongguo Renmin Yinhang Bangongshi, *1981 Jinrong guizhang*, 242.

44 The one exception was in Guangdong and Fujian. State Council document 1981.100 admitted that the value of some commodities had to be lower than the domestic-market retail price. Still, the reduction could not exceed 20 percent.

45 "Guanyu xianqi diaohui weijing pizhun cunfang zai jingwai waihui de tongzhi" [Circular on transferring back foreign exchange deposited outside the country without permission], State Council document 1981.20, issued on 31 January 1981, in Zhongguo Renmin Yinhang Bangongshi, *1981 Jinrong*, 377.

46 "Duiwaihui, guijinshu he waihui piaozheng deng jinchu guojing de guanli shexing xice" [The detailed administration regulations for importing and exporting foreign exchange, precious metals, and foreign exchange instruments], issued by the State General Administration for Foreign Exchange Controls on 10 August 1981, in *ZRGJFX*, 332.

47 "Guanyu quxiao guonei danwei tongguo siren gouwu jinkou zi guonei zhifu Renminbi de tongzhi" [Circular on abolishing the practice of domestic units of purchasing import materials through private individuals and converting payment into renminbi], Huiguanzi 1981.799, issued by the State General Administration for Foreign Exchange Controls et al. on 28 July 1981, in Zhongguo Renmin Yinhang Bangongshi, *1981 Jinrong*, 246.

48 "Fasong 'Zhonghua Renmin Gongheguo jingnei jigou jieshou qiaozi, waizi daikuan he faxing waibi zhaijuan de zhanxing guanli banfa'" [Dispatching the "Temporary Administration Methods for Organizations within the PRC Receiving Overseas Chinese Capital, Foreign Capital, and the Issuance of Foreign

Debentures"], Huiguanzi 1981.478, issued by the State General Administration for Foreign Exchange Controls et al. on 11 July 1981, in *DJFZH*, 411.

49 "Guanyu tiaoji waihui gongzuo de jige wenti de yijian" [Views on some problems with redistributing foreign exchange], Huiguanzi 1981.505, issued by the State General Administration for Foreign Exchange Controls et al. on 17 April 1981, in Zhongguo Renmin Yinhang Bangongshi, *1981 Jinrong*, 382.

50 "Guanyu fufa 'Guanyu waihui edu tiaoji gongzuo zhanxing banfa' de tongzhi" [Circular on issuing "Temporary methods for redistributing foreign exchange quotas"], Huiyezi 1981.376, issued by the State General Administration for Foreign Exchange Control et al. on 4 August 1981, in *DJFZH*, 432.

51 "Dui weifan waihui guanli youguan fajin ji jiangin de zhanxing chuli banfa" [Temporary measures for dealing with fines and bonuses in cases of disobeying the foreign exchange administration], Huiguanzi 1981.1183, issued by the State General Administration for Foreign Exchange Control on 24 December 1981, in *DJFZH*, 429.

52 Discussions on "Guanyu jianguo yilai dang de ruogan lishi wenti de jueding" [Decision on certain historical problems since the country's establishment] were conducted throughout 1980. The decision, which criticized past excesses, was finally adopted at the Sixth Plenum of the Eleventh Party Congress. See *SQYZWX*, 788–847; Zhonggong Zhongyang Dangshi Yanjiushi, *Zhonggong dangshi dashi nianbiao*, 435, 436, 444.

53 Si, *Guoneiwai dashiji*, 21.

54 Hu Yaobang, "Gaohao dangfeng de jige wenti" [Several problems in improving party style], in *SQYZWX*, 574.

55 Zhao Ziyang, "Dangqian de jingji xingshi he jinhou jianshe fangzhen," in *SQYZWX*, 1042.

56 Ma et al., *Jingshen wenming cishu*, 785. For a description of "socialist spiritual civilization," see Zhao Ziyang, "Dangqian de jingji xingshi," *SQYZWX*, 1042–50.

57 The *Wujiang simei* (five emphases and four beautifications) campaign and the military's *Siyou, san jiang, liang bupa* (four haves, three stresses, and two fear nots) campaign. See Ma et al., *Jingshen wenming cishu*, 786; Si, *Guoneiwai dashiji*, 5; Zhonggong Zhongyang Dangshi Yanjiushi, *Zhonggong dangshi dashi nianbiao*, 442; and *DXPWX*, 392.

58 Deng Xiaoping, "Guanyu sixiang zhanxianshang de wenti de tanhua," in *DXPWX*, 344.

59 Ma et al., *Jingshen wenming cishu*, 787; Si, *Guoneiwai dashiji*, 27.

60 *SJTN*, 1985: 619.

61 "Guangdong, Fujian liangsheng huiyi jiyao de pishi," [Comment on the "Summary of the Conference on Guangdong and Fujian Provinces"], Central Committee document 1981.27, translated in Reardon, "China's Coastal Development Strategy (I)," 69.

62 Reardon, "China's Coastal Development Strategy (I)," 69.

63 Such restricted goods included grains and fertilizer. Also see "Guanyu duijinkou guanli shixing banfa gebie wenti zhanxuo xiugai de tongzhi" [Circular on

temporary revisions for various problems with the trial methods for import administration], Maojinguanzi 1981.293, issued by the MFT et al. on 18 August 1981, in *DJFZH*, 351.

64 "Guanyu yange kongzhi jixie shebei jinkou de tongzhi" [Circular on strictly controlling machinery equipment imports], State Council document 1981.6, issued by the State Council on 14 January 1981, in *DJFZH*, 864.

65 Reardon, "China's Coastal Development Strategy (I)," 78.

66 "Guangdongsheng di wu jie renmin daibiao dahui changwu weiyuanwei gonggao" [Proclamation issued by the Standing Committee of the Fifth People's Congress of Guangdong Province], No. 6, issued on 24 December 1981, *ZJTN*, 1983:50.

67 "Guanyu jianjue daji zousi huodong de yijian" [Views on resolutely attacking smuggling activities], issued by the Shenzhen Party Committee and the Shenzhen Peoples' Government on 24 March 1981. Reflecting Guangdong's concerns about smuggling, this document was issued two weeks after Liang Xiang replaced Wu Nansheng as first party secretary of Shenzhen.

68 Reardon, "China's Coastal Development Strategy (I)," 77–78.

69 Reardon, "China's Coastal Development Strategy (I)," 78.

70 Luo, "The Shenzhen 'Earthquake,'" W1.

71 Chen and Xue, "Xiwang zhichuang."

72 Chen Yun, "Jiaqiang jihua jingji" [Strengthen the planned economy], 25 January 1982, in *SQYZWX*, 1134.

73 Chen Yun, "Dui jingji gongzuo," *SQYZWX*, 1057–60.

74 Chen Yun, "Jiaqiang jihua jingji," *SQYZWX*, 1134.

75 Reardon, "China's Coastal Development Strategy (II)," 21.

76 *Shenzhen tequbao*, 29 November 1982.

77 This possibly included the bribery/smuggling case of Yu Tianzhang, which involved more than 100 people in nine provinces, cities, and SARs, and RMB 28,500. See Si, *Guoneiwai dashiji*, 21.

78 Chen Yun, "Dui jingji gongzuo de jidian yijian," *SQYZWX*, 1059.

79 Hu Qiaomu, "Ruhe kandai fandui zousi douzheng" [How one should view the struggle against smuggling], 12 February 1982, in Hu, *Hu Qiaomu wenji*, 3:194.

80 Zhao, *Prisoner of the State*, 103.

81 Hu Qiaomu, "Ruhe kandai," in *Hu Qiaomu wenji*, 3:192.

82 Hu Qiaomu, "Ruhe kandai," 3:193.

83 Ball, *Russia's Last Capitalists*.

84 Hu Qiaomu, "Ruhe kandai," in *Hu Qiaomu wenji*, 3:193-94. On the Soviet Union's cruel form of collectivization, see Fitzpatrick, *Stalin's Peasants*.

85 Hu Qiaomu, "Ruhe kandai," 3:194.

86 Hu Yaobang, "Guanyu duiwai jingji guanxi wenti" [Problems concerning foreign economic relations], speech to the CCP Secretariat Conference on 14 January 1982, in *SQYZWX*, 1113.

87 Hu Qiaomu, "Ruhe kandai," in *Hu Qiaomu wenji*, 3:192.

88 Chen Yun, "Dui jingji gongzuo de jidian yijian," *SQYZWX*, 1060.

89 Zhao Ziyang, "Guanyu Guowuyuan 1982 nian shangbannian de gongzuo bushu"

[Drawing up the State Council work itinerary for the first half of 1982], speech to the State Council on 29 January 1982, in *ZZYWJ*, 1:395.

90 Zhao Ziyang, "Daji zousi baisi jixu guanche zhixing teshu zhengce he linghuo cuoshi" [To fight against smuggling and fight selfishness and continue to fully carry out special policies and flexible measures], delivered to the Guangdong and Fujian Provincial Conference on 12 February 1982, in *ZZYWJ*, 1:415–18.

91 Zhao Ziyang, "Weirao tigao jingji xiaoyi zuohao gongye jiaotong he zhengge jingji gongzuo" [Focusing on raising economic efficiency and doing a good job in improving industry, transportation, and the entire economy], 4 March 1981, in *ZZYWJ*, 1:432–46.

92 Zhao Ziyang, "Weirao tigao jingji xiaoyi," *ZZYWJ*, 1:432–46.

93 Zhao Ziyang, "Guanyu dangqian jingji gongzuo de jige wenti" [Several problems in current economic work], report presented to 22nd meeting of the standing committee of the fifth national people's congress, 8 March 1982, in *SQYZWX*, 1195.

94 The talk with the Moroccan premier occurred on 25 February 1982. Quoted in Wang Zhengming, *Sanzhong quanhui yilai*, 107.

95 "Guanyu 'san fan' douzheng de zhishi" [Directive on fighting the "three evils"], issued by the CCP Central Committee on 30 November 1951, in *ZRGJGD*, 27; "Guanyu kaizhan fandui xinghui, fandui toushui loushui, fandui daoqie guojia caichan, fandui tougong jianliao he fandui daoqie jingji qingbao de douzheng de zhishi" [Directive on launching the struggle to oppose bribery, tax evasion, the theft of state property, shoddy workmanship, and use of inferior materials, as well as the theft of economic information], issued by the CCP Central Committee on 26 January 1952, in *ZRGJGD*, 29.

96 Meisner, *Mao's China*, 96.

97 As vice premier, chairman of the finance and economy commission, and minister for heavy industry, Chen Yun had fully supported those campaigns. See Chen Yun's speech to the Preparatory Representative Conference of the National Alliance for Industry and Commerce, presented on 20 June 1952, in *ZRGJD*, 71–72; Zhonggong Renminglu Bianxiu Weiyuanhui, *Zhonggong renming lu*, 590. The comparison could also have been made by Hu Qiaomu.

98 Zhao Ziyang, "Weirao tigao jingji xiaoyi zuohao gongye jiaotong he zhengge jingji gongzuo" [Focusing on raising economic efficiency and doing a good job in improving industry, transportation, and the entire economy], 4 March 1981, in *ZZYWJ*, 1:432–46.

99 "Guanyu daji jingji lingyu zhong yanzhong fanzui huodong de jueding" [Decision to attack the serious criminal activities in the economic area], Central Committee document 1982.22, issued by the CCP Central Committee and the State Council on 13 April 1982, in *SQYZWX*, 1241–55.

100 Hu Qiaomu, *Hu Qiaomu wenji*, 3:193.

101 Deng Xiaoping, "Jianjue daji jingji fanzui huodong" [Resolutely combat criminal economic activities], in *DXPW*, 357.

102 Zhonggong Zhongyang Dangshi Yanjiushi, *Zhonggong dangshi dashi nianbiao*, 454.

103 Deng Xiaoping, "Jingjian jigou shi yichang geming" [Streamlining organizations constitutes a revolution], in *DXPWX*, 351–56.

104 Reardon, "China's Coastal Development Strategy (II)," 22.

105 Central Committee document 1982.22, in *SQYZWX*, 1241–55.

106 "Guanyu yancheng yanzhong pohuai jingji de fanzui de jueding" [Decision to severely punish criminals who damage the economy], approved by the NPC Standing Committee on 8 March 1982, in *YJFZDWX*, 205.

107 Central Committee document 1982.22, in *SQYZWX*, 1241–55; Deng Xiaoping, "Jingjian jigou shi yichang geming," *DXPWX*, 351–56; Zhao, *Prisoner of the State*, 103.

108 Zhonggong Zhongyang Dangshi Yanjiushi, *Zhonggong dangshi dashi nianbiao*, 456–57.

109 Zhao Ziyang, "Weirao tigao jingji xiaoyi zuohao gongye jiaotong he zhege jingji gongzuo" [Focusing on raising economic efficiency and doing a good job in improving industry, transportation, and the entire economy], 4 March 1981, in *ZZYWJ*, 1:432–46.

110 Li, *Breaking Through*, 154.

111 Ehara, "Expansion of China's Foreign Economic Relations," 12.

112 "Guanyu Guowuyuan jigou gaige wenti de jueyi" [Decision on the State Council's organizational reform], approved by the NPC on 8 March 1982, in Zheng, Han, and Zheng, *Zhongguo jingji*, 204. In addition, the State Council clearly established the responsibilities of the SPC, the SEC, and the State Science and Technology Commission on 5 May 1982. The Agricultural and Energy Commissions and other assorted bureaus were placed under the SEC. See "Guanyu Guowuyuan buwei jigou gaige shishi fang'an de jueding" [Decision on the organizational reform plans for the State Council's ministries and commissions], adopted by the NPC on 4 May 1982, in Zhang Zerong, *Zhongguo jingji tizhi gaige jishi*, 277; *ZRGJGD*, 470–71.

113 "Guanyu zai zhuyao kou'an sheli tepaiyuan banshichu he 'Duiwai jingji maoyi tepaiyuan banshichu zhanxing tiaoli' de qingshi" [Request for instructions on establishing a special representative office and regarding "The temporary regulations for the office of the special foreign economic and trade representative"], submitted by MOFERT and approved by the State Council on 15 July 1982, in *ZRGJGD*, 474.

114 "Guanyu bufen wuzi jihuawai chukou shixing xukezheng banfa de qingshi baogao" [Report and request for instructions on the methods of implementing the export permit system for some materials exported outside the plan], State Council document 1981.179, submitted by the SIEAC et al. and approved by the State Council on 28 December 1981, in *DJFZH*, 263; *ZRGJD*, 455. Those eleven categories are: (1) crude, heavy, and refined oil; (2) coal; (3) steel: sheets, strips, plates of medium thickness, welded, square blanks; (4) pig iron, coking coal, ferroalloy, chromium ore; (5) plate glass; (6) nonferrous metals: copper, aluminum, lead, zinc, tin, cobalt, bismuth, refined molybdenum ore and its products, tellurium; (7) wood: lumber, sawed, plywood; (8) cement from large or medium-size cement factories; (9) natural rubber; (10) sodium carbonate, caustic soda,

polyethylene, polypropylene, phosphate rock, iron sulfate ore, sulfur, benzene anhydride, liquid hydrocarbon; (11) rice, soybeans, corn, sugar, cotton, rosin, tung oil, flue-cured tobacco.

115 "Guanyu ruogan shangpin zhengshou chukou guanshui de qingshi" [Request for instructions on collecting export duties on certain commodities], State Council document 1982.70, submitted by the Ministry of Finance et al. and approved by the State Council on 30 April 1982, in *SQYZWX*, 121; *ZRGJGD*, 470; also see point 1 in "Guanyu zhuajin zuohao huobi huilong gongzuo he yange kongzhi huobi toufang de tongzhi" [Circular on paying close attention to monetary circulation and strictly controlling the money supply], State Council document 1982.75, issued on 6 May 1982, in Zhongguo Shehui Kexueyuan Faxue Yanjiusuo, *Zhongguo jingji guanli fagui wenjian huibian*, 2, 1149.

116 "Guanyu waimao chukou shangpin shixing fenlei jingying de guiding de qingshi" [Request for instructions concerning the categorization of foreign trade export products] and "Guanyu waimao chukou shangpin shixing fenlei jingying de guiding" [Regulations on implementing category administration of foreign trade export products], State Council document 1982.5, submitted by the MFT and approved by the State Council on 7 January 1982, in *DJFZH*, 303.

117 The twenty-three commodities included grains, oils and oil-bearing crops, tung oil, cotton yarn, cotton gray cloth, cotton-nylon yarn, cotton-nylon gray cloth, silk, tungsten and tungsten products, antimony and its products, tin, coal, coking coal, cement, sponge titanium, iron ore, iron sheets, unprocessed and refined oil, petroleum, bulk liquid chemicals, naphtha, and heavy water.

118 Commodities such as red beans, jellyfish, chestnuts, frozen pork, dyed cotton cloth, rosin, sewing machines and accessories, and ceramics.

119 "Guanyu jixu kongzhi shehui jituan goumaili de baogao" [Report on continuing to restrict institutional purchases], State Council Office document 1982.25, issued on 20 March 1982, in *Zhongguo jingji guanli fagui wenjian huibian* 2, 907.

120 "Guanyu gaijin jixie shebei jinkou shencha gongzuo de tongzhi" [Circular on improving examination of machinery equipment imports], State Council document 1982.33, issued on 20 February 1982, in *DJFZH*, 857; "Yinfa 'Guanyu jixie shebei jinkou shencha gongzuo de ruogan juti guiding' de tongzhi" [Circular on the publication of "Several specific regulations on examination of mechanical equipment importation"], Jingji 1982.43, issued by the SEC on 29 May 1982, in *DJFZH*, 883; "Guanyu yange kongzhi liangyou jiagong jixie jinkou de tongzhi" [Circular on strictly controlling the importation of edible-oils processing machinery], Shanggongzi 1982.23, issued by the Ministry of Commerce on 4 August 1982, in Jingji Kexue Chubanshe, *Shangye zhengce fagui huibian*, 1982, 753.

121 "Guanyu zhanting jinkou huaxian zhiwu shencha fanwei de tongzhi" [Circular on the examination and approval procedures for synthetic textiles whose importation has temporarily been suspended], Shangfangzi 1982.1, issued by the Ministry of Commerce on 23 March 1982, in *Shangye zhengce fagui huibian, 1981*, 93.

122 "Guanyu yinfa 'Jinchukou xukezheng guanli gongzuo zuotanhui jiyao' de tongzhi" [Circular on the publication of "The Summary of the Conference on Import-

Export Permit Management Work"], Waijingmaoguanchuxuzi 1982.132, issued by MOFERT on 21 November 1982, in *DJFZH*, 265–76.

123 "Guanyu Zhongguo Renmin Yinhang de zhongyang yinhang zhineng jiqi zhuanye yinhang de guanxi wenti de qingshi" [Request for instructions on the problem of the relationship between the PBOC's function as a central bank and its relationship with the other specialized banks], submitted by the PBOC and approved by the State Council on 14 July 1982, in *ZRGJGD*, 474.

124 "Guanyu yange zhizhi waihui fangmian weifa luanji xingwei de jueding" [Decision to strictly control the violation of foreign exchange laws and discipline], issued by the CCP Central Committee and the State Council on 17 July 1982, in *ZRGJGD*, 474.

125 . "Guanyu banfa 'Guanyu jiaqiang liucheng waihui edu guanli de zhanxing banfa' de tongzhi" [Circular on the publication of "The temporary measures for strengthening administration of retained foreign exchange"], Yinfazi 1982.244, issued by the PBOC et al. on 26 November 1982, in *DJFZH*, 477.

126 "Guanyu pizhuan dangqian shiban jingji tequ gongzuozhong ruogan wenti de jiyao de tongzhi" [Circular promulgating the "Summary of certain problems concerning the implementation of the special economic zones"], Central Committee document 1982.50, in Reardon, "China's Coastal Development Strategy (I)," 25–37.

127 "Guanyu zhuanfa 'Shenru chijiude kaizhan "Wujiang simei" huodong zhengqu shehui zhuyi jingshen wenming jianshe de xinshengli' de tongzhi" [Circular on the transmittal of "The deepening and extension of carrying out the 'five stresses and four beauties' campaign and achieving a new victory in socialist spiritual civilization construction"], issued by the CCP Central Committee on 28 May 1982, in *SQYZWX*, 1285–98.

128 "Guanyu shenru kaizhan 'Wujiang simei' huodong de baogao" [Report on deepening the campaign for "five stresses and four beauties"], issued by the CCP Central Committee Secretariat and reported by Xinhua News Agency on 17 February 1982; also see "Dongyuan qilai, zhazha shishi zhuahao 'Quanmin wenming limao yue' huodong de lianhe tongzhi" [Joint circular on motivating everyone to implement in a down-to-earth manner "National Culture and Courtesy Month"], issued by the CCP Propaganda Ministry et al. on 25 February 1982, cited in Ma et al., *Jingshen wenming cishu*, 789.

129 Zhao Ziyang, "Zhengqu shehui fengqi he dangfeng de genben haozhuan" [Fighting to fundamentally turn around common practice and the party], 26 February 1983, in *ZZYWJ*, 2:24–26.

130 "Guanyu yanjin jinkou, fuzhi, xiaoshou, bofang fandong huangse xialiu luyin luxiang zhipin de guiding" [Regulations strictly prohibiting the importation, reproduction, sale, or broadcasting of reactionary, pornographic, and obscene recordings and tapes], issued by the CCP Central Committee and the State Council and reported by Xinhua News Agency on 12 March 1982, in Ma et al., *Jingshen wenming cishu*, 789.

131 "Guanyu yanjin zhizu Gang'ao'tai lianhuanhua deng shukan de tongzhi" [Circular on prohibiting the lending of picture books and other materials from Hong

Kong, Macao, and Taiwan], issued by the Ministry of Culture et al. on 12 May 1982, in Guojia Tigaiwei Jingji Guanlisi, *Siying he geti jingji shiyong fagui daquan*, 717.

132 Xu, Mao, and Wu, "Guanyu jingji tequ jianshezhong."

133 Ruan, "Establishment of Special Zones," 47–48.

134 For State Council document 1979.202, see Reardon, "China's Coastal Development Strategy (I)," 9–18; for State Council document 1979.233, see *ZRGJGD*, 358.

135 For example, see *Renmin ribao*, 8 June 1981.

136 Chen Yun, "Dui jingji gongzuo de jidian yijian," *SQYZWX*, 1059.

137 Chen Yun, "Jiaqiang jihua jingji," *SQYZWX*, 1134.

138 "'Guangdong, Fujian liangsheng zuotanhui jiyao' de tongzhi" [CCP Transmits and Approves the "Circular on the Summary of the Guangdong and Fujian Conference"], Central Committee document 1982.17, translated in Reardon, "China's Coastal Development Strategy (I)," 83.

139 Reardon, "China's Coastal Development Strategy (I)," 82–83.

140 Reardon, "China's Coastal Development Strategy (I)," 85.

141 Luo, "The Shenzhen 'Earthquake,'" W1–8.

142 Hongyi Lai, "SEZs and Foreign Investment in China," 78.

143 *Shenzhen tequbao*, 29 November 1982.

144 Zhonggong Shenzhen Shiwei Bangongting, *Shenzhen tequ fazhan*, 196–98; *SJTN*, 1985: 621–23; "Guanyu Liang Xiang deng tongzhi renzhi de tongzhi" [Circular on the formal appointment of Comrade Liang Xiang and others], Shenzhen Government document 1982.4, issued 4 January 1982, cited in *ZJTN*, 1983: 373; Zhu Jianru, *Zhongguo zuida*, 165.

145 Shenzhenshi Renmin Zhengfu Bangongting, *Shenzhen jingji tequ*, 22.

146 *SJTN*, 1983: 374.

147 "Guanyu jiaqiang Guangdong, Fujian liangsheng jinkou shangpin guanli he zhizhi sihuo neiliu de zhanxing guiding" [Temporary regulations on strengthening commodity import administrations of Guangdong and Fujian provinces and preventing the transference of smuggled goods to the interior], State Council document 1982.111, issued on 17 August 1982, in *YCKTGWX*, 2:631–33.

148 The "seventeen imported commodities" included vehicles, motorcycles, bicycles, sewing machines, televisions, tape recorders, watches, cameras, electric fans, washing machines, electronic calculators, refrigerators, VCRs, videotapes, chemical fibers, and their manufactured products. Restrictions included both complete products and unassembled pieces.

149 "Guanyu jieshou Huaqiao he Gang'ao tongbao juanzeng" [Concerning the acceptance of gifts from overseas Chinese and Hong Kong and Macao compatriots], State Council document 1982.110, issued in August 1982, as cited in "Haiguan dui Huaqiao, Gang'ao tongbao juanzeng wuzi guanli guiding" [Customs regulations on managing material gifts from overseas Chinese and Hong Kong and Macao compatriots], in *YCKTGWX*, 2:574–76.

150 "Guanyu yange jinzhi ge diqu, ge bumen he qiye tongguo waishang, Qiaoshang he Gang'ao shangren zai guonei zhuanshou daomai wo chukou huowu de guiding" [Regulations strictly forbidding every locality, department, and enterprise

from using foreign businessmen, overseas Chinese businessmen, and HK and Macao businessmen to resell Chinese export materials on the domestic market], issued by MOFERT on 26 August 1982, in *DJFZH*, 330; "Guanyu yinfa xiuding de 'Haiguan dui jiagong zhuangpei he zhongxiaoxing buchang maoyi jin-chukou huowu jianguan he zhengmianshui shishi xice' de tongzhi" [Circular on publication of the revised "Detailed regulations on the monitoring and tax-ation on the imported and exported materials from processing and assembling and medium to small sized compensation trade ventures"], Waijingmaoguanzi 1982.4, issued by MOFERT on 1 October 1982, in *YCKTGWX*, 1:349–53.

151 Reardon, "China's Coastal Development Strategy (I)," 73.

152 "Guanyu zai tequ yu feitequ fenjiexian shang jianli tequ guanlixian, zuzhi she-fang he guanli de jueding" [Decision to establish between the SEZ and non-SEZ boundary an SEZ administration line and organize its defense and administra-tion], issued by the State Council in 1982, in *ZJTN*, 1983: 370; Liang Wensen, *Zhongguo jingji tequ*, 66–75.

153 Chen Yun, "Jiaqiang jihua jingji," *SQYZWX*, 1134.

154 Chen Yun, "Jiaqiang jihua jingji," *SQYZWX*, 1134.

155 Zhonggong Shenzhen Shiwei Bangongting, *Shenzhen tequ fazhan*, 195; *SJTN*, 1985: 620. It was formally announced by the Shenzhen government on 4 January 1982 in "Guanyu Liang Xiang deng tongzhi renzhi de tongzhi," Shenzhen Gov-ernment document 1982.4, *ZJTN*, 1983:373. The literature is unclear about the fate of the "Lao Bao'an" cadre. The original investigation of Shenzhen cadre stated that 80 percent of the members were corrupt.

156 Shenzhen Shiwei Gaige Lingdao Xiaozu Bangongshi, *Shenzhen tequ fazhan*, 9. For an excellent analysis of administrative reforms, see Wong and Chu, *Mod-ernization in China*, 180–84; Xianggang Zhuanshang Xuesheng Lianhui, *Jingji tequmian mianguan*, 28–38.

157 *Wen wei pao*, 24 June 1982; Xianggang Zhuanshang Xuesheng Lianhui, *Jingji te-qumian mianguan*, 30–31; Crane, *Political Economy*, 52–55.

158 *SJTN*, 1985: 623. For a different interpretation, see Crane, *Political Economy*, 50–55.

159 Conference papers are reprinted in Sun Ru, *Qianjinzhong de Zhongguo*.

160 Li, *Breaking Through*, 158.

161 *Renmin ribao*, 3 December 1982.

162 Zhao Ziyang, "Jianshe Zhongguoshi shehui zhuyi" [Building a Chinese style of socialism], 15 September 1980, in *ZZYWJ*, 1:88–91.

Chapter Four

1 Schram, "'Economics in Command?'" 433.

2 Vogel, *Deng Xiaoping*, 418–19.

3 Vogel, *Deng Xiaoping*, 413.

4 Zhao Ziyang, "Dui woguo yanhai diqu fazhan waixiangxing jingji de zhanluë sikao," [Strategic thinking concerning China's coastal areas developing an outward-oriented economy], in *ZZYWJ*, 4:305–12.

5   "Guanyu dali fazhan duiwai maoyi cengjia waihui shouru ruogan wenti de gui-
    ding" [Regulations on the problems of devoting a major effort to expand foreign
    trade and foreign exchange revenue], State Council document 1979.202, issued
    on 13 August 1979, in Reardon, "Coastal Development Strategy (I)," 9.

6   Zhao, *Prisoner of the State*, 102.

7   "Pizhuan Jinchukou Guanli Weiyuanhui guanyu Jing, Jin, Lu sanshi chukou
    gongzuo zuotanhui jiyao de baogao" [Approval of the Import-Export Admin-
    istration Commission report on the conference on Beijing, Tianjin, and Shang-
    hai export work], State Council document 1979.233, in *ZRGJGD*, 358.

8   "Guanyu Jing, Jin, Lu sanshi di'erci chukou gongzuo zuotanhui de baogao" [Report
    from the Beijing, Tianjin, and Shanghai export work conference], State Council
    document 1980.145, 28 May 1980, translated in Reardon, "Coastal Development
    Strategy (II)," 43.

9   Zhao, *Prisoner of the State*, 152.

10 Lin Jinzhi, *Huaqiao huaren yu zhongguo geming he jianshe*, 478–84.

11 Zhao, *Prisoner of the State*, 153; Reardon, *Reluctant Dragon*, 120.

12 Shambaugh, *Making of a Premier*.

13 Zhao, "Guanyu jingji fazhan zhanlüe de jige wenti" [Several problems regarding
    the economic development strategy], speech to the entire State Council, 14 April
    1981, in *ZZYWJ*, 1:172–74.

14 Zhao, *Prisoner of the State*, 153.

15 Zhao Ziyang, "Duiwai jingji maoyi lingyu de sixiang yao jiefang [We must liber-
    ate our thinking in foreign economic trade area], speech at the Central Party
    Secretariat, 27 and 20 July 1981, in *ZZYWJ*, 1:202.

16 Zhao, "Guanyu jingji fazhan," *ZZYWJ*, 1:173–74.

17 Canto, Joines, and Laffer, *Foundations of Supply-Side Economics*.

18 See, for instance, Koziara and Yan, "Distribution System for Producers' Goods,"
    689–702.

19 Joniak-Lüthi, "Han Migration to Xinjiang," 155–74.

20 "Tongzhi pizhuan 'Yanhai jiu sheng, shi, zizhiqu duiwai jingji maoyi gongzuo
    zuotanhui jiyao'" [Circular promulgating the "Summary of the Conference of
    Nine Provinces, Municipalities, and Autonomous Regions on Foreign Economic
    Trade Work"], issued by the Central Committee and State Council on 15 January
    1982, translated in Reardon, "Coastal Development Strategy (II)," 45–98.

21 Central Committee, "Guanyu jiaqiang zhengfa gongzuo de zhishi" [Directive on
    strengthening political and legal work], in Zhonggong Zhongyang Dangshi
    Yanjiushi, *Zhonggong dangshi dashi nianbiao*, 454.

22 Reardon, "Coastal Development Strategy (II)," 45–46.

23 Reardon, *Reluctant Dragon*, 122–23.

24 Fieldwork in Foshan, Guangdong, China, 1987.

25 See Reardon, "Coastal Development Strategy (II)," 47–48.

26 "Guanyu pizhun Changjiang Nantonggang, Zhangjiagang duiwai gouji chuanbo
    kaifang de jueding" [Decision to approve the opening of the ports of Nantong
    and Zhangjiagang to foreign shipping], issued by the NPC Standing Committee
    on 19 November 1982, in *YCKTGWX*, 1:181.

27 "Guanyu tiaozheng Zhuhai jingji tequ qucheng fanwei wenti de pifu" [Approval of readjusting the area of the Zhuhai SEZ], Guohanzi 1983.117, issued by the State Council on 29 June 1983, in *YCKTGWX*, 1:112.

28 "Jiakuai Hainan kaifa jianshe wenti taolun jiyao" [Summary of a discussion on the problem of accelerating Hainan Island's development and construction], Central Committee document 1983.11, circular issued by the Central Committee and State Council on 1 April 1983, translated in Reardon, "Coastal Development Strategy (II)," 83–96. For greater detail about SEZ policy changes during the 1983–85 period, see Crane, *Political Economy*, 76–107.

29 "Guanyu Taiwan tongbao dao jingji tequ touzi de tebie youhui banfa" [Special treatment accorded to Taiwanese compatriots investing in the special economic zones], State Council document 1983.57, issued on 5 April 1983, in *YCKTGWX*, 1:123.

30 For a general overview, see Harding, *China's Second Revolution*, 187–88.

31 Ruan, "Establishment of Special Zones and Economic Strategy," 47–48.

32 "Zhonggong zhongyang zhengzhiju huiyi tongbao" [Central Committee Political Bureau notice], issued on 5 December 1980, in *SQYWX*, 558.

33 For an excellent analysis of the campaign against spiritual pollution, see Schram, "'Economics in Command?,'" 437–49; Fewsmith, *Dilemmas of Reform*; Gold, "Just in Time!," 947–74; Brugger and Kelly, *Chinese Marxism in the Post-Mao Era*.

34 Deng Xiaoping, "Dang zai zuzhi zhanxian he sixiang zhanxianshang de poqie renwu" [The party's pressing responsibility to organize the political and ideological lines], in *DXPWDS*, 36–48; Mackerras, "'Party Consolidation,'" 175–86; Baum, *Burying Mao*, 157.

35 Reardon, *Reluctant Dragon*, 87–88.

36 For a comprehensive analysis of the Hong Kong issue, see Vogel, *Deng Xiaoping*, 487–511.

37 Deng Xiaoping, "Women dui Xianggang wenti de jiben lichang" [Our fundamental position on the Hong Kong problem], in *DXPWX*-3, 313.

38 Deng Xiaoping, "Yige guojia, liangzhong zhidu" [One country, two systems], 22 and 23 June 1984, in *DXPWX*-3, 58–61.

39 Loh, *Underground Front*, 129–43.

40 Baum, *Burying Mao*, 161–63; Su Tiren, *Deng Xiaoping*, 771.

41 "Dangqian nongcun jingji zhengce de ruogan wenti" [Several issues in the countryside's current work], issued by the Central Committee on 1 January 1984, in *ZRGJGD*, 521; "Guanyu kaichuang shedui qiye xin jumian de baogao" [Report on starting the new phase of community and team enterprises (TVEs)], issued by the Central Committee and State Council on 1 March 1984, in *ZRGJGD*, 528; "Guoying qiye chengben guanli tiaoli" [Regulations on state-owned enterprise administration], issued by the State Council on 5 March 1984, in *ZRGJGD*, 528; "Guanyu renzhen zhuahao qiye niukui zengying gongzuo de baogao" [Report on implementation of transforming enterprises from profit-loss to profit-making enterprises], approved by the State Council on 3 May 1984, in *ZRGJGD*, 534; "Guanyu 'Guangdong, Fujian liangsheng jixu shixing texu zhengce, linghuo cuoshe de huiyi jiyao' de tongzhi" [Circular on the "Summary of the Conference on Guangdong and Fujian Provinces' continuation to implement special policies

and flexible measures"], State Council document 1985.46, issued on 28 March 1985, in *YCKTGWX*, 1:82–87.

42　Zhao, *Prisoner of the State*, 126.

43　Shiping Zheng, "New Era in Chinese Elite Politics," 193.

44　Yang Shangkun was second provincial party secretary from December 1978 to March 1979 and was subsequently promoted to first party secretary of Guangzhou, a post he held until June 1981.

45　Wang, "Women jianli jingji tequ."

46　Su Tiren, *Deng Xiaoping*, 698–99; Li, Lanqing, *Breaking Through*, 173–74.

47　Deng Xiaoping, "Banhao jingji tequ, cengjia duiwai kaifang chengshi" [Make a success of the SEZs and open more cities to the outside world], in *DXPWX*-3, 51.

48　Deng Xiaoping, "Banhao jingji tequ," *DXPWX*-3, 52.

49　Fieldwork in Beijing, September 1984.

50　Fieldwork in Beijing, October 1984.

51　"Communiqué of the Third Plenary Session of the 12th Central Committee of the Chinese Communist Party," *FBIS*, 22 October 1984, K1–9. For an analysis of the Third Plenum's decision on price reform, see Bernstein, "China in 1984," 38–41.

52　Zhao Ziyang, "Guangdong yao jixu zai gaige kaifang he tequ jianshe zhong zou zai qianmian" [Guangdong must continue to take the point in the reforms and opening and SEZ construction], 21–29 November 1984, in *ZZYWJ*, 2:547.

53　Naughton, "The Third Front," 351–86; Reardon, *Reluctant Dragon*, chap. 4.

54　For the quotations in this paragraph, see Zhao Ziyang, "Shenzhen tequ yao wei quanguo gaige kaifang tigong jingyan" [The Shenzhen SEZ must provide its experiences in reforms and opening for the entire country], 27 November 1984, in *ZZYWJ*, 2:561–62.

55　"'Guanyu Guangdong, Fujian liangsheng jixu shixing teshu zhengce, linghuo cuoshi de huiyi jiyao' de tongzhi" [Notice on the "Brief on special policies and flexible measures in Guangdong and Fujian provinces"], State Council document 1985.46, issued on 28 March 1985, in *YCKTGWX*, 1: 82–87.

56　Hu Qiaomu, "Dui Fujian gongzuo de jidian xiwang" [Several requests regarding Fujian work], in Hu Qiaomu, *Hu Qiaomu wenji*, 3:212–14.

57　Hu Qiaomu, "Dui Fujian," 3:216.

58　Hu Qiaomu, "Dui Fujian," 3:217.

59　Chu, "China's Special Economic Zones," 77–89.

60　Breslin, "Politics of Chinese Trade," 1179–99.

61　Bogye, "Memorandum."

62　Fieldwork, Shenzhen University, August 1986–February 1988.

63　Ngai and Chan, "Global Capital, the State, and Chinese Workers," 383–410.

64　For more detail, see Breznitz and Murphree, *Run of the Red Queen*, 160–94; Fuller, *Paper Tigers, Hidden Dragons*, 81–93.

65　"Who's Afraid of Huawei?" *Economist*, 4 August 2012. For a broader analysis, see Harwit, "Building China's Telecommunications Network," 311–32; Arvanitis and Jastrabsky, "Un système d'innovation régional," 14–28.

66　Rogers and Ruppersberger, *Investigative Report*.

67　Haggard, "ZTE Case."

68 Cendrowski, "Is the World Big Enough for Huawei?"; Huang Guo, "20 Years History of ZTE Corporation."

69 Fan, "Catching Up through Developing Innovation ," 364; "Huawei: The Long March," *Economist*.

70 Fan, "Catching Up," 367.

71 Wong and Lee, "Welfare in a Stratified Immigrant Society," 218–19; Warner and Ng, "Ongoing Evolution of Chinese Industrial Relations," 1–20.

72 Chang, "Making of the Chinese Bankruptcy Law," 341.

73 "Guanyu guli waishang touzi de guiding" [Regulations on encouraging foreign investment], State Council document 1986.95, issued on 11 October 1986, in *YCKTGWX*, 3:83–85.

74 "Special Economic Zone must continue to be 'special'—congratulating the 15th anniversary of the establishment of the Shenzhen Special Economic Zone," *Liaowang* 34 (21 August 1995), 1, translated in *FBIS—China*, 25 September 1995, 39.

75 Crane, *Political Economy*, 108–45.

76 State Council document 1985.46, *YCKTGWX*, 1:82–87.

77 Deng Xiaoping, "Banhao jingji tequ," *DXPWX*-3, 52.

78 Li, *Breaking Through*, 179–80.

79 "Yanhai bufen chengshi zuotanhui jiyao" [Summary of the conference of some coastal municipalities], Central Committee document 1984.13, translated in Reardon, "China's Coastal Development Strategy (II)," 49–66.

80 Reardon, "China's Coastal Development Strategy (II)," 66.

81 Yeung and Hu, *China's Coastal Cities*.

82 Li, *Breaking Through*, 181; fieldwork in Guangzhou, 1986.

83 Li, *Breaking Through*, 182.

84 The May Fourth Movement of 1919 was a protest against the older Confucian values and promoted a Chinese cultural renewal based on the Western ideals of science and democracy." See Schwarcz, *Chinese Enlightenment*.

85 "Guanyu pizhuan 'Changjiang, Zhujiang Sanjiaozhou he Minnan xia zhang quan sanjiao diqu zuotanhui jiyao de tongzhi'" [Circular promulgating the "Summary of the Conference on the Yangtze, Pearl River Deltas, and the Xiamen, Zhangzhou, Quanzhou Triangle Area in Southern Fujian"], Central Committee document 1985.3, issued on 18 February 85, in *YCKTGWX*, 1:74–81.

86 Central Committee document 1984.13, in Reardon, "China's Coastal Development Strategy (I)," 49–66.

87 Central Committee document 1984.13, in Reardon, "China's Coastal Development Strategy (I)," 50.

88 Central Committee document 1984.13, in Reardon, "China's Coastal Development Strategy (I)," 57.

89 See, for example, Li, *Breaking Through*, 186–95, for a story about the problems Tianjin encountered as a new open coastal city and ETDZ.

90 Zhao, "Guanyu jingji fazhan," *ZZYWJ*, 1:173–74.

91 Zhao Ziyang, "Zhenxing Shanghai, chongfen fahui quanguo jingji zhongxin de zuoyong" [Revitalize Shanghai, fully develop its utility as our country's economic

center], speech at the Shanghai Economic Work Conference, 9 December 1984, in *ZZYWJ*, 2:563–72.

92 Zhao Ziyang, "Guanyu gaizao he zhenxing Shanghai gei Zhongyang de bao-gao" [Report to central leaders on the transformation and revitalization of Shanghai], submitted on 29 December 1984, in *ZZYWJ*, 2:594–98.

93 Zweig, *Internationalizing China*, 90.

94 Zhao Ziyang, "Guanyu yanhai diqu jingji fazhan de jige wenti" [Several problems of coastal economic development], 20 December 1984, in *ZZYWJ*, 2:577–87.

95 Zhao, *Prisoner of the State*, 109–10.

96 Central Committee document 1984.13, in Reardon, "China's Coastal Development Strategy (I)," 57.

97 "Guanyu pizhun guojia gaoxin jishu chanye kaifaqu he youguan zhengce guiding de tongzhi" [Circular on the approval of the National Industrial Development Zones for New and Advanced Technology and their policies and regulations], approved by the State Council on 6 March 1991. The NIDZNAT designation was approved for Wuhan, Nanjing, Shenyang, Tianjin, Xian, Chengdu, Weihai, Zhongshan, Changchun, Harbin, Changsha, Fuzhou, Guangzhou, Hefei, Chongqing, Hangzhou, Guilin, Zhengzhou, Lanzhou, Shijiazhuang, and Jinan. For more information, see Meng, "Theory and Practice of Free Economic Zones," 86–89.

98 Central Committee document 1984.13, in Reardon, "China's Coastal Development Strategy, (I)," 64–65.

99 For a comprehensive list of these official documents from the 1984–85 period, see *YCKTGWX*, 1:185–271.

100 Tsai, *Back-Alley Banking*; Mai and Shih, *Taiwan's Economic Success*.

101 "Guowuyuan guanyu Wenzhoushi jinyibu duiwai kaifang youguan wenti de pifu" [State Council approval concerning the problems of further opening up Wenzhou Municipality], State Council letter 1985.36, issued on 14 March 1985, in *YCKTGWX*, 1:204–5.

102 "Wenzhou Yongqiang Jichang zhengshi gengming wei Wenzhou Longwan Guoji Jichang" [The Wenzhou Yongqiang Airport has officially changed names to the Wenzhou Longwan International Airport], 9 May 2013, accessed on 12 November 2013, *Phoenix News*, http://news.ifeng.com/mil/air/hkxw/detail_2013_05/09 /25122104_0.shtml.

103 The first group included Dalian, Caohejing, Fuzhou, Guangzhou, Hongqiao, Lianyungang, Minhang, Nantong, Ningbo, Qingdao, Qinhuangdao, Tianjin, Yantai, and Zhanjiang ETDZs. The second group included Beijing, Changchun, Chongqing, Dongshan, Guangzhou Nansha, Hangzhou, Harbin, Huizhou Dayawan, Kunshan, Rongqiao, Shenyang, Urumchi, Weihai, Wenzhou, Wuhan, Wuhu, Xiaoshan, and Yingkou. For the State Council approvals, see *YCKTGWX*, 1:185–271.

104 Alan Liu, "The 'Wenzhou Model,'" 703–6.

105 Tsai, *Capitalism*, 155.

106 Liu, "The 'Wenzhou Model,'" 704–6.

107 Yeung, *Foreign Investment and Socio-economic Development*.

108 See "Guanyu kaifa he kaifang Pudong wenti de pifu" [Approval of the develop-
     ment and opening of Pudong], Central Committee and State Council document
     1990.100, issued on 2 June 1990, in *YCKTGWX*, 5:44–45.

109 For instance, see Zhu Rongji, "Kaifa xibu diqu zhuyao cong sange fangmian
     zhuoshou" [Starting primarily from three different areas to develop western
     China], delivered on 29 October 1999, in Zhu Rongji, *Zhu Rongji jianghua shilu*,
     342–48.

110 Kong Xiaoqi, "China Launches Major Economic Zone."

111 Reardon, *Reluctant Dragon*, 133–34, 153–54.

112 For more detailed analysis, see Lo, "Recent Spatial Restructuring," 293–308.

113 Walker, "40 Years On," 451.

114 For instance, see Schottenhammer, *Emporium of the World*.

115 For instance, see Luo and Howe, "Direct Investment and Economic Integration,"
     746–69.

116 Fieldwork in Shenzhen, Foshan, Shahe, Zhuhai, Zhongshan, and Guangzhou,
     1985 and 1986–88.

117 Zhao Ziyang, "Guanyu kaifang Zhujiang sanjiaozhou he Changjiang, sanjiao-
     zhou gei zhongyang de qingshi" [Request instructions from Central Leaders
     concerning opening the Pearl River Delta and Yangtze River Delta], submitted
     on 29 December 1984, in *ZZYWJ*, 2:601.

118 Zhao, "Guanyu kaifang Zhujiang sanjiaozhou," *ZZYWJ*, 2:600.

119 Zhao, "Guanyu kaifang Zhujiang sanjiaozhou," *ZZYWJ*, 2:601.

120 Zhao Ziyang, "Zai Changjiang, Zhujiang sanjiaozhou he Minnan sanjiao diqu
     zoutanhui jieshu de jianghua" [Concluding speech to the Conference on the
     Yangtze and Pearl River Delta and the Minnan Triangular Area], in *ZZYWJ*,
     3:47.

121 Fieldwork, Guangzhou, 1987. For more analysis of the coastal cities' desire to
     be granted greater decision-making rights, see Zweig, *Internationalizing
     China*, 60–64, 80–87. For an excellent analysis of provincial leaders' initiatives
     to develop Northeast China in the 1980s, see Freeman, "China's Reform
     Challenge."

122 For a complete list of the cities and counties involved in the economic regions,
     see Central Committee document 1985.3, *YCKTGWX*, 1:81.

123 For more information on general tax reforms in the 1980s and the consolidated
     industrial-commercial tax, see Zhai, "Tax Legislation of the People's Republic
     of China," 208.

124 Ma Hong, "'China-Style' Socialist Modernization," 1.

125 For the opening of the coastal regions, see Central Committee document 1985.3,
     YCKTGWX, 1:74–81.

126 Central Committee document 1985.3, *YCKTGWX*, 1:74.

127 Zhao, "Zai Changjiang, Zhujiang sanjiaozhou he Minnan," *ZZYWJ*, 3:54.

128 George Lin, "Metropolitan Development," 383–406.

129 Deng Xiaoping, "Banhao jingji tequ," *DXPWX*-3, 52.

130 Fieldwork, Hainan, January–February 1985. For more on Hainan and Lei Yu, see
     Vogel, *One Step*, 275–309.

131 For an updated account of the Yulin submarine base, see Cook, "China's Most Important South China Sea Military Base." Zhao Ziyang approved moving the base farther east to help Sanya develop more comprehensively. See Vogel, *One Step Ahead*, 304.

132 "Guanyu zai dalu zhongzhi xiangjiaoshu de chubu jihua de baogao" [Report on the initial plans to establish a natural rubber plantation in China], approved by the Central Committee on 13 August 1951, in *ZRGJGD*, 27, 29.

133 Zhu De, "Cengjia chukou chanpin," 34-35.

134 Xi Zhongxun, "Guangdong de jianshe ruhe dagan kuaishang," in Xi, *Xi Zhongxun wenxuan*, 283-84.

135 World Bank, "Implementation Completion Report."

136 "Hainandao wenti zuotanhui jiyao" [Conference report on the Hainan problem], State Council document 1980.202, approved and transmitted on 24 July 1980, in *YCKTGWX*, 1:25-32; Reardon, "China's Coastal Development Strategy (II)," 67-82.

137 State Council document 1980.202, Reardon, "China's Coastal Development Strategy (II)," 79.

138 Chen Yun, *Chen Yun tongzhi wengao xuanbian*, 118.

139 "Hainandao wenti zuotanhi jiyao" [Summary of the Hainan Island conference], State Council document 80.202, issued on 24 July 1980, translated in Reardon, "Coastal Development Strategy (II)," 77.

140 "'Jiakuai Hainandao kaifang jianshe wenti taolun jiyao' de tongzhi" [Circular on the "Discussion Summary on the Problems of Accelerating Hainan Island's Opening and Construction"], Central Committee document 1983.11, issued by the Central Committee and the State Council on 1 April 1983, in *YCKTGWX*, 1:58-64; Reardon, "China's Coastal Development Strategy (II)," 83-96.

141 Zhao Ziyang, "Dui kaifa Hainandao wenti de piyu" [Written comment on the problem of developing Hainan Island], issued on 10 December 1982, in *ZZYWJ*, 1:665.

142 "Circular" approving/transmitting "Jiakuai Hainan kaifa jianshe wenti taolun jiyao" [Summary of a discussion on the problem of accelerating Hainan Island's development and construction], Central Committee document 1983.11, approved and transmitted by the Central Committee and State Council on 1 April 1983, translated in Reardon, "Coastal Development Strategy (II)," 87.

143 Reardon, "Coastal Development Strategy (II)," 90.

144 Reardon, "Coastal Development Strategy (II)," 91.

145 Reardon, "Coastal Development Strategy (II)," 88-91.

146 Reardon, "Coastal Development Strategy (II)," 93.

147 Reardon, "Coastal Development Strategy (II)," 94.

148 "Guanyu dangqian Hainandao qingkuang he xuyao bangzhu jiejue wenti de huibao de tongzhi" [Circular of the SEZ Office's report on the current situation on Hainan Island and the necessary help to resolve the issue], State Council document 1985.142, issued by the State Council Office on 16 December 1985 and approved by the State Council on 24 December 1985, in *YCKTGWX*, 1:87-96.

149 Vogel, *One Step Ahead*, 292–93; *Renmin ribao*, 1 August 1985.

150 Crane, *Political Economy*, 109.

151 Koziara and Yan, "Distribution System," 689–702.

152 Zhao Ziyang, "Zhazha shishi de ba Hainan de kaifa jianshe sheye jinxing xia qu" [Vigorously implementing the task of opening and developing Hainan], delivered on 14 February 1986, in *ZZYWJ*, 3:288.

153 "Guanyu jiaqian waihui guanli de jueding" [Decision on strengthening foreign currency administration], State Council document 1985.38, issued on 13 March 1985, in *YCKTGWX*, 2:513–14.

154 Crane, *Political Economy*, 112.

155 "Guanyu jianjue zhizhi jiudi zhuanshou daomai huodong de tongzhi" [The circular on firmly prohibiting profiteering on local resale of goods], issued by State Council on 13 March 1985, in *ZRGJGD*, 589.

156 "Guanyu yange kongzhi yinjin caise dianshiji zhuangpeixian he caise xianxiangguan shengchaixian de tongzhi" [Circular on strict control of import of color TV and kinescope production line], issued by State Council on 22 April 1985, in *ZRGJGD*, 608.

157 "Guanyu jiaqiang dianbingxiang hangye guanli, kongzhi mangmu yinjin de baogao" [Report on strengthening administration in refrigerator industry, control blind importation], State Council notice approving the report of the National Planning Commission, National Economic Commission, and the Ministry of Light Industry on 15 June 1985, in *ZRGJGD*, 619.

158 "Guanyu jiaqiang qiche jinkou guanli de tongzhi" [Notice on strengthening automobile import administration], issued by State Council on 15 October 1985, in *ZRGJGD*, 649.

159 "Guanyu jixu baoliu dongnan yanhai sansheng gongshang xingzheng guanli jiguan jisi jianchazhan de baogao" [Report on continuing to maintain the industrial and commercial administrative checkpoints to suppress smuggling in three southeastern coastal provinces], issued by National Industrial and Commercial Administrative Bureau, approved by State Council Office on 25 October 1985, in *ZRGJGD*, 652–53.

160 Crane, *Political Economy*, 110.

161 Zhao Ziyang, "Dangqian de jingji xingshi he jingji tizhi gaige" [The current economic situation and reforms of the economic system], government work report presented on 27 March 1985 to the third session of the Sixth NPC, in *ZZYWJ*, 3:120.

162 Deng Xiaoping, "Gaige shi Zhongguo de dierci geming" [Reform is China's second revolution], *DXPWX*-3, 113–14.

163 "Guanyu jiaqiang dui Guangdong, Fujian liangsheng jinkou shangpin guanli de tongzhi" [Notice on strengthening import administration in Guangdong and Fujian], issued by the State Council on 7 December 1985, in *ZRGJGD*, 660.

164 Zhao, "Zhazha shishi," *ZZYWJ*, 3:287–96.

165 Zhao, "Zhazha shishi," *ZZYWJ*, 3:288.

166 Zhao, *Prisoner of the State*, 184.

167 Zhao, *Prisoner of the State*, 211.

168 Zhao Ziyang, "Guanyu Hainan jiansheng choubei gongzuo de jige wenti" [Several problems involving the preparatory work to establish Hainan province], 11 September 1987, in *ZZYWJ*, 4:170–72.

169 Zhao, "Guanyu Hainan jiansheng," *ZZYWJ*, 4:170.

170 Zhao Ziyang, "Yanzhe you Zhongguo tesi de shehui zhuyi daolu de qianjin" [Progressing along the Chinese-style socialist road], report presented to the Thirteenth Party Congress, 25 October 1987, in *ZZYWJ*, 4:237–39.

171 Zhao, "Guanyu Hainan jiansheng," *ZZYWJ*, 4:170. For more detail about the establishment of the new province and its "small government" approach, see Brødsgaard, *Hainan*.

172 Zhao, "Guanyu Hainan jiansheng," *ZZYWJ*, 4:171.

173 "'Guanyu Hainandao jinyibu duiwai kaifang jiakuai jingji kaifa jianshe de zuotanhui jiyao' de tongzhi" [Circular on the Conference on the Further Opening to the Outside World and the Acceleration of Economic Construction], State Council document 1988.24, issued on 14 April 1988, in *YCKTGWX*, 3:14–21.

174 State Council document 1988.24, *YCKTGWX*, 3:15.

175 "Guanyu kongzhi chongfu jinjin, zhizhi duotou duiwai de baogao de tongzhi" [Circular on controlling import duplication and stopping too many organizations involved in foreign negotiations], State Council document 1985.90, submitted by the State Economic Commission on 28 June 1985 and approved by the State Council on 12 July 1985, in *YCKTGWX*, 2:420–25.

Chapter Five

1 Chen Yun, "Jingji xingshi yu jingyan jiaoxun" [The economic situation and lessons from experience], in *SQYZWX*, 601–2.

2 Pearson, *Joint Ventures*, 122.

3 World Bank, *East Asian Miracle*.

4 Vogel, *Deng Xiaoping*, 223–24.

5 Davie and Carver, "China's International Trade," 28; World Bank, *Socialist*, 2:462.

6 Zhao Ziyang, "Guanyu guowai daiquan wenti de yifengxin" [A letter on the foreign loan problem], 25 July 1980, in *ZZYWJ*, 1:52–53.

7 Long, *Liyong waizi gailun*, 253, 288, 300; Kokubun, "Politics," 19–44; Davie and Carver, "China's International Trade," 27.

8 For more information on the use of foreign capital, see Reardon, *Reluctant Dragon*, chap. 7.

9 Zhao Ziyang, "Huijian Shijie Yinhang daibiaotuan de tanhua" [Discussion with the World Bank delegation], 16 July 1980, in *ZZYWJ*, 1:48–52.

10 Zhao, "Huijian Shijie Yinhang daibiaotuan de tanhua," *ZZYWJ*, 1:48–52.

11 Zhao Ziyang, "Haishang shiyou kantan kaifa bixu gao duiwai hezuo" [In carrying out offshore oil exploration and development we must cooperate with foreigners], speech in March 1981, in *ZZYWJ*, 1:157–58; State Council, "Guanyu yu waishang hezuo kantan kaifa shiyou gongzuo tongyi guikou de jianyi" [Opinion

on relevant administration of cooperative exploration and development of oil resources with foreigners], submitted by the Ministry of Petroleum and approved by the State Council on 12 June 1980, in *ZRGJGD*, 389.

12 Katori, "Cable from Ambassador Katori to the Foreign Minister."

13 Harold, "Freeing Trade"; Hui, *Politics of China's Accession*; Jacobson and Oksenberg, *China's Participation in the IMF*; Pearson, "The Case of China's Accession," 337–70; Pearson "China's Integration," 161–205; Pearson, "Major Multilateral Economic Institutions," 207–34; Wei Liang, "China's WTO Negotiation Process," 683–719; Lardy, *China in the World Economy*, 141–43.

14 Li, Lanqing, *Breaking Through*, 375.

15 State Council, "Guanyu canjia guanshui yu maoyi zongxieding de qingshi" [Request for instructions concerning China's participation in GATT], 25 December 1982, in Harold, "Freeing Trade," 133–36.

16 Li, *Breaking Through*, 376; Davis and Wilf, "Joining the Club."

17 A. Doak Barnett, *China's Economy in Global Perspective*, 527–31.

18 Pearson, "China's Integration," 169. Also see Moore, *China in the World Market*, 80–110; Ryan, *Playing by the Rules*, 152–67.

19 Zhao Ziyang, "Xiwang huifu Zhongguo Guanmao Zongxieding tiaoyueguo de diwei" [Hoping to resume China's seat in the GATT], discussion with Arthur Dunkel, 10 January 1986, in *ZZYWJ*, 3:254.

20 Zhao, "Xiwang huifu Zhongguo Guanmao," *ZZYWJ*, 3:254. For the actual letter, see Li, *Breaking Through*, 376–77.

21 Lardy, *Foreign Trade*, 50; Jacobson and Oksenberg, *China's Participation in the IMF*, 139–52; Reardon, "Rise and Decline," 281–303.

22 Zhao, *Prisoner of the State*, 152–53. Zhao describes his efforts in the 1960s to increase Guangdong's exports in order to accelerate its economic recovery from the GLF. For early analysis of the coastal development strategy, see Yang, Dali, "China Adjusts," 42–64.

23 For the literature published around the 1980s on export-led growth and its effect on domestic industrial development, see Balassa, *Process of Industrial Development*; Helpman and Krugman, *Market Structure and Foreign Trade*; Chow, "Causality," 55–63; Haggard, *Pathways*. These studies culminated with World Bank, *East Asian Miracle*.

24 Fewsmith, *Dilemmas of Reform*, 214–17. Also see Gewirtz, *Unlikely Partners*, 194–98.

25 Zweig, *Internationalizing China*, 261.

26 As the Hong Kong dollar was pegged to the devalued U.S. dollar, global production gravitated toward Hong Kong.

27 Zhao Ziyang, "Zai Zhongyang Gongzuo Huiyi jiesushi de jianghua" [Speech at the conclusion of the Central Committee Work Conference], in *ZZYWJ*, 4:271.

28 Chase, *Trading Blocs*, 232–35; Borrus, Ernst, and Haggard, "Introduction," 12–13; Pearson, *Joint Ventures*, 32, 94–95.

29 Thorbecke and Salike, "Understanding Foreign Direct Investment."

30 Zhao Ziyang, "Zai Zhongyang Gongzuo Huiyi," *ZZYWJ*, 4:271.

31 Zhao Ziyang, "Zai Zhongyang Gongzuo Huiyi," *ZZYWJ*, 4:271.

32 Zhao, *Prisoner of the State*, 149–50.

33 Zhao Ziyang, "Dui woguo yanhai diqu fazhan waixiangxing jingji de zhan-luë sikao" [Strategic thinking concerning China's coastal areas developing an outward-oriented economy], *ZZYWJ*, 4:305–12.

34 Zhao Ziyang, "Dui woguo yanhai diqu fazhan," *ZZYWJ*, 4:305.

35 Zhu De made the same comments on 9 October 1957. See Wang Xiangli, "Zhu De jingji sixiang," 45.

36 Zhao Ziyang, "Zai Zhongyang Gongzuo Huiyi," *ZZYWJ*, 4:306.

37 Zhao Ziyang, "Dangqian jingji gongzuozhong ying yanjiu jiejue de xin wenti" [New problems arising in our current economic work that need research and resolution], delivered at State Council Standing Committee meeting discussing economic work, 18 September 1982, in *ZZYWJ*, 1:567–71.

38 Huang, Yasheng, *Capitalism with Chinese Characteristics*, 78–85.

39 Zhao, "Dui woguo yanhai diqu fazhan waixiangxing jingji," *ZZYWJ*, 4:308.

40 Lardy, *Foreign Trade*, 39, 145.

41 Zhao, "Dui woguo yanhai diqu fazhan waixiangxing jingji," *ZZYWJ*, 4:311.

42 Zweig, *Internationalizing China*, 111.

43 Zhao Ziyang, "Gei jingji tequ fazhan waixiangxing jingji yi xin de dongli he xin de zhengce" [Giving new force and policy to develop an outward-oriented SEZ economy], delivered on 30 December 1987, in *ZZYWJ*, 4:331.

44 "Yinfa Zhongguo (Shanghai) ziyou maoyi shiyanqu zongti fang'an de tong-zhi" [Circular to publish the comprehensive plan to establish China (Shanghai) free-trade experimental zone], State Council document 2013.38, issued on 27 September 2013, accessed 3 October 2019, http://finance.ifeng.com/a/20130927/10773237_0.shtml. Wan et al., "Policy and Politics," 1–6.

45 Baum, *Burying Mao*, 236. Hu Qili was closely associated with Zhao Ziyang and Hu Yaobang and a member of the Standing Committee from 1987 until 1989, when he was ousted for his opposition to the old guard's 6.4 Tiananmen crackdown. Qiao Shi was a Standing Committee member from 1987 to 1992, and supported Deng Xiaoping's military response to the 6.4 demonstrations.

46 Zhao, *Prisoner of the State*, 68.

47 Baum, *Burying Mao*, 218.

48 Gewirtz, *Unlikely Partners*, 197–98.

49 Zhao, *Prisoner of the State*, 146.

50 Zhao, *Prisoner of the State*, 146–47.

51 Fewsmith, *Dilemmas of Reform*, 215–16. Fewsmith argues that Zhao failed to promote the concept of the great international cycle, as "no ministry of the State Council ever formally endorsed proposals for implementing the great international cycle" (216). While Zhao Ziyang specifically mentioned the concept at the Central Work Conference of 5 November 1987, Zhao did not promote the concept further but instead incorporated the idea into his concept of an outward-oriented economy.

52 Zhao Ziyang, "Yanhai diqu jingji fazhan de zhanlüe wenti" [The problem concerning coastal economic development strategy], in *ZZYWJ*, 4:342–55.

53 Zhao, *Prisoner of the State*, 151; Wedeman, *From Mao to Market*, 36–37.

54 Zhao, "Yanhai diqu jingji fazhan de zhanluë wenti" *ZZYWJ*, 4:344.

55 Pearson, *Joint Ventures*, 87.

56 Kueh, "Foreign Investment and Economic Change," 638.

57 Zhao, "Yanhai diqu jingji fazhan de zhanluë wenti," *ZZYWJ*, 4:345.

58 Zhao, "Yanhai diqu jingji fazhan de zhanluë wenti," *ZZYWJ*, 4:346.

59 Zhao, *Prisoner of the State*, 151–52.

60 Zhao, "Yanhai diqu jingji fazhan de zhanluë wenti," *ZZYWJ*, 4:348.

61 Zhao, "Yanhai diqu jingji fazhan de zhanluë wenti," *ZZYWJ*, 4:350.

62 For more background on the problems of learning foreign administration skills, see Pearson, *Joint Ventures*, 177–82.

63 Zhao, "Yanhai diqu jingji fazhan de zhanluë wenti," *ZZYWJ*, 4:352.

64 For more information about China's policies in the 1980s on foreign technology transfer, see Pearson, *Joint Ventures*, 145–53.

65 Zhao, "Yanhai diqu jingji fazhan de zhanluë wenti," *ZZYWJ*, 4:353.

66 Zhao, "Yanhai diqu jingji fazhan de zhanluë wenti," *ZZYWJ*, 4:355.

67 Zhao, "Yanhai diqu jingji fazhan de zhanluë wenti," *ZZYWJ*, 4:342.

68 Zhao, *Prisoner of the State*, 146; Yang, Dali, "China Adjusts," 54–58.

69 Zhao, *Prisoner of the State*, 131.

70 Zhao, *Prisoner of the State*, 147.

71 Zhao, *Prisoner of the State*, 147–48.

72 Imbalances did occur. See Jian and Fleisher, "Regional Income Inequality," 141–64. For interior-economy criticisms, see Yang, Dali, "China Adjusts."

73 Zhao, *Prisoner of the State*, 149.

74 Li Peng, "Zhengfu gongzuo baogao" [Government work report], delivered on 25 March 1988, in *YCKTGWX*, 3:2–3.

75 "Guanyu kuoda Minnan sanjiaozhou jingji kaifangqu fanwei de fuhan" [Letter in reply to expanding the Minnan Delta economic region], State Council Office letter 1988.2, issued on 26 January 1988, in *YCKTGWX*, 3:74.

76 "Guanyu kuoda yanhai jingji kaifangqu fanwei de tongzhi" [Circular on expanding the area of the open coastal economic regions], State Council document 1988.21, issued on 18 March 1988, in *YCKTGWX*, 3:72–74.

77 "Guanyu kuoda Guangdongsheng yanhai jingji kaifangqu fanwei de pifu" [Approval to expand the area of the Guangdong open coastal economic regions], State Council letter 1988.96, issued on 28 June 1988, in *YCKTGWX*, 3:74–75.

78 Zhao Ziyang, "Caiqu jiji taidu duidai waimao gaigezhong chuxian de wenti" [Adopting a proactive outlook on dealing with problems arising with foreign-trade reforms], 30 January 1988, in *ZZYWJ*, 4:363–65. For more on the problems of the foreign trade corporations, see Yang, Dali, "China Adjusts," 56–57.

79 Dziubla, "International Trading Companies," 422–96.

80 "'Shenpi duiwai maoyi qiye youguan wenti de guiding' de tongzhi" [Circular on "Endorsing the regulations regarding certain problems with foreign trade corporations"], Waijing maoguan tizi 1988.167, issued on 21 May 1988, in *YCKTGWX*, 3:332–35. These are the detailed regulations mandated by State Council document 1988.22, "Guanyu yanhai diqu fazhan waixiangxing jingji de ruogan buchong guiding" and "Guanyu jiakuai he shenhua duiwai maoyi tizhi gaige ruogan wenti de guiding" [Regulations on dealing with certain problems of accelerating and

deepening foreign trade structural reforms], State Council document 1988.12, that are cited in Waijing maoguan tizi 1988.167, in *YCKTGWX*, 3:332–35.

81   Zhao Ziyang, "Luoshi yanhai jingji fazhan zhanluë de liang ge guanjian wenti" [Two key problems facing the implementation of the coastal economic development strategy], delivered on 7 March 1988, in *ZZYWJ*, 4:402–4.

82   "Guanyu yanhai diqu fazhan waixiangxing jingji de ruogan buchong guiding" [Supplementary regulations on the coastal areas developing an outward-oriented economy], State Council document 1988.22, issued on 23 March 1988, in *YCKTGWX*, 3:11–15.

83   Also see Zweig, *Internationalizing China*, 117–20.

84   See Phylaktis and Girardin, "Foreign Exchange Markets in Transition," 215–35.

85   "Guanyu shixing 'Guli Taiwan tongbao touzi de guiding' ruogan wenti de tongzhi" [Circular on the implementation problems of the "Regulations to Encourage the Investment of Taiwanese Compatriots"], State Council document 1988.41, issued on 3 July 1988, in *YCKTGWX*, 5:67–69.

86   "Guanyu pizhuan yanhai diqu duiwai kaifang gongzuo huiyi jiyao de tongzhi" [Circular approving the summary of Conference on the Coastal Opening to the Outside], 1–3 December 1988, State Council document 1989.5, in *YCKTGWX*, 3:46–53.

87   "Zai zhili zhengdunzhong jinyibu shishi yanhai jingji fazhan zhanluë" [While managing reorganization, to further implement the coastal economic development strategy], delivered on 3 December 1988, in *ZZYWJ*, 4:569–71.

88   State Council document 1989.5, *ZZYWJ*, 3:46–58.

89   Solinger, *China's Transition*, 276–77.

90   "Guanyu tiaozheng chukou xukezheng guanli shangpin mubiao ji fazheng danwei de tongzhi" [Circular approving the revision of the export permit commodity list and units issuing permits], MOFERT document 1989.7, issued in January 1989, in *YCKTGWX*, 5:97–107.

91   "Guanyu yinfa 'Difang bumen ziyou waihui jinkou pei'e shangpin zhanxing guanli banfa' de tongzhi [Circular on the publication of "The Temporary Administrative Regulations for Localities and Departments Using Free Foreign Exchange to Import Regulated Products"], State Planning Commission and MOFERT document 1989.16, issued on 11 January 1989, in *YCKTGWX*, 5:108–12.

92   "Guanyu yinfa 'Quanguo maoyi chukou shouru shangjiao zhongyang waihui de rogan guiding' de tongzhi" [Circular on the publication of "Certain Regulations concerning the Transfer of Foreign Exchange Earned From Exports to the Central Government"], State Administration of Foreign Exchange and MOFERT document 1989.26, issued on 14 January 1989, in *YCKTGWX*, 5:139–43.

93   Saich, "Rise and Fall," 186, 199.

Conclusion

1   Baum, *Burying Mao*, 5–9.

2   Hall, "Policy Paradigms," 291.

3   Hu Deping, "Essay."

4 "Guanyu jianguo yilai dang de ruogan lishi wenti de jueyi" [Resolution on Certain Questions in Our Party's History since the Founding of the PRC], adopted by the sixth plenum of the eleventh Central Committee on 27 June 1981, in *SQYZWX*, 788–846.

5 "China Corrects a Slip in Ideology," *New York Times*, 11 December 1984, A4.

6 *Beijing Review*, 30 August 1985, 20, as cited in Chen Jie, "The Impact," 26.

7 Deng Xiaoping, "Zai quanti renminzhong shuli fazhi guannian" [Developing a legal perspective among the whole people], 28 June 1986, *DXWX*, 3:163–64. For a detailed analysis of this period, see Baum, *Burying Mao*, 193–205.

8 Goldman, "A New Relationship," 510–11; Deng Weizhi, "Enhance Liberal Atmosphere," *Jiefang ribao*, 21 May 1986, 4.

9 Zhao Ziyang, "Guanyu zhengzhi tizhi gaige yantao gongzuo gei Zhongyang Changwei de xin" [A letter to the Political Bureau's Standing Committee concerning political structural reform discussions], submitted on 23 September 1986, in *ZZYWJ*, 3:452–53.

10 For the discussion group's letter describing their first meeting, see Zhao Ziyang, "Guanyu zhengzhi tizhi gaige wenti gei Zhongyang Zhengzhiju Changwei de xin" [Letter to the Standing Committee of the Political Bureau concerning the problem of political structural reform], issued on 18 November 1986, in *ZZYWJ*, 3:490–93.

11 Zhao Ziyang, "Guanyu zhengzhi tizhi gaige wenti" [The problem of reforming the political structure], in *ZZYWJ*, 3:468–77.

12 Zhao Ziyang, "Guanyu dangzheng fenkai" [Regarding the separation of party and state], delivered on 14 October 1987, in *ZZYWJ*, 4:202–6.

13 Baum, *Burying Mao*, 198–99.

14 Baum, *Burying Mao*, 201; fieldwork in Shenzhen, 1986–87.

15 Goldman, *Sowing the Seeds*, 17.

16 Zhao, *Prisoner of the State*, 172–77, 183–84; Vogel, *Deng Xiaoping*, 584–85.

17 Zhao Ziyang, "Zai chunjie tuan baihui shang de jianghua" [Speech to the Chinese New Year's celebration of the Communist Youth League], 29 January 1987, in *ZZYWJ*, 4:21–22.

18 Fieldwork, Guangzhou, January 1987.

19 Zhao, "Zai chunjie tuan baihui shang de jianghua," *ZZYWJ*, 4:24.

20 Zhao, *Prisoner of the State*, 211.

21 Baum, *Burying Mao*, 210.

22 Zhao Ziyang, "Guanyu caoni shisanda baogao dagang de shexiang gei Deng Xiaoping tongzhi de xin" [Letter to Comrade Deng Xiaoping on some thoughts concerning the draft outline for the 13th Party Congress report], 21 March 1987, in *ZZYWJ*, 4:47–48.

23 Baum, *Burying Mao*, 210–11, 213; fieldwork, Shenzhen, 1987; Su, "Decade of Crises," 349.

24 Zhao, "Zai chunjie tuan baihui shang de jianghua" [Speech to the Spring Festival group meeting], 29 January 1987, in *ZZYWJ*, 4:23.

25 Zhao, *Prisoner of the State*, 239. Also see Zhao Ziyang, "Zai xuanchuan, lilun, xinwen, dangxiao ganbu huiyishang de jianghua" [Speech to the Party School on Propaganda, Theory, and News], 13 May 1987, in *ZZYWJ*, 4:96–104.

26 Su, "Decade of Crises," 350–51.

27 Zhao, *Prisoner of the State*, 240; Baum, *Burying Mao*, 216.

28 Zhao Ziyang, "Yanzhe you Zhongguo tesi de shehui zhuyi daolu de qianjin" [Moving forward by following a Chinese-style socialist road], 25 October 1987, in *ZZYWJ*, 4:217–54.

29 Zhao, "Yanzhe you Zongguo tesi de shehui zhuyi daolu qianjin," *ZZYWJ*, 4:217–54; "Guanyu jianguo yilai dang de ruogan lishi wenti de jueyi" in *SQYZWX*, 788–846.

30 For an in-depth analysis, see Baum, *Burying Mao*, 220–22.

31 Zhao Ziyang, "Guanyu dangzheng fenkai" [On separating the party and the state], 14 October 1987, in *ZZYWJ*, 4:202–6.

32 Su, "Decade of Crises," 349–50; Zheng, Shiping, "New Era in Chinese Elite Politics," 197–200. For a discussion of the party-state, see Xia, *People's Congresses and Governance*.

33 Kathy Long, "Zhao Ziyang: yiming zhonggong buxiang jizhu de gaige xianfeng" [Zhao Ziyang: A reform pioneer who the Communist Party does not want to remember], *BBC News (Chinese)*, 24 January 2019. Retrieved on 22 April 2020, https://www.bbc.com/zhongwen/simp/chinese-news-46977041.

34 Zhao, *Prisoner of the State*, 269–73.

35 Solinger, "Commerce," 104; Reardon, *Reluctant Dragon*, chap. 1.

36 Baum, *Burying Mao*, 213; Zhao, *Prisoner of the State*, 238–40.

37 Yang, Dali, "China Adjusts," 60–61.

38 Shambaugh, "Dynamics of Elite Politics," 103–11. Dickson, *Red Capitalists in China*.

39 Zhao, *Prisoner of the State*, 149.

40 Jiang Zemin, "Jiang Zemin zongshuji zai qingzhu jianguo sishi zhounian dahuishang de jianghua jielu" [Excerpts from General Secretary Jiang Zemin's talk commemorating the 40th anniversary of the founding of the PRC], 29 September 1989, in *YCKTGWX*, 5:9–11.

41 "Pizhuan yijiu jiuling nian jingji tequ gongzuo huiyi jiyao de tongzhi" [The approval and transmittal of the summary of the 1990 SEZ Work Conference], State Council document 1990.32, issued on 28 May 1990, in *YCKTGWX*, 5:39–44.

42 "Guanyu kaifa he kaifang Pudong wenti de pifu" [Approval of the development and opening up of Pudong], Central Committee and State Council document 1990.100, issued on 2 June 1990, in *YCKTGWX*, 5:44–45.

43 "Jiang Zemin zongshuji zai qingzhu Shenzhen jingji tequ jianli shi zhounian zhaodaihui shang de jianghua" [General Secretary Jiang Zemin's speech to the 10th anniversary celebration of establishment of the Shenzhen SEZ], delivered on 26 November 1990.

44 Naughton, "Western Development Program," 253–96.

45 Zhonggong Shenzhen Shiwei Xuanchuanbu, *1992 Chun Deng Xiaoping yu Shenzhen*.

46 Liang, Wei, "China's WTO Negotiation Process," 693–99. For a Chinese insider's view, see Li, *Breaking Through*, 377–84.

47 Colvin, "It's China's World."

Bibliography

Amsden, Alice H. "Why Isn't Everyone Experimenting with the East Asian Model to Develop? Review of *The East Asian Miracle*." *World Development* 22, no. 4 (April 1994): 627–33.

Arvanitis, Rigas, and Eglantine Jastrabsky. "Un système d'innovation régional en gestation: Le cas du Guangdong" [A regional system of innovation in gestation: The case of Guangdong]. *Perspectives Chinoises* 92 (2005): 14–28.

Bachman, David M. *Chen Yun and the Chinese Political System*. Berkeley, CA: Center for Chinese Studies Research Monograph, 1985.

———. "Differing Visions of China's Post-Mao Economy: The Ideas of Chen Yun, Deng Xiaoping, and Zhao Ziyang." *Asian Survey* 26, no. 3 (March 1986): 292–321.

Balassa, Bela. *The Process of Industrial Development and Alternative Development Strategies*. Princeton, NJ: International Finance Section, Department of Economics, Princeton University, 1981.

Ball, Alan M. *Russia's Last Capitalists: The Nepmen, 1921–1929*. Berkeley: University of California Press, 1990.

Barnett, A. Doak. *China's Economy in Global Perspective*. Washington, DC: Brookings Institution, 1981.

Barnett, Vincent. "Soviet Commodity Markets during NEP." *Economic History Review* 48, no. 2 (May 1995): 329–52.

Barson, Joy. "Special Economic Zones in the People's Republic of China." *China—International Business* 4 (1981): 461–94.

Baum, Richard. *Burying Mao: Chinese Politics in the Age of Deng Xiaoping*. Princeton, NJ: Princeton University Press, 1994.

———. "The Road to Tiananmen: Chinese Politics in the 1980s." In *The Politics of China: The Eras of Mao and Deng*, 2nd ed., edited by Roderick MacFarquhar, 340–471. Cambridge, UK: Cambridge University Press, 1997.

Bernstein, Thomas P. "China in 1984: The Year of Hong Kong." *Asian Survey* 25, no. 1 (1985): 33–50.

———. "Introduction: The Complexities of Learning from the Soviet Union." In Bernstein and Li, *China Learns from the Soviet Union*, 7–14.

Bernstein, Thomas P., and Hua-Yu Li. *China Learns from the Soviet Union, 1949–Present*, edited by Thomas P. Bernstein and Hua-Yu Li. Lanham, MD: Lexington Books, 2010.

Blyth, Mark. *Great Transformations: Economic Ideas and Institutional Change in the Twentieth Century*. Cambridge, UK: Cambridge University Press, 2002.

Bogye, Janos. "Memorandum, 'Re: Information Related to China,'" September 30, 1986. History and Public Policy Program Digital Archive, Historical Archives of the Hungarian State Security (ÁBTL). Obtained by Peter Vamos and translated by Katalin Varga. Accessed on 3 October 2019. http://digitalarchive.wilsoncenter.org/document/119998.

Breslin, Shaun. "The Politics of Chinese Trade and the Asian Financial Crises: Questioning the Wisdom of Export-Led Growth." *Third World Quarterly* 20, no. 6 (1999): 1179–99.

Breznitz, Dan, and Michael Murphree. *The Run of the Red Queen: Government, Innovation, Globalization, and Economic Growth in China*. New Haven, CT: Yale University Press, 2011.

Brinton, Crane. *The Anatomy of Revolution*. New York: Vintage, 1965.

Brødsgaard, Kjeld Erik. *Hainan: State, Society, and Business in a Chinese Province*. New York: Routledge, 2008.

Brooks, Sarah M., and Marcus J. Kurtz. "Capital, Trade, and the Political Economies of Reform." *American Journal of Political Science* 51, no. 4 (October 2007): 703–20.

Brown, Shannon R. "China's Program of Technology Acquisition." In *China's Four Modernizations*, edited by Richard Baum, 153–73. Boulder, CO: Westview Press, 1980.

Brugger, Bill, and David Kelly. *Chinese Marxism in the Post-Mao Era*. Stanford, CA: Stanford University Press, 1990.

Bruton, Henry J. "A Reconsideration of Import Substitution." *Journal of Economic Literature* 36, no. 2 (June 1998): 903–36.

Caizhengbu Waihui Waishi Caiwusi, ed. *Feimaoyi waihui zhidu huibian* [Collection of documents concerning the noncommercially earned foreign exchange system]. Beijing: Zhongguo Caizheng Jingji Chubanshe, 1991.

Canto, Victor A., Douglas H. Joines, and Arthur B. Laffer. *Foundations of Supply-Side Economics: Theory and Evidence*. New York: Academic Press, 1983.

Cendrowski, Scott. "Is the World Big Enough for Huawei?" *Fortune*, 1 February 2017.

Chan, Thomas, Edward K. Y. Chen, and Steve Chin. "China's Special Economic Zones: Ideology, Policy and Practice." In *China's Special Economic Zones: Policies, Problems, and Prospects*, edited by Y. C. Jao and C. L. Leung, 87–104. Hong Kong: Oxford University Press, 1986.

Chang, Ta-kuang. "Making of the Chinese Bankruptcy Law: A Study in the Chinese Legislative Process." *Harvard International Law Journal* 28 (1987): 333–72.

Chase, Kerry A. *Trading Blocs: States, Firms, and Regions in the World Economy.* Ann Arbor: University of Michigan Press, 2005.

Chen Donglin. "Chen Yun yu 70 niandai duiwai jingji gongzuo de xin kaituo" [Chen Yun and the new opening in foreign economic work in the 1970s]. In Zhu Jiamu. *Chen Yun he tade shiye* [Chen Yun and his career]. Vol. 2: 1092–1103. Beijing: Zhongyang Wenxian Chubanshe, 1996.

Chen Wanshan and Xue Wei. "Xiwang zhichuang" [Window of hope]. *Renmin ribao*, September 15, 1987.

Chen Yun. *Chen Yun tongzhi wengao xuanbian* [Selections of Comrade Chen Yun's manuscripts (1956–62)]. Beijing: Renmin Chubanshe, 1981.

———. *Chen Yun wenxuan* [Chen Yun's selected works]. Vol. 3. Beijing: Renmin Chubanshe, 1995.

———. *Chen Yun wenxuan, 1956–1985* [Chen Yun's selected works]. Beijing: Renmin Chubanshe, 1986.

Cheng, Chu-yüan. "The Modernization of Chinese Industry." In *China's Four Modernizations*, edited by Richard Baum. Boulder, CO: Westview Press, 1980.

Cheng, Li, and Lynn White. "Elite Transformation and Modern Change in Mainland China and Taiwan: Empirical Data and the Theory of Technocracy." *China Quarterly* 121 (March 1990): 1–35.

———. "The Thirteenth Central Committee of the Chinese Communist Party: From Mobilizers to Managers." *Asian Survey* 28, no. 4 (April 1988): 376–98.

Cheremukhin, Anton, Mihail Golosov, Sergei Guriev, and Aleh Tsyvinski. "Was Stalin Necessary for Russia's Economic Development?" NBER Working Paper 19425. Cambridge, MA: National Bureau of Economic Research, September 2013.

Childs, Marquis William. *Sweden: The Middle Way.* New Haven, CT: Yale University Press, 1936.

Chow, Peter CY. "Causality between Export Growth and Industrial Development: Empirical Evidence from the NICs." *Journal of Development Economics* 26, no. 1 (1987): 55–63.

Chu, David K. W. "China's Special Economic Zones: Expectations and Reality." *Asian Affairs* 14, no. 2 (Summer 1987): 77–89.

———. "Population Growth and Related Issues." in Wong and Chu, *Modernization in China*, 131–39.

Chun, Han Wong. "China's Museums Rewrite History to Boost Xi." *Wall Street Journal*, August 20, 2018.

Chung, Yen-lin. "The CEP of the Utopian Project: Deng Xiaoping's Roles and Activities in the Great Leap Forward." *China Journal* 69 (2013): 154–71.

Collier, David. "Understanding Process Tracing." *PS: Political Science and Politics* 44, no. 4 (2011): 823–30.

Colvin, Geoff. "It's China's World. *Fortune*. 22 July 2019. Accessed on 22 April 2020. https://fortune.com/longform/fortune-global-500-china-companies/

Commission of the Central Committee of the Communist Party of the Soviet Union, ed. *History of the Communist Party of the Soviet Union (Bolsheviks), Short Course*. Moscow: Foreign Languages Publishing House, 1939.

Commission on Growth and Development. *The Growth Report: Strategies for Sustained Growth and Inclusive Development*. Washington, DC: World Bank Publications, 2008.

Cook, Damen. "China's Most Important South China Sea Military Base." *The Diplomat*, March 9, 2017.

Crane, George T. *The Political Economy of China's Special Economic Zones*. Armonk, NY: M. E. Sharpe, 1990.

Dangdai Zhongguo Congshu Bianjibu, ed. *Dangdai Zhongguo de jingji tizhi gaige* [Economic structural reforms of contemporary China]. Beijing: Zhongguo Shehui Kexueyuan Chubanshe, 1984.

Dangdai Zhongguo de Jingji Guanli Bianjibu, ed. *Zhonghua Renmin Gongheguo jingji guanli dashiji* [A chronicle of the PRC's economy and administration]. Beijing: Zhongguo Jingji Chubanshe, 1986.

Davie, John L., and Dean W. Carver. "China's International Trade and Finance." In U.S. Congress, Joint Economic Committee, *China under the Four Modernizations*, 19–47. 97th Cong., 2d sess., 1982.

Davies, Robert William. "Changing Economic Systems: An Overview." In *The Economic Transformation of the Soviet Union, 1913–1945*, edited by Robert William Davies, Mark Harrison, and S. G. Wheatcroft, 1–23. Cambridge, UK: Cambridge University Press, 1994.

Davis, Christina L., and Meredith Wilf. "Joining the Club: Accession to the GATT/WTO." *Journal of Politics* 79, no. 3 (2017): 964–78.

Deng Xiaoping. *Deng Xiaoping wenxuan, 1975–1982* [The selected works of Deng Xiaoping]. Beijing: Renmin Chubanshe, 1983.

———. *Deng Xiaoping wenxuan, di san juan.* [The selected works of Deng Xiaoping, vol. 3]. 3 volumes. Beijing: Renmin Chubanshe, 1993.

———. *Jianshe you Zhongguo tese de shehui zhuyi (Zengdingben)* [Construction of socialism with Chinese characteristics (revised and enlarged edition)]. Beijing: Renmin Chubanshe, 1987.

———. *Jianshe you Zhongguo teshi de shehui zhuyi* [Building socialism with Chinese characteristics]. Beijing: Renmin Chubanshe, 1984.

———. "Remarks on Successive Drafts of the "Resolution on certain questions in the history of our party since the founding of the People's Republic of China." In *Selected Works of Deng Xiaoping, Vol. 2 (1975–1982).* Accessed on 14 April 2020. https://dengxiaopingworks.wordpress.com /2013/02/25/remarks-on-successive-drafts-of-the-resolution-on-certain -questions-in-the-history-of-our-party-since-the-founding-of-the-peoples -republic-of-china/

Deng, Yong, and Fei-Ling Wang. "Introduction: Toward an Understanding of China's World Views." In Christensen, Thomas J., John Garver, Hu Weixing, Huang Yasheng, Wan Minggang, Bin Yu, Zhang Ming Jiu, *In the Eyes of the Dragon: China Views the World II.* Lanham, MD: Rowman & Littlefield, 1999, 1–19.

Dickson, Niall. "UK Politics: What Is the Third Way?" BBC News. Accessed on 22 April 2017. http://news.bbc.co.uk/2/hi/458626.stm.

Dittmer, Lowell. *Liu Shao-Chi and the Chinese Cultural Revolution: The Politics of Mass Criticism.* Berkeley: University of California Press, 1974.

Domínguez, Jorge I. *Technopols: Freeing Politics and Markets in Latin America in the 1990s.* University Park: Pennsylvania State University Press, 1997.

Dong Yun. "Ta zhuyi xiqu waimian de xinxian jingyan" [He pays attention and derives new experiences from the outside]. *Haishihua* 2 (1985): 2–4.

Donnithorne, Audrey. "New Light on Central-Provincial Regulations." *Australian Journal of Chinese Affairs* 10 (1983): 97–104.

Dziubla, Robert W. "International Trading Companies: Building on the Japanese Model." *Northwestern Journal of International Law & Business* 4, no. 2 (Fall 1982): 422–96.

Economy, Elizabeth, and Michel Oksenberg, eds. *China Joins the World: Progress and Prospects.* New York: Council on Foreign Relations Press, 1999.

Ehara, Noriyoshi. "The Expansion of China's Foreign Economic Relations." *China Newsletter* 49 (March/April 1984): 12.

Fairbank, John King. *The United States and China.* Cambridge, MA: Harvard University Press, 1972.

Fan, Peilei. "Catching Up through Developing Innovation Capability: Evidence from China's Telecom-Equipment Industry." *Technovation* 26, no. 3 (March 2006): 359–68.

Feuchtwang, Stephan, and Athar Hussain. *The Chinese Economic Reforms.* New York: St. Martin's Press, 1983.

Fewsmith, Joseph. *Dilemmas of Reform in China: Political Conflict and Economic Debate.* Armonk, NY: M. E. Sharpe, 1994.

Fitzpatrick, Sheila. *Stalin's Peasants: Resistance and Survival in the Russian Village after Collectivization.* New York: Oxford University Press, 1996.

Fong, Lee Mo-Kwan. "Tourism: A Critical Review." in Wong and Chu, *Modernization in China,* 79–88.

Freeman, Carla P. "China's Reform Challenge: The Political-Economy of Reform in Northeast China, 1978–1998." PhD diss., Johns Hopkins University, 1998. UMI Number 9920717.

Friedman, Edward. "Maoism, Titoism, Stalinism: Some Origins and Consequences of the Maoist Theory of the Socialist Transition." In *The Transition to Socialism in China,* edited by Mark Selden and Victor Lippit, 159–214. Armonk, NY: M. E. Sharpe, 1982.

Fuller, Douglas B. *Paper Tigers, Hidden Dragons: Firms and the Political Economy of China's Technological Development.* New York: Oxford University Press, 2016.

George, Alexander L., and Andrew Bennett. *Case Studies and Theory Development in the Social Sciences.* Cambridge, MA: MIT Press, 2004.

Gewirtz, Julian. *Unlikely Partners: Chinese Reformers.* Cambridge, MA: Harvard University Press, 2017.

Giddens, Anthony. "Socialism and After." In *The Third Way: The Renewal of Social Democracy,* 1–23. Malden, MA: Polity Press, 1998.

———. *The Third Way and Its Critics.* Malden, MA: Polity Press, 2000.

Gold, Thomas B. "'Just in Time!': China Battles Spiritual Pollution on the Eve of 1984." *Asian Survey* 24, no. 9 (1984): 947–74.

Goldman, Merle. "A New Relationship between the Intellectuals and the State in the Post-Mao Period." In *An Intellectual History of Modern China,* edited by Merle Goldman and Ou-Fan Lee. Cambridge, UK: Cambridge University Press, 2002.

———. *Sowing the Seeds of Democracy in China: Political Reform in the Deng Xiaoping Era.* Cambridge, MA: Harvard University Press, 1994.

Gong'anbu Zhengce Falü Yanjiushi, ed. *Youguan tong jingji fanzui zuo douzheng de wenjian xuanbian* [A selection of public documents relating to the struggle against economic crimes]. Beijing: Qunzhong Chubanshe, 1982.

Gu Shutang, ed. *Tianjin jingji gaikuang* [Economic conditions of Tianjin]. Tianjin: Tianjin Renmin Chubanshe, 1984.

Guangdong Nianjian Bianji Weiyuanhui, ed. *Guangdong nianjian, 1987* [Guangdong yearbook, 1987]. Guangzhou: Guangdong Renmin Chubanshe, 1987.

"Guanyu shouquan Guangdongsheng, Fujiansheng renmin daibiao dahui ji qi changwu weiyuanhui zhiding suoshu jingji tequ de gexiang danxing jingji fagui de jueding" [Resolution concerning the authorization of the people's congresses and their standing committees of Guangdong province and Fujian province to formulate various specific economic regulations for their respective special economic zones] adopted at the Twenty-First Session of the Fifth NPC Standing Committee on 26 November 1981. English translation in *SJTN*, 1985: 208.

Guoji Maoyi Wenti Bianjibu, ed. *Zhongguo duiwai maoyi wenti yanjiu* [Research on China's foreign trade problems]. Beijing: Jingji Guanli Chubanshe, Gaige Chubanshe, 1988.

Guojia Tigaiwei Jingji Guanlisi, ed. *Siying he geti jingji shiyong fagui daquan* [Comprehensive collection of private and individual economic laws and regulations]. Beijing: Renmin Chubanshe, 1988.

Guojia Wuziju Yanjiushi, ed. *Wuzi guanli falü huibian, 1949–1985* [Collection of commodity management laws]. Beijing: Zhongguo Wuzi Chubanshe, 1987.

Guowuyuan Tequ Bangongshi and Guowuyuan Bangongting Mishuju, eds. *Yanhai chengshi kaifang he tequ gongzuo wenjian xuanbian* [A selection of public documents relating to the opening of the coastal cities and the special economic zones]. Beijing: Guowuyuan Tequ Bangongshi, Bangongting Mishuju, May 1986.

———. *Yanhai chengshi kaifang he tequ gongzuo wenjian xuanbian, di 3–4 ji* (A selection of public documents relating to the opening of the coastal cities and the special economic zones, vols. 3–4). Beijing: Guowuyuan Tequ Bangongshi, Bangongting Mishuju, July 1989.

———. "The ZTE Case." *North Korea: Witness to Transformation* (blog). Peterson Institute for International Economics, 15 March 2017. Accessed on 26 April 2020. https://www.piie.com/blogs/north-korea-witness-transformation

Guo Xuezhi. "Dimensions of *Guanxi* in Chinese Elite Politics." *China Journal* 46 (2001): 69–90.

Haggard, Stephan. *Pathways from the Periphery: The Politics of Growth in the Newly Industrializing Countries*. Ithaca, NY: Cornell University Press, 1990.

Haggard, Stephan, and Robert Kaufman, eds. *The Politics of Economic Adjustment: International Constraints, Distributive Conflicts, and the State*. Princeton, NJ: Princeton University Press, 1992.

Hall, Peter A. "Policy Paradigms, Social Learning, and the State." *Compara-*
tive Politics 25 (April 1993): 275–96.

Hall, Peter A., and Rosemary C. R. Taylor. "Political Science and the Three
New Institutionalisms." *Political Studies* 44, no. 5 (1995): 936–57.

Hamrin, Carol Lee. "Competing 'Policy Packages' in Post-Mao China."
Asian Survey 24, no. 5 (May 1984): 487–518.

Han, Donglin, and David Zweig. "Images of the World: Studying Abroad
and Chinese Attitudes towards International Affairs." *China Quarterly*
202 (2010): 290–306.

Hanshou Xuexi Ziliao Bianjizu, ed. *Gongye jingji guanli fagui xuanbian*
[Collection of industrial economic management laws, vols. 1–4]. Beijing:
Zhongguo Renmin Daxue Hanshou Xueyuan, 1985.

Harding, Harry. *China's Second Revolution: Reform after Mao.* Washington,
DC: Brookings Institution, 1987.

Harold, Scott. "Freeing Trade: Negotiating Domestic and International Obstacles on China's Long Road to the GATT/WTO, 1971–2001." PhD diss.,
Columbia University, 2008.

Harwit, Eric. "Building China's Telecommunications Network: Industrial
Policy and the Role of Chinese State-Owned, Foreign and Private Domestic Enterprises." *China Quarterly* 190 (2007): 311–32.

———. *China's Automobile Industry: Policies, Problems, and Prospects.*
Armonk, NY: M. E. Sharpe, 1995.

Hasan, Sabiha. "Yugoslavia's Foreign Policy under Tito (1945–1980)—II,"
Pakistan Horizon 34, no. 4 (Fourth Quarter 1981): 62–103.

Hassard, John. "Multiple Paradigm Research." In *Sociology and Organi-*
zation Theory: Positivism, Paradigms and Postmodernity, 88–110. Cambridge, UK: Cambridge University Press, 1993.

Helpman, Elhanan, and Paul R. Krugman. *Market Structure and Foreign*
Trade: Increasing Returns, Imperfect Competition, and the International
Economy. Cambridge, MA: MIT Press, 1985. Hofheinz, Roy, Jr. "The Autumn Harvest Insurrection." *China Quarterly* 32 (October–December
1967): 37–87.

Hong, Lijian. "Provincial Leadership and Its Strategy toward the Acquisition
of Foreign Investment in Sichuan." In *Provincial Strategies of Economic*
Reform in Post-Mao China: Leadership, Politics, and Implementation,
edited by Peter T. Y. Cheung, Jae Ho Chung, and Zhimin Lin, 372–411.
Armonk, NY: M. E. Sharpe, 1998.

Hou, Xiaojia. "'Get Organized': The Impact of Two Soviet Models on the
CCP's Rural Strategy, 1949–1953." In Bernstein and Li, *China Learns from*
the Soviet Union, 167–96.

Howell, Jude. *China Opens Its Doors: The Politics of Economic Transition*. Boulder, CO: Lynne Rienner, 1993.

Howlett, Michael, and M. Ramesh. *Studying Public Policy: Policy Cycles and Policy Subsystems*. New York: Oxford University Press, 2003.

Hu Deping. "Essay: Hu Yaobang and the Test of Truth." *Caijing*, June 20, 2008.

Hu Qiaomu. *Hu Qiaomu wenji, di san juan* [Collected works of Hu Qiaomu, vol. 3]. Beijing: Renmin Chubanshe, 2012.

Hua Guofeng. "Report on the Work of the Government." *Peking Review*, 10 March 1978, 7–41.

Huang, Guo. "20 Years History of ZTE Corporation." *ZTE Communications* 2 (28 March 2005).

Huang, Yasheng. *Capitalism with Chinese Characteristics: Entrepreneurship and the State*. Cambridge, UK: Cambridge University Press, 2008.

Huang, Yitian. "Policy Experimentation and the Emergence of Domestic Voluntary Carbon Trading in China." *East Asia* 30, no. 1 (March 2013): 67–89.

Huang Zhenzhao and Chen Yu. *Xiwang zhichuang* [Window of hope]. Beijing: Guangming Ribao Chubanshe, 1984.

"Huawei: The Long March of the Invisible Mr. Ren." *Economist*, June 2, 2011.

Investment Promotion Bureau of the Ministry of Commerce, People's Republic of China. "Guanyu qingli guifan shuishou deng youhui zhengce de tongzhi" [Notice regarding cleaning up and regulating various taxes and other preferential policies]. Accessed 7 July 2015. http://fdi.govol.cn /1800000121_23_71979_0_7.html.

Jian, Chen, and Belton M. Fleisher. "Regional Income Inequality and Economic Growth in China." *Journal of Comparative Economics* 22, no. 2 (1996): 141–64.

Jiang Zemin. *Jiang Zemin wenji* [The collected works of Jiang Zemin]. Vol. 1. Beijing: Renmin Chubanshe, 2006.

Jinan Daxue Jingji Xueyuan Jingji Yanjiusuo and Shenzhenshi Kexue Jishu Xiehui. *Zhongguo jingji tequ yanjiu*, 1984 [Research on China's Special Economic Zones]. Guangzhou: n.p., 1984.

Jingji Kexue Chubanshe. *Shangye zhengce fagui huibian, 1982* [Collection of Laws and Regulations concerning Commerce Policies, 1982]. Beijing: Jingji Kexue Chubanshe, 1983.

Johnston, Alastair Iain, and Robert S. Ross, eds. *Engaging China: The Management of an Emerging Power*. New York: Routledge, 1999.

Joniak-Lüthi, Agnieszka. "Han Migration to Xinjiang Uyghur Autonomous Region: Between State Schemes and Migrants' Strategies." *Zeitschrift Für Ethnologie* 138, no. 2 (2013): 155–74.

Ju, Zhongyi. "'New Economic Group' versus 'Petroleum Group.'" In *Policy Conflicts in Post-Mao China*, edited by John P. Burns and Stanley Rosen, 192–97. Armonk, NY: M. E. Sharpe, 1986.

Kampen, Thomas. "Chinese Communists in Austria and Germany and Their Later Activities in China." *Asian and African Studies* 11, no. 1–2 (2007): 21–30.

———. *Mao Zedong, Zhou Enlai and the Evolution of the Chinese Communist Leadership.* Copenhagen: Nordic Institute of Asian Studies, 2000.

———. "Wang Jiaxiang, Mao Zedong and the 'Triumph of Mao Zedong-Thought' (1935–1945)." *Modern Asian Studies* 23, no. 4 (1989): 705–27.

Katori, Yasue. "Cable from Ambassador Katori to the Foreign Minister, 'Prime Minister Visit to China (Foreign Ministers' Discussion—Regarding the Participation of China in the ADB).'" March 25, 1984, History and Public Policy Program Digital Archive, 2002-113, Act on Access to Information Held by Administrative Organs. Accessed 3 October 2019. http://digitalarchive.wilsoncenter.org/document/119554.

Kong, Hanbing. "The Transplantation and Entrenchment of the Soviet Economic Model in China." In *Mao and the Economic Stalinization*, 153–66.

Kong, Xiaoqi. "China Launches Major Economic Zone." *Caixin Global*, 2 April 2017.

Kotkin, Stephen. *Stalin. Vol. 1, Paradoxes of Power, 1878–1928.* New York: Penguin Press, 2014.

Koziara, Edward Clifford, and Chiou-shuang Yan. "The Distribution System for Producers' Goods in China." *China Quarterly* 96 (1983): 689–702.

Kueh, Y. Y. "Foreign Investment and Economic Change in China." *China Quarterly* 131 (1992): 637–90.

Kuo, Cheng-tian. "Chinese Religious Reform." *Asian Survey* 51, no. 6 (November–December 2011): 1042–64.

Lai, Hongyi. *Foreign Trade and Economic Reform in China, 1978–1990.* Cambridge, UK: Cambridge University Press, 1992.

———. *Reform and Non-State Economy in China: The Political Economy of Liberalization Strategies.* New York: Palgrave Macmillan, 2006.

———. "SEZs and Foreign Investment in China: Experience and Lessons for North Korean Development." *Asian Perspective* 30, no. 3 (2006): 69–97.

Li Fuchun. *Li Fuchun xuanji* [Collected works of Li Fuchun]. Beijing: Zhongguo Jihua Chubanshe, 1992.

Li, Hua-Yu. "Instilling Stalinism in Chinese Party Members: Absorbing Stalin's *Short Course* in the 1950s." In Bernstein and Li, *China Learns from the Soviet Union*, 107–30.

———. *Mao and the Economic Stalinization of China, 1948–1953*. Lanham, MD: Rowman & Littlefield, 2006.

Li, Lanqing. *Breaking Through: The Birth of China's Opening-Up Policy*. Hong Kong: Oxford University Press, 2009.

Li Xiannian. *Li Xiannian lun caizheng jinrong maoyi, 1950–1991* [Li Xiannian's discussions on finance and trade, 1950–1991]. Vols. 1 and 2. Beijing: Zhongguo Caizheng Jingji Chubanshe, 1992.

Li Xiannian Bianxiezu. *Li Xiannian zhuan, 1949–1992* [The biography of Li Xiannian, 1949–1992]. Beijing: Zhongyang Wenxian Chubanshe, 2009.

Li Xiaoxian, ed. *Duiwai maoyi yuanli yu shiwu jiaocheng* [Text on the principles and practices of foreign trade]. Shanghai: Shanghai Renmin Chubanshe, 1986.

Li Yongchun, Shi Yuanqin, and Guo Xiuzhi. *Shiyijie sanzhong quanhui yilai zhengzhi tizhi gaige dashiji* [Chronicle of political structural reforms since the eleventh plenum]. Beijing: Chunqiu Chubanshe, 1987.

Li Zhongjie, Xu Yaoxin, and Wu Li. *Shehui zhuyi gaigeshi* [A history of socialist reforms]. Beijing: Chunqiu Chubanshe, 1988.

Liang, Wei. "China's WTO Negotiation Process and Its Implications." *Journal of Contemporary China* 11, no. 33 (2002): 683–719.

Liang Wensen. *Zhongguo jingji tequ de jinxi he weilai* [Current and future prospects of the Chinese SEZ economies]. Hong Kong: Xianggang Jingji Daobaoshe, Shenzhen Daxue Tequ Jingji Yanjiusuo, 1988.

Liang Xiang. "Construction and Development in the Shenzhen Special Economic Zone." *Foreign Broadcast Information Service—China* (24 January 1986): P1.

Lieberthal, Kenneth, and Michael Oksenberg. *Policy Making in China: Leaders, Structures and Processes*. Princeton, NJ: Princeton University Press, 1988.

Lin, George C. S. "Metropolitan Development in a Transitional Socialist Economy: Spatial Restructuring in the Pearl River Delta, China." *Urban Studies* 38, no. 3 (2001): 383–406.

Lin, Guijun, and Ronald M. Schramm. "China's Foreign Exchange Policies since 1979: A Review of Developments and an Assessment." *China Economic Review* 14, no. 3 (2003): 246–80.

Lin Jinzhi, ed. *Huaqiao huaren yu Zhongguo geming he jianshe* [Overseas Chinese involvement in the revolution and construction of China]. Fuzhou: Fujian Renmin Chubanshe, 1993.

Linz, Juan J., and Alfred Stepan. *Problems of Democratic Transition and Consolidation*. Baltimore, MD: Johns Hopkins University Press, 1996.

Liu, Alan P. L. "The 'Wenzhou Model' of Development and China's Modernization." *Asian Survey* 32, no. 8 (August 1992): 696–711.

Liu Shaoqi. *Liu Shaoqi lun xin Zhongguo jingji jianshe* [Liu Shaoqi's speeches on economic construction in new China]. Edited by Zhonggong Zhongyang Wenxian Yanjiushi. Beijing: Zhongyang Wenxian Chubanshe, 1993.

Liu Yuezhou. "Shenzhenshi chuanghui nongye fazhan qingkuang ji tihui" [Understanding how Shenzhen earns foreign exchange and develops its agricultural sector]. *Nongye Quhua* 6 (1988): 1–20.

Liu Yuji and Zou Yinghao. *Duiwai kaifang zhengce wenda* [Questions and answers on the opening policy]. Beijing: Falü Chubanshe, 1983.

Lo, C. P. "Recent Spatial Restructuring in Zhujiang Delta, South China: A Study of Socialist Regional Development Strategy." *Annals of the Association of American Geographers* 79, no. 2 (June 1989): 293–308.

Loh, Christine. *Underground Front: The Chinese Communist Party of Hong Kong*. Hong Kong: Hong Kong University Press, 2010.

Long Chucai. *Liyong waizi gailun* [An introduction to the use of foreign capital]. Beijing: Zhongguo Duiwai Jingji Maoyi Chubanshe, 1985.

Lowenthal, Richard. "Development vs. Utopia in Communist Policy." In *Change in Communist Systems*, edited by Chalmers Johnson. Stanford, CA: Stanford University Press, 1970.

Luo Ping. "The Shenzhen 'Earthquake' and Inner-Party Struggle." *Zhengming*, August 1, 1985, 9–13, translated in *FBIS-China*, 7 August 1985, W1–8.

Luo, Qi, and Christopher Howe. "Direct Investment and Economic Integration in the Asia Pacific: The Case of Taiwanese Investment in Xiamen." *China Quarterly* 136 (1993): 746–69.

Lüthi, Lorenz. *The Sino-Soviet Split: Cold War in the Communist World*. Princeton, NJ: Princeton University Press, 2008.

Ma, Hong. "'China-Style' Socialist Modernization, and Issues of Economic Restructuring." In *A Collection of Ma Hong's Works on Economic Reform*, edited by China Development Research Foundation, 1–46. New York: Routledge, 2014.

Ma Lianhui, Sun Zhen, Zhao Cunfang, Guan Zhemin, and Yang Qiao, eds. *Jingshen wenming cishu* [Dictionary on spiritual civilization]. Beijing: Zhongguo Zhanwang Chubanshe, 1986.

MacFarquahar, Roderick. *The Origins of the Cultural Revolution, Vol. 1: Contradictions Among the People*. New York: Columbia University Press, 1974.

———. *The Origins of the Cultural Revolution, Vol. 2: The Great Leap Forward 1958–1960*. New York: Columbia University Press, 1983.

———. *The Origins of the Cultural Revolution, Vol. 3: The Coming of the Cataclysm 1961–1966*. New York: Columbia University Press, 1997.

Mackerras, Colin. "'Party Consolidation' and the Attack on 'Spiritual Pollution' in Retrospect." *Australian Journal of Chinese Affairs* 11 (January 1984): 175–86.

Macmillan, Harold. *The Middle Way*. London: Macmillan, 1938.

Mai, Chao-Cheng, and Chien-Sheng Shih, eds. *Taiwan's Economic Success since 1980*. Northampton, MA: Edward Elgar Publishing, 2001.

Malle, Silvana. *The Economic Organization of War Communism, 1918–1921*. Cambridge, UK: Cambridge University Press, 2002.

Mao Zedong. *Jianguo yilai Mao Zedong wengao* [Post-1949 manuscripts of Mao Zedong]. Edited by Zhonggong Zhongyang Wenxian Yanjiushi. Vols 1–. Beijing: Zhongyang Wenxian Chubanshe, 1990–.

———. *Mao Zedong sixiang wansui* [Long live Mao Zedong thought]. N.p., 1969.

———. *Mao Zedong wenji* [The collected works of Mao Zedong]. Vols. 6–8. Edited by Zhonggong Zhongyang Wenxian Yanjiushi. Beijing: Renmin Chubanshe, 1999.

———. *Mao's Road to Power: From the Jinggangshan to the Establishment of the Jiangxi Soviets, July 1927–December 1930*. Armonk, NY: M. E. Sharpe, 1995.

———. *Miscellany of Mao Tse-Tung Thought (1949–1968)*. Arlington, VA: Joint Publications Research Service, 612690-1, 1974.

———. *Selected Works of Mao Tsetung, Vol. 4*. Beijing: Foreign Languages Press, 1961.

———. *Selected Works of Mao Tsetung, Vol. 5*. Beijing: Foreign Languages Press, 1977.

Meisner, Maurice. *Mao's China*. New York: Free Press, 1977.

Meng, Guangwen. "The Theory and Practice of Free Economic Zones: A Case Study of Tianjin, People's Republic of China." PhD diss., Ruprecht-Karls University of Heidelberg, 2003.

Minzhengbu Xingzheng Quhuachu. *Zhonghua Renmin Gongheguo xingzheng quhua shouce* [PRC administrative divisions handbook]. Beijing: Guangming Ribao Chubanshe, 1986.

Mishler, William, and Richard Rose. "Generation, Age, and Time: The Dynamics of Political Learning during Russia's Transformation." *American Journal of Political Science* 51, no. 4 (October 2007): 822–34.

———. "What Are the Origins of Political Trust? Testing Institutional and Cultural Theories in Post-Communist Societies." *Comparative Political Studies* 34, no. 1 (2001): 30–62.

Moltz, James Clay. "Divergent Learning and the Failed Politics of Soviet Economic Reform." *World Politics* 45, no. 2 (January 1993): 301–25.

Moore, Thomas G. *China in the World Market: Chinese Industry and International Sources of Reform in the Post-Mao Era.* Cambridge, UK: Cambridge University Press, 2002.

Naughton, Barry. *Growing Out of the Plan: Chinese Economic Reform 1978–1993.* Cambridge, UK: Cambridge University Press, 1996.

———. "The Third Front." *China Quarterly* 115 (September 1988): 351–86.

———. "The Western Development Program." In *Holding China Together: Diversity and National Integration in the Post-Deng Era*, edited by Barry Naughton and Dali Yang, 253–96. Cambridge, UK: Cambridge University Press, 2004.

Oborne, Michael. *China's Special Economic Zones.* Paris: Organization for Economic Co-operation and Development, 1986.

Oi, Jean. "Fiscal Reform and the Economic Foundations of Local State Corporatism in China." *World Politics* 45, no. 1 (October 1992): 99–132.

Pantsov, Alexander V., and Steven I. Levine. *Deng Xiaoping: A Revolutionary Life.* New York: Oxford University Press, 2015.

———. *Mao: The Real Story.* New York: Simon & Schuster, 2012.

Pearson, Margaret M. "The Case of China's Accession to the GATT/WTO." In Lampton, *Making of Chinese Foreign and Security Policy*, 337–70.

———. "China's Integration into the International Trade and Investment Regime." In *China Joins the World: Progress and Prospects*, edited by Elizabeth Economy and Michel Oksenberg. New York: Council on Foreign Relations Press, 1999, 161–205.

———. *Joint Ventures in the People's Republic of China: The Control of FDI under Socialism.* Princeton, NJ: Princeton University Press, 1992.

———. "The Major Multilateral Economic Institutions Engage China." In Johnston and Ross, *Engaging China*, 207–34.

Phylaktis, Kate, and Eric Girardin. "Foreign Exchange Markets in Transition Economies: China." *Journal of Development Economics* 64 (2001): 215–35.

"Ping Lin Biao de 'Zhengzhi bianfang'" [Criticizing Lin Biao's Strategy of "Political Frontier Defense"]. *Jiefang junbao*, 15 October 1978.

Po Di. "Shenzhen lingdaoceng de mingzheng andou" [Clear infighting within the Shenzhen leadership]. (April 1987): 54–56.

Pye, Lucian. "How China's Nationalism Was Shanghaied." *Australian Journal of Chinese Affairs* 29 (January 1993): 107–33.

Qing, Simei. "The Eisenhower Administration and Changes in Western Embargo Policy against China, 1954–1958." In *The Great Powers in East Asia 1953–1960*, edited by Warren I. Cohen and Akira Iriye, 131–36. New York: Columbia University Press, 1990.

Radchenko, Sergey. *Unwanted Visionaries: The Soviet Failure in Asia at the End of the Cold War*. New York: Oxford University Press, 2014.

Ramo, Joshua Cooper. *The Beijing Consensus*. London: Foreign Policy Centre, 2004.

Reardon, Lawrence C., ed. and trans. "China's Coastal Development Strategy, 1979–1984 (I)." Special issue, *Chinese Law and Government* 27, no. 3 (May–June 1994): 1–95.

———, ed. and trans. "China's Coastal Development Strategy, 1979–1984 (II)." Special issue, *Chinese Law and Government* 27, no. 4 (July/August 1994): 1–96.

———. "Learning How to Open the Door: A Reassessment of China's 'Opening' Strategy." *China Quarterly* 155 (September 1998): 479–511.

———. *Reluctant Dragon: Crisis Cycles and Chinese Foreign Economic Policy*. Seattle: University of Washington Press, 2002.

———. "The Rise and Decline of China's Export Processing Zones." *Journal of Contemporary China* 5 (November 1996): 281–303.

———. "Shifting Global Paradigms and Obama's Adaptive Foreign Policy." In *The Obama Presidency: Promise and Performance*, edited by William Crotty, 103–26. Lanham, MD: Lexington Books/Rowman and Littlefield, 2012.

Renmin Ribaoshe Gongshangbu, ed. *Zhongguo duiwai kaifang gongzuo shiwu shouce* [Practical handbook for China's opening to the outside]. Beijing: Gongshang Chubanshe, 1987.

Rogers, Mike, and C. A. Dutch Ruppersberger. *Investigative Report on the U.S. National Security Issues Posed by Chinese Telecommunications Companies Huawei and ZTE*. Permanent Select Committee on Intelligence, U.S. House of Representatives, 112th Congress, 2nd session, October 8, 2012.

Ruan, Ming. "Establishment of Special Zones and Economic Strategy." *Fujian luntan* 2 (April 1982): 47–48.

Ryan, Michael P. *Playing by the Rules: American Trade Power and Diplomacy in the Pacific*. Washington, DC: Georgetown University Press, 1995.

Saich, Tony. "The Rise and Fall of the Beijing People's Movement." *Australian Journal of Chinese Affairs* 24 (1990): 181–208.

Schoenhals, Michael. "Cultural Revolution on the Border: Yunnan's 'Political Frontier Defence.'" *Copenhagen Journal of Asian Studies* 19 (2005): 27–54.

Schottenhammer, Angela, ed. *The Emporium of the World: Maritime Quan-zhou, 1000–1400.* Vol. 49. Leiden: Brill, 2001.

Schram, Stuart R. "'Economics in Command?' Ideology and Policy since the Third Plenum, 1978–1984." *China Quarterly* 99 (September 1984): 417–61.

———. "Mao Zedong a Hundred Years On: The Legacy of a Ruler." *China Quarterly* 137 (March 1994): 125–43.

Schwarcz, Vera. *The Chinese Enlightenment: Intellectuals and the Legacy of the May Fourth Movement of 1919.* Vol. 27. Berkeley: University of California Press, 1986.

Shambaugh, David L. "The Dynamics of Elite Politics during the Jiang Era." *China Journal* 45 (2001): 103–6.

———. *The Making of a Premier: Zhao Ziyang's Provincial Career.* Boulder, CO: Westview Press, 1984.

Shanghai Shehui Kexueyuan. *Shanghai jingji (1949–1982)* [Shanghai economy (1949–1982)]. Shanghai: Shanghai Shehui Kexueyuan Chubanshe, 1984.

Shenzhen Jingji Tequ Nianjian Bianji Weiyuanhui. *Shenzhen jingji tequ nianjian* [Shenzhen Special Economic Zone yearbook], various years. Hong Kong: Xianggang Jingji Daobao Chubanshe, n.d.

Shenzhenshi Duiwai Xuanchuanchu and Xianggang Xinwanbao. *Zhongguo jingji tequ shouce* [Handbook of the Chinese SEZs]. Hong Kong: Shenzhen Duiwai Xuanchuanchu, Xinwanbao, 1984.

Shenzhenshi Renmin Zhengfu Bangongting, ed. *Shenzhen jingji tequ jiben qingkuang jieshao* [Introduction to the basic conditions of the Shenzhen SEZ]. Shenzhen: n.p., 1983.

Shi Zhe. "'Zhong Su youhao tongmeng huzhu tiaoyue' qianding shimo" [The entire story of signing the "Sino-Soviet Treaty of Friendship, Alliance, and Mutual Assistance"]. *Dang de wenxian* 25 (1992): 52–57.

Si Fu. *Guoneiwai dashiji, 1981* [Major foreign and domestic events of 1981]. Beijing: Renmin Chubanshe, 1982.

Solinger, Dorothy J. *China's Transition from Socialism.* Armonk, NY: M. E. Sharpe, 1993.

———. "Commerce: The Petty Private Sector and the Three Lines in the Early 1980s." In *Three Visions of Chinese Socialism*, edited by Dorothy J. Solinger. Boulder, CO: Westview, 1984.

"Special Economic Zone must continue to be 'special'—congratulating the 15th anniversary of the establishment of the Shenzhen Special Economic Zone," *Liaowang* 34 (21 August 1995), p. 1, translated in *FBIS-China* (25 September 1995), 38–39.

Su, Shaozhi. "A Decade of Crises at the Institute of Marxism-Leninism-Mao Zedong Thought, 1979–89." *The China Quarterly* 134, (June 1993): 335–51.

Su Tiren, ed. *Deng Xiaoping shengping quanjilu* [A comprehensive record of Deng Xiaoping's life]. Beijing: Zhongyang Wenxian Chubanshe, 2004.

Sun Ru. *Qianjinzhong de Zhongguo jingji tequ* [Chinese special economic zones on the move]. Beijing: Zhongguo Caizheng Jingji Chubanshe, 1983.

Sutton, Anthony. *Western Technology and Soviet Economic Development, 1917 to 1930*. Stanford, CA: Hoover Institution on War, Revolution and Peace, 1968.

Tan Qingfeng, Yao Xuecong, and Li Shusen, eds. *Waimao fuchi shengchan shijian* [The practice of supporting foreign trade production]. Beijing: Zhongguo Duiwai Jingji Maoyi Chubanshe, 1984.

Teets, Jessica C. *Civil Society under Authoritarianism*. Cambridge, UK: Cambridge University Press, 2014.

Teiwes, Frederick C. "The Establishment and Consolidation of the New Regime: 1949–57." In *The Politics of China: The Eras of Mao and Deng*, 2nd ed., edited by Roderick MacFarquhar, 5–86. Cambridge, UK: Cambridge University Press, 1997.

———. "The Paradoxical Post-Mao Transition: From Obeying the Leader to 'Normal Politics.'" In *The Nature of Chinese Politics: From Mao to Jiang*, edited by Roderick Unger, 55–94. Armonk, NY: M. E. Sharpe, 2002.

———. *Politics at Mao's Court*. Armonk, NY: M. E. Sharpe, 1990.

Teiwes, Frederick C., and Warren Sun. "China's Economic Reorientation after the Third Plenum: Conflict surrounding 'Chen Yun's' Readjustment Program, 1979–80." *China Journal* 70 (July 2013): 163–87.

———. "China's New Economic Policy under Hua Guofeng: Party Consensus and Party Myths." *China Journal* 66 (July 2011): 1–43.

Thorbecke, Willem, and Nimesh Salike. "Understanding Foreign Direct Investment in Asia." ADBI Working Paper 290. Tokyo: Asian Development Bank Institute, 2011.

Tong Xiaopeng. *Fengyu sishinian, 2* [Forty-year storm, vol. 2]. Beijing: Zhongyang Wenxian Chubanshe, 1996.

Trotsky, Leon. *The Revolution Betrayed*. 5th. ed. Atlanta: Pathfinder, 1972.

Truex, Rory. "Consultative Authoritarianism and Its Limits." *Comparative Political Studies* 50, no. 3 (June 2014): 329–61.

Tsai, Kellee S. *Back-Alley Banking: Private Entrepreneurs in China*. Ithaca, NY: Cornell University Press, 2002.

———. *Capitalism without Democracy: The Private Sector in Contemporary China*. Ithaca, NY: Cornell University Press, 2007.

Twelfth National Congress of the Communist Party. "Constitution of the Communist Party of China (1982)." *Beijing Review*. Accessed on 22 April 2017. http://www.bjreview.com.cn/90th/2011-04/12/content_357495.htm.

UN Development Programme. *First Country Programme for the People's Republic of China*. DP/CP/CPR1. United Nations Development Programme, 18 February 1982. http://web.undp.org/execbrd/archives/sessions/gc/May-1982/DP-CP-CPR-1.pdf.

Vogel, Ezra. *Canton under Communism*. New York: Harper and Row, 1969.
———. *Deng Xiaoping and the Transformation of China*. Cambridge, MA: Harvard University Press, 2011.
———. *One Step Ahead in China: Guangdong under Reform*. Cambridge, MA: Harvard University Press, 1990.

Walder, Andrew. *China under Mao: A Revolution Derailed*. Cambridge, MA: Harvard University Press, 2015.
———. *The Waning of the Communist State: Economic Origins of Political Decline in China and Hungary*. Berkeley, CA: University of California Press, 1995.
Walker, Kenneth R. "40 Years On: Provincial Contrasts in China's Rural Economic Development." *China Quarterly* 119 (1989): 448–80.
Wan, Zheng, Yang Zhang, Wang Xuefeng, and Jihong Chen. "Policy and Politics behind Shanghai's Free Trade Zone Program." *Journal of Transport Geography* 34 (2014): 1–6.
Wang Dao'nan. "Shekou gongyequ de jumin shenghuo" [The lives of the inhabitants of the Shekou Industrial Area]. *Shehui* 5 (1984): 24–26.
Wang, Dong. "The Discourse of Unequal Treaties in Modern China." *Pacific Affairs* 76, no. 3 (Fall 2003): 399–425.
Wang Shouchun and Li Kanghua. *Zhongguo duiwai jingji maoyi de xinfazhan* [The new developments of China's foreign economic trade]. Beijing: Duiwai Maoyi Jiaoyu Chubanshe, 1986.
Wang Wenyang, ed. *Jingji tequ* [Special economic zones]. Beijing: Zhongguo Zhanwang Chubanshe, 1983.
Wang Xiangli. "Zhu De jingji sixiang xuexi biji (xia)" [Study notes on Zhu De's economic thinking (part 2)]. *Dang de wenxian* 12 (1989): 44–48.
Wang Zhen. "Women jianli jingji tequ de zhengce shi zhengque de" [Our establishment of the SEZ policy was correct]. In *Zhongguo jingji tequ wenxian ziliao, di san juan* [The collected materials concerning China's SEZs, vol. 3]. Edited by Guo Maojia, Zhong Jian, and Zhong Ruoyu. Beijing: Shehui Kexue Wenxian Chubanshe, 2010.
Wang Zhengming. *Sanzhong quanhui yilai jingji zhengce yu fagui shuyao* [Commentary on the economic policies, laws and regulations issued since the Third Plenum]. Beijing: Falü Chubanshe, 1984.

Wang Zhiye and Zhu Yuanzhen. *Jingji tizhi gaige shouce* [Handbook on economic structural reforms]. Beijing: Jingji Ribao Chubanshe, 1987.

Warner, Malcolm, and Ng Sek Hong. "The Ongoing Evolution of Chinese Industrial Relations: The Negotiation of 'Collective Contracts' in the Shenzhen Special Economic Zone." *China Information* 12, no. 4 (1998): 1–20.

Watson, Andrew, ed. *Mao Zedong and the Political Economy of the Border Region.* Cambridge, UK: Cambridge University Press, 1980.

Wedeman, Andrew H. *From Mao to Market: Rent Seeking, Local Protectionism, and Marketization in China.* Cambridge, UK: Cambridge University Press, 2003.

"Wenzhou Yongqiang Jichang zhengshi gengming wei Wenzhou Longwan Guoji Jichang" [Wenzhou Yongqiang Airport has officially changed its name to the Wenzhou Longwan International Airport]. *Fenghuang wang,* May 9, 2009.

Wheatcroft, S. G., R. W. Davies, and J. M. Cooper. "Soviet Industrialization Reconsidered: Some Preliminary Conclusions about Economic Development between 1926 and 1941." *Economic History Review* 39, no. 2 (May 1986): 264–94.

"Who's Afraid of Huawei?" *Economist,* August 4, 2012.

Wong, Kwan-yiu, and David K. Y. Chu, eds. *Modernization in China: The Case of the Shenzhen Special Economic Zone.* Hong Kong: Oxford University Press, 1985.

Wong, Linda, and Grace Lee, eds. "Welfare in a Stratified Immigrant Society: Shenzhen's Social Policy Challenge." In *Economic and Social Development in South China,* edited by Steward MacPherson and Joseph Y. S. Cheng, 208–28. Cheltenham, UK: Edward Elgar, 1996.

World Bank. *China: External Trade and Capital.* Washington, DC: World Bank, 1988.

———. *China, Socialist Economic Development.* Vols. 1–3. Washington, DC: World Bank. 1983.

———. *The East Asian Miracle: Economic Growth and Public Policy.* New York: Oxford University Press, 1993.

———. *Implementation Completion Report: China, Daguangba Multipurpose Project.* Report No. 19700, 23 September 1999. Accessed 3 October 2019. http://documents.worldbank.org/curated/en/863231468023964694/pdf/multi-page.pdf.

World Steel Association. *World Steel in Figures 2014.* Brussels, Belgium: World Steel Association, 2014.

Wu Qunce, Qu Chifeng, Zheng Weibiao. "Tequ jingji tiaojian de bianhua gei jingshen wenming jianshe dailai de yixie xinwenti" [New problems of constructing spiritual civilization caused by SEZ changes], in Sun Ru, *Qianjinzhong*, 358–72.

Wu Wutong. *Duiwai maoyi jichu zhishi gailun* [Introduction to the basics of foreign trade]. Beijing: Duiwai Maoyi Jiaoyu Chubanshe, 1986.

Xi Zhongxun. *Xi Zhongxun wenxuan* [Selected writings of Xi Zhongxun]. Beijing: Zhongyang Wenxuan Chubanshe, 1995.

Xia, Ming. *The People's Congresses and Governance in China: Toward a Network Mode of Governance*. New York: Routledge, 2008.

Xianggang Zhongguo Jingji Tequ Nianjian Bianjibu. *Zhongguo jingji tequ nianjian* [Chinese special economic zone yearbook,]], various years. Hong Kong: Xianggang Jingji Tequ Nianjian Chubanshe, 1983.

Xianggang Zhuanshang Xuesheng Lianhui, ed. *Jingji tequmian mianguan* [Views on the SEZs]. Hong Kong: Guangjiaojing Chubanshe, 1983.

Xinhua. "The birth of an important decision." *Foreign Broadcast Information Service—China*, 18 June 1984, K3.

Xiong Bingchuan and Xu Bang, eds. *Shekou shouce* [Shekou handbook]. Nanchang: Jiangsu Renmin Chubanshe, 1987.

Xu Dixin. "Jiji wending, banhao jingji teque" [In an active and balanced fashion manage the SEZs]. *Fujian luntan* (April 1981): 2–6.

———. *Zhongguo shehui zhuyi jingji kaizhanzhong de wenti* [Problems in Developing China's Socialist Economy]. Beijing: Zhongguo Shehui Kexue Chubanshe, 1982.

Xu Xuehan, Mao Rongfang, and Wu Jian. "Guanyu jingji tequ jianshezhong de jige wenti" [Several problems encountered in SEZ construction]. *Renmin ribao*, 13 September 1982.

Yang, Dali L. "China Adjusts to the World Economy: The Political Economy of China's Coastal Development Strategy." *Pacific Affairs* 64, no. 1 (1991): 42–64.

Yeh, Anthony G. O. "Planning: Infrastructure, Labour and the Environment in Shenzhen." In Wong and Chu, *Modernization in China*, 108–30.

Yeung, Godfrey. *Foreign Investment and Socio-economic Development: The Case of Dongguan*. Houndsmills, Basingstoke, UK: Palgrave, 2001.

Yeung, Yue-man, and Xu-wei Hu, eds. *China's Coastal Cities*. Honolulu: University of Hawai'i Press, 1992.

Yu, Miin-ling. "'Labor Is Glorious': Model Laborers in the PRC." In Bernstein and Li, *China Learns from the Soviet Union*, 231–58.

Yu Shicheng. *Deng Xiaoping yu Mao Zedong* [Deng Xiaoping and Mao Zedong]. Beijing: Zhonggong Zhongyang Dangxiao Chubanshe, 1995.

Zhai, Jianxiong. "Tax Legislation of the People's Republic of China and Its Information Sources." *Revenue Law Journal* 8, no. 1 (1998): 207–15.

Zhang, Eping, and Kim Lem. "Chen Yun's Role after the Cultural Revolution." *Asian Affairs* 12, no. 1 (Spring 1985): 41–58.

Zhang Suiqiang. "Zhiqing taogang yanjiu de ruogan sikao" [Some reflections on the study of educated youth escaping to Hong Kong]. *Dangdai Gang'ao yanjiu* 34, no. 1 (2012): 128–35.

Zhang Zerong, ed. *Zhongguo jingji tizhi gaige jishi (Sichuan)* [Chronology of China's Economic Structural Reforms (Sichuan)]. Chengdu: Sichuan Kexue Jishu Chubanshe, 1986.

Zhao Ziyang. *Prisoner of the State: The Secret Journal of Premier Zhao Ziyang.* Edited by Bao Pu, Renee Chiang, and Adi Ignatius. New York: Simon and Schuster, 2009.

———. *Zhao Ziyang wenxianji (1980–1989)* [The collected works of Zhao Ziyang (1980–1989)]. Vols. 1–4. Hong Kong: Chinese University Press, 2016.

Zhejiangsheng Sifating and Zhejiangsheng Duiwai Jingji Maoyiting. *Duiwai jingji falü zhengce huibian* [A selection of foreign economic laws and policies]. Zhejiang: Zhejiangsheng Sifating, Zhejiangsheng Duiwai Jingji Maoyiting, March 1985.

Zheng Derong, Han Mingxi, and Zheng Xiaoliang. *Zhongguo jingji tizhi gaige jishi* [Chronology of China's economic structural reforms]. Beijing: Chunqiu Chubanshe, 1987.

Zheng, Shiping. "The New Era in Chinese Elite Politics." *Issues and Studies* 41, no. 1 (2005): 190–203.

Zhonggong Renminglu Bianxiu Weiyuanhui, ed. *Zhonggong renming lu* [Biographies of Chinese Communist personages]. Taibei: Guoli Zhengzhi Daxue Guoji Guanxi Yanjiu Zhongxin, 1983.

Zhonggong Shenzhen Shiwei Bangongting. *Shenzhen tequ fazhan de daolu* [The development of the Shenzhen SEZ]. Beijing: Guangming Ribao Chubanshe, 1984.

Zhonggong Shenzhen Shiwei Xuanchuanbu. *1992 Chun Deng Xiaoping yu Shenzhen* [1992 Spring Deng Xiaoping and Shenzhen]. Shenzhen: Haitian Chubanshe, 1992.

Zhonggong Shenzhen Shiwei Zhengce Yanjiushi, ed. *Diaocha yanjiu huibian* [Collection of investigative and research reports]. Shenzhen: Zhonggong Shenzhen Shiwei Zhengce Yanjiushi, 1984.

Zhonggong Zhongyang Dangshi Yanjiushi. *Zhonggong dangshi dashi nianbiao* [Chronology of major historical events of the Chinese Communist Party]. Beijing: Renmin Chubanshe, 1987.

Zhonggong Zhongyang Shujichu Yanjiushi Lilunzu, ed. *Diaocha yanjiu, 1979–1980* [Investigation and research, 1979–80]. Beijing: Zhonggong Zhongyang Dangxiao Chubanshe, 1983.

Zhonggong Zhongyang Wenxian Yanjiushi, ed. *Chen Yun wenji* [The collected works of Chen Yun]. Vol. 3. Beijing: Zhongyang Wenxian Chubanshe, 2005.

———. *Liu Shaoqi nianpu (1898–1969)* [A chronicle of Liu Shaoqi's life (1898–1969)]. Vol. 2. Beijing: Zhongyang Wenxian Chubanshe, 1996.

———. *Mao Zedong wenji, 7* [Collected works of Mao Zedong, vol. 7]. Beijing: Renmin Chubanshe, 1999.

———. *Sanzhong quanhui yilai zhongyao wenxian xuanbian* [Selected important documents since the Third Plenum] Beijing: Zhongyang Wenxian Chubanshe, 1998.

———. *Sanzhong quanhui yilai zhongyao wenxian xuanbian* [Selected important documents issued since the Third Plenum]. Beijing: Renmin Chubanshe, 1984.

———. *Sanzhong quanhui yilai zhongyao wenxian xuanbian* [Selected important documents issued since the Third Plenum]. Beijing: Renmin Chubanshe, 1982.

———. *Zhou Enlai jingji wenxian* [Zhou Enlai's economic documents]. Beijing: Zhongyang Wenxian Chubanshe, 1993.

———. *Zhou Enlai nianpu (1949–1976)* [A chronicle of Zhou Enlai's life (1949–1976)]. 2 vols. Beijing: Zhongyang Wenxian Chubanshe, 1997.

Zhongguo Duiwai Jingji Maoyi Nianjian Bianji Weiyuanhui. *Zhongguo duiwai maoyi nianjian, 1984* [China's foreign economic trade yearbook, 1984]. Beijing: Renmin Chubanshe, 1984.

Zhongguo Renmin Cidian Bianjibu, ed. *Zhongguo renming dacidian: Xianren dangzhengjun lingdao renwujuan* [Dictionary of China's important personages: Current party, government and military leaders edition]. Shanghai: Shanghai Cishu Chubanshe, Waiwen Chubanshe, 1989.

Zhongguo Renmin Yinhang Bangongshi, ed. *1981 Jinrong guizhang zhidu xuanbian, di er juan* [A selection of rules and regulations concerning the 1981 financial system, vol. 2]. Beijing: Zhongguo Jinrong Chubanshe, 1983.

Zhongguo Renmin Yinhang Bangongshi, ed. *1981 Jinrong guizhang zhidu xuanbian, shangce, xiace* [A selection of rules and regulations concerning the 1981 financial system, vols. 1, 2]. Beijing: Zhongguo Jinrong Chubanshe, 1983.

Zhongguo Renmin Yinhang Jihuasi, ed. *Lilü wenjian huibian* [A collection of documents on interest rates]. Beijing: Zhongguo Jinrong Chubanshe, 1986.

Zhongguo Shehui Kexueyuan and Faxue Yanjiusuo, eds. *Zhongguo jingji guanli fagui wenjian huibian* [Laws, regulations, and documents relating to China's economic administration, vol. 1]. Jilin: Jilin Renmin Chubanshe, 1985.

———. *Zhongguo jingji guanli fagui wenjian huibian, xiace* [Laws, regulations, and documents relating to China's economic administration, vol. 2]. Jilin: Jilin Renmin Chubanshe, 1987.

Zhongguo Shehui Kexueyuan and Zhongyang Dang'anguan, eds. *Zhonghua Renmin Gongheguo jingji dang'an ziliao xuanbian: gongye juan, 1949–1952* [A collection of archival materials on the PRC economy: Industry, 1949–1952]. Beijing: Zhongguo Wuzi Chubanshe, 1996.

———. *Zhonghua Renmin Gongheguo jingji fagui xuanbian, 1979.10–1981.12* [Collection of economic laws and regulations of the People's Republic of China, October 1979–December 1981]. 2 vols. Beijing: Zhongguo Caizheng Jingji, 1982.

Zhonghua Renmin Gongheguo Caizhengbu Bangongshi, ed. *Caizheng guizhang zhidu xuanbian, 1981* [A selection of financial rules and regulations]. Beijing: Zhongguo Caizheng Jingji Chubanshe, n.d.

"Zhonghua Renmin Gongheguo Guangdongsheng jingji tequ tiaoli" [Regulations of Guangdong province on special economic zones], approved at the Fifteenth Session of the Standing Committee of the Fifth NPC on 26 August 1980. English translation in *SJTN*, 1985: 201–7.

Zhou Enlai, ed. "Diyige wunian jihua de jingyan he jiaoxun" [The experiences and lessons to be learned from the First Five-Year Plan]. In *Zhou Enlai jingji wenxuan* [A selection of Zhou Enlai's economic works], edited by Zhonggong Zhongyang Wenxian Yanjiushi, 278–328. Beijing: Zhongyang Wenxian Chubanshe, 1993.

Zhu De. "Cengjia chukou chanpin, fazhan Hainan jingji" [Increase export products, develop Hainan's economy). In *Dang de wenxian*, 53:34–35, 1996.

Zhu Jianru, ed. *Zhongguo zuida de jingji tequ: Shenzhen* [China's largest SEZ: Shenzhen]. Hong Kong: Guangjiaojing Chubanshe, 1983.

Zhu Rongji. *Zhu Rongji jianghua shilu, di san juan* [Zhu Rongji on the record, vol. 3]. Beijing: Renmin Chubanshe, 2011.

Zhu Yuanshi. "Liu Shaoqi yijiusijiunian mimi fang Su" [Liu Shaoqi's secret 1949 trip to the Soviet Union]. *Dang de wenxian* 21 (1991): 74–89.

Zhuhai Jingji Nianjian Bianji Weiyuanhui. *Zhuhai jingji nianjian, 1979–1986* [Yearbook of Zhuhai's economy, 1979–1986]. Guangzhou: Guangdong Renmin Chubanshe, n.d.

Zuo Chuntai and Song Xinzhong, eds. *Zhongguo shehui zhuyi caizheng jianshi* [A simple history of Chinese socialist finance]. Beijing: Zhongguo Caizheng Jingji Chubanshe, 1988.

Zweig, David. *Internationalizing China: Domestic Interests and Global Linkages.* Ithaca, NY: Cornell University Press, 2002.

Index

Harvard East Asian Monographs
(most recent titles)